RELATIONSHIP MANAGEM ....
AND THE MANAGEMENT
OF PROJECTS

Relationship Management and the Management of Projects is a guide to successfully building and managing relationships as a project manager and in the project business.

Relationship management is a core skill for any project business to develop capabilities and manage the interface with projects, providing guidance to project managers as they negotiate with business partners and coordinate between business functions. Whatever the structures and procedures an organization has and whatever the project management tools and techniques, they are only as good as the hands they are in. Yet relationship management, though a well-established discipline, is rarely applied to the process-driven world of project management.

This book is a much-needed guide to the process of enhancing these skills to boost firm performance, team performance and develop collaborative practices. Hedley Smyth guides you through the processes of relationship management examining the theory and practice. This book highlights the range of options available to further develop current practices to ensure a successful relationship management in all stages of a project's lifecycle.

Relationship Management and the Management of Projects is valuable reading for all students and specialists in project management, as well as project managers in business, management, the built environment, or indeed any industry.

Hedley Smyth is Director of Research for the Bartlett School of Construction and Project Management, University College London. He has worked extensively in industry and academia and has been published in many leading journals and authored a wide range of books.

This is a comprehensive work that shows how productivity and effectiveness in projects can be improved by mobilising the under-utilised asset of social relations. This book provides a guide on how to structure the project in a robust task-oriented way that engenders the outwards orientation and trust that underlies all value-creation in projects.

Magnus Gustafsson, PBI Research Institute, Finland

Projects are not islands and neither is the management of projects. As this book argues, we need to consider projects and project management in light of relationship management. This book is an excellent contribution to the theory of the management of projects and to our understanding of how projects and project business are formed in a relational context. It offers fresh ideas for both theorists as well as practitioners. It tackles a host of important topics, including trust building in project business, social capital in projects, moral issues in project business, and the development of long-term and short-term relationships for better projects and more successful project business.

Jonas Söderlund, Professor, BI Norwegian Business School, Norway

RELATIONSHIP MANAGEMENT AND THE MANAGEMENT OF PROJECTS

Hedley Smyth

Routledge
Taylor & Francis Group

LONDON AND NEW YORK

First published 2015
by Routledge
2 Park Square, Milton Park, Abingdon, Oxon OX14 4RN

and by Routledge
711 Third Avenue, New York, NY 10017

Routledge is an imprint of the Taylor & Francis Group, an informa business

© 2015 Hedley Smyth

British Library Cataloguing in Publication Data
A catalogue record for this book is available from the British Library

Library of Congress Cataloging-in-Publication Data
Relationship management and the management of projects / Hedley Smyth.
    pages cm
  Includes bibliographical references and index.
  1. Project management.   2. Interorganizational relations.   3. Interpersonal relations.   4. Business networks–Management.   5. Management.   I. Title.
    HD69.P75S6145 2014
    658.4′04–dc23
    2014009632

ISBN: 978-0-415-70510-3 (hbk)
ISBN: 978-0-415-70512-7 (pbk)
ISBN: 978-1-315-88998-6 (ebk)

Typeset in Bembo
by Apex CoVantage, LLC

Printed and bound in Great Britain by
CPI Group (UK) Ltd, Croydon, CR0 4YY

This book is dedicated to Nikki, Claire and Phoebe

CONTENTS

FIGURES

TABLES

FACT BOXES

PREFACE

I first became interested in relationship management through relationship marketing, which I had largely been intuitively applying in practice, coming back into academia as the paradigm was beginning to gain traction. Relationship management was seen early on as a crucial part of embedding the function across operations. From this, Nick Thompson, a former PhD student, now an academic, kindled an interest in trust as a key component of any relationship. In parallel, the relational contracting was being adopted by many clients for many projects through partnering and supply chain management. Relationships had become currency and trust became a byword for good collaborative working. If industry were saying that relationships and trust in particular were important, there was scope to test whether they were proverbially 'putting their money where their corporate mouth is'. So I began over a decade of research work to examine the extent to which relationships in general and trust in particular have been taken seriously.

One or two people who view 'soft' management issues as remote see some of this work as somewhat normative, but that rather misses the point. There is nothing normative about investigating on the basis of saying: 'this is what the theory says, this is what you are doing, here is the issue, now how seriously are you taking this in practice?' Reflecting on the extent of dissonance between theory and practice, and seeing the current trends in projects in terms of client demands and their complexity, does raise some normative issues, which relationship management can contribute to filling. This is where the conceptual connection between relationship management and the management of projects resides. Project businesses and the project multi-organizational project teams are increasingly going to need more diverse and richer sets of capabilities in order to successfully complete projects (assuming the failure rate merely stays constant). They cannot stand still and probably will not survive on so doing. Too many project businesses have relied upon clients taking initiatives and driving through change. That arguably is an unrealistic assumption on which to rely in the next phase of maturity. This book therefore aims to distil some of the issues that will help equip project businesses as well as examine the state of current play in managing relationships across project businesses.

Relationships are foundational to individual development and social development. Communication or voice is the barometer of any relationship, but relationships are more than this. Yet where there is a loss of voice, a loss of relationship follows. People are social beings and provide the basis for the creation of value. This begs that question as to why relationships are paid little direct attention, especially in project management. The attention relationships do receive tends to be indirect in research and practice. There is a reluctance to deal with these issues. Some are socially and psychologically uncomfortable and have ethical implications too. However, aggregated abstinence results in falling short in relation to clients and other stakeholders, letting staff down by keeping job satisfaction amongst the lowest common denominator and at a sectoral level run the risk of market failure. There are ethical factors at play here too.

This book is one of a pair, the other being *Market Management and Project Business Development*, which has a narrower remit but shares a common set of influences in its gestation with some useful topic interplay between the two for those that wish to explore. They are both standalone works.

The book builds upon this body of research in relationship management and poses a number of challenges for research and practice, asking *to what extent are relationships managed by project businesses, in what ways are relationships managed at an operational level through systems in teams and by teams*, and *what is the extent of the issue between the theoretical principles applied in practice and the theory?* Answering these questions is intrinsically interesting, but of greater significance is to examine the implications and consequences of the answers for performance. Performance is meant in a twofold sense – the bearing on the project business and the performance of the project in delivering benefits to the client and other stakeholders.

The book is written to provide a challenge in ways that will help inform future research, have an impact through teaching, and perhaps persuade the reflective practitioner in order to have both a direct and indirect impact upon future practice.

H. S.
London, UK

ACKNOWLEDGEMENTS

I would like to thank The Bartlett School of Construction and Project Management at University College London for supporting this endeavor, especially for the sabbatical. Peter Morris encouraged me to write this book. Subsequent support came from Andrew Edkins. My colleagues have carried the burden of my absence during my sabbatical, especially for administrative duties, exam marking and supervision. I particularly single out Satu Teerikangas, Stephen Pryke, John Kelsey and Illona Kusuma for their support. I wish to thank colleagues at PBI in Finland, who hosted me during some of the writing period, especially Kim Wikström and Magnus Gustafsson. I would also like to thank the BI Norwegian Business School, who also accommodated me for a few days during writing, especially Jonas Söderlund and Anne Live Vaagaasar. I have been fortunate to work with other scholars on publications that have underpinned parts of this work. They are cited in the book, and I thank them for their help and insight. I thank Peter Morris, Anne Live Vaagaasar and Magnus Gustafsson for their valuable comments and feedback on an earlier draft of the book.

ABBREVIATIONS

30Rs	thirty types of relationship
B2B	business-to-business
BATNA	best alternative to a negotiated agreement
BIM	building information modelling
BU	business unit
CAT	climate assessment tool
CLV	customer or client lifetime value
CRM	customer relationship management
DMU	decision-making unit
ECG	emotionally competent group
ECI	emotional competence inventory
EQ-i	emotional quotient inventory
ERP	enterprise resource planning
FTM	full-time marketer
GDP	gross domestic product
H&S	health and safety
HRM	human resource management
IQ	intelligence quotient
IT	information technology
KPI	key performance indicator
MoP	management of projects
MSCEIT	Mayer–Salovey–Caruso emotional intelligence test
P³M	project, programme and portfolio management
PBI	Project-Based Institute
PFI	project finance initiative
PMBoK®	Project Management Body of Knowledge
PMI	Project Management Institute

PMO	project management office
PPP	public private partnerships
PTM	part-time marketer
ROI	return on investment
SI	substantive issue
T5	Terminal 5, London Heathrow Airport
TCA	transaction cost analysis
TEIQue	trait emotional intelligence questionnaire
TMO	temporary multi-organizational project team
UK	United Kingdom

1

IN THE BEGINNING THERE ARE RELATIONSHIPS

Introduction

This book is about relationships and their management. It is located in the *social space of conduct* for project businesses and projects. Therefore, it forms part of organizational behaviour, which is how the features of the organization affect the way people work. It also resides at the interface between organizational behaviour and systems integration, where systems are high-level processes drawing together activities to deliver value to customers profitably. Collaboration, integrated teams and forms of relational contracting, for example partnering and supply chain management, have all received a great deal of attention in the management of projects over the last two or more decades. Teamwork, learning, social and psychological contracts and other aspects of organizational behaviour have also received attention. The relationships between people, through which value is created, have been overlooked in comparison to their significance in the performance of projects and their benefits. Success in project management is based more on human factors than on tools and techniques (e.g. Slevin and Pinto, 1986; Pinto and Slevin, 1988; Morris and Pinto, 2004; Pryke and Smyth, 2006). It is the relationships that articulate project teams; the tools and techniques of project management are means. It is the relationships that articulate the interface with the project business, supported by systems with specific procedures. It is the relationships that articulate the interaction with customers and other network organizations.

Most project businesses are unaware of the totality stored in the capabilities of their staff. Directors will say 'people are our biggest asset' and then fail to support them and hardly invest in their collective development. Employers worry that the best staff will be enticed to another employer, hence the reticence to invest in their development. It has been found that only 3 per cent of companies effectively develop and progress their staff: *Developing and exploiting creative capabilities calls for a systematic strategy* (Robinson, 2001: 3). Managers leave much to individual responsibility, in ways that are unsupported and without authority or sufficient empowerment. Staff remain unaware of their full creative capacities, and taking initiatives can have adverse consequences that look risky to individuals. One of the most creative means is the interaction between people. Interactions are enriched by their frequency, how well these are organized and how well people get on working together. These serial interactions are called *interpersonal relationships,* and where groups of actors, especially key decision-makers, represent their employer, these form the basis of *inter-organizational relationships.* The management of interpersonal and inter-organizational relationships is *relationship management.* Relationship management is more than effective interpersonal relationships. Relationship management is the systematic approach to managing intra-organizational and inter-organizational relationships articulated by procedures and behavioural codes. It has gradually been becoming part of the management of projects (MoP) through systematic strategies and action, albeit largely partial at present.

The moves towards relationship management have been tentative and incremental in both research and practice. There are two main reasons. The first is that relationships are always located in context. People behave differently because individuals and groups are simply different, which is the human agency issue where will and choice lead to unpredictable action and behaviour (e.g. Hartshorn, 1997). Both behaviour and action are influenced by the organization of the project business, the project organization and its goals. They are influenced by the project content and task conduct. Relationships are also located in the broader context of market, regulatory, political and other institutional factors. Yet that is precisely why they need managing. The diversity of influences and forces render unmanaged relationships high risk (Nooteboom et al., 1997; Das and Teng, 2001), yet central to excellent performance of project businesses and the performance of projects for customers and other stakeholders (Pryke and Smyth, 2006). Thus, context does not exclude systematic guidance to relationship formation and behaviour.

Relationships cannot be structured in deterministic fashion by management. Human agency counters this outcome, but they can be guided. Systematic guidance and behavioural procedures exert some control and are designed to do just that, yet do not exclude human agency. They provide potential consistency through compliance and room for individuals and teams to shine and, in so doing, try to reinforce what is 'good' and squeeze out much of the 'bad'. Hence, there is explicit or implicit *structuring* in relationships that guide relationship formation and development (cf. Giddens, 1979, 1981). There is a delicate balance between facilitation and control. Dictatorial measures to control behaviour and action are inefficient and ineffective, demotivating the people from whom management are trying to get the best. Draconian measures are also morally inappropriate. Yet, relationships cannot be left to individual responsibility alone. Facilitation is one of the management tasks in practice.

The second reason is that researchers and management seem to be somewhat uncomfortable addressing relationships directly. Context is one factor, the concern for being too dictatorial is rightly another concern, but the third is that it requires time, effort and investment from management. This is compounded by market factors that encourage project businesses to keep investment, overheads, indeed all transaction costs to a minimum (e.g. Linder, 1994; Gruneberg and Ive, 2000). This is effective short-term, but long-term, it adds to administrative and legal costs, reduces effective cash flow management and can render the project business a liability to the customer or client rather than an asset. Project businesses have been described as hollowed-out firms (Green et al., 2008) with insufficient attention being given to human issues (Leading Edge, 1994; cf. Bredin and Söderlund, 2006). Investment can lead to opportunities to develop capabilities to add value and save costs.

Relationships have been providing an increasing focus. Zou et al. state: *A relatively new management approach – relationship management (RM) has gained increasing attention from both researchers and practitioners* (2014: 266). Reliance upon contractual relations requires support from 'established relationships' prior to any project (Cheung et al., 2006); hence, a relationship management approach is expanding its field of application (e.g. Teicher et al., 2006; Cheung and Rowlinson, 2011; Zou et al., 2014; cf. Zineldin, 2004). There is a close link with other areas of management in project management research and practice. Governance especially through authority and trust, systems integration, teamworking and leadership are obvious examples. External 'drivers' arising from relational contracting initiatives such as partnering and supply chain management have advocated collaborative and cooperative working, where cooperation concerns coordination and integration, arising from interdependencies between organizations or their members (e.g. Lawrence and Lorsch, 1967a; 1967b) and collaboration develops out of cooperation at a more sophisticated level to integrate the contributions of differentiated functions under conditions of high complexity and uncertainty (e.g. Anvuur and Kumaraswamy, 2008). Systems draw together at a 'high level' activities from other functions and their subsystems internally and externally with the aim of integrating the totality. Integration comes about through sets of procedures, which are called coordinating mechanisms as mid-level procedures. They are defined as dynamic social practices comprising prescribed standards, defined processes, behavioural programmes and other procedures that are relatively stable and guide practice (Jarzabkowski et al., 2012: 907). Some procedures are routines, which can be lower level 'how-to-do' activities (Parmigiani and Howard-Grenville, 2011) that include specified actions, codes of conduct that induce and are defined as regular and predictable patterns of behaviour (Nelson and Winter, 1982: 14). Relationships feed into these systems and have both coordinating and routinized roles. To the extent that the systems, their coordinating mechanisms and routines are effective as inputs, they yield capabilities and support competencies as organizational outputs in project businesses and teams that can be decisive in the marketplace for delivering value and realizing profit.

Relationship management provides the focus for the book, and the evidence will be presented to support the case outlined. Relationships are therefore essentially practice based due to context, yet there are theories and concepts that can be mobilized to guide the structuring of relationships, giving room for manoeuvre for individuals and groups to develop their strengths in behaviour and action. Where effectively developed relationships are dynamic, whether initially driven by interpersonal behaviour, market drivers, internal initiative and supported by systems that cascade to the level of behavioural programmes and codes of conduct, meeting bottom-up influences of individual action, behavioural influences, norms and organizational culture as interactive and iterative forces of relationship development. Where there is will to develop effective relations and systems to support their development relationship management feeds project management functions and nurtures positive action. This gives rise to a consistent service delivery on a project and across projects via the programme management, which bundle projects together to expend resource on coordinated project management methodologies and capability development to improve performance, provide continuity and consistent service provision. It offers increased opportunity to add value for the customer or client and may yield higher job satisfaction for those involved, thus further enhancing motivation and performance.

Relationships are thus contingent upon what has gone before. There are organizational path dependencies in terms of context and in themselves; thus a contingent and recursive trajectory for development exists, which is far from mechanistic, yet limits the options. Therefore, relationship management put in place systems and procedures to favour certain sorts of options that suit the project business and the market in which it positioned.

Relationship management draws upon a disparate set of concepts within the management literature, for example from governance, systems integration, relationship marketing, group emotional intelligence and organizational culture, as well as being connected in ways to be examined later with relational contracting in transaction cost economics. It is closely related with other functional project management methods and tools as these implicitly embody relations in their operation. There is a conceptual management case for pulling these threads together. Effective relationship management requires investment to spread, embed and coordinate across the project business organization. Projects and their teams are frequently socially and spatially dislocated from the rest of the project business, hence the 'corporate centre', which means that relationship management cannot be assumed to be automatically transferred from the 'corporate centre' into the project and the temporary multi-organizational (TMO) project team (Cherns and Bryant, 1984). Projects are temporal, and their organization is temporary, and therefore, more enduring processes are needed to span projects at the corporate or programme management levels, that is, managed by the project business (cf. Jones and Lichenstein, 2008).

Relationships are founded upon trust. Good relationships build commitment, which provides a key relationship indicator (Wilson, 1995; Jones et al., 2011). Strong relationships, sometimes referred to in terms of relationship *ties* and *bonds,* help solicit personal and social identification with a goal, purpose and with an organization. Much of the significant content of relationships and their management falls between the interpersonal level in socio-psychology and organizational behaviour in management research, and it is this middle ground that has received scant attention in research and a great deal of practice. In research, Kreiner (1976, 1995) probably comes closer than anyone, but then backs off as others seem to do. Pryke (2012) looks at relationships, including those between people, but not relationship dynamics and how they function.

The long-term trend in practice has been towards flatter organizational structures, and decentralized management creates scope for relationship development linked directly to performance (Mayer et al., 1995; Jones and George, 1998), implying a greater reliance upon relationships and their management. The long-term trend is towards increased outsourcing to specialist providers emphasizing the need for effective internal relationships to help coordinate and integrate inter-organizational working. Outsourcing links forward to supply chains, their management and industrial networks, which are considered during the book. The increasing complexity of projects brings relationship management increasingly into focus as project management tools and techniques need subtle application and articulation, especially from the perspective of the project business occupying the role of systems integrator (Davies et al., 2007; Smyth, 2015). Techniques predicated upon simple cause-effect outcomes and linear models for managing projects are insufficient for purpose and relationships provide important mediation, enabling and leverage of appropriate outcomes. Effective relationship management at the project level requires management at the level of the project business to achieve these ends.

Relationships provide a basis of social coordination mechanisms (Jones et al., 1997; Martinsuo and Ahola, 2010). Kumaraswamy et al. (2005) identified the most important relational project team building factors as the capabilities and competencies the project business has built, the learning and training policy, considerable care taken in the selection of project partners and responsibility delegation, previous interactions and trust building, and finally compatible organizational culture and long term focus. All five factors have been shown to have beneficial relational outcomes. As relationships are central to value creation, it would be expected that all five factors are indirectly influenced through relationships, but the last three are dependent upon firm and inter-organizational relational inputs. This echoes the work of Davies with others (Davies and Brady, 2000; Hartmann et al., 2010; Artto et al., 2011). In inter-organizational relationships, three stages of bonding have been proposed: cooperation, collaboration and coalescence (Thompson and Sanders, 1998). Other stages have been proposed (e.g. Boddy et al., 2000; Donaldson and O'Toole, 2001). Dwyer et al. (1987) point to the iterative nature and therefore development is not mechanistic, nor linear. Relationships are contingent, iterative and recursive in development. Consistent effectiveness can lead to depth of relationship development and maintenance to the extent these become embedded, but this is typically not automatic, management intervention needed to achieve embeddedness. Nor is the embedded nature of relationships necessarily 'good' as biased and corrupt practices can become embedded and managed accordingly. Generally management seeks to enhance what is seen as 'good' as there is a business case where short-term and individualistic agendas are not too dominant or where the firm is used to bestow individual power in a broader social domain.

Inter-organizational bonds in the form of economic exchanges or governance structures are embedded in interpersonal and social relationships (Heide and John, 1990; Young-Ybarra and Wiersma, 1999). Schakett et al. (2011) found social bonds or ties account for 44 per cent of service quality variance, whereas governance accounts for 36 per cent and economic bonds account for 27 per cent of service quality variance. Relationships are about performance as a factor and facilitator of effective and efficient performance. An important driver is the alignment between internal relational capabilities (Ritter et al., 2004) in order to help achieve successful outcomes (Meyer et al., 1993; Miller, 1996). Yet scarce resources limit investment and there is no single way to manage relationships. Focus is a management matter, drawing from different theoretical and applied approaches. Project governance is said to structure relationships in project management (Müller, 2011). This view lends a great deal of influence to governance as a structuring mechanism of coordination. How actor relationships are conducted on the ground may be misaligned in practice with structuring from the 'corporate centre' of the project business. It lacks sufficient detailed management of relationships to configure project services and performance. Relationships are interactive and the actions of one affect others who act back to moderate relationship development across a group, team or network. The evolution can lead to inconsistent behaviour. While behaviour cannot be standardized, it can be regularized to a degree. Relationship management across departmental boundaries and teams, and especially organizational boundaries and in networks are subject to emergent behaviour and instability, yet need relatively stability and consistency for effective performance. Relationship management practices and systems established at the corporate level and applied in projects provide a more robust frame of guidance and specificity for detailed action. The relationship management system interfaces with other systems and helps integration of these other project business systems and project management practices. The choice of relationship management theory and application feeds into the business model, which is defined as configurations of interrelated capabilities, their governance and processes to align them and articulate output (Storbacka and Nenonen, 2009). How the capabilities are configured within the business model begin to scope and shape the services provided (Romme, 2003) of which relationship management is one.

Outsourcing is common across most sectors; therefore, configuration includes integration of supply chains and across industrial networks. Relationships articulate networks (Dubois and Gadde, 2000; Pryke, 2012). Research on inter-organizational relationships shows there has been a high failure rate for such relationships due to their complexity (Barringer and Harrison, 2000). Project businesses outsource non-core activities as part of risk management, but spreading risks raises coordination issues. Coordination and control arising from the division of project work and responsibilities across organizations cause a *plethora of highly visible project failures and challenges* (Hui et al., 2008: 7). Governance of the exchange is procurement and contract driven and is therefore insufficient. A proactive approach to relationship management emanates from firms prior to market exchanges. Therefore inter-organizational relationship management is also an important feature for consideration.

This book is therefore about *relationship management* in *project businesses* and *projects*. Relationship management is located in the social space of conduct, specifically in organizational behaviour. Organizational behaviour is a substantial field of knowledge. It has been given proportionately less research attention in the project business domain and arguably not as much attention at the project management level, although there is a redress of balance underway. Integration and a systems approach is well established, yet still a growing part of, the project literature (Morris et al., 2011). The interface between organizational behaviour and systems integration in project businesses is certainly underdeveloped. Relationships and their management provide important coordinating mechanisms and routines to support other activities as well as relationship management requiring its own system and specific sets of procedures, that is, coordination mechanisms and routines.

The term *project businesses* distinguishes firms with projects as the core business, or project-based suppliers, P-form organizations and main contractors which are some of the other terms used for organizations undertaking projects from other firms that conduct projects as part of their broader set of core operational activities. The term project-based organization (e.g. Hobday, 2000; Artto et al., 2011) is closest to project businesses, but includes firms that source in-house. P-form and project business arise from the Scandinavian school, which tend to stress the internal management logic (e.g. Söderlund and Tell, 2009; Wikström et al., 2009). *Project businesses* are specialist producers and service providers that undertake projects as the primary mode of organizing and can be divided into systems integrators, systems advisors on and providers of integrated solutions (Davies et al., 2007). *Project business* is the term used in this book signifying these independent firms where the core business is undertaking projects. Project businesses solicit contracts in the marketplace. They operate in sectors from industrial construction (e.g. Eccles, 1981), shipbuilding (e.g. Martinsuo and Ahola, 2010), oil and gas (e.g. Merrow, 2011), and IT (e.g. Sauer and Reich, 2009) to sectors such as fashion (Uzzi, 1997), film (e.g. DeFillippi and Arthur, 1998; Bechky, 2006), media (e.g. Miles and Snow, 1986; Windeler and Sydow, 2001) and events management (Pitsis et al., 2003). The link between the 'corporate centre' and the project is the project management office (PMO) (Lycett et al., 2004; Crawford, 2006; Aubry et al., 2008). For project businesses a finer grain of analysis is preferred based around the 'corporate centre' managing at portfolio, programme and project levels (P^3M).

Projects are time bound and thus temporary activities conducted by temporary multi-organizational project teams (TMOs) delivering non-standard content (Cherns and Bryant, 1984; Packendorff, 1995). The organizations behind the projects, especially firms for which projects are the core business, are relatively stable as are many or most client organizations (Winch, 2013). Projects are 'skill containers' for execution (Winch, 2013) involving at least two 'permanent' and one temporary organization. Projects are a significant constituent of gross domestic product (GDP) in most economies. Industrial project business is one the largest sectors worldwide (Hadjikhani, 1996; Miller and Lessard, 2000) and continues to grow (Wikström et al., 2010; Liinamaa, 2012). The overall contribution of projects to an economy varies, but a range of 25–35 per cent contribution to GDP has been estimated (McKeeman, 2002; EURAM SIG, 2012). Estimates depend upon definitions applied. Some recent adapted usage of 'project' include:

- *Projectization* involves taking organizational profit centres and turning them into temporary dedicated teams (Peters, 1992);
- *Projectification* involves turning some organizational functions into project activities as distinct and 'separate' project functions, for example new product development (Midler, 1995);
- *Projectivization* is more sociological in seeing certain societal activities as projects (Eksted et al., 1999);
- *Project intensification* involves using the project form of organization to accelerate delivery of activities (Bredin and Söderlund, 2006).

Projects are about producing outcomes in the temporary organization, supported by project business processes. Traditional execution has its focus as efficiency with outputs as the primary objective, yet efficiency in time, cost and scope does not necessarily lead to project success in terms of delivering benefits in use to the sponsor or owner. It may not even yield benefits for the provider or other external stakeholders. Front-end project definition has a focus upon effectiveness within a budget (e.g. Morris, 2010; 2013). Yet the range of management functions does not necessarily lead to delivering benefits from the viewpoint of the sponsor; nor is value necessarily added through project management (Pryke and Smyth, 2006). The traditional execution places prime emphasis upon tools and techniques. The front-end MoP places primary emphasis upon functions, such as systems and contingencies. These are important, yet largely overlooked, relationships. There is some attention given to people, particularly leadership, teamwork and collaborative practices. Yet how relationships work and how they are managed and can be managed remain largely overlooked in research and practice. And projects continue to fail. Estimates state 65 per cent of industrial projects exceeding US$1bn failed to meet business objectives (Porter, 2011; cf. Morris and Hough, 1987). Relationships are one of the current frontiers for management.

Project relationships can be temporary and lack continuity and consistency of organizational setting: new encounters and relationships take place whenever a new project is started (Prencipe and Tell, 2001: 1374). It is what Grabher (2004) refers to as an *action locality*. This can induce ambiguity about norms and routines, and conflicts surface around protocols and processes for using available systems

(Bredin and Söderlund, 2011). Some project businesses retain a core of project staff, hiring in others for specific roles according to demand (Whitley, 2006). This is efficient in transactional terms, hence efficiency in controlling resource inputs, but not necessarily effective as project management methodologies, capabilities and consistency of service provision is compromised due to loss of continuity and systematic coordination. It also affects competence development long-term (Engwall, 2003). People working on projects may move from their current project to a new project on an individual basis, with other team members, or may move organizations for their next project. The discontinuity of working with others can lead to tensions in relation to operational effectiveness.

The book begins to unpack and develop issues of relationship management in the project context in theory and practice. Yet is the issue about a lack of theory or applied practice – a thorny issue and one that cannot easily be resolved? Researchers have made successive calls for theory building (Ghoshal, 2005; Suddaby et al., 2011), but there has been far more theory developed than has been adequately applied. Research and application in social science faces the challenge that the object of our study changes as it is studied and as application begins because of the research undertaken and iterations in practice (e.g. Kaplan, 1964; Ghoshal, 2005). Theory helps us to scope and construct the project management field that is perceived to be necessary to undertake projects. Some commentators argue a coherent theorization of project management already exists or can be induced (e.g. Lundin and Söderholm, 1995; Shenhar, 2001; Andersen, 2006; Turner, 2006). It is more generally accepted that project management and the broader conception of MoP does not constitute a domain defined by a single theory or discrete theoretical propositions (e.g. Shenhar, 2001; Cicmil and Hodgson, 2006; Jacobsson and Söderholm, 2011; Söderlund, 2011a). It is necessary to draw on multiple disciplines and apply the results. Relationship management spans several disciplines, for example psychology, sociology and management, and the ethnographic approach of anthropology.

Rationalist approaches to examination, particularly positivism, have dominated the study of project management and inform the bodies of knowledge (Smyth and Morris, 2007), for example PMI's PMBoK® (2013). In recent years, an increasing number of academics have addressed action and behaviour through a sociological approach (e.g. Morris and Geraldi, 2011; Morris et al., 2011; Morris, 2013) and a critical perspective comparing how project management is rationally presented, and how it is conducted on the ground (e.g. Hodgson and Cicmil, 2007; Bresnen and Marshall, 2011). Traditional approaches of focusing upon rationality and objectivity, tools, techniques and task have made significant contributions yet have fallen short of resolving all the main problems in project management on their own terms. Other approaches using observation, theorization and critical perspectives can be added to enrich theory and practice. Some are implicitly used as criticism of the market system and attendant bureaucracy for projects. However, projects take place in the market and organizational context and the immediate objective is to make the most of the situation. This is a work in progress and addressing relationships remains an under-researched area.

There are coordination and control issues within the project business from a rationalist perspective. Cicmil and Marshall (2005) found that structural intervention, such as contractual arrangements, is insufficient to balance project performance and control on the one hand and the processes of cooperation, collaboration and learning on the other due to the complexity of projects. They propose the project as essentially to be a process of *becoming* in order to capture complexity with the inherent uncertainties, ambiguities and paradoxes in content and in the power relations via influence and deference. This echoes the approach of Kreiner (1995, 2012). The rational planning of projects is a function of general experience and client demands around time–cost–quality rather than a function of actual events and frequently content at a detailed level. The project plan or *map* precedes the *territory* whereby the map is limited in its ability to answer the key issues as it tries to impose convergence rather than face the tendencies for divergence in practice (Lowe et al., 2010; cf. Schumacher, 1977). Relationships can be part of convergent or divergent trends; there is no mechanistic approach to rational or interpretative multi-layered analysis (cf. Burns and Stalker, 1961). The issues faced are therefore more than a function of project content or type. There are broader issues in the institutional levels of policies, markets and organizations through the project business and project. These are the variables that encapsulate the reality of what actually affects behaviour on projects (Bresnen, 1991).

Yet relationships are not a panacea. Just because they are managed does not make them intrinsically good. They can be dysfunctional if badly managed and they will serve whatever goals are in place (cf. Baier, 1994), for example corrupt practices (Gummesson, 2000). However, where they are well managed, the benefits are considerable and arguably increasingly necessary. This implies a strong normative trajectory. There is no more normative content presented here than in most management research. It is industry that has been advocating collaborative practices and thus presents the agenda to take stock of the substantive issues of theory and practice. Project demands and the challenges faced are arguably growing, posing substantive challenges between theory and practice. Projects are growing in complexity. The 'easy projects' have been done, for example as oil and gas exploration becomes more difficult, urban renewal and infrastructure megaprojects provision challenging and client demands increase across the board. This means that projects are not only technically demanding, but also increasingly demanding in service content and delivery. Effective relationships are necessary to meet the plethora and complexity of project goals. Dysfunction and high levels of project failure will probably not be eradicated, but the (lack of) relationship management need not be the source and is a means of mitigation and improvement. However, the path is more than a rational, objective and cognitive one. Emotions, intuitively informed behaviour and judgments will continue to aid sense making and decision-making. Researchers try to abstract the rational economic factors from emotional and moral factors. In relationships, they are bound together on the ground. Indeed, it is a case for all human endeavour and social constructions (Berger and Luckmann, 1967), whether they are project plans or markets. Markets are not pre-given but socially constructed (Polanyi, 1944; Abolafia, 1996), which can dysfunction on grounds of ineffective relationships and immoral action. The market is not simply economic or financial; there is a moral economy that is necessary for the financially driven economy to survive. This is not an argument on moral grounds *per se*, but on the basis that (i) markets need sufficient moral behaviour at an aggregate and thus macro-level to merely survive, (ii) relationships are harbingers of morality levels and (iii) relationships and attendant morality are part of social capital that appreciates with use (cf. Nahapiet and Ghoshal, 1998). Morality is distinguished from moralism and legalism, which are typically dysfunctional. Morality adds to the asset base; moralism and legalism add to the cost base of a project business. Projects have shared reputations for being adversarial, harbouring opportunism with guile and incurring on-costs, even if short-term transaction costs appear lower.

Theory is practical on application. Project businesses continue to endeavour to meet the challenges placed before them by clients, and some are proactive in anticipating challenges and developing capabilities to be competitive and future demands. Theory helps with this, informing types of strategic action and relationship management provides a theoretical and conceptual way forward. Practice also develops on the ground, identifying ways forward through reflective practice and learning which induces new conceptual means and opportunities to apply practice in strategic ways or 'strategy as practice' to coordinate activities (Jarzabkowski et al., 2012; cf. Whittington, 1996).

This book shares a concern for general patterns and particular issues of significance in relationship management and MoP. It acknowledges objectivity and subjectivity in practice and research, finding neither preference for one or another, but examines what forces seem to be at play for actual and possible events (Smyth and Morris, 2007).

Aims and objectives

Aims

The *main aim* of the book is to set out how theoretical developments and developments in practice for relationship management apply. An overarching *aim* is to develop a systematic and operational focus for *relationship management* in projects. Relationships are anchored in projects and in project businesses. Relationships are dynamic and subject to change on an interpersonal level and thus offer a challenging topic for examination. Put these in not one organizational setting, the project business, but in a nexus of organizations of the TMO, suppliers and other stakeholders and relational complexity abounds. Relationships mitigate risk even though they are also a source of risk too and hence need managing. It is the act of management that reduces complexity through developing formal and harnessing informal routines. The purpose is not only to reduce risk but also to provide a *consistent* service to clients and *add value* through the relationships into the project content and for the service experience. These in turn add capability and reputational value to the project business. There is evidence to support this from different relationship management theories, yet for some concepts the evidence examined is purely based in the theoretical logic and potential that scopes the substantive issues of theory and practice, and thus is awaiting empirical evidence through application in the field.

A specific *aim* is to focus upon the detailed conceptual and applied content of relationship management, especially as the content relates back to a systematic approach. Systems necessarily imply constraints. The more closed they are, the more constraints there are. Relationship management needs to be reasonably open. This is not only because the market and project environments in which they are located are subject to change, but more significantly because a balance is needed to achieve a consistent service on the one hand and scope on the other hand for creative problem solving and innovation levered through the experience and skill sets of the personal actors. In other words, relationship management facilitates getting the best from people rather than shutting them down. This is far from easy, especially as much current management thinking and practices are still locked into a linear flow-line production-orientated mindset.

This book builds upon this body of research in relationship management and poses a number of important questions that challenge the project domain as a discipline and in practice:

1. *To what extent are relationships managed by project businesses?* Relationships are powerful and firms cannot determine how they operate, but they can influence how they are conducted. There is no overall pattern to this and practices are still emerging in research and practice. Many project businesses only indirectly manage relationships and leave a great deal of behaviour and action to individual responsibility. Sometimes, there is a lack of support to individuals and for managing risk (Smyth, 2013a) that have the effect of constraining actors in taking responsibility and being creative (cf. Robinson, 2001).

2. *In what ways are relationships managed at an operational level through systems in teams and by teams?* There are two main dimensions. The first is the project business–project interface. Relationship management requires resource commitment and needs coordinating at the 'corporate centre' to be in place for every project. These are portfolio management and programme management functions, and thus relationship management operates at all three levels of P³M. The second main dimension is along the project lifecycle to provide a consistent service on any one project. The link with programme management is again made at the need of each project where internal and external relationships need to be maintained. This is especially so where there is a client programme of work (cf. Hadjikhani, 1996) or where the project business has its own programme of work where continuity and consistency of service are needed (Smyth, 2015).

3. *What is the extent of the issues between the theoretical principles applied in practice and the theory?* The partial and tentative adoption of direct relationship management constrains the ability to mobilize direct data. Indirect management of relations is more prevalent, especially in response to market and procurement drivers, for example, through supply chain management, partnering and

other collaborative or alliance practices. To a large extent, the theory–practice domain is the frontier for exploration. The book attempts to contribute to the discussion on the theoretical side, and the extent of the issue with practice is for businesses to map so realistic assessments can be made in the future. Practices are emerging, and so some terrain is already mapped and is reported upon.

The answers provided in theory and practice have significant implications for clients, owners and society at large. Beginning to address these questions in this chapter requires the following:

A. A theoretical and applied focus upon measures (and changes) that can be made – the internal functions that are under management guidance and control.
B. Theory and concepts are highly practical, yet application can be challenging: if it was all easy it would have been done long ago. Yet application can have profound effects upon business performance.
C. Positive effects on business performance require other functions and processes to be aligned and, where necessary, mutually adjusted and configured for effective performance, including satisfying work for staff.

Above all, the aim is to improve performance. This is the litmus test. Where relationship management is perceived to improve performance, then the justification is evident. Short-term return on investment (ROI) calculations cannot always attribute effects to specific investment causes in terms of financial, management and personnel investment, which renders such assessments problematic. If investment is clearly not yielding returns, then there are three possible reasons. First, the payback is long-term and perhaps indirect, which begs the question as to whether to proceed or exit on an affordable loss basis. Second, the relationship management principles may have been poorly applied and managed, which again questions whether to proceed with further adjustments or to withdraw. Third, the theory may simply be wrong or perhaps inappropriate for the particular project business or for the particular project market. Performance improvement, if any, is seen at a more detailed level. Hence, some specific objectives are also required in relation to MoP and project businesses.

Objectives

Four objectives have been set for a relationship approach to MoP:

(1) Exploring interpersonal and inter-firm relationships at the project interface: client-project, team-contractor, stakeholders and supply chain relations.
(2) Examining different concepts for understanding and for the inception, development and management of relationships.
(3) Analysing the formation and development of relationships in ways that can aid project delivery for contractors and project success for clients.

(4) Highlighting some of the key issues that require development, theoretically, through applied research and in practice.

(Pryke and Smyth, 2006: 5)

What is needed is a structured approach to relationship management. Relationships perforate organizational boundaries, supported by communications and relationship management. Organizational structures facilitate or constrain relationship management top-down and bottom-up and for cross-functional working to support integration. Formal routines based upon relationships are part of an integrated 'hard' and 'soft' system with management and human resource policies that can encourage and incentivize relationship development. These are frequently partial, emerging from existing practice and harnessed by management as part of a broader set of capabilities (Parmigiani and Howard-Grenville, 2011). Informal routines can support an ethical nurturing of people to help mobilize trust, emotional intelligence and other reflective practice. These processes occur implicitly and misaligned if left unmanaged. Thus, a lack of relationship management is likely to constrain relationship development and reduce value delivered to clients whether value is defined in terms of quality or functionality in use in relation to cost or perceived value that includes interpretative and emotional factors among client decision-makers and users.

Therefore, the objectives are to explore relationships at the three levels of managing projects suggested by Morris et al. (2011) – project management, MoP and institutional management. It is MoP level that is pivotal for relationship management for projects and how this relates to the project business where the appropriate systems are embedded.

There are three important issues that project management will need to further address in academia and practice, namely value, context and impact (Morris, 2013). Value means the benefits configured at the front-end and delivered during execution. In terms of relationship management, value is not something that is *out there* and has to be captured for the project. Value is configured *here* in and through relationships. To put it conceptually, value is not objective and external, but is intrinsically embedded and levered through the social capital in which project businesses have invested. Context is meant as all the specific features for the project and in its environment that influence how the project strategy is formed at the front-end and implemented during execution. In terms of relationship management, context is both something to be managed through relationships and recognizing relationships as part of the context. Impact is meant in terms of the usefulness of any project for the client, stakeholders and society. Impact flows from the benefits delivered, and shifts the focus from project management as the means towards the usefulness of projects. In terms of relationship management, impact includes the value embodied in the project as it is put to use and the service experience received throughout.

Flowing from the above, the following additional *objectives* are identified:

1. Improve understanding of relationships and their management in project businesses from the viewpoint of academe in research and learning and from the viewpoint in practice;

2. Improve selection of the most appropriate theories and concepts for relationship management, their application and detailed implementation from theory to practice;
3. Improve understanding of the implications of relationship management for the overall management of project businesses.

There are a number of theories of relationship management and theoretical lenses through which relationship management can be viewed, which are covered in separate chapters:

1. *Relational contracting*: the transactional approach emanating from market drivers, procurement routes and contracts,
2. *Relationship management*: a systematic approach to organizational behaviour, which has its roots in relationship marketing,
3. *Emotional intelligence*: an emergent and albeit contentious behavioural conceptualization with its roots in interpersonal skills,
4. *Trust theory and development*: an operational and behavioural approach to develop relationships and create value,
5. *Organizational culture*: a social container in which organizations and relationships develop.

These are evaluated in the context of organizational behaviour, systems integration and decision-making. Each of these theories and their concepts are highly practical on application. Their mobilization in practice takes the conceptual principles and processes in order to generate particular capabilities. Such capabilities are over and above those required to deliver projects at the threshold level, whether it is MoP in film, oil and gas, IT, property development or any other sphere. The threshold level can be seen as meeting minimum requirements. Being able to consistently deliver above that level requires what are termed *dynamic capabilities* (e.g. Helfat, 1997; Teece et al., 1997; Eisenhardt and Martin, 2000; Helfat and Peteraf, 2003) or *core competencies* (e.g. Prahalad and Hamel, 1990; Hamel and Prahalad, 1996). Core competencies are developed, owned and managed by the firm through structuring and processes derived from conceptual principles associated with a theoretical choice of relationship management. It is a moot point as to where core competencies end and dynamic capabilities begin. Dynamic capabilities are processes between functions that help to improve effectiveness of operations. Relationships management can comprise a dynamic capability where the relationship enhances effectiveness and is the medium for adding value. There is overlap between the two concepts and a lack of complete clarity of definition across the literature. The shared attribute is that whether they are developed top-down or emerge bottom–up, they both need investment to develop, especially to spread and embed the concept across the organization. For ease of purpose they will be referred to as the *relationship management capabilities* henceforth, and thus, whether and how resources are allocated to develop and support, this capability can be theoretically located in the resource-based view (RBV) of the firm. RBV is a theory of competitive advantage that states how resources are allocated and sets the competitive ground upon which the firm competes (Wernerfelt, 1984; Barney, 1991).

Relationship management capabilities can take two forms. Relationship management can be an *organizational capability* (Davies and Brady, 2000), systems and procedures developed and embedded for rolling out at programme level and operationalized for each project. Relationship management can also be a *project capability* (Brady and Davies, 2004), procedures and behaviours developed at project level in response to the procurement drivers of relational contracting or in response to other project demands. A project-based relational capability can be harnessed to develop into an organizational capability of relationship management.

Market competition theoretically drives improvement, so it could be expected that capabilities of advantage in the current market will eventually become standard requirements in certain segments. Implementation of a relationship management capability is likely to be incrementally refined and developed on its own terms and in conjunction with other activities, and thus project business can develop the next stage as competitors either emulate or develop their own form of relationship management.

Defining the scope

Establishing the definition of terms used is difficult because relationship management has different meanings through each theoretical lens. Yet definitions are needed in order to provide a common reference point for the overall analysis and discussion.

Definition and scope of terms

Relationship management

Söderlund (2012) draws attention to the importance of relationships through the work of Sayles and Chandler (1971) who identified three types of relationship:

1. Organizations and users;
2. Sequential relationships, pertinent to programme and project lifecycles;
3. Integrated relationships.

Management on a functional basis per se is only one facet, especially where complex sets of requirements, complex technology and complex industrial networks of suppliers are involved. Wasserman and Faust discuss relationships as:

> A collection of ties of a specific kind among members of a group is called a relation. For example . . . the set of formal diplomatic ties maintained by pairs of nations in the world, are ties that define relations.
>
> (1994: 20)

There has been a considerable research attention given to formal relationships and relational routines (Bayliss et al., 2004; Bygballe et al., 2010), but less attention has been given to informal aspects (Bresnen and Marshall, 2002; Kadefors, 2004; cf. Parmigiani and Howard-Grenville, 2011). Kreiner consistently analyzed people, behaviour and their relationships on projects (Christensen and Kreiner, 1991, cited in Hällgren et al., 2012; Kreiner, 2012). Even as far back as the Banwell Report (1964) in the United Kingdom, the importance of long-term relationships was being stressed. Yet, it was only recently that a relationship approach was seriously considered as a conceptual lens for project management (Pryke and Smyth, 2006). As Pryke has stated:

> The quality of relationships is a key element in the success of a project. The quality may be the product of a range of factors and therefore a consequence of a whole series of dynamic issues. In this way a project team is the recipient of those relationships and how they develop, both within the project team and with those who are externally feeding into the project. However, relationships are also **managed.**
>
> (2012: 51, emphasis in original)

Interactions between people provide the basis for relationship formation. Interactions can be communication or economic exchanges, but relationships describe a deeper connection between people. Frequency of interaction is usually a precondition, but an emotional connection is necessary to form *interpersonal relationships.* In organizations, such as project businesses, the emotional connection is coupled with a functional one, for example business development, procurement, bid management and project management. The organization of effective relationships between groups of actors, especially key decision-makers, is necessary for the formation of *inter-organizational relationships.* Relationships and their management encompass both internal interpersonal and inter-organizational relationships. Relationship management has been scoped in this way:

> Relationship management involves analysis, investment in relationships and a clear view of the wider value that can be gained from each relationship and which extends beyond the straightforward features of the product that is exchanged.
>
> (Ford et al., 2003: 5)

In the business setting, a commercial purpose is linked to the functions undertaken:

> The emphasis is on people and adding value. This is achieved through servicing, gaining competitive advantage through more effective working

> relationships rooted firmly in a systematic context, and through delivering
> effective value. The outcome of the relationship is profit.
>
> (Smyth, 2000: 192)

Relationships are therefore formed through communication and interaction, going beyond these surface phenomena to be initiated around aligned purpose, shared understanding and trust to form ties or bonds, and they can lead to enhanced personal and social identification. *Ties* or *bonds* are often the terms used to convey the emotional–functional–commercial linkage, which embody the subjective and non-cognitive aspects alongside the objective and rational content and assessment of relationships. Relationships can be equality based, yet are also embedded in power and authority. With more power comes more responsibility, which has moral connotations. Whatever way business is structured and organizational behaviour conducted: *All business is based on relationships. The firm only has to make them visible and meaningful* (Grönroos, 2000: 20).

Internal relationship management provides the foundation for developing strong external relationships with clients, suppliers and other stakeholders. But strong project business ties with clients or suppliers do not automatically lead to strong ties in the TMO project team or coalition. It depends upon the interface between each team and the 'corporate centre' and the interface between the organizations represented in the TMO. Strong interpersonal ties can develop, but these may be relatively independent of each organization. Rapid formation of teams can lead to sets of functional and dysfunctional relationships with separate cultural and relationship norms being established in comparison to the 'corporate centre'. Relationship management structures relations systematically to induce alignment and functionality. A relationship approach has been defined in terms of: . . . *project performance and client satisfaction achieved through an understanding of the way in which a range of relationships between people, between people and firms, between firms as project actors operate and can be managed* (Pryke and Smyth, 2006: 4).

Inter-organizational relationships can be formalized and structured through transactions. They start as informal at the front-end prior to a transaction within an industrial network of suppliers or as a community of practice around other shared interests, such as knowledge domains and disciplines (Wenger, 1998). They can be formalized at the front-end as teams are allocated during the bid stage, but this presents the first challenge of service consistency. Without relationships management a change of team may change the service experience for the client and their representatives, whereas relationship management provides a frame of reference so that the base service line remains consistent throughout, enhanced by the interpersonal, and group relationship skills over and above meeting the requirements of the system and procedures.

Risk management is a central concern to project businesses and to project management operations. Risk has traditionally been a prime focus and certainly has been elevated higher than relationships in management thinking. Yet, relationships comprise an important part of risk management. Relationships occupy a paradoxical position. Relationships are a major source of risk, *human risk factors*, inducing uncertainty (Thevendran and Mawdesley, 2004), yet are also a significant source of mitigating risks (Smyth and Thompson, 2005; Pryke and Smyth, 2006). Effective relationships mitigate risks because they have affirmative effects upon other actors, reducing the possibility of opportunistic behaviour among others. Relationships mitigate other risks by enabling creativity, problem solving and innovation to overcome project risks. Effective relationships are a financial asset to the project business and client, whereas poor or adversarial relationships are a financial liability to both the client and supplier (Gustafsson et al., 2010; Smyth et al., 2010; cf. Porath et al., 2011).

The management of projects

Projects are social activities conducted by individuals, their actions and through interaction (Winter and Szcepanek, 2009). Project management applies tools and techniques that are socially constructed artifacts (cf. Berger and Luckmann, 1967), for example, work breakdown methods, critical path analysis or last planner, method statements, and project management methodologies such as Waterfall or SCRUM. Once applied in context, they tend to be used as the 'natural order' to determine action, for example, the exclusion of emergent requirements as deviations (Smyth, 2013b), or can be used politically to legitimize a project and secure organizational resources (e.g. Flyvbjerg et al., 2003). Engwall (2012) draws attention to the decoupling of the rhetoric to use PERT on Polaris and the action on the ground, thereby illustrating how tools and techniques for application are also tools of legitimation. In application, the tools and techniques serve the purpose of those managing the project rather than the project per se. Research and practice have arguably for too long focused upon the tools and the techniques, functions and attendant systems rather than what is at the heart of projects: people and content. It is people and the relationships between people that work well or badly, pursue self-interests from the personal through to institutional levels. The tools and techniques are only as good as the hands they are in. The functions are as good as the systems and their integration. But all rely upon effective relationships. Organizational relationships start prior to the project front-end through stable interactions formed during business development and in organizational networks. Leadership is a further factor, but leadership can be over-emphasized. Only so much is done because of leadership and only so much can be done despite the leadership. Most management theorization has tried to focus upon what is good leadership rather than research the good and the bad, the two sides of the functional/dysfunctional coin among many leaders and managers.

The track record of projects remains poor despite the considerable attention given to project management over the decades (Morris and Hough, 1987; Miller and Lessard, 2000; Flyvbjerg et al., 2003). The project, including its tools and techniques, is not the end in itself. The project is the means to an end. Quality content releases the potential to derive quality impact in use. However, the end in terms of benefits and impact is more difficult to assess during execution and often impossible to measure. Opting for the measurable, meeting requirements within time–cost–quality/scope, has the effect of focusing researchers and practitioners upon the means as an end in itself. This has the side effect of inducing a task and project management focus, which is the equivalent of the production focus in other sectors (Handy, 1997; Pryke and Smyth, 2006). This loses sight of client needs in terms of the project being the means to achieve or provide the preconditions for other worthwhile endeavours. A complimentary client and service focus is needed as all projects render services in order to achieve their ends (Smyth, 2015).

The project as a means to move towards an envisaged future state (e.g. Kreiner, 1995, 2012; Pitsis et al., 2003), which is emerging rather than known (Winch, 2010; Smyth, 2013a) and a service with a client focus to compliment the task focus, has renewed emphasis upon benefits delivery. A complimentary back-end focus to the front-end one offered by MoP helps scope the potential and defines known requirements (Morris, 2013). Dalcher (2012: 653) recently reviewing the work of Morris and Hough (1987), provided an interesting insight: *The work suggests that securing the underpinning conditions, which appear to be most akin to hygiene factors, will go a long way towards delivering positive outcomes to projects.* Taking this further, hygiene factors are those factors that are necessary but not decisive: their absence causes problems but their presence falls short of yielding optimal or high-performance outcomes (cf. Herzberg, 1968). In other words, other factors need to be present to achieve successful outcomes, however defined. This may be a prime reason why research into project management has been broadening its remit, arguably over several waves from the project management or execution focus, through MoP with a front-end and increasingly a back-end focus, towards more institutional foci (Morris and Geraldi, 2011; Morris et al., 2011; Morris, 2013). Relationship management can therefore be perceived as an overlooked factor in project management. Beyond that, relationship management can be seen as a capability of enhancement conceived as a dynamic capability or core competency.

Operations and operations management in project businesses is therefore broader than the project. This is seen in two detailed ways. First is that some functions are located in the 'corporate centre' that inform and form part of operations such as procurement and estimating, technical services, and health and safety. Second is the operational link between the strategic front-end and project execution. These ways provide different lenses to operations management (Smyth, 2015). Relationship management is therefore more than a strategic concept for application; it drills down through systems and procedures as formal and informal routines to affect the implementation of MoP.

Organizational structuring of the project business

The picture is evolving with the 'third wave' of project management. Execution is the first wave. MoP can be considered the second wave of developing the domain. The third wave is broader still embracing the institutional context (Morris et al., 2011) and includes the organizational context of the project business, covering:

- Theoretical foundations and history of project management;
- Focus upon societal, sectoral, and firm levels, including business units;
- The linkages between firm and project;
- Strategy, the role of innovation and injection into the project level;
- Governance and control;
- Leadership, trust and competence development;
- The project in its industrial network.

The shift over the last 20 years has been from a predominant 'management as control' issue towards management as a set of coordinating mechanisms to enable and facilitate effective implementation. This has been evident in the types of contract used, alignment or goals, processes and incentives, and collaborative and relational practices (Smyth and Pryke, 2008; Morris et al., 2011). The trend points towards relationship management at institutional to project levels in order to meet increased demands in technical content and service provision.

Adopting and implementing relationship management is part of a larger system. The existing organization has structures and processes. New relationship management capabilities are to be aligned with existing structures and processes by managing out the rigidities and path dependencies where these exist (cf. Gilbert, 2005). How are organizations designed and how do they evolve? Organizational design is about the structure (Haberstroh, 1965; Weick, 2003). Project businesses are generally structured with reasonable simplicity, but the functional and departmental boundaries tend to be rather rigid, rendering cross-functional coordination an integration issue and encouraging 'mental silos'. Two conditions need to be met where the boundaries are flexible and perforated:

1. Those working within each structural boundary or 'silo' are not inward facing ('silo mentality');
2. There are systems and procedures articulating the interfaces between the structures without increasing net costs and increase effectiveness.

(Smyth, 2015)

Addressing these issues is the management task. What action is needed? The structures are probably working well. The need is to address interface management, which is difficult as taken-for-granted thinking is often fossilized and the problems remain unseen. Interface management is a major issue for most project businesses. Relationships at the interface have largely been overlooked to date because they are contextual and because management is somewhat uncomfortable directly addressing these. Relationship management helps to bring more certainty to context and erase some idiosyncratic elements of behaviour and action. To date, the consequences of the absence of relationship management is manifested in many ways, including:

1. IT or other systems provide links for data and information transmission, for example, ERP, CRM, and BIM, but this is confined to data transference. The data and information are only as good as the collective hands they are in; people turn them into knowledge through coordination and application. To coordinate this for organizational effectiveness, a parallel human system is needed, and that includes a relationship management system, especially at the functional interfaces.
2. Each function or department operates with its own system, frequently operating separately. Relationship management is a systematic means for management to link otherwise disconnected subsystems, for example, linking business development with procurement to help identify and lever value at the front-end for particular projects.
3. Idiosyncratic behaviour, self-interested behaviour, opportunism with guile (for career purposes or in contract implementation), and unaligned informal routines that emerge in the 'corporate centre' or within TMO project teams.

A relationship management system frames action and behaviour in order to help coordinate functional subsystems and to provide consistent service across projects as part of programme management. It may drill down to a finer level of consideration, implementing a behavioural code of conduct at project level as a routine. This frames detailed action yet is indeterminate within it. It provides simple points of guidance to deliver a consistent service yet leave room for the interpersonal and social skills, the creative and problem-solving interaction to be manifest. A behavioural code of conduct provides assurance against self-interested behavioural norms (Elster, 1989; Lyons and Mehta, 1997), with the aim of squeezing out much adversarial behaviour and opportunism with guile (cf. Das and Teng, 1998), eradication or reduction of manipulation and deceit (Powell, 1990a). Behaviour combines rational and intuitive action (Misztal, 1996) and a code can highlight action that otherwise might go overlooked or uncorrected. Transgression in any relationship has consequences beyond the interpersonal and thus affects firms and inter-organizational relations (Jones et al., 2011). A code is not present to measure behaviour as this will tend to render it legalistic and constraining, thus self-defeating.

The most important relationship is between the project director on the client side and the project manager on the supply side (Merrow, 2011). Relationship development at the front-end is important, typically originating in the selling stage (Smyth, 2015). Clients tend to skimp at this stage, Merrow estimating that

3–5 per cent of the total budget should be spent at this stage to define and plan a project. Merrow goes onto saying that the roots of problems are not down to 'bad team chemistry' or 'lack of teamwork' during executions, but are to be *found in the fundamentals of the project and how it was shaped* at the front-end (2011: 159). This is supported in general and includes the strategic setting up of operational relationships.

The front-end offers opportunities providing organizational behaviour is articulated effectively. Edkins et al. (2013) state that across functional groups, there is a greater range of intellectual, personality types, data and experience compared to the execution stages. Communication, an alignment of attitudes and a common leadership vision are important facilitators (Alshawi and Faraj, 2002; Ankrah et al., 2009; Baiden and Price, 2011). Those individuals that provide operational coordination across internal and external organizational boundaries are termed *boundary spanners* (Leifer and Andre, 1978) and relationship management provides a common frame of reference to facilitate interaction and build swift trust (Meyerson et al., 1996). Where there is relationship commitment, people are more tolerant of occasional relationship transgressions (Duck, 1982) or opportunism (Gundlach et al., 1995), because individual relationships are supported from and form part of a base of social capital (Nahapiet and Ghoshal, 1998), and at the interpersonal level, psychological contracts act as a further deterrent for transgression (cf. Rousseau, 1990).

Intuition plays a significant role in organizational behaviour. While relationship management and behavioural codes may have effect in providing a baseline of service consistency, ruling out the more idiosyncratic behaviour, intuition plays and will continue to play an important role. Management and team decision-making are informed by intuitive judgment. Instinct where experts lean upon predisposition and experience in reflex mode is inappropriate. There is a middle ground between reflex reaction and the cognitive rationality of the plan to guide action. Here relationships provide a medium in which to develop agreed actions based upon considered judgment that includes experience and expertise that employs sense making and heuristics to give informed meaning to decisions and actions that combines intuition and cognition (see Kahneman et al., 1982; Weick, 1995, 2003; Dreyfus and Dreyfus, 2005; Edkins et al., 2013).

Definition and scope of relationship management issues for theorization and practice

A brief summary of the main theory–practice issues is provided at this point. These *Substantive Issues* (SIs) are significant under any conception of relationship management, but even more so where relationships are recognized as the means to identify, capture, deliver and co-create value. These issues of relationship awareness and management occur at several levels, many of which are presented here.

SI no. 1: *Organizational Behaviour* emphasizes the point that behaviour is more than individual or self-organized activity in small groups. It is informed by and informs organizational culture, and it is guided by systems and procedures. Yet, mismatches frequently exist between the functional systems and behaviour on the ground, which compromises integration, adding value, achieving efficient operations and effective service delivery. Management tend to over-simplify structures, making the boundaries rigid, thereby encouraging 'silo mentalities' (Smyth, 2006; Smyth, 2013a; Smyth, 2015; cf. Simon, 1979). Research tends to focus upon the systems, whereby management becomes a reified object of study, structured around depersonalized and sometimes dehumanized concepts. Analysis can centre on governance, boundaries, functions and business units rather than relationally driven interactions and decision-making. Researchers can conflate ownership with senior management, and senior with operational management, where analysis tends to be discussed from the *individual project manager's (PM's) perspective* (cf. Engwall, 2003: 790; Frame, 2002).

SI no. 2: *Relationship Management Theory* seeks conceptual means to articulate interpersonal relations and organizational behaviour in order to support integration, lever (added) value, induce service consistency on and across projects in practice. This requires theory to inform the structuring and implementation of relationship management. There is an absence of a unified theory of relationship management, trends and influences emanating from theories of relational contracting, emotional intelligence, relationship marketing and organizational culture. There is an applied need to move from disparate theorization towards *coherent conceptual principles* for application to overcome difficulties that can otherwise appear intangible at this 'soft end' of the management spectrum.

SI no. 3: *Socio-psychological Issues* provide the conceptual link between manifested individual behaviour and informal routines. This includes cognitive action and rational decision-making on the one hand and intuitive behaviour on the other. The range of relationship issues attached to theory and practice include personal and individual identity, social contracts and self-interest that is out of line with the interests of the employer and client. The project management domain has increasingly encompassed a broader remit in scope from project management to MoP, and institutional factors (Morris, 1994, 2013). The roots of project management in engineering have arguably led to some resistance among researchers to encompass the gamut of disciplinary influences germane to practice. People do not behave rationally and cognitively all the time and management has insufficient time and resource to do so. Evaluation, interpretation and other sense making activities are central to the management role for making judgments and assessments. These embody intuitive and experiential thinking, using heuristic rules of thumb in order to be decisive. These decisions and actions are occasionally undertaken individually, but more common is to undertake such action in decision-making units (DMU) of small groups or teams. The role and functioning of relationships remains underplayed in these contexts.

SI no. 4: *Conceptual and Applied Hierarchical Integration* ranges from strategy formulation and investment set at board level, feeding into and forming part of portfolio management, through strategy implementation and configuration of capabilities and support at programme level for roll out onto projects. In addition, there is the injection into projects from functional roles and departments, such as procurement, to guide project management. Therefore, this theory–practice challenge is about the degree of integration and the fragmentation and, in some instances, dislocation of functions that constrain integration. Relationship management is part of this hierarchy in terms of the strategy and design of a system is top-down, albeit building on informal routines bottom-up where possible (cf. Parmigiani and Howard-Grenville, 2011; Jarzabkowski et al., 2012). Portfolio, programme and project management (P^3M) is thus a core element of vertical integration. Capabilities are devised or identified and embedded top-down of which relation management is one. It is also a coordinating mechanism for integration in its own right. Projects are influenced and shaped top-down by formal and informal routines in several ways. Organizational culture resides at the top of the hierarchy, its form influencing all that flows into the routines that configure project management. It is also located at the bottom in the form of habits, group norms and actions that are aggregated up to renegotiate the climate and culture. Relationships are articulated through the culture and thus contribute to the culture through both the formal and informal routines. Formal routines include organizational procedures that build into a systematic approach or system that are designed to regulate organizational behaviour and guide interpersonal and personal behaviour. The management of relationships in relation to cultural factors in the conceptual hierarchy has yet to receive extensive analysis in project management research. At an applied level, this raises questions over the pertinence of detailed measures, for example behavioural codes of conduct. Professional codes that prohibit certain acts and indirectly guide behaviour are accepted in principle with little questioning, yet behavioural codes are focused on particular activities such as health and safety rather than generally applied in project management, despite being commonplace in many service industries. In sum, effective P^3M provides a layered approach to integrated implementation.

SI no. 5: *Conceptual and Applied Horizontal Integration* shares some of the features raised under the previous substantive issue, but instead of a hierarchical or vertical set of integration issues, this challenge focuses upon boundary spanning, cross-functional working and co-location issues to facilitate integration. The horizontal dimension has direct effect on project lifecycles from the front of the front-end where business development conceptually resides through to after-care service, total asset and facility management functions where these are integrated into project delivery, as they are for some PPP-type IT and infrastructure projects. Departmental and functional management is therefore frequently horizontal and coordination is necessary for the project delivery organization, especially in the project business in the role of systems integrator. In-house projects also require cross-functional working. Boundary spanning has become a pertinent issue, which includes formal and informal routines. Formal routines have tended to cover formal communication, systems and procedures. Informal routines have tended to focus upon co-location of staff to help facilitate routines that improve coordination and encourage problem solving. Relationships are dealt with indirectly by these means, an issue that needs investigation whereby a relationship management system, formal or informal, articulates and supports the delivery of integrated solutions at the programme level and over project lifecycles.

SI no. 6: *The Project Preoccupation* is the project centric view falling into the general remit of a production orientation. Most other sectors have added a complimentary customer orientation and are increasingly being more service orientated. Projects remain largely anchored in the historic model, overlooking a complimentary *client and service focus.* This has been the case for both research and practice. Some incremental shift has been taking place over the last 15 years and more progress has been made in research along service lines, while the gradual evolution in practice has been incorporating a marginally greater client orientation. The project as a unit of analysis is task and project management focused which reinforces risk management as a main management activity. The expertise and effort associated with project management is largely seen as an end in itself rather than the means to an end that focuses upon benefits delivery. The technical content, and thus the meeting of requirements, only constitutes a small part of the activity and a small part of benefit delivery. Managers tend to hide behind the uniqueness of projects as explanations for failing to regularize other issues such as relationship management. Relationship management is an important component to addressing these issues and increasing consistency and continuity.

SI no. 7: *The Task Orientation* flows from the project management focus within the preoccupation with the project. It is an *inwards-* rather than *outwards-*facing view of activity. The task focus is about getting the job done, seen through the lens of meeting time and minimum requirements in practice. Practitioners might baulk at the idea that they are insufficiently outwards focused. There is far more of an outwards focus covering client, health and safety and other regulatory issues, and external stakeholders. Behind these areas, which regulatory regimes and client demands have largely forced, remains an essentially task orientation to meet the requirement to time, cost and quality/scope (Handy, 1997; Pryke and Smyth, 2006). This inwards focus is informed by technical expertise and experiential knowledge rather than deep understanding of clients and the benefits in use they require and how the project is conducted from their viewpoint. Tensions can emerge between inward focused, task-orientated project teams and a strategy-focused business with a wider view of the organization (Lycett et al., 2004). This issue has been partly addressed from a market management and marketing perspective (Smyth, 2015). The majority of industries have moved from the production and goods perspective towards an increasingly service approach with an outward focus. The prevailing project perspective is that services reside downstream (Davies, 2004) rather than commencing at the front of the front-end prior to even securing a contract (Smyth, 2015). Most project businesses have yet to shift from a task orientation. Relationship management provides a means to aid potential transition. The conceptualization of project management embodies flexibility, a strong element concentrating upon developing and refining task content and conduct as the means to improve success. All activities have to be performed well, but resolving problematic areas resides more in the breadth of project management consideration than in project task.

SI no. 8: *Relational Contracting* remains an area of conceptual confusion. There is a transition to be made in practice from emergent practices of relational contracting on a project and project capabilities on a client programme of projects. A common response to the intuitive and cognitive appreciation of the problems has come in the form of relational contracting – alliances, partnering, supply chain management – from clients/sponsors and delivery providers. Relational contracting is about contracts of exchange and underpinning social contracts too in some of the literature that emanates in the marketplace. Relationship management is about management processes and capabilities that emanate from the firm that are built and developed by management to inform what happens in the marketplace. This is the transition. Relationship management requires proactive initiative and investment at enterprise level whereas relational contracting is largely reactive. This conceptual confusion renders a challenge for applied understanding and may be an important factor in management awareness of the opportunity and being able to articulate any transition from relational contracting practices of alliancing, supply chain management and partnering into a more comprehensive and integrated approach to managing relationships in projects.

SI no. 9: *Systems Integration* is related to other issues, the emphasis here being a de-emphasis upon internal risk management in favour of an increased emphasis towards managed integrated supply chains and clusters of knowledge services as well as technical capabilities. As project businesses in the systems integrator role, these businesses are well positioned to manage supply chains in all tiers to identify, capture and co-create (added) value to enhance integration. Supply chains are currently used as a means of decentralizing and managing risk. The integrator role requires engagement to improve technical and technological content, align service provision and add value using relationships management as one means to achieve holistic integration. Relationship management articulating business development–procurement–supply chain management interfaces, project management-supply chain management/supplier interfaces are important to achieve integration. This is a source of value on its own terms and is a lever for value in managing suppliers and supply chains. Integration from external actors is only as strong as internal integration.

SI no. 10: *Market Functioning* in research tends to focus upon competitive advantage. In reality, only a few project businesses can have advantage in any project sector, segment or tier of the market. Some are able to develop particular strengths, yet often this gives advantage through differentiation rather than direct comparative advantage. The management of project businesses tends to first focus on survival and second upon any forms of substantive differentiation that yield advantage. This theory–practice issue is considerable. Relationship management is potentially one way to start addressing the issue. The benefits are a source of advantage and help develop other sources of differentiation and competitive advantage. Adopted innovations in project management have arisen from projects conducted in-house and from clients in the marketplace. Reactiveness can stave off adoption. Suppliers including main contractors and other delivery partners tend to be reactive as part of the survival mode. Investment increases short-term risks, and most managers shy away from such investment, encouraged by pay incentive schemes and the need to account for short-term shareholder value. This keeps investment low at the firm level and induces fragmented markets of intense competition. There are some signs of change and more firms may change to meet the increasing complexity of demands. Relationship management provides opportunity (and attendant risk) to manage complexity. Addressing such issues help suppliers to become more competitive and possibly may become necessary in the upper-market tiers in order to survive.

What are the implications of these theory–practice gaps? This depends on, to borrow from Aristotle (2004), what is 'good'. A 'good' project technically, judged by technical input and expertize, may nonetheless leave the client and stakeholders dissatisfied. Projects are simply 'skill containers' for execution (Winch, 2013). What is the price of failure as assessed by others rather than the 'experts'? What is the real underlying problem? What are the benefits of success? These are the core agenda. Yet those engaged with project management have allowed themselves to focus too much on the means to the extent it has become the 'end'. Projects are more than delivering to technical requirements using command and control tools and techniques. Projects deliver a range of benefits using creativity and problem solving. Tools and techniques are needed to deliver the benefits, but their effective application is the start rather than the end point. There is a septic problem, which is the tendency to look at the symptoms or presenting problem in isolation from the root causes. This problem is evident in projects as the axis is increasingly shifting towards demands for creative, innovative and flexible services. This is one reason for the increasing use of the project as a mode of delivery. However, project management is still dominated by a mindset focused on a production and task focus rather than a client and service focus with the consequence that project management is seen as an end in itself rather than the means to delivering benefits and having impact.

Structure of the book

The book draws upon established theories and conceptualization of management as it pertains to and is 'translated' into MoP. It draws upon empirical evidence, including case material from other researchers and published elsewhere. It also includes some evidence that is reported for the first time and some evidence that has been presented to limited audiences, such as academic seminars and conferences. Four main forms of representation are used: the written work, diagrammatic figures, tables and fact boxes.

The organization and brief outline of the chapters are provided next. **Chapter 2** is the first of several chapters that takes an established area of theory and teases out the pertinent concepts of relationship management. *Relational contracting* from transaction cost analysis provides the focus for this first look at theories. This may be the most familiar territory as a considerable amount of research has been conducted using relational contracting concepts of alliances, partnering and supply chain management and more general notions of collaborative working. This is a reflection of practice in project sectors although implementation of the concepts has tended to be partial in practice. The main economics and management literature will be briefly introduced, and then the relevance to asset specific markets and project businesses in particular will be examined. Conceptual alignments and misalignments, hence strengths and weaknesses, are evaluated and an assessment of the pertinence of this theory concludes the chapter.

Chapter 3 is the next one to consider a theory. It is the first of several chapters where the relationships link to a strategic core competency or dynamic capability. The chapter introduces the concept of *relationship management* derived and developed from *relationship marketing* theory. The focus is based upon two premises. The first is that marketing is a function that pervades all activities whether there are separate marketing and sales departments or not. The second premise is that supplier–customer relations are only as strong as the internal relationships. Therefore this theory starts with inter-organizational relationship management, which leads to internal relationship management. Translating this into the project business raises challenges between the corporate or project business–project interface to secure service consistency. This raises some of the strengths and weaknesses of the theory in relation to both the literature and context. An evaluation is made at the end of the chapter.

Knowledge management and *organizational learning* could have been proposed as a core competence underpinning relational factors. Socialization and explicit knowledge and learning are closely linked to relationships, hence potentially forming a separate chapter or an important part of this. Knowledge management and learning has a huge body of literature behind it and has received considerable attention in project management literature (e.g. Scarborough et al., 2004). It is an area where it is arguably easier to connect and transfer the relationship principles from theory and practice into the domains of organizational knowledge and learning. The project management literature is also way ahead of practice in this respect, where studies have shown that take up of cognitive and formal knowledge management practices have been sparse (e.g. Smyth, 2010). Nahapiet et al. however provide a particularly pertinent quote for this book:

> Projects bring together people with diverse skills and expertise for the purpose of solving problems or performing specific tasks. The aim and impact of project groups come from the capacity to build strength by combining difference . . . [and] project groups can draw people together and build a sense of shared destiny and identity.
>
> (2005: 9)

Knowledge management and learning constitute core competencies and capabilities. There are multiple conceptual approaches, another of which is addressed in **Chapter 4,** which considers the challenging and contentious area of emotional intelligence. It integrates a range of concepts and ideas that traditionally are treated separately in research terms, especially from using positivist and quantitative approaches. It is also embodies high levels of abstraction. These challenge some ideas as to what constitutes a theory or a coherent model. The strengths on the other hand are its holistic approach, which is precisely what resonates with practitioners. There is also an approach to relationship management in certain theorizations, which is explored in the chapter. The strengths and weaknesses at a more detailed level are brought together at the end in the project business and project context.

Chapter 5 takes the fourth body of theory, which is less strategic conceptually, but of great tactical import, namely *trust* and its importance in relationship management. Trust has received considerable attention in project sectors over the last two decades, particularly in connection with the implementation of relational contracting (**Chapter 2**). There is some confusion, especially in practice, as to whether trust is present by circumstance and context or can be developed and nurtured through management action. There is considerable amount about how to foster trust on the ground in this chapter. This is considered for managing trust in internal and external organizational relationships. This chapter examines the evidence for the development and management of trust as an important part of relationship management.

Organizational culture is the topic of **Chapter 6.** This is one of the 'softest' management issues, which is typically misused, either when a new chief executive comes in and says that they are going to change the 'organizational culture', or when management says something is 'all down to the organizational culture', suggesting it is beyond their reach to influence and control. The former position inflates the collective power of management; the latter underplays the power of management. The influence of organizational culture and the scope to manage it in connection to relationship management is therefore the topic of consideration for this chapter.

Chapter 7 represents a departure from the introduction of theoretical lenses through which relationship management can be examined and applied. *Organizational behaviour, cross-functional working* and *systems integration* provide three applied and linked concepts with which management grapple in project businesses and for which relationship management is an integral part whether it is present (or absent) implicitly or whether it is explicitly developed. Relationship formation is practice based (Nahapiet et al., 2005), providing a solid ground for this examination. Projects tend to be considered at technical, strategic and institutional levels (Morris and Geraldi, 2011), although relationship formation can be developed and structured through the strategic application of institutional influences. This chapter therefore builds upon issues of organizational and social culture in this particular applied setting.

Chapter 8 drills down further to the level of decision-making as a crucial function, where effective relationship management enhances the quality of decision-making and addresses some of the self-interested agendas that serve neither the project business nor clients. On the positive and proactive dimensions, relationship management applied to decision-making aids adding technical and service value, and hence performance improvement.

Chapter 9 examines the consequences of relationship management in the MoP context as a means to enhance *service provision*. The application over project lifecycles and for programme management within the project business is examined. The conceptual role of social capital, and relationship management as an important part of social capital, is particularly considered. This chapter leads onto *technical and technological provision,* which is set out in **Chapter 10**, and addresses issues of value creation and delivery and the effects of the task orientation that pervades project management. The role of relationship management as a soft skill set for the management of technology and technical expertise is an important issue addressed in this chapter.

Chapter 11 returns to issues of trust and confidence in relationships and their management. Relationships per se are benign, it depends how they develop in practice, and trust is a neutral moral concept as relationships and trust serve the prevailing or dominant ethical and moral climate. The main argument is centred on the *moral economy* as necessary component of a function market, which is expressed through relationships and relational activities and aggregated up from micro levels of operation. Thus, whether morality in business is thought to be 'good' and there is contention as to what the moral interests of a business are, it is the argument of *necessity* that sufficient morality is present at macro and micro levels for the market to effectively function. The chapter focuses mainly on the micro level of exchange and transaction for the management of ethics and morality through trust and relationship management in project businesses.

Chapter 12 considers the increasing 'projectization' of society and the role of projects in the financial and moral economies. It will sum up the main issues covered, including the contribution made to the substantive issues identified in this chapter around theorization and practice. *Recommendations* for research and for reflective practice are made. Drawing the threads together to provide the progression of how the book develops has been attempted in Figure 1.1. This indicative guide acts as a signpost as to how this book builds, showing the relationship management conceptual lenses and applied approaches build into a holistic approach to effective business and operational performance. Some of the recurring

Relationship management as an integral part of project business strategy and the management of projects at the operations level	Relationship management as an additional and integral means of managing projects	Chapters 1, 11 and 12
Towards the application of relationship principles organized through routines, coordination mechanisms and structured into systems to provide and generate capabilities to deliver integrated added value projects and services that are decisive in the marketplace	Business model with relationship management as part of the service, performance and earning logic	Chapters 6, 7, 9, 10 and 11
Towards the application of relationship principles organized through routines, coordination mechanisms and structured into systems to provide and generate capabilities to deliver integrated added value projects and services that enhance the management of projects and meet the most complex project challenges	Internal and network collaboration Service and management of projects focused Innovation and systems integration Internal, project team and network capabilities	Chapters 4, 6, 7, 8 and 9
Towards the application of relationship principles organized through routines, coordination mechanisms and structured into systems to provide capabilities to guide and support individual and functional activity to meet minimum requirements	Capability identification and development bottom-up and top-down Systematic development Internal integration	Chapters 3, 4, 5 and 7
Towards the application of relationship management principles to support individual action in separate and independently structured and organized functions for transactional meeting of minimum requirements at adequate or satisfying performance levels	Governance and contracts Awareness creation of relationships and collaboration practices Emergent service attributes	Chapters 2, 3 and 4
Organizational behaviour comprising discrete actions in separate and independently structured and organized functions for transactional meeting of minimum requirements at adequate or satisfying performance levels	Transactional management Risk management, task and project management focus Reliance upon technical expertise	Chapters 1, 2 and 9

FIGURE 1.1 Mapping relationship management as a means of managing project businesses and projects

issues are flagged up in the middle column and the third column providing an indicative guide in relation to the chapters.

Audiences and benefits

The primary audience for this book is academic. There are two specific academic audiences. First are those researchers in the field of projects, project management and MoP. This includes the project environment, project business, project management and all P³M levels. It includes those researching issues of organizational behaviour in projects and project businesses. It may also be of interest to researchers in the general field of management because projects have become a major channel of delivery. The second academic audience are students, principally PhD researchers, master's students and, to a more limited degree, undergraduate students interested in the field, especially for dissertations.

The secondary audience is practitioners. Those in project businesses, especially the reflective practitioner and senior management who wish to progress their businesses will be stimulated with theories and applied principals to adopt with some lessons learned from previous research and practice. There is a crossover between practice and education for those studying part-time courses, which should prove fertile ground for encouraging reflective practice.

Conclusion

The social space of conduct in which project businesses and projects reside, contain many challenges for performance. As Pryke found through applying social network analysis to a series of construction and development projects:

> The existence of long-term supplier relationships and the relatively intense management of these relationships were central. Major construction clients began to realise that collaborative long-term relationships provided both a threat and opportunity: the threat of escalating costs and poor performance from service providers, but the opportunity to collaborate and integrate within the context of those long-term relationships.
>
> (2012: 48)

This is a balanced assessment of the value of relationships. Pryke was building upon the relationship approach using social network analysis, particularly in the inter-organizational context, arguing that organizations are not necessarily the critical focus for project delivery – the network is. This book also builds upon the relationship approach to managing projects (Pryke and Smyth, 2006; Smyth and Pryke, 2008). Here the emphasis is upon internal relationship management, which then affects inter-organizational management. It has been argued elsewhere that the role of the project business as a systems integrator is under medium to long-term threat unless short to medium-term action is taken to address market management and business development (Smyth, 2015). One way to improve performance and indirectly manage the market is to develop relationship management. It is not the only way, but this book will argue it will become an increasingly important recognized role for the project business, especially the systems integrator role. Clients want value and added value, especially added service value. Project businesses that respond will be those that survive, and the best will gain competitive advantage. The trends are present in the market, and evidence is building up in management practice. The theoretical review provided in this book provides a timely way to articulate these issues, which will lend awareness and equip management for action.

The chapter has introduced some key issues for research and practice, namely:

1. To what extent are relationships managed by project businesses?
2. In what ways are relationships managed at an operational level through systems in teams and by teams?
3. What is the extent of the issue between the theoretical principles applied in practice and provided by theory?

The book has been scoped to explore and examine a theoretical and applied focus upon relationships, their management and implications. Application of theory and concepts were set out and the challenge of implementation investigated to improve projects and business performance. Business performance requires other functions and processes to be aligned and mutually adjusted and configured for effectiveness with financial performance, marketing and human relations, thus offering reward for the owners, satisfying work for staff and satisfaction for clients.

Ten substantive issues have been identified to provide detailed focus to begin to address these key issues. A theoretical and applied focus upon measures and changes is and can be developed in and across project businesses in highly practical ways, which are challenging at times. The aim is to have an effect upon business performance. Efficient business and project performance and effective outcomes are located in the social space of conduct, and relationship management is at the heart of good performance.

2

RELATIONAL CONTRACTING

Introduction

Exchange can take place without either party knowing each other interpersonally or inter-organizationally, that is without a direct relationship between individuals and organizations, especially in consumer markets. Relationships predate an exchange in many markets, particularly in business-to-business (B2B) markets, and especially in asset-specific and project markets. Economics tends to render relationships exogenous, subsequently reintroducing them and pushing them to the periphery of consideration, even though they are central to articulating the exchange and managing transactions. One exception is *relational contracting,* a concept for managing the exchange within transaction cost economics. Transaction cost analysis (TCA) is a substantial subject, and relational contracting is an important topic within the knowledge domain. The chapter will therefore try to draw out the pertinent aspects from a relationship viewpoint.

Relational contracts are built upon relationships of 'trust' and collaboration rather than discrete exchanges. It will be argued that 'trust' in relational contracting is more accurately defined as *confidence* in the context of this examination of relationship management. The relationships can become long-term, spanning transactions. They are designed to promote and encourage collaborative and cooperative working for mutual benefit, so-called win-win outcomes, although the notion of equal shares is frequently idealistic because of market power, the balance of power between organizations at any point in the exchange and any dependencies that may build up through the relationship.

Relational contracts are market and procurement driven. This can be depicted as developing relationships reactively rather than proactively on the supply side, but as will be seen, this can form a basis for transitioning to proactive relationship management, although it is a moot point whether a degree of proactivity is always needed for long-term maintenance within relational contracting.

To begin to address issues of relational contracting for relationship management and management of projects (MoP), the following are investigated:

A. Relational contracting as a form of transaction management in the market and for relationship management in project businesses in theory and practice.
B. Implementation and adoption of relational contracting principles top-down for structuring, governing, and therefore coordinating and integrating activities in the hierarchy, and for setting the parameters of horizontal integration across programmes and along project lifecycles.
C. Management recognition of constraints and barriers posed by relational contracting for management coordination mechanisms across organizational and inter-organizational boundaries.

The main message is about the paradoxical role of relational contracting in trying to manage relationships in the market without addressing internal or organizational relationship management directly, brought about by reintroducing relationships into economics and hence management retrospectively. It is particularly paradoxical as management is so often assumed out of the exchange process and market operations, yet it assumes absolute management control and coordination within the firm upon its reintroduction.

The traditional approach to project management has been:

1. To approach the project from the time that the contract has been signed, and execution is the main management role, with a focus upon cost control yet sometimes treating certain financial matters as peripheral, even though stage payments, claims and final accounts bring these financial matters back into play through the contract. Many issues in practice are negotiated relationally within the 'spirit' rather than terms of contracts.
2. To conduct the project within the framework of the so-called iron triangle of *time–cost–quality/scope*. The ultimate goal is to deliver product and service benefits to the client and, where possible, optimize impact for other external stakeholders, although the means can take precedence over achieving the desired outcomes.

MoP additionally focuses upon the front-end and therefore engages with the business development, bid management and contract negotiations. The front-end is important in relational contracting to set up the framework and terms for conducting the contract. The arrangement may be project specific, for example project partnering, or long-term, for example strategic partnering and supply chain management with framework agreements (e.g. Green and McDermott, 1996). The relationship between client and project business or between project businesses in the supply chain is a standing one and long-term, whether formally enshrined in a framework agreement or informal alliancing.

An overview of relationship management under relational contracting is depicted in Figure 2.1. However, to understand relational contracting prior to exploring it

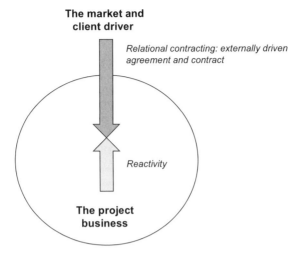

FIGURE 2.1   Reactive relationship building and response to relational contracting

further in the context of relationship management, an overview of TCA is necessary and is covered in the next section.

Relational contracting in theory and practice

TCA economics yet has a strong management dimension posing the question as to what is the most efficient way to manage activities. The main choice is between hierarchy and the market. Another way of putting this is to examine whether it is more efficient to manage production in-house or to outsource and subcontract activities – the 'make or buy' question (Coase, 1937; 1988).

The 'make' option benefits from economies of scale and scope and from the integration of activities. The 'buy' option is an extension of the division of labour to source goods and services from specialist suppliers (Gibbons, 2010). TCA posits three types of contract: classical, neoclassical and relational (Williamson, 1993; Macneil, 2000). Classical contracts are based on exchanges where any prior relationship before or during the transaction is irrelevant both financially and legally. They are predicated upon the market as the mediator to bring an exchange into being through alignment of interests expressed through the exchange. Neoclassical contracts bring parties together through supply and demand factors at the point of exchange, and any interaction between the parties incurs a cost for the transaction. Neoclassical contracts recognize financial and legal issues in the exchange process because contracts per se are unable to determine all parameters and the associated costs of management and resolution, the transaction costs. Relational contracts are necessary where people are working together, for example the employer–employee relation, or where demanding contracts require a degree of collaboration and cooperation, for example in partnering, partnership, supply chain management, joint venture and other alliancing contracts whether collaboration is formal or informal. The three types of contract can be viewed along a continuum of discreteness where the classical contract is the most discrete with no relationship assumed and relational contracts having the least discretion due to relational linkages.

The classical contract is largely untenable in B2B project markets; neoclassical contracts have high levels of bounded rationality, uncertainty and attendant risk in project markets. Contracts are necessarily incomplete and some level of negotiations will be necessary once a contract is signed and payments require adjustment. There are consequences to neoclassical contracts in markets of asset specificity and high uncertainty levels. It assumes a high level of procurement and project management knowledge in being able to assess the capabilities of bids, value for money received and the level of value added (meeting requirements) and added value (beyond meeting minimum requirements). These capabilities on the client side come from specialist knowledge and expertise, the latter being attained education, experientially and through past contractual relationships with suppliers. Yet one of the consequences of outsourcing, the 'buy' decision, is frequently to reduce in-house costs, hence reduce in-house expertise. This feeds into a long-term issue as whether firms that extensively outsource become hollowed out to the extent that they run down internal technical skills and relational capabilities. The residual relational capabilities alone are insufficient to compensate (Parmigiani and Mitchell, 2010). This has been found to be an issue in project markets (Green et al., 2008). The running down of in-house skills and capabilities is a particular issue in the aftermath of economic downturns. Clients become less able or incapable of making judgments as to what they will receive at the front-end and are receiving from the supplier during execution. This current problem is experienced in client bodies (Merrow, 2011; Winch and Leiringer, 2013). The solution is to either increase outsourcing by buying in consultant expertise to advise upon integrated solutions or to build up in-house capabilities again. In either case, a closer relationship is needed. Reliance upon the consultant where mutual understanding and reflective practice are needed implies a strong relationship between the parties. In-house capability development relies upon re-establishment of relationships with suppliers to build up experiential expertise as a minimum requirement for decision-making and performance assessments. In both cases, there is a degree of relational contracting, implicitly, if not formalized explicitly.

What are the key relationship issues seen through the TCA lens? They include the following:

- '*Atmosphere*' – culture, climate and norms are compressed into and to an extent conflated into a single term, which characterize how relationships are being structured and feel at the point of exchange and during transaction administration.
- Human agency, and thus human behaviour, is largely perceived as a negative influence. *Self-interest* is seen as dominating, pursued even where it is at the expense of others, that is, opportunism, sometimes with intent in the form of opportunism with guile. Self-interest is frequently expressed through the

principal-agent problem, representing the relationship where the one party looks after its own interests disproportionately to the interests of the other party (Jensen and Meckling, 1976; Milgrom and Roberts, 1992; for projects see Ive and Gruneberg, 2000; Winch, 2002). It encompasses two main sub-elements:

a. *Adverse selection* – where there are high levels of uncertainty due to insufficient information. This inhibits producing complete contracts and where the information available is held asymmetrically between the parties in the exchange. The result is the party or organization concerned will select an inappropriate supplier or client with which to work. The risk is that the supplier or client will take advantage of circumstances, especially through the incompleteness of the contract.

b. *Moral hazard* – where decisions and related actions incur risk for the other party rather than the risk being incurred by the decision-making party, project team or organization.

- *Uncertainty* and inter-organizational *bounded rationality* (Simon, 1955, 1979) mainly manifested in connection with the incomplete contracts and the barriers posed by organizational boundaries to effective relationship formation and information exchange.

These relationship views prevail with different degrees of emphasis whatever contract form is chosen in TCA terms. Frequency of contact and frequency of contract can ease matters, but clients can switch supplier or suppliers refuse to work for the client. Relational contracting tries to counteract these tendencies. There are positive views of relationships central to exchange, which are socially orientated. The work of Lyons and Mehta (1997) located within the TCA tradition is one example. Going further, the cluster of output around social capital (e.g. Nahapiet and Ghoshal, 1998; Nahapiet et al., 2005; Rocha and Ghoshal, 2006) emphasizes that people and the organizations they represent can and do pursue what is 'good' where it makes business sense. In other words, it offers an alternative market position, one that is increasingly demanded by customers and clients requiring complex bundles of products and service. Therefore a strong business case exists to be socially orientated and conduct activities to the 'good' (cf. Aristotle, 2004). Whether there is a business case in any one context is dependent upon a number of factors, governance of the economic and contractual relations being one significant factor.

Therefore, related to 'make or buy' is governance and hierarchy, which have relationship implications too. If the 'make' option is selected, governance is internal and conducted through the hierarchy. Relationships are based upon hierarchical control, authority and power and rely upon international employer–employee relational contracts embodying trust and confidence. If the 'buy' option is chosen, then the types of contract frame governance. Authority (and power), price (incentives) and trust provide the three-way means on a trade-off basis and for combinations (Bradach and Eccles, 1989).

Classical contracts place primacy on price, based upon the absence of relationship recognition; therefore, price is claimed to determine how the transaction is governed. Neoclassical contracts place greater emphasis authority to resolve thorny issues, and thus power in the marketplace is used. Typically, the client will retain the command position in the dyadic relationship, although the balance of power switches in serial exchanges and contracts. This is significant for most projects, which are rarely structured as single exchanges, typically comprising a series of stage payments, each carrying transaction cost, albeit flowing from a single contract.

Relational contracts endeavour to give greater emphasis to trust and confidence. The term *trust* in TCA generally refers to 'calculative trust' (Williamson, 1993), which is entirely cognitive and tends towards a probability statement and therefore is more akin to *confidence*, where trust is more based on conviction and vulnerability (e.g. Mayer et al., 1995; Rousseau et al., 1998; Smyth et al., 2010). Lewicki and Bunker define 'calculative trust' in narrow terms:

> . . . on-going, market-orientated, economic calculation whose value is derived by determining outcomes resulting from creating and sustaining the relationship relative to the costs of maintaining or severing it.
>
> (1996: 120)

If calculation 'determines outcomes', then this requires scant trust yet some confidence. Confidence and more so trust are required where outcomes cannot be determined nor guaranteed. Puranam and Vanneste (2009) approached trust from the governance perspective and showed different relationships between governance and trust, which may coexist: (a) trust may enhance the impact of governance on performance, (b) governance may reduce the level of trust between exchange partners, and (c) *ex-ante* trust in projects may influence the level of governance complexity. This indicates that trust or confidence is a mediator for governance; that is, the governance structure and ethics in a project. Many have shown trust lowers transaction costs (e.g. Das and Teng, 1998; Dyer and Chu, 2003; Gulati and Nickerson, 2008) and raises the propensity to collaborate (Gulati and Nickerson, 2008). Trust encourages information flow, which can reinforce trust building other factors being favourable (Carson et al., 2003). This approach sees governance as a dynamic outworking on the ground, whereas a great deal of TCA sees it more deterministically structured in the contract and exchange from which certain outcomes automatically flow. This is idealistic, failing to reflect the dynamics of exchange lifecycles; specifically, project governance is a turbulent process over project lifecycles (Morris, 2009) and therefore requires management. This implies the management of trust rather than seeing it as flowing from structuring governance.

Economic exchange and social exchanges used to be considered as different. Economic value was largely considered as the tangible output from production, whereas value theory has broadened to recognize the role of behaviour and thus trust, the knowledge economy and intangible services, social benefits and other facets that have been drawn together and developed under the service-dominant logic (S-DL) (Vargo and Lusch, 2004). The economic exchange is now recast as a social exchange incorporating the co-creation of value as a foundational principle of exchange, value realization and service provision (Vargo and Lusch, 2004, 2008). Therefore, relationships have social value, comprising technical and service value, in evidence through co-creation, which includes both collaborative working on an activity and the perceived value derived in use.

Social exchange can be particularly pertinent where a single transaction is considered in the context of serial exchanges. This occurs on projects in two ways. First, discrete exchanges pursued with self-interest on the supply side can result in the failure to build reputation or the loss of market reputation. For programmes of work on the client side offering repeat business opportunities in principle encourages suppliers to adopt a more outward and social orientation (Ring and Van de Ven, 1992; Lyons and Mehta, 1997; Levitt et al., 1999; Henisz et al., 2012). Second, project exchanges typically comprise series of transactions, structured as stage payments, which can lead to a social orientation, but can yet encourage opportunism, sometimes with guile, as power shifts during the project lifecycle (Gruneberg and Ive, 2000; Smyth, 2015). *Displaced agency* is where actors fail to take responsibility (Henisz et al., 2012), for example for providing a con-sistent service over a project lifecycle or take decisions that make business sense at the project level, yet compromise the ability to secure repeat business from a client programme. Social exchange, instead of being primarily articulated through legal contracts, is articulated through socio-psychological contracts and enabled through social skill sets (Rousseau, 1990; see for projects Pryke, 2012). Relational contracts, such as project partnering, are *a formal intervention designed to overcome the tendency to manage projects in an adversarial fashion* (Larson, 1997: 188). Relational contracts can obscure a fundamental issue. They assume that market or hierarchical decisions are rational. It is people who make decisions and they do so on the basis of goals they set (Gibbons, 2010; cf. Cyert and March, 1992). Yet the goals may dominate in the delivery of a project, which may serve client interests, staff interests, or mainly serve the self-interest of managers or the firm owners, either in the form of direct trade-offs or in some combination.

Macaulay (1963) argues from a legal perspective that contracts are only as good as the relationships. A social orientation and socio-psychological contracts are more likely to induce decisions in the interest of the firm and its owners despite seeming irrational from an economic perspective. Schakett et al. (2011) found that service quality was only 27 per cent attributable to economic bonds (exchange and transaction), 36 per cent to a structural bond (contractual), and that 44 per cent was attributable to social bond (norms and social contracts), pointing towards the importance of relationships. The economy *is also a relational economy since the structure and quality of relationships are a major influence both on the creation and exploi-tation of knowledge* (Nahapiet et al., 2005: 4). This statement was made in relation to the notion of the *knowledge economy*. The same can be said if using the broader concept of the *service economy* (cf. Uzzi, 1997; Vargo and Lusch, 2004). This macro-level conceptualization, when unpacked at the level of the exchange, includes the structure and quality of relationships as a major influence on value created. At the level of exchange, relationships are formally structured through the contract, but the reality is that they are socially constructed by and through management and working practices that form socio-psychological contracts. Task interdependencies are articulated through relationships and their coordination (Gittell, 2001). Interdependencies tend to reduce hierarchy and place greater emphasis upon behavioural control. Herein lies the difference with relational contracts. They structure collaborative working at a general contract level, but not detailed action and behaviour. They are socially incomplete. Socio-psychological contracts do begin to structure behaviour and action. For structuring, management is needed to provide a frame or system to guide action and behaviour, which becomes part of the relationship structuring of a project and transitions from relational contracting towards a relationship management system.

Incomplete contracts are not simply a drafting problem in the face of complexity, but a function of information asymmetry too. Information exchange is necessary up, down, and across the organization to complete a contract (Galbraith, 1974), and here the lines are truly blurring between relational contracting driven by external factors and when these begin to impact internally beyond being reactive towards a more proactive approach that is management driven rather than procurement driven. This is placed in the context of social agendas associated with the exchange process increasing. For example, external stakeholder management and corporate social and environmental responsibility are factors of growing importance. The prevailing economic assumptions barely relate to what happens on the ground (see also **Chapter 12**).

Many argue that relational contracts require norms of obligation and cooperation to coordinate the exchange (e.g. Bradach and Eccles, 1989). Macneil (2000) put forward a relational contracting approach that gives prominence to the social relations in which contracts take place. Such relations are guided by ten contractual norms or behaviour patterns: (1) role integrity, (2) reciprocity, (3) implementation of planning, (4) effectuation of consent, (5) flexibility, (6) contractual solidarity, (7) restitution, reliance and expectation interests, (8) creation and restraint of power, (9) propriety of means and (10) harmonization. Whether these ten norms are satisfied because the individuals and teams work in accordance with these norms out of their own volition or whether management needs to frame action and behaviour to induce alignment because it cannot be left to individual responsibility is where the blurring occurs. Recent evidence in the project arena concerning a client orientation shows that management leave a great deal to individual responsibility who act in different ways, often using the same concepts and business jargon, such as 'client drivers', to explain and label the different behaviour (Smyth, 2013a, 2014). In project environments, overreliance of individuals taking responsibility around shared norms and informal routines perhaps cannot yet be relied upon. In other words, structuring action or deferring responsibility to individuals is shown to be insufficient.

Olsen, Slater and Hult (2005) more recently applied three norms in the project context for relational contracting: (i) solidarity, (ii) reciprocity, and (iii) flexibility. This is fewer than Macneil offered. There is a lack of agreement as to what is necessary. Seven elements have been claimed as required to induce team cooperation by Prasad (1996):

- *Communications*: the precursor to effective collaboration. Communication is free, and open exchange of information among the teams induces a shared understanding and working together (Sullivan, 1988).
- *Commitment*: focused management and empowered teams define the tasks and prioritize areas to make breakthrough opportunities. Goals and objectives, duration, utility, complexity, expected results, and key success factors (cf. Wilson, 1995; Jones et al., 2011).
- *Collaboration*: collaboration seeks out the unplanned and unpredictable events in development beyond a traditional structure and methods of communication and teamwork: a process of value creation (cf. Anvuur and Kumaraswamy, 2008).
- *Consensus*: project team and management members may disagree on some issues, but team support on the requirements and a commitment to project objectives is essential, reinforced throughout the project lifecycle (Prasad, 1996).
- *Compromise*: there is compromise and input from every discipline so that simultaneous development of the product, process, and equipping can be achieved.
- *Continuous improvement*: product or process design teams work toward waste elimination, focusing upon enhancing productivity and profitability through improvements in quality and time (Imai, 1986).
- *Coordination*: actors performing interdependent activities work to prescribed goals, supported through resource allocation, synchronization, group decision-making, communication and common detailed objectives (Malone, 1991). Partnerships are formed among all disciplines involved in the project, and communication links are formally established and utilized.

These are important issues but largely fail to address the direct management relationships at a detailed level of organizational and team behaviour. Perhaps understanding is still lacking as to what relational contracts require on the ground and contexts pose challenges. Yet, many of the above features are supported by strong bonds and work ties, informal norms and direct relationship management within the 'make' decision of in-house production, and therefore one way of looking at relational contracting is to view it as getting the best from outsourcing through a competitive edge to avoid complacency and escalating cost structures, yet getting similar benefits through collaboration as those achieved through internal coordination and relational contracts. In this sense, relational contracting is akin to a domestic market (Campbell, 1995). The domestic market brings discussion to the archetype relational contract between employer and employee whereby they are not seeking a dyadic relationship but are on the same 'side' in shared endeavor to complete sets of activities successfully.

Relational contracting, relationship management and the management of projects

Relational contracting is conceptually relevant for the provision of specific assets. Nishiguchi (1994) found four types of specific assets, namely, physical assets such as specialist tools for manufacture, dedicated assets which are related to specific sales and contracts, human assets such as learning by doing and developing customer-specific social capital, and site assets such as a building facility and other infrastructure. Projects can cover all four types of specific assets in various combinations, and partnerships were most successful where there were high levels of human and site assets involved.

MoP, and specifically the development of the front-end strategy for the project, is an important part of the structuring of the project. The overt process of scoping the project strategy and defining the requirements is a central function of MoP on the client side and for project businesses seeking to prequalify and bid. Project businesses have to assess their strategy towards the project as far as it is known. They frequently have influence in shaping projects (Cova et al., 2002; Cova and Salle, 2011). This starts during the sales process through business development, implicitly through relationships developed and explicitly through relationship marketing approaches (Smyth, 2015; **Chapter 3**). Marketing and business development are conceptually instigated at the front of the front-end in project businesses and constitute part of the service delivered. At the rudimentary level, this includes conveying track record and capabilities against the background of market reputation and corporate brand to give reassurance service to the prospective client. At a comprehensive level, it involves offering advice and shaping the content and execution too.

Relationships are therefore implicitly present from the outset of any project. An informal elementary level of relationship management is implicitly included at an interpersonal level dependent upon how the individuals interact. This does not constitute a relationship management system for the project business as it is left to individual responsibility. Relational contracting, through partnering, partnerships, supply chain management or other alliance mechanisms, is largely reactive to procurement drivers from the market. The front-end strategy for the project business is conceptually employing an integrated approach to its internal coordination and sourcing value from the supply chain. This is the systems integrator role (Davies et al., 2007). Relationships therefore play an important role in two respects at the front-end:

1. *Employer–employee relational contract*: two parties collaborating and part of that function is to perform actions to support integration vertically in the hierarchy and cross-functionally between departments and roles at any one time and along the project lifecycles. The relational contract is therefore supported by internal integration, hence team working between individuals where a social contract is relied upon within other managerial systems and operations. Relational contracts do not ensure coordination unless articulated by management through an explicit relationship management system.

2. *Inter-organizational relational contracts*: practices to drive collaborative in the marketplace, the assumption being that internal coordination is in place, structured through governance, especially trust and confidence. Systems are necessary to facilitate the technical and other management functions to integrate all internal contributions and components towards effective delivery. Relational contracts from the market can exert some force to help relational coordination internally, but as the analysis has shown to date, there is a somewhat ambiguous, even paradoxical position occupied by such contracts between external drivers for collaboration and the extent to which social norms and socio-psychological contracts are engendered internally to develop effective relationships and informally generate sound relational practices. This is supported elsewhere in other research (e.g. Cheung et al., 2006; Teicher et al., 2006; Zou et al., 2014).

Internal functions often suffer from a lack of integration, leading to the so-called silo mentality and a lack of communication and relationship development necessary to compensate for the disconnect between functional subsystems (Fact Box 2.1).

FACT BOX 2.1 RELATIONSHIPS, THE EXTENT OF INTEGRATION AND RELATIONAL CONTRACTING

UKCo, a major international engineering contractor, reported that they lack integration. Their highly decentralized structure inhibits integration. Portfolio and programme management are underdeveloped, the result being a lack of systematic integration along project lifecycles from the front-end and to close out. The integration of different business units (BUs) is also reported to be a work-in-progress. Within BUs, functional departments view integration as 'upstream and downstream' with activities and tasks flowing through their department or function for discrete inputs. Some functions are becoming more centralized, for example Procurement.

EUCo, a major international contractor, demonstrated variable ability to integrate internal activities. Business Development Management worked better than Bid Management along project lifecycles to monitor and learn. Bid Managers, drawn from Estimation, Planning and Project Management, lacked appreciation of the 'bigger picture'. Senior management believe value is being lost between prequalification and bid submission. They were suffering a low strike rate at bid stage. It has been stated: *the lack of integrated systems, including relationship management systems, is a large contributory factor* (Smyth, 2013a: 8–9).

AntCo, an international construction and property development group, work discretely by function but not in 'a joined up way'. It was stated that the benefits are obvious when integration is achieved: *They do work fantastically*

(Continued)

> **FACT BOX 2.1** (Continued)
>
> *well together if they are joined together in the right way.* AntCo exhibits silo think-
> ing, inducing 'creative tension'. Knowledge is picked up mostly by osmosis
> with people coming up the 'delivery ranks'. Learning is 10 per cent training,
> 20 per cent is mentoring and 70 per cent is gained through job experience. They
> depend upon internal governance and trust. There are regular project reviews
> and a Head of Governance calls the people to account. A Bid Manager further
> noted that there are spatial divisions by floor allocation, which structurally rein-
> forces the silos, amplifies the negativity of enclaves and inhibits integration.
>
> EuroCo, an international construction contractor, exhibited silo approaches
> with a traditional project performance focus. It was said there are *disconnected
> systems* and this *leads to a waste of resources by incurring 'so much repetition'.*
> Specifically in connection with relational contracting, it was found the intent to
> collaborate with clients lacked support beyond integrative efforts to add 'short-
> term technical value for projects'. Internal and external relationships are not
> systematically spanning whole project lifecycles (Smyth and Kusuma, 2013).
>
> In sum, successfully integrated 'hard' systems require parallel 'soft',
> human systems to make the hard systems work. In the absence of integrated
> hard systems, the soft systems become more critical. None of these project
> businesses had formal relationship management systems, but all were work-
> ing in markets where relational contracting is applied by key clients.
>
> *Sources*: Interviews conducted with directors, senior management, departmental and
> project managers, 1st and 2nd quarters of 2012; Smyth (2013a); Smyth and Kusuma
> (2013).

Relational contracts are therefore no guarantee to more effective collaborative
working in the marketplace if internal collaboration is weak or not enhanced via
social contracts of collaboration among employees in addition to their relational
contracts and not supported by integrated management systems in which relationship management is present. Misalignments of strategic elements can incur relational
dysfunction during execution and hence invoke defensive behaviour from within
project businesses, rendering relational contracts with clients largely rhetorical (cf.
Green and May, 2003; Green, 2011). Yet, contracts are usually met because of the
good relationships between the parties, where these develop by individuals taking
responsibility, cultural norms and implicit if not explicit relationship management
routines; indeed, these are positive reinforcements if there is a programme of work
that extends beyond a single project. Relationships in this way are self-reinforcing
(Merrow, 2011). However, Merrow (2011) is not an advocate of formal relational
contracts, having data on oil and gas projects to show that most have failed. This
has been corroborated through other empirical studies (e.g. Harrigan, 1988; Kogut,
1988). This might suggest that the lack of adequate relationship management is
a general problem or it may suggest that it is largely irrelevant.

There are qualified successes too. Relational contracting is based on sustainable relationships and trust as a primary governance mechanism in order to induce so-called win-win outcomes for both the client and contractor. The development of trust between organizations is seen as a function of the length of the relationship between them (Bresnen and Marshall, 2000). This is dependent upon a number of factors:

a.   The length (and depth) of relationship established at the front-end from business development, through bid management and handover into execution;
b.   The continuity of staff over project lifecycles;
c.   The extent of serial contracts of repeat business and relationship continuity between contracts (Hadjikhani, 1996);
d.   Robust internal systems of integration;
e.   Strength of internal relationships and trust (Smyth, 2008a).

Client or customer loyalty for repeat business and profit generation can only be as strong as internal loyalty among staff (Reichheld, 1996), loyalty being underpinned by trust, which in the marketplace can only be as strong as internal trust on either side of the dyadic relationship (Smyth, 2008a). This takes the discussion beyond relational contracts in the marketplace to an internal focus and an overt relationship management system, which extends beyond the dyadic relationship between project business and client.

The Terminal 5 project at London Heathrow Airport is frequently held up as an archetypal relational contract. Risk absorption and collaborative working for innovation (Davies et al., 2009). It was a highly successful construction and engineering project. It was organized around the 'T5 agreement', whereby the client, British Airports Authority or BAA, absorbed the project risk as a means to engender innovation and collaboration. Despite employing multiple attributes of relational contracting, in some important respects mechanisms to ring-fence the profit and to set targets reasserted price governance of classical contracts (Gil et al., 2011). This shows that relational contracts can achieve considerable benefits for the client and project businesses, despite experience in other sectors (e.g. Merrow, 2011), but it also shows that the full scope is seldom implemented in practice because of the degree of difficulty and that clients are reluctant to let go of some hierarchical control through market power (e.g. Campbell, 1995; Smyth and Edkins, 2007; cf. French and Raven, 1958). Megaprojects not only give sufficient time to overcome temporal barriers to aligned behaviour, but there also benefits from continuity, for example many key decision-makers moving from Terminal 5 to the London Olympics 2012, and then Cross Rail in the United Kingdom.

On most contracts, behavioural blockages are a common source of frustrating relational contracting initiatives (e.g. Cheung et al., 2003; Crespin-Mazet and Portier, 2010). One issue is the social and sometimes spatial distance between the instigators and those responsible for implementation. The decision-makers adopting relational contracting are seldom those responsible for implementation (Salk and

Simonin, 2003; Janowicz-Panjaitan and Noorderhaven, 2009). The distance is twofold, created by the market and organizational hierarchies. While relational contracting has fallen short of the original expectations in modern times (e.g. Smyth, 2010; Green, 2011; Merrow, 2011), some benefits have been evident too. Bresnen and Marshall (2000) identified the following benefits of partnering: increased productivity, early contractor and supplier involvement, focus upon learning and continuous improvement, increased client satisfaction and a greater stability of workload. Integrated team working has been forthcoming, especially in Hong Kong (e.g. Kumaraswamy et al., 2005), where collaboration is supported by social obligations. Others have found positive evidence across different continents where relationships have proved significant (e.g. Larson, 1997; Love et al., 2010; Eriksson and Pesämma, 2007; Henisz et al., 2012). Drawing on a range of evidence, Pryke (2012) states collaborative relations induce a customer focus, a mechanism for problem resolution, open book accounting, means for continuous improvement, commitment to objectives and long-term aims and innovation with greater equality between the organizations. Partnering between several organizations influences other organizations in the network involved in projects (Bygballe et al., 2010).

Thus, relational contracting on the supply side is not deterministic. Introducing relational contracting does not mechanically lead to collaboration. It may induce favourable conditions, but more is necessary on the supply side that emanates from management. This is clear from the variation in research findings, supported by conceptual logic derived from management theory. The theory–practice issue indirectly alluded to by Merrow (2011) on the lack of success on oil and gas relational contracts may be partly answered from the above analysis.

The same problems reside on the demand side. Clients have been responsible for poor implementation. There are several known factors:

- Clients moving to relational contracts have subsequently run down their in-house capabilities to secure cost savings and are less able to assess whether they are going to get or receive value for money (Merrow, 2011; Winch and Leiringer, 2013).

  a. Different forms and meaning (Saad et al., 2002; Crespin-Mazet and Portier, 2010);
  b. Reluctance to invest resources upfront (Smyth, 2004) and resistance to structural change (Crespin-Mazet and Portier, 2010);
  c. Lack of programme development on the supply side to manage operational relationships (Smyth and Edkins, 2007);
  d. Clients changing the ground rules disincentivize investment and so continuous improvement tend to be 'thrown over the wall' to suppliers through several tiers until the original objectives and purposes are lost in the social distance of supply chains (Smyth, 2006);
  e. Time, cost and quality issues have failed to improve – the incentive structures on quality are largely unchanged, there are rarely under-runs on alliance contracts, and operability failures have increased (Merrow, 2011).

- Clients have insufficiently intervened through supply chain management when contractors have failed to provide adequate response:

    a. Demanding a shift from the traditional project focus to programme management;
    b. Driving relational contracting to reach beyond the next supply tier below the main contractor (cf. Mason, 2008);
    c. Requiring robust systems with appropriate coordinating mechanisms to transfer lessons learnt and continuous improvement between projects (cf. Bresnen et al., 2004; Smyth, 2010);
    d. Value co-creation induced by strengthening relationships along project lifecycles and between projects (cf. Hadjikhani, 1996; Cova et al., 2002; Smyth and Fitch, 2009; Smyth, 2015).

Establishing a relationship relies upon commitment, which from an economics perspective can be construed as a factor of lock-in (Donaldson and O'Toole, 2001) and thus has negative overtones, although the purpose of any contract is lock-in. Relationships require sustenance over project lifecycles (Love et al., 2011), although relational contracting as a concept does not demand this. Relational contracting is market and procurement driven rather than driven by internal management, and investors and managers cannot rely upon contractual remedies. Overreliance on contracts for negotiating outcomes is *frequently met with bitter disappointment* (Henisz et al., 2012: 42). Project partnering is easier than strategic partnering as strong relationships require close cooperation, and this is difficult to replicate across projects (Gadde and Dubois, 2010). However, it is less effective as discussed (Green and McDermott, 1996).

Additional support for relational approaches comes from the broader industrial and supply network. Projects are conducted within production networks (e.g. Dubois and Gadde, 2000; Beamish and Biggart, 2012; Pryke, 2012; cf. Håkansson and Snehota, 1995) and communities of practice (e.g. Eccles, 1981; cf. Wenger, 1998). The industrial network is insufficient in itself to sustain a relational approach. Relationships between the main contractor and the client are central to the organizational culture, climate and behavioural norms and 'atmosphere' of relational contracting. Relational contracts do not necessarily penetrate deep into supply chains. Conversely, this relative autonomy can mean that relational alliances are informally formed in supply chains with the project business acting as systems integrator. Thus, other supply chain members occupy significant relational positions through supply chain management (Saad et al., 2002; Meng, 2012), but they are not decisive or necessarily causal in producing positive outcomes. Evidence produced by Meng (2012) from 400 respondents in project partnering in construction found that cost overruns are likely to occur, although the amount of overruns was lower on average compared to other types of contract. This may be an indicator of the ability to negotiate work content as latent requirements emerge, although other works suggests that the contractor default position is to treat emergent requirements as deviations to be rejected or responded to on a minimal basis (Smyth, 2013b). There may be other reasons for the marginal improvement in meeting cost targets and budgets.

Clearly, there is evidence pointing to positive and negative features of relational contracting. Despite the attention it has received, analysis of the causal outworking at detailed levels of operation remains sparse to secure a picture of the types of situation where the causal powers of relational contracts yield to other more causal processes. The contextual contingencies and conditions that have causal powers to affect relational contracting one way or the other have therefore yet to be fully unpacked and articulated (cf. Smyth and Morris, 2007). What we do know is that there is a 'grey area' between the market and procurement drivers of relational contracting during execution and the need to implement systematic management practices requiring formal systems and procedures to endure successful implementation. There is clear evidence that relational contracting is insufficient to guarantee all the desired outcomes to date. The trigger points for implementing robust systems with client and especially supplier firms may also be contextual depending on organizational culture, existing systems, norms and informal routines in relation to each project. Internal relationship management systems are distinct from relational contracting. They are more than and conceptually distinct from relational contacting. Relational contracting does however offer management a stimulus and catalyst to transition to proactive relationship management.

Conclusion

Relational contracts within TCA occupy a curious and somewhat paradoxical position in project markets. First, project businesses are driven to keep overheads and investments low due to uneven market demand over economic cycles and 'lumpiness' of annual workload evidenced through bids and attendant strike rates. This provides a driver to outsource in order that project businesses do not carry costly capacity that is idle at any one time, and second, projects tend to embody the production of specific assets of complexity of high risk. Asset specificity might be thought to provide a driver to produce in-house in order to integrate inputs and to avoid negative negotiation through 'haggling' (Masten, 1984; cf. Williamson, 1985). In practice, market drivers tend to outweigh project drivers as outsourcing is and has become increasingly prevalent in project sectors in order to manage risk and pursue survival strategies.

Despite the considerable focus upon relational contracting over the last two and a half decades, research has hardly considered the interplay and effects of long-term alliances and collaborative working upon relationships and how they have developed (Bygballe et al., 2010). This chapter has analyzed *relational contracting* as a form of transaction management in the market and for relationship management in project businesses in theory and practice. It finds a tension between the two, in particular that relational contracting is dependent upon factors outside its conceptual remit for applied success. Specifically, it depends upon management response in the project business and an area of repetitive occurrence is needed to help facilitate relationship development in the supplier and client organizations in order to engender an adequate relational interface between the client and supplier.

The implementation and adoption of relational contracting principles top-down for structuring, governing, and therefore coordinating and integrating activities in the hierarchy and setting the parameters for horizontal integration across programmes and along project lifecycles have also been examined. Governance is insufficient to structure relationships, despite its conceptual emphasis upon calculative trust or confidence. It assumes too much in the outworking of practices. A broader network approach was also addressed but considered insufficient to sustain relational contracting between client and project business. Management recognition of constraints and barriers posed by relational contracting for coordination mechanisms across organizational and inter-organizational boundaries were therefore addressed in outlining the arguments.

A map of the relationship characteristics is provided in Table 2.1 as a means to distill some of the main relationship implications that arise from the analysis.

A number of theory–practice issues were addressed in the chapter, which are set out in relation to the descriptions of the issues that were previously presented (**Chapter 1**). Only those substantive issues that relational contracting directly addresses are reviewed below.

SI no. 3: *Socio-psychological Issues* are addressed through the *intuitive behaviour and judgment* that relational contracting assumes to be aligned yet does not directly address – at most therefore an indirect and partial influence to addressing this issue, but relational contracting can have the effect of strengthening the sense of these socio-psychological contracts through existing routines and management action. There is however nothing mechanistic in relational contracting that automatically addresses this issue.

SI no. 6: *The Project Preoccupation* is addressed by moving towards a greater *client focus* based upon collaborative working. Relational contracting may extend beyond a single project into a programme through strategic partnering and framework agreements for example. However many relational contracts are one-off events, for example project partnering, or treated as one-off events by project businesses even if part of a large client programme.

SI no. 8: *Relational Contracting* moves away from a market and procurement driven approach towards relational capabilities that flow from the contract and governance based upon trust, which may shift ground towards *internally induced relationship management*. Alliances, partnering, supply chain management are employed on the demand side. Transition to relationship management on the supply side is underpinned by competencies and capabilities, and it requires strategic investment by the enterprise at the portfolio management level to be cascaded down through programme management to the project. This has occurred on a limited basis in practice among project businesses because structuring relational contracts does not automatically induce necessary capability development.

SI no. 10: *Market Functioning* in seeking *competitive advantage* through relational contracting is weak as most project businesses are reactive rather than

TABLE 2.1 Relational contracting and the management of relationships

Markets	Structural features	Possible/probable power relations	Behaviour	
			Interpersonal	*Organizational level*
Client	Market and procurement drivers, structured through a contract or an associated agreement or framework. The project businesses have developed programme management. Project-level collaboration.	Conceptually **cooperative**. A tendency for the client to revert towards a more **competitive** approach for selection and a **command** position for project execution. The result is an *interdependent* and 'domestic' market relationship in general, but a *dependent* sub-contract relationship. Equality norms needed to balance equity and power norms in practice.	Reliant upon goodwill and socio-psychological contracts.	No explicit relationship management required. There is an assumption that the contract and associated governance initiates good relations and management automatically have all other necessary attributes in place.
Suppliers	Relational contracting between client and main contractor are not necessarily cascaded down the supply chain. Successive suppliers 'throw the responsibility over the wall' to the next tier.	**Cooperation** and *interdependency* often yield to either a **competitive** and *independent* approach or to the purchaser occupying a **command** position with suppliers being *dependent* subcontractors. Mutual cooperation and joint development of working practices and co-created value is rare.	Relationships largely rely on personal disposition, and informal routines, typically developed from habits of the key decision-makers.	No explicit relationship management required. Some informal routines may get embedded and become formal ones.
Staff (employees and contract staff)	Inherently relational contracts.	**Cooperative**. An *interdependent*, and domesticated market. Relationships between peers and in teams rely upon socio-psychological contracts derived from norms and individuals/teams taking responsibility rather that firm management.	A legal contract facilitated by goodwill and psychological contracts between employer and employee.	
Recruitment	Potentially relational contracts. No requirement to recruit those with strong interpersonal skills.	A reputation for a **cooperative**, *domesticated* market for employees. *Interdependence* prevails, although contract staff may experience a more competitive and *independent* market.	Usually the employer is in a commanding position and potential employees are in competition, hence the weighting is towards an *independent* buyer's market.	

proactive, and thus, the outcome is dependent upon the extent that the previous issues are addressed.

An additional comment can also be made about **SI no. 2**, which concerns ***Relationship Management Theory***. The description points towards the disparate theorization in existence. Relational contracting provides one theoretical option, yet is narrow in its remit. Indeed, it has been a source of some considerable confusion across the literature as to how far it constitutes relationship management on its own terms, and some commentators have failed to distinguish it from internally driven relationship management, preferring the structural 'remedy' induced through contracts and related governance. Thus, articulating organizational behaviour generally and relationship management in particular is hampered by different theorization on relational contracting, rendering application difficult at the 'soft end' of the management spectrum in practice.

The main contribution has been to explore relational contracting directly through the broader theoretical lens of relationship management. This provides a different starting point from the majority of the literature that commences with the project. There are several main *recommendations* for research that flow from the analysis regarding project businesses and projects:

A. Research into relational contracting has still to unpack when and under what circumstances the tipping point is reached to invoke proactive relationship management. This involves investigating a range of different project types and contexts, including how relationships are structured both in respective organizations and in the dyadic relationships.
B. Research into the detailed influence and impact of social and psychological contracts internally and in the market relationships under relational contracting.
C. The influence of different organizational cultures, norms and informal routines remain a largely under-researched area in relational contracting.

There are several main *recommendations* for practice that flow from the analysis and echo some of the recommendations from the previous chapter:

1. Investigating opportunities and means to transition from relational contracting to internal relationship management in project businesses.
2. Consideration of aligning behaviour, especially habitual behaviour, that has developed as informal routines, to programme management and to project management where temporary multi-organizational project teams (TMOs) have to be swiftly established with a greater risk of misalignment in the temporal context.
3. Overreliance upon individuals and individualism versus control of behaviour and action is an important area of management about which greater awareness and practice experience can be exchanged in project businesses and for project operations.

In summary, the adoption of relational contracting is far from a guaranteed recipe for collaborative working, but helps to stimulate a more thoughtful and reflective approach to the way relationships are conducted in practice with potentially beneficial results. It does not constitute a coherent relational approach either upon its own conceptual terms nor in practice, yet it provides a basis to transition to a more coherent approach. The next chapter addresses one such approach towards which a project business can transition.

3

THE MARKET, MARKETING AND RELATIONSHIP MANAGEMENT

Introduction

Modern work is social, conducted through relationships with others in groups and teams. Relationships contribute to performance, job satisfaction, and managing of clients and stakeholders. Effective inter-functional interfaces are key to internal performance and hence performance in the marketplace (Kohli and Jaworksi, 1990; Slater and Narver, 1995; Biemans et al., 2010). The internal interfaces are relational. A lack of established relationships among project decision-makers and actors reduces the success of positive project outcomes (Söderlund and Andersson, 1998).

Relationships are therefore a vital ingredient to undertaking activities and doing them well. Yet relationships are not just about doing. Gilligan (1982) claimed that relationships are about *voice*. This is more than open communication as voice is about being heard for who you are before being heard for what you do. We are 'human beings' before we are 'human doings' (Smyth, 2008a). In establishing business relationships, people often move too quickly to purpose and goal achievement in their interactions. People need confirmation that they have understood what has been communicated, that they have been listened to, and that they have some value as a person. They are not just a source of business information that is to be gathered. Being valued and knowing that you are valued is evidenced in subtle ways. This is important because work is a major source of self-worth and identity. This arises from building deep relationships that recognize others for who they are. Perhaps it is not at all surprising that 75 per cent of new business is lost at the first contact (Harvey, 1988). Managers tend to move too quickly to exhortation, whereas most people want to receive (genuine, not gratuitous) encouragement first (Smyth, 2000). Empathy and effort require sensitivity through emotional investment. This forms part of the development of social capital.

A key link between the individual, the team and business is how relationships are managed. Relational contracting does not entirely address this issue (Cheung et al., 2006; Teicher et al., 2006; Zou et al., 2014), although it can contribute an important element and aid transition to a more proactive management approach (**Chapter 2**). A relationship approach is needed to develop potential performance (Pryke and Smyth, 2006; Smyth and Pryke, 2008). Specifically, relationship management concepts and a system for adoption and implementation are necessary. This begs the question about relationships and relationship management. The conceptual origins of *relationship management* for this chapter have their roots on relationship marketing. Relationship marketing, especially in business-to-business (B2B) contexts, is a paradigm of securing work through building and adding value through relationships (Berry, 1983; Levitt, 1983). As the paradigm emerged some 30 years ago, it was realized that for it to work, there has to be systematic cross-functional working to manage the relationships and delivery according to the promises made (e.g. Grönroos, 2000; Gummesson, 2000; Ford et al., 2003).

The awareness of relationship management remains partial. Zou et al. (2014) found in the PPP context that only 25 per cent of those surveyed thoroughly understand relationship management, while 30 per cent had some familiarity with relationship management, and only 10 per cent perceived their organization to have systematic procedures in this respect.

The aims of this chapter are to address:

A. Relationship management as a system and set of management practices for project businesses in theory and practice.
B. Relationship management and its contribution to the management of projects.
C. The strengths and weaknesses of relationship management in theory and application across organizational and inter-organizational boundaries.

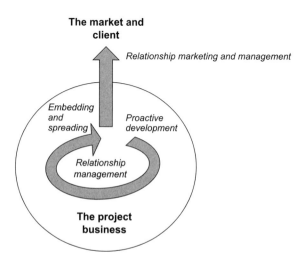

FIGURE 3.1 Proactive relationship building and relationship management

A main message concerns the theory–practice issue, that is, the significant yet neglected contribution that relationship management makes to the effective project business performance and for MoP. For the project contribution, project businesses need to develop and embed support measures in routines to guide team action and behaviour at programme and project levels. An overview of relationship management is depicted in Figure 3.1. From its origins in relationship marketing, it has been adopted as part of a management approach, which is explored in the next section.

Relationship management in theory and practice

Relationships

Relationships are more than economic exchange and interactions between people. They start with communication, develop through voice and understanding with complementary and/or shared values and norms. Foundational to relationship development is trust, which is a sense or conviction comprising both intuitive and cognitive assessment of others, based upon their behaviour (e.g. Gustafsson et al., 2010). As the quality of any interpersonal relationship grows, the cognitive aspect increases as more is known about the other person or parties, but this does not render it any less subjective because the emotional content increases too.

Experience or affect has long been recognized in business, and emotion is being given increasing recognition (e.g. Fineman, 2003; Andersen, 2013; cf. Smith, 1759). What we feel, how feelings motivate us and get translated into action vary according to predispositions, values, context and task. The same feelings may evoke different behaviour and actions from different people. The relationship and business context may help guide a relationship, yet this does not automatically invoke certainty. Relational risk derived from human agency is important. A greater frame of reference is needed to add greater predictability or probability of action. This is where management of an organization enters the picture. Relationships develop between individuals *in* the organizational context and *between* the individual and the organization. This is depicted in Figure 3.2, showing the influence of emotion on behaviour from individuals and the relationship management system and organizational behaviour. Relationships also take the form of individuals representing

FIGURE 3.2   The relationship between the individual and organizational behaviour

the organization: internally, as line managers and senior management for example, or externally, to another party or organization. This gives three types of business relationship: (i) interpersonal in the organization, (ii) individual-to-organization, and (iii) inter-organizational relationships where individuals or teams represent the organizations.

The management literature on relationship management envisages various stages of relationship development both organizationally and inter-organizationally. Although terminology differs, a summative typology can be set out as:

> *Relationship Commitment* as an investment in development for relationship building → *Relationship Quality* suitable for the functional purposes at hand indicating the formation of *Relationship Ties or Bonds* → *Relationship Strength* as an asset contributing to social capital with long term implications for *Performance* including *Relationship Revenue* and *Profit* in customer contexts.

This does not occur by happenstance, but rather through management, hence relationship management in a holistic and systematic way, both internally and across organizational boundaries for clients and other stakeholders. The roots of relationships management are dyadic, hence the link to relationship marketing.

Relationship marketing

Rust and Zahorik (1993) state that the provision of service or production of a product offered for sale should be aimed at satisfying identified needs of the targeted customers. In B2B industrial markets, including markets for specific assets, relationship marketing was defined in terms of being: *Marketing oriented toward strong, lasting relationships with individual accounts* (Jackson, 1985: 2).

Relationship marketing is about systems to build client and stakeholder relationships in order to add value and secure work. A key premise of relationship marketing is that it is only as effective if the value is delivered in the product, service or project context. Thus, relationship marketing develops systems of relationship management to orchestrate value delivery (e.g. Christopher et al., 2002). Relationship management is twofold. First, customers or clients are to be proactively managed over their lifecycle, posing questions as to what the lifetime value is in terms of revenue and profit – the relationship revenue and profit in the above typology rendering a customer or client lifetime value (CLV). Effective relationship management increases opportunities for repeat business and profit, hence feeds back into marketing to increase CLV. Thus, how well the inter-organizational relationships are managed by those managing the supply side from selling through to operations, delivery and aftersales service affects firm performance. Second, staff relationships are to be managed, which can be motivated by operational performance, job satisfaction or from a marketing perspective to deliver value propositions: *Marketing management should be broadened into marketing-oriented company management* (Gummesson, 2000: 14).

Relationship management

Organizational systems fail. There are many reasons why, including a lack of cross-functional working and misaligned systems (e.g. Reyck et al., 2005; Shehu and Akintoye, 2010), implementation issues between the business model, strategies and tactics used on the ground (cf. Barrett and Fudge, 1981). Poorly designed systems cannot be effectively implemented – for example, IT systems that do not work for the user and/or lack a parallel human system (e.g. Reinartz et al., 2004; King and Burgess, 2008). Relationships articulate these systems, but are only coordinated for the purpose if there is a relationship management system, sets of coordinating mechanisms and routines, for example behavioural programmes, relationship monitoring and management procedures and behavioural codes. Good internal relationship systems provide the basis to articulate inter-organizational relations: *Relationship management involves analysis, investment in relationships and a clear view of the wider value that can be gained from each relationship and which extends beyond the straightforward features of the* [operations and] *product that is exchanged* (Ford et al., 2003: 5).

Relationship management represents a step beyond contractual approaches. It displaces the unit of analysis from transactions to the broader context for projects – internal and external relationships and associated processes for their functioning. If mature individual relationships are a competence, then the function might be expressed along the following lines:

$$\text{Relationship Competence} = f(\text{Knowledge} + \text{Skills} + \text{Behaviour}) \times \text{Experience}$$

If these are orchestrated in their development and coordination as relationship management, which can be perceived as a core competency or dynamic capability (e.g. Hamel and Prahalad, 1996; Teece et al., 1997), then the organizational function might be expressed along the following lines:

$$\text{Organizatioanal Relationship Management Competence} = f(\text{Relationship Management System} \times \text{Behavioural Programme} \times \text{Behavioural Code} \times \Sigma \text{Individual Social Competence}) \times \text{Reputation}$$

Organizational relationships can be conceived at four management levels:

1. *Relationship management system* – a subsystem to frame the way in which individuals relate to each other in general terms allowing other systems, procedures, codes and discretion to be more influential. A relationship management system facilitates integration at the interface between functions and for individuals to enable cross-functional working and lifecycle coordination.
2. *Behavioural programme* – a set of procedures to undertake roles, functions and activities that may include tailored yet aligned differences within the system according to function, for example health and safety, client management, agile project management methodologies.

3. *Behavioural codes of conduct* – simple and memorable rules for forming and maintaining team and interpersonal relationships.
4. *Line management* – modelling and oversight to ensure that initiative is enhancing behaviour and action to increase effective performance and add value.

A relationship management system is the top level of systematic operation and works to aid other formal and informal routines (cf. Storbacka et al., 1994). There are investments to formulate and implement a system to enable distinctive attributes and differentiating features to shape the organization and support effective product and service delivery. These attributes and features are dynamic in application and come in the form of technical and service threshold competencies to enhance performance and core competencies to add value. Thus, relationship management helps articulate what Davies and Brady have termed in project environments as *organizational* and *project capabilities* (Davies and Brady, 2000; Brady and Davies, 2004). Indeed, the relationship management system as a differentiator adds to the dynamic capabilities and aids value delivery in the market place (Smyth, 2015; cf. Möller, 2006).

Behavioural programmes are commonplace in organizations today, for example for leadership, health and safety (H&S), and as part of broader change programmes. It has been found regarding H&S behavioural programmes that cross-functional absorption of the precepts at the 'corporate centre' is weak, hence, vertical implementation to the project level is weak. It took a longitudinal 7-year programme in one project business to achieve a 60 per cent decline in accident frequency (Roberts et al., 2012). For relationship management, implementation requires incremental development and reinforcement at the behavioural level below the system to spread and embed effective management. This includes relationship

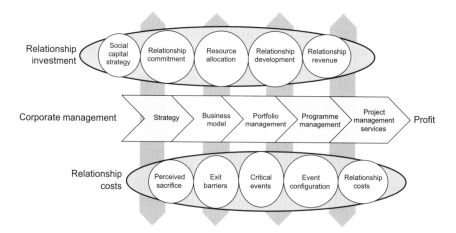

FIGURE 3.3 Internal relationship management system

Source: Developed from Storbacka et al., 1994; adapted from Pryke and Smyth, 2006.

considerations as an integral part of quality and scope in the time-cost-quality/ scope of the so-called iron triangle.

Behavioural codes drill down to a finer grain of action. They are commonplace, for example ethical codes and professional codes of conduct. For relationships, behavioural codes provide more specific guidance upon relationship development and sustenance. The level at which the rules are pitched can be varied:

- A detailed applied level, such as recording in a day journal the key points and follow up action among colleagues, team members and for clients and their networks;
- Mid-order mapping of individuals by role, power and influence, motivation and behaviour, and their preferred modes of interaction and response;
- Evaluative measures of reflective practice on skills of listening, acknowledgement and understanding others, and self-evaluation of performance in relationship building/maintenance, decision-making and operational performance.

The main aim is to have a few rules that are sufficiently memorable. Some businesses have given staff credit or business card size memos to carry around, and the key behavioural programme elements can be on one side and the specific codes on the other. These codes can be built up and developed over a long programme, adding new ones as each previous set is internalized. Issues of sensitivity and the tension between public and privately held information can pose issues to consider depending upon the country of operation and legislative requirements.

External relationships are also important. Thirty types of relationship (30Rs) have been developed under four categories: classic market relationships, special market relationships, mega relationships and nano or internal relationships (Gummesson, 2000) – see Table 3.1. This mainly focuses upon inter-organizational relationships, indicating the challenge of managing different relationship types.

The management of projects

Developing relationships at the front-end and for execution has pertinence to internal project teams and temporary multi-organizational project teams (TMOs). The 30Rs have been analyzed in project contexts on PPP and PFI-type (where PPP stands for public private partnerships and PFI for project finance initiative) projects where:

> The findings for the first three categories of the 30Rs are all negative, indicating weak, dysfunctional relationships between the parties both across the organisations and across the range of projects. The special market relationship category, in which PFI/PPP is centrally located, is particularly dysfunctional.
>
> (Smyth and Edkins, 2007: 238)

TABLE 3.1 Relationship types from a relationship marketing perspective

Relationship category	Number	Relationship type
Classic market relationships	R1	The classic dyad
	R2	The classic triad
	R3	The classic network
Special market relationships	R4	Relationships via full-time marketers (FTMs) and part-time marketers (PTMs)
	R5	The service encounter
	R6	The many-headed customer and the many-headed supplier
	R7	The relationship to the customer's customer
	R8	The close versus the distant relationship
	R9	The relationship to the dissatisfied customer
	R10	The monopoly relationship
	R11	Customer as 'member'
	R12	The e-relationship
	R13	Parasocial relationships
	R14	The non-commercial relationship
	R15	The green relationship
	R16	The law-based relationship
	R17	The criminal network
Mega relationships	R18	Personal and social networks
	R19	Mega marketing
	R20	Alliances change the market mechanisms
	R21	The knowledge relationship
	R22	Mega alliances that change the basic conditions for marketing
	R23	The mass media relationship
Nano relationships	R24	Market mechanisms are brought inside the firm
	R25	The internal customer relationship
	R26	Quality and the customer orientation
	R27	Internal marketing
	R28	The two-dimensional matrix relationship
	R29	The relationship to external providers of marketing services
	R30	The owner and financier relationship

Source: Adapted from Gummesson (2000).

Where the . . .

> . . . private sector management is reactive rather than proactive role in managing relationships . . . public sector [was found] to be particularly weak in consistently managing the interface with the private sector, particularly in ways that engender collaboration through trust.
>
> (Smyth and Edkins, 2007: 239)

Relationship management requires awareness and commitment in senior management. Operationally, it requires exploration and development through commitment *to* engender cooperation, collaboration and coalition (e.g. Wilson, 1995; Thompson and Sanders, 1998) and commitment to targeted relationships, which individually invoke interdependence and inter-organizationally interdependence (Campbell, 1995) or dependent lock-in (Donaldson and O'Toole, 2001). A relationship management system has been developed for project businesses – see Figure 3.4. How might a relationship management system be developed at a more detailed level? There are multiple ways this can be achieved. Figure 3.5 sets out one generic overview of how some of the elements for relationship management system can be drawn together. Care needs to be taken. A balance needs to be achieved between being too dictatorial on the one hand, which will make implementation more challenging and the systems will arguably be counterproductive in the long run, and too weak and ineffective on the other hand. Similarly, it needs to be sufficiently integrated to be coherent on its own terms as a frame of guidance with sufficient room for manoeuvre to let staff adjust what they are doing to context and tailor responses to clients and stakeholders. This is a thorny issue of balance. The key evaluative question as to how much latitude is whether particular actions help to reinforce the relationship without

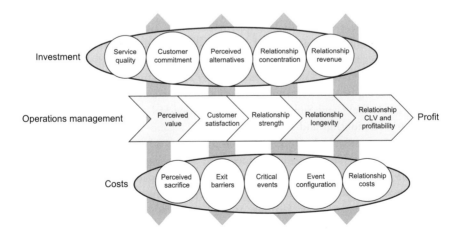

FIGURE 3.4 Relationship marketing and management systems

Source: Smyth, 2015 Figure 4.6.

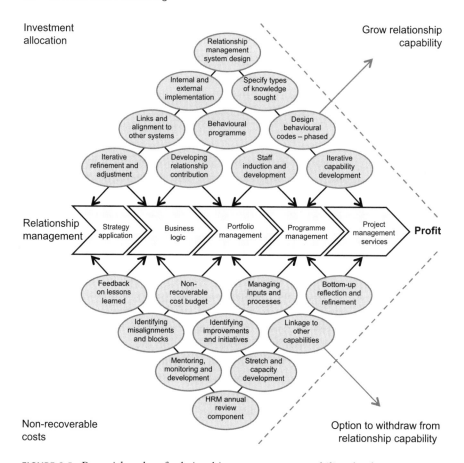

Investment allocation

Grow relationship capability

Non-recoverable costs

Option to withdraw from relationship capability

FIGURE 3.5 Potential paths of relationship management capability development

undermining the system. For example, research has shown evidence across IT sectors that project managers tend not to adhere to the project management methodologies required. The stated justification is tailoring to client needs and context, although on close examination, the most common practice is about accommodating personal 'comfort zones' despite the client and employer interests (Wells, 2011; Wells and Smyth, 2011). Here, individual and team action undermines any relationship and system.

The way a system is developed connects directly to other systems. One example is to link relationship management directly to supply chain management systems for value identification, leverage and delivery at the interfaces of business development, procurement, bid management and project management to maximize fit and added value. Another example is to link relationship management with knowledge management, especially significant areas of tacit knowledge on projects, in industrial networks and communities of practice. This can also be linked to human resource management (HRM) through annual reviews where relationship management and tacit knowledge development are an explicit part of personnel reviews and a key element of promotion.

At the individual level people need to be equipped with basic interpersonal skills on listening, reflecting and internalizing where necessary, on asking open-ended questions, and then follow up questions and reflection. For example, business developers are going beyond soliciting information on project pipelines in order to build deep relationships to gain understanding of issues a project or programme is addressing, how it fits with the client strategy and what the significant business or organizational issues are that underlie client operations in order to identify what is of value, where value can be added and how projects can be shaped. Another example is where the project manager is building supply chain relationships in order to examine a deep understanding about how work packages can be configured and integrated on the ground, and how components will physically interface to minimize redesign and rework. Building information modelling (BIM) will increasingly provide a platform to resolve problems, yet effective relationships underpin the practical means of resolution in timely, effective and efficient ways.

Relationships are external with clients, suppliers and other stakeholders. Relationship alignment with clients and lower supply chain tiers is important to induce effective inter-functional interfaces (Kohli and Jaworksi, 1990; Slater and Narver, 1995; Biemans et al., 2010). The advocacy of relational contracting provides part recognition of this importance. The intelligent client should be in a position to establish their needs and select the right private sector organization and people to fill this need (Czerniawska, 2002). Furthermore: *The intelligent client should also be able to maximise value from the private sector by managing the relationships and increasing the value that is added by these private sector participants* (Aritua et al., 2009: 5).

The implications of these requirements in terms of the skills sets and capabilities may be addressed at three levels: the individuals, the project team, the programme and the organization (Aritua et al., 2009). Aritua and colleagues advocate a 'client champion' – presumably in the owner decision-making unit (DMU) – requiring analytical and conceptual thinking to meet strategic aspirations and flexibility to cope with change. Similar comments can be made about the supply chain where the project business acting as the systems integrator is sourcing from project businesses providing systematic, integrated solutions from subcontractors and suppliers. The purpose of supply chain management is to improve performance through the relationships (e.g. Bygballe et al., 2010). It was found that clients of the construction industry using alliances seek to learn from their supply chains, especially the first tier main contractor. Clients look for cooperative attitudes supported by conducive behaviour: *the correct attitudes and behaviour were key to making long-term programmes and alliances successful* (Butcher and Sheehan, 2010: 42). Conversely, contractors who join a supply chain and try to then impose their way of doing things induce 'annoyance' (Butcher and Sheehan, 2010). As French and Raven note (1958: 84): *the use of coercive power should reduce the legitimate power.*

Thus, using market power or authority derived from the supply chain hierarchy erodes the more decentralized and egalitarian relationships based upon equality rather than equity norms necessary for effective relationship development. There is sufficient hierarchy embedded in market relations to structure exchanges without it dominating at the level of behaviour and action.

It is the understanding of depth of collaboration that distinguishes the relational contracting outcomes from relationship management ones. A transaction typically has a distinct beginning, short duration and an end point for a project or programme. The tasks come first and the relationships follow. In relationship management, the relationship comes first and the task flows from it to achieve business and project goals. Such relationships are potentially enduring, having a life independent of any project, interpersonally through respect and sometimes friendship and inter-organizationally through reputation and goodwill. This has been described in terms of cooperative power, shifting thinking to long-term interests of the project business and the CLV, that is, a shift from a transactional to a relationship mindset (Aarseth and Sorhaug, 2009).

Relationship building

Recent relationship management research into PPP projects found the top four factors for success to be (Zou et al., 2014):

1. Commitment and participation of senior executives;
2. Defining the objectives;
3. Integration of different divisions;
4. Multi-disciplinary team.

Relationship commitment is a key construct and an antecedent of inter-organizational cooperation at both the organizational commitment and interpersonal levels (Morgan and Hunt, 1994). Relationship commitment, development and maintenance are part of delving *deeply into the customer's world of product use in their situations* (Woodruff, 1997: 150, cited in Helkkula et al., 2012: 59). Commitment is associated with strong relationships, a social orientation, high-repeat business levels (e.g. Morgan and Hunt, 1994; Martinsuo and Ahola, 2010; Jones et al., 2011), cooperation (Powell, 1990b; Heide and Miner, 1992) and tolerance (Agnew et al., 1997). Relationship commitment is also a deterrent to opportunistic behaviour (Powell, 1990b; Heide and Miner, 1992). It is important to build strong relationships that have depth and breadth, variously termed *relationship quality* (Grönroos, 2000), *strong ties* (Granovetter, 1973, 1985) or *bonds*. Strong internal ties come first. Dyadic interpersonal cooperation advances ahead of inter-organizational cooperation. Psychological contracts are interwoven here – see Figure 3.6.

Establishing relationships takes care; listening and acknowledging the other party is important – as discussed some 75 per cent of contacts fail to develop a relationship. Three types of interaction can be identified:

FIGURE 3.6 Managed relationship in inter-organizational relations

1. *Symbolic interaction*, where vision and purpose are identified and the rules of inter-action intuitively negotiated, yet guided by a relationship management system;
2. *Substantive interaction*, where there is purpose and thus specific content;
3. *Administrative interaction*, where related actions are monitored and reported.

Clients do not distinguish between interpersonal and inter-organizational relationships, accepting the individual as representative of the firm unless subsequent evidence is provided to the contrary (Jones et al., 2011). Therefore for example, inconsistent behaviour in managing projects and relationships between project managers is taken by clients to mean inconsistent service provision between projects by the same project business. This has been the case and why an increasing number of clients are only legally contracting with project businesses if they can formally negotiate consistency of DMU personnel on a project and continuity of the DMU across a programme – managing themselves what project businesses had previously failed to manage. This is one main reason why relationship management is necessary, another being value, the two being linked as relationship are a means to deliver value, especially service value, which is the core offer of the systems integrator project business.

However, project businesses should not confuse implementing the system as the solution to relationship management. It is an important part, providing the frame of guidance. As Handy (1996) notes, systems thinking explains everything, yet predicts little. Action and behaviour resides in the hands of individuals and responsibility ultimately rests with them. The relationship management systems sets expectations so that the criteria for action are shared and individuals have parameters within which to take initiative, solve problems, for creativity to shine through, and apply interpersonal skills. Employees will know that relationship performance will be evaluated if it is built into HRM and part of annual staff appraisal requirements. Porath et al. (2011) demonstrate a direct relationship between staff and customer satisfaction through *employee commitment* and *organizational behaviour*. Civil relationships increase job satisfaction as employees value good working relationships.

Strong relationships are unhealthy where the organizational culture is highly egalitarian or so inward looking that it is isolated as an organization. Under these conditions, strong organizational identity leads to in-group favouritism (e.g. Tajfel, 1974; Brewer, 1979). This invokes the mobilization of bias in decision-making

(Bachrach and Baratz, 1973) and potentially unethical behaviour both internally and in the marketplace.

Relationship management can help reduce or eliminate errant behaviour. Customers have been reporting an increase of witnessing incivility in supplier workplaces, this being defined as insensitivity, disrespect and rudeness (Cortina et al., 2001). Employees have supported this evidence and claimed it lowers morale, reduces productivity and increases staff churn (Pearson and Porath, 2009). There is growing evidence that customers or client representatives who witness incivility perceive it as a reflection on the firm (Porath et al., 2011), remembering that customers perceive interpersonal interactions and relationships as representative of the firm (Jones et al., 2011). Witnessing incivility is thought to reduce *commitment* and customers implicitly or explicitly blame the organization for having insufficient policies and procedures in place (Acquino et al., 2006).

The tolerance among clients and their representatives of uncivil behaviour among project business staff may be greater at the 'heavy' end, for example construction and engineering, where blame and shame tactics internally and adversarial relationships in the dyadic relationship are traditionally more prevalent, although this is largely unsubstantiated. Assuming it is the case, uncivil behaviour is relative and will have positive and negative effect against the perceived sector norms. If the assumption is false, then the case for behavioral programmes for relationship development, procedures anchored in systems and in particular behavioural codes of conduct is stronger than in other sectors with high norms of civil behaviour.

Contract staff pose particular problems within TMOs because they are seen to represent the project business. The implication is that project businesses cannot just 'shop and drop' contract staff onto projects, but need thorough induction on behavioural programmes along similar lines that occur for best practice H&S. They also need to be made aware of key system elements and behaviours within any behavioral code.

Adverse selection was noted as an issue with relationship implication in relational contracting (**Chapter 2**). Developing strong relations is a way to overcome many of the issues. In other words, instead of waiting to sign a contract and then developing the dyadic relation, the objective is to develop strong relationships from the outset of qualifying suppliers and clients (Smyth, 2015). This provides a solid basis upon which to make selection, using criteria, such as those proposed by Cook and Hancher (1990): high quality experienced firms, cultural compatibility, resources and capability alignment, and scope for further relationship development.

It is risky for clients and systems integrators to become too dependent upon any one supplier. Over-dependency leads to clients questioning the value for money received. Strong relationships can be formed with suppliers nested in a small yet competitive panel of suppliers. Project businesses also need a range of clients to avoid putting 'too many eggs in one basket', and benefit from developing organizational and project capabilities through working with a range of clients. Leading project businesses follow the pattern of around 80 per cent of turnover and profit coming from 20 per cent of the client base. A contribution of 10–20 per cent per key client is reasonable, but towards the upper end of that range, a premium profit is to be expected to justify the additional risk. The type of client exhibits diversity to spread the risk and maximize opportunity for developing a range of core competencies and capabilities to maintain a competitive position and justify earning any premium profit from the client perspective.

Supply chain and other network initiatives tend to focus upon cost and waste elimination, frequently uncritically resulting in value being leaked. Expenditure incurred at the cost level is largely inseparable from the investment level (Grönroos, 2000). Cost elimination can erode the service experience and invariably compromises value in use. Cost elimination from the budget often reappears in the form of non-recoverable costs (Smyth, 2015). Value-focused team networks with good relationships achieve successful outcomes with focused relationship-based teams (Kumaraswamy and Anvuur, 2008). Network coordination has been expressed in the oil and gas sector in this way:

> . . . megaprojects always contain a large number of interfaces. An interface occurs whenever independent or even quasi-independent functions or organizations come into contact. Interface management is an issue for even small projects. . . . In many respects, the task of megaproject management is centered around the effective management of the interfaces. The interfaces are opportunities for conflicts and misunderstandings to occur. They are the places where things tend to 'fall between the cracks'.
>
> (Merrow, 2011: 184)

The system integrator role is to ensure integration, pulling in the resources, capabilities and supplies from networks. This involves resolving conflicts, improving misunderstandings and adding value through interface management. Effectively managing network organizational relationships is in the interest of project businesses (e.g. Dubois and Gadde, 2000; Pryke, 2012; cf. Håkansson and Snehota, 1995; Christopher et al., 2002; Ford et al., 2003). The influence of solutions providers such as professional consultants upon major construction contractors in the systems integrator role is set out in Fact Box 3.1.

Relationships and the project lifecycle

Many project businesses stress the importance of relationship building. In the absence of a relationship management system, relationship building is left to individual responsibility. The purpose and process of building relationships has been found to mean different things and to be conducted in different ways within each company (Smyth, 2013a). Yet similar language, such as 'responding to client drivers' and 'using right behaviours', is used to describe the meaning and processes, hence

FACT BOX 3.1 IDENTIFYING THE SIGNIFICANCE OF RELATIONSHIP MANAGEMENT AT THE SYSTEMS INTEGRATOR–INTEGRATED SOLUTIONS PROVIDER INTERFACE

The civil engineering division of a major international construction contractor acting as a systems integrator, was actively developing relationships with professional consultants in the integrated solutions provider role. It undertook an investigation into leading design and cost consultants with which they worked or would like to work. A series of interviews were conducted with top-level management.

The top design consultancy operating in rail, highways and energy said this systems integrator business acted with a transactional or 'jobbing attitude'. One Group Director of a major consultancy stated the business:

> . . . need to understand the interaction between design and construction process. Design is not a commodity or something separate from the construction process. Design requires encapsulating the concept and articulating it to something that is defined. In general, we usually do not get the recognition to the difficulty of our role. We have to deliver something that is efficient/effective and also economic to build.

The contractor was said to be quite aggressive in its dealings with consultants treating them the same as any part of their supply chain. Behaviour varied enormously between projects partly because of the personnel and partly as to whether the consultant was appointed by the client or novated under a design and build-type contract.

The Chairman of one of the top design consultancies commented it is better for them to address what is *the maximum value that they can get from this project and not instead asking for a minimum price*. A Group Managing Director of a major consultancy stated:

> When things are going the wrong way, then a positive differentiator is how you handle them and start to agree how are both parties going to fix . . . and resolve the conflict. This also helps trust to be built and also having an open-transparent discussion; with also space for constructive criticism; but avoid having a blame culture!

The essence of the issues and problems being brought forward in the investigation is about effective relationship management. Professional consultants provide a good 'sounding board' as they are knowledge providers and are guided by professional codes of practice to deliver solutions, which places a higher premium upon relationships as a base line of operation.

Source: Fitch et al. (2010).

disguising the differences. It was recognized that it is *all about people and relation-ships,* and; *boils down to some trusted relationships,* there was:

> . . . no guidance about how to build and manage relationships i) through **relationship systems,** ii) through **procedures** to address types, continuity and coordination of relationships, and iii) **behavioural codes of conduct** to establish norms and specific guidance on behaviour.
>
> (Smyth, 2013a: 6, emphasis in original)

The emphasis of the above research was at the front-end; however, the consequence was that there was an absence of relationship handover between functions and along project lifecycles. Where there was a rudimentary key account management or client management function, the focus was largely project specific and failed to address relationship consistency within a project and continuity across project lifecycles (cf. Cova et al., 2002; Hadjikhani, 1996; Skaates and Tikkanen 2003; Cova and Salle, 2005). Discontinuity and the lack of management of the 'sleeping relationship' has been a management issue in careers and for projects (Faulkner and Anderson, 1987; Hadjikhani, 1996). The issue is summarized as follows: *when a project is terminated, it will leave a sediment of trust* (Hadjikhani, 1996: 20; cf. Faulkner and Anderson, 1987: 323) and *this sediment is eroded over time,* but *the success of a project often depends largely on the capacity the supplier had in maintaining the relationship with the customer independent of economic activity* (Cova et al., 2002: 20). Continuity of people and context is absent in many temporary organizations, and therefore norms and common practices are ineffectively developed (Bresnen et al., 2004), organizational discontinuity occurs due to financial management around transaction cost management, resource allocation at portfolio level, especially for staffing, and the lack of project business programme management to coordinate services across and for projects is absent (Smyth and Lecoeuvre, 2014). All of these issues interconnect with relationship management.

Inconsistency of service provision can be improved by using the *relay team* model to have orchestrated handovers. This helps transfer the essential elements of client understanding and knowledge (Smyth, 2000, 2004). A relay team could form one part of structuring relationship management. *Key account management* (McDonald et al., 1997; Kempeners and Van der Hart, 1999) operating a project and programme level provides another means, which can also be part of a rela-tionship management system (Smyth, 2015). However, consistency is best served by continuity of personnel over the project lifecycle and programme, which many clients have been increasingly demanding as project businesses have been slow to recognize they need to manage service consistency.

An inconsistent service arises where there is personnel change, especially in the absence of a relationship management system. The main cause of personnel change on project teams is that the management transfers key members onto another project. This is driven by short-term bid management tactics and financial control to minimize transaction costs. The so-called A-team on an existing project is proposed for a project at bid stage. Once started, the A-team members are moved off the project taking their understanding of the client and the tacit learning about the existing project, typically without a considered handover as the B-team takes over. This may be serial over a project lifecycle. The hidden management costs, the increase in project costs and the loss of reputation and repeat business due to a reduction in service value are seldom accounted for or even understood (Smyth, 2015). Financial considerations to minimize transaction costs mean that senior management are unprepared to sanction having project management staff 'on the bench' between projects. Some companies do, for example IBM, which provides an available resource for future projects. Staff that are 'on the bench' are able to support bids or undertake other productive work, for example helping to embed new project capabilities across teams, during what would otherwise be 'downtime'. This also helps build internal relationships and enables knowledge transfer. Having staff on the bench interacting and engaging in internal relationship building helps provide continuity of service across projects.

Relationship quality or strong relationships are derived from the way in which relationships are built and managed. During execution, practitioners often cite 'open communication' as the main means to build and maintain relationships. But communication has to be with purpose. This drives the business need for interaction, but relationship quality is more than communication. On the ground, relationships are built through a series of acts, episodes and serial interaction (Grönroos, 2000). Relationship management helps these interactions – whom, where, when, why and especially how interactions are conducted. This interaction is appreciative of other actors and has been described as *dialogical,* where dialogue develops into mutual responsiveness and associated action (Ballantyne and Varey, 2006). On occasions the only purpose is to maintain the relationship in which case a short meeting or even brief exchange is sufficient. Additional meetings of happenstance in the industrial network are useful means of reinforcement and sometimes provide latitude and gives rise to new ideas and initiatives.

Human resource management (HRM) has an important role to introduce policies to support relationship management internally and externally. HRM is about the strategic management of people and the relationships between them. Policies set the context for organizational behaviour, working with other functions to align operational functions and routines. This definition is broader than the function of an HRM department, yet most of the crucial areas for management are the cross-functional and inter-departmental ones in the modern business, and particularly in project businesses where boundaries are over-determined culturally and operationally, creating mental silos and operational barriers to integration. For the individual, career progression is often related to line manager sponsorship and the informal networks of individual project managers for whom others work. For example, a major international contractor informed new staff at induction that progression was on merit. There were no criteria as to what merit constituted, and in practice this meant whether 'your face fitted' as far as the line manager was concerned. Good practice develops a systematic approach to HRM, strategically developed in and with the HRM function and tactically steering HRM at operations level to provide a frame within which discretion is applied (Clark and Wheelwright, 1992), rather than discretion and favouritism determining outcomes. There are four HRM areas of practice (Bredin and Söderlund, 2006), which are relevant to relationship management:

1. *Flows* – how the flow of people is managed and allocated to roles and to projects and teams (cf. Smyth, 2000, 2004, 2014).
2. *Performance* – how people contribute to the development of capabilities (cf. Davies and Brady, 2000; Brady and Davies, 2004).
3. *Involvement* – how people participate in strategic and tactical decision-making and influence the control of work and working conditions (cf. Herzberg, 1968; Hedberg et al., 1997).
4. *Development* – nurture, personal development plans and related development programmes to support individual development (cf. Beer et al., 1984).

The project as the unit of management focus tends to neglect the corporate level and how this cascades down through portfolio and programme management to the project level. Relationships need to be socially embedded (Jones and Lichtenstein, 2008) either informally, which takes longer than projects allow, or through a relationship management system at corporate or programme level for application on projects.

Relationship building through a relationship management system does not necessarily guarantee quality relationships, especially in a TMO where a number of relationships are being built swiftly from scratch. A relationship management system provides a frame and guides consistency – a form of social control to help align action and behaviour – yet it is people who build relationships. Each relationship is different depending upon the people. The totality of relationships in a TMO will build the character of interactions and the norms for inter-organizational interaction. The emanating routines will form the basis of the inter-organizational relationships at the TMO level. Holmen and Pedersen (2010) found in the construction industry that habits around existing relationships are hard to change. The nature of the project is insufficient alone to induce high commitment levels to the project and among those working on it, within the TMO and among suppliers. One factor is project affinity, which contributes to successful TMO working (Dainty et al., 2005). Affinity is akin to 'project chemistry' (Nicolini, 2002). The importance of emotions has been recognized in organizational behaviour but less so in project management (Fineman, 2003; Dainty et al., 2005). Cascading relationship management to the project level helps address these issues.

Programmes and projects are temporal, which has implications for embedding relationships. Temporal embeddedness may create mechanisms and informal routines that shape the coordination of collaborative working depending upon the duration of a project and to the disposition of the team, which surrenders a great deal to individual and team responsibility within temporal constraints. Temporal embeddedness is affected by several factors (Clark, 1985). Entrainment is the transitive pacing of embedding measures. It is based upon the rhythm of the project or programme, unfolding events and discrete tasks (e.g. Nandhakumar and Jones, 2001; Manning, 2008; Söderholm, 2008; cf. Ancona and Chong, 1996). Current management is primarily conducted through risk management at project and programme levels (Geraldi et al., 2010) rather than relationship management from the corporate or programme level, although there are successful examples of relationship management (Smyth and Fitch, 2009). Non-routine tasks are more difficult to frame and embed at the temporal level without a system above the project level (cf. Orlikowski and Yates, 2002). Therefore the inherently transitive and temporal nature of projects induce difficulty in socially embedding routines as part of structuring routines unless the projects are of long duration with continuity of personnel, hence the need to mobilize a relationship management process inherited from the 'corporate centre'. Routines emerge from past practices and norms carried into projects and routines emerge, which are partial (cf. Parmigiani and Howard-Grenville, 2011), which helps frame the TMO culture and can be nurtured through project management within the temporality to enhance operational performance.

Temporal embeddedness is also affected by the dispositions of team members that help shape the TMO organization culture, norms and routine behaviours. Relational contracting is more egalitarian and norms of equality are expected to be the fore. However, hierarchy derived from market power and organizational norms of equity can quickly emerge. Merit and authority are the positive aspects, yet behaviour based upon rivalry and jealousy, and to some extent suspicion and disdain quickly invoke a stratification of personnel at a more detailed level than ascribed roles and job titles. In film projects, humour is used in positive ways to accelerate and compress activity to meet deadlines (Bechky, 2006), whereas in construction projects, humorous behaviour is motivated towards blame and shame and used to subtly define the pecking order so when something goes wrong it becomes easy to pin on a weak team member (Smyth, 2000). This induces weak relational ties (Granovetter, 1973, 1985). Such behaviour may establish coordinating routines in tension with relational contracting (Portes, 1998; Jones et al., 1997). In addition, different cultural norms due to background can create conflict negotiating norms and establishing routines (cf. Coleman, 1988).

However, there are two views on the temporal nature of projects:

1. Projects have a short lifecycle (transactional resource exchange) and are thus temporary (e.g. Foord et al., 1988; Hadjikhani, 1996).
2. Projects are underpinned by long-term relationships, both in the employer organization and in the broader network (e.g. Dubois and Gadde, 2000; Pryke, 2012).

This is more than internal relationship management. Managing client and supplier relations between projects, the so-called *sleeping relationship*, is a key ingredient on a programme level, thus in periods of potential discontinuity, the other key ingredient being the relationships across the industrial network that embed both the project business and the key client DMU members in a set of stable relationships that provide common reference points (cf. Håkansson, 1982; Håkansson and Snehota, 1995).

In terms of continuity of maintaining relational ties, this is only possible long-term. Framework agreements, strategic partnering and ongoing informal alliances through relational contracts are all ways of helping to foster conditions for relationship sustenance. However, there are also disruptive factors on the client side, which pose challenges for relationship continuity under relational contracting. The client can become complacent, running down its capabilities, and unhealthy dependencies develop as discussed in regard to the supply side. In addition, the mobility of buyer operating in international markets and career progression can lead to personnel discontinuity on the client side. Consequently, negotiation is a temporary activity (e.g. Salacuse and Rubin, 1990) and can be driven by short-term goals to forge an agreement, whereby being prepared to absorb any negative long-term behavioural implications is the *best alternative to a negotiated agreement* (BATNA) (e.g. Mnookin et al., 2000). Hence relationship management in the marketplace supports relationship sustenance where relational contracting falls short and teases out clients and suppliers with inadequate commitment.

The more complex the technology or technical content of the project, the more dependent the client is upon the supplier. Effective relationships become more critical under such conditions. In sum, relational contracts are insufficient and where interdependencies grow up, effective relationships become even more important, all prompting the need for a more rigorous and integral approach to managing relationships and maintaining these over project and programme life-cycles. Suppliers and subcontractors are a key part of value and added value delivery. Relationships in supply chains and the broader industrial network are important (e.g. Dubois and Gadde, 2000). Holmen and Pedersen (2010) found barriers around attitudes, behaviour and habits in supply chains, but systems integrators have been weak in relationship management associated with supply chain management (Mason, 2008; Smyth, 2013a). Pryke (2012) has found reciprocity to an important informal relationship mechanism in supply chain management (Fact Box 3.2). Reciprocity arises out of the interpersonal and inter-organizational relationship ties.

Identifying external stakeholders and knowing how to approach stakeholder management has been found to be problematic for project businesses and their project managers during execution (Jepsen and Eskerod, 2009). This is a challenge, but developing relationship management procedures located in a relationship management system will help identify and develop relationships due to the increased outward focus and may guide timing of relationship formation. This is a neglected area for relationship management to investigate (Polonsky, 1995; Payne et al., 2005), although some work has been carried out in project management (Smyth, 2008b). There is insufficient management preparation given to potential external stakeholders because they anticipate difficulties in mapping the interests (Payne et al., 2005) and are somewhat fearful of invoking unwarranted responses for being proactive (Jepsen and Eskerod, 2009). Some project sectors are better at managing stakeholders than others. The oil and gas sector tends to resist responding to local content requirements internally and externally, largely on 'ideological' rather than

FACT BOX 3.2 COLLABORATIVE WORKING ON FOUR DEVELOPMENT PROJECTS

Four major property development contracts were investigated to examine the network relationships. Relationships are not a substitute for contracts, but it has been found that where collaborative practices are extensively applied, fewer contractual linkages exist, potentially reducing the scope for disputes, but there is a growth in reliance upon strong ties with a relatively small number of significant individual actors. Less monitoring existed across the four projects and two projects did not use an independent cost consultant to advise on cost control.

One project controlled costs through close client management of second tier firms in the supply chain – a principle that can be applied by systems integrator project businesses to the second tier systems providers of integrated solutions in the chain of subcontractors and suppliers.

Another project employed prime contracting principles with a performance incentive structure to encourage cost control. On all four projects, the proactive use of supply chain management was used developed over a client programme of work. For example, client capability was used to foster innovative and problem-solving capabilities in close working with the supply chain on one project, whereas on another the prime contractor led supply chain management.

Repetition was an important factor not only for delivering (added) value but also for cost control. Whilst projects are different in content, and the form of contract may differ over a programme, the learning of effective collaborative working is long term and predicated upon relationship ties in a network of organizational and individual actors. Overall, it was found:

- Collaborative relationships applied over a programme of work obviate the need for extensive networks dealing with financial, progress and design matters.
- Effective supply chain management requires a single, prominent actor within the project coalition.
- A client procurement strategy includes aligned *performance incentives and incorporates all the relevant actors (including consultants)* as a means to induce value for money out of all suppliers, and developing such measures requires a high level of client capability on how value is configured, how parties interface and structure incentives (2012: 211).

The currency of exchange in networks was found to be reciprocity, and the contract binding was found to be the psychological contracts in the relationships. This enabled effective collaborative working. Payment was therefore for collaborative working, and the tangible works was the by-product rather than the payment being for the works per se.

Source: Quoted and developed from Pryke (2012).

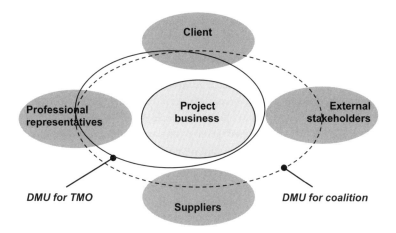

FIGURE 3.7   The scope of the decision-making unit

'logical' grounds (Merrow, 2011). Yet, stakeholder management has become a growth activity.

Towards personal and social identification

A deep relationship is established and deeply embedded when there is identification, especially mutual identification between the parties. Identification gives the individual a sense of self (e.g. Tajfel, 1974; Appiah, 2005) and the organization a sense of support. Inter-organizationally, identification builds inter-organizational interdependence. This is problematic with external stakeholders initially opposed to a project. Engagement can be distancing around different values and desired outcomes.

Social identification with external actors is underpinned by internal identification in and with the employer organization. Employees, as discussed, enter into relational contracts and into psychological contracts (Rousseau, 1990; **Chapter 2**). A sense of *membership* arises from self-selection and affirmation that the decision to apply for a post was correct. Self-enrollment links self-selection to psychological contracts (Andersen, 2013). Management have been adding weight to this perception and the potential for employees to go a step further, that is affinity, then identification, by reducing top-down authority and control over recent decades, emphasizing *delegation, empowerment* and encouraging staff to be their *authentic self* as they take responsible action. This apparent 'freedom' embodies tension and conflict, because management want employees to have room to manoeuvre, provided they comply with organizational requirements, as Luhmann recognized some decades ago: *Thus 'emancipation' becomes management's last trick: denying the difference between superior and subordinate and thus taking away the subordinate's power base* (1979: 180).

While employees always conceptually had power in the sense that they choose to defer to management under a contract, the reality is that the tensions only serve to constrain employee initiative because of the mixed messages given. Thus a relationship management system might appear to be moving towards greater equality at work, yet it overtly offers a guiding framework to provide the necessary degree of conformity and gives sufficient room to show individuality, be authentic, respond to internal and client relationships with sensitivity and empathy without tension or 'trick'. It is performing the same reference point that professional codes, club rules or family discipline provide.

Membership is a complex phenomenon. It exists between the purpose and goals of the business, as manifested at the operative level of the employee, and the motives of the individual. This has been called the *zone of indifference,* where both employer and employee can exhibit some indifference towards the needs of the other party (Barnard, 1968; Luhmann, 1996). Thus, relationship management cannot effect identification, only support its development. Engagement occurs through communication; relationship building helps form bonds, and employees feel more able and want the employer to increasingly give them room for manoeuvre while, at the same time, being appreciative and encouraging of management actions (Ekman, 2012). Yet, the greater the sense of identification, the less they feel they need managing. They may need less management too, but there are tensions too, which relate to wider cultural issues (**Chapter 6**). Identification is in the category of outcome rather than effect and helps define the scope and limits of relationship management.

What the analysis on relationship management has shown is that the management intervention extends beyond the limits and scope of relational contracting. It is a more comprehensive approach, which has been adopted by some project businesses. For other project businesses, this is a paradox, whereby management recognize the importance of relationships in their business and for business performance yet do little to manage relationships.

Conclusion

Relationship management, as derived and developed from relationship marketing, offers a more comprehensive approach compared to relational contracting to improve performance (cf. **Chapter 2**) and increase client and staff retention. It offers a systematic approach, yet there are a number of weaknesses that need to be drawn together. First, most of the theoretical development has emphasized inter-organizational relationships more than internal ones and has overlooked TMO teams specifically. Second, while there are numerous approaches offered to categorizing relationships in terms of types and processes involved, a detailed analysis of the types and implications for management are not always teased out. This leads to the third weakness of scant detailed direction or guidance as to how relationships are developed in terms of action and behaviour. This third criticism is problematic because contexts vary and relationships themselves are contextual. In this sense, it raises the initial ethical concern of establishing a balance between (dictatorial) control and (disparate and inconsistent) action left to individual responsibility. The analysis argued that systematic relationship management frames action sufficiently to provide consistency of service provision while leaving room for manoeuvre to be creative and solve problems with individual and team initiative. Further guidance is needed at the level of behavioural programmes nested below an overarching relationship management system. The relationship management literature largely does not address this level, being more content with the detailed outcomes and effects of relationship marketing and management. The chapter has begun to address the level of behavioural programmes and codes of conduct.

Addressing the behavioural level could imply strict requirements for compliance in the way that H&S behavioural programmes do for example. That would be inappropriate for relationship management. A more responsive approach is needed to allow accommodation of contextual issues and tailoring to the team setting and client needs. Tailoring is within a framework rather than despite the framework provided by a system and programme.

Simon (1969) drew attention to the need for deep knowledge to resolve operational problems and that this knowledge is held by specialists. This deep knowledge is more than technical and is embedded in relationships. Relationship management starts in the project business. The effects of relationship management are taken into the marketplace. Relationship management helps transition from relational contracting and transforms market exchange, especially by adding value from the client perspective.

Top management in most project businesses is still grappling with relationship management, recognizing the value of relationships yet backing off managing them. The current tendency is to largely leave relationships to individual responsibility. Consequently multiple opportunities are missed to effectively manage value creation and delivery in integrated ways, with the consequence that project businesses are failing to get closer to meeting their performance potential.

The aims of this chapter have been to address relationship management as a system of management for project businesses in theory and practice. Setting up, spreading and embedding of the relationship management strategy occurs independently of any project. The theory has been investigated at the levels of strategy, systems, organizational behaviour and behavioural codes. The issues of transference into practice have been examined, particularly at the programme level, for cross-functional working, and along project lifecycles. The detailed issues, for example infusion into TMOs, continuity of team personnel, and integration into the DMU helped address the contribution of relationship management to MoP. The strengths and weaknesses of relationship management in theory and application across organizational and inter-organizational boundaries have been pointed out and drawn together above.

A main message has been the extent to which the management of project businesses has yet to adequately embrace and embed relationship management in any systematic way. There is overreliance upon individual responsibility. Relationship management offers scope for consistent service provision and added technical value through creativity at the front-end and enhanced problem-solving in execution.

The short-term economic drivers to minimize investment and operating costs that often dominate project business thinking are arguably unsustainable in the way that client demands are increasing and project complexity is on the increase too. A summary map of the relationship characteristics is provided in Table 3.2, which builds upon and develops many of the relationship issues raised.

There were a number of research and practice issues carried forward from **Chapter 1** that were addressed, as set out below.

SI no. 1: *Organizational Behaviour* provides a detailed conceptual setting for relationship management, which is directed towards enhancing opportunities for the delivery of integrated solutions through improvements in *integrated management*. While a relationship management system adds to the structuring of the organization, the objective is to frame dynamic social processes. Cross-functional integration is facilitated through a more proactive approach to the management of organizational behaviour.

SI no. 2: *Relationship Management Theory* has been developed through the approach derived and developed from relationship marketing. Management has recognized the significance of relationships but have yet to fully articulate the need and develop the means of application. The chapter helps to create a bridge by developing understanding in theory and for practice.

SI no. 4: *Conceptual and Applied Hierarchical Integration* is dependent upon implementation of a robust system, designed and implemented top-down. Practitioners have partially implemented elements, but comprehensive approaches implemented with rigor remain nascent. Projects are shaped by formal and informal routines, therefore relationship management systems require robust linkage between the corporate centre and projects, which may be implemented through P^{3}M, especially programme management.

SI no. 5: *Conceptual and Applied Horizontal Integration* is also articulated through a robust relationship management system, helping to link a series of functional systems towards *integrated solutions*. Formal routines have tended to cover formal communication, technical systems and procedures, relationship management adding a 'soft' system.

SIs no. 6 and **7: *The Project Preoccupation*** and ***The Task Orientation*** are indirectly addressed because a relationship management system shifts the ground towards a broader view of service provision and client benefits through adding value and considering how project management is conducted from the front-end into the post-completion stages.

SI no. 9: *Systems Integration* is addressed by adding a conceptually more holistic approach which in practice can facilitate systems integration through relationships delivering value and from a relationship management system potentially linking up with other subsystems.

SI no. 10: *Market Functioning* is challenged by relationship management in terms of mainstream economics, a systems and its use being a source of social capital development to improve performance in the market and being a means to develop dynamic capabilities of competitive advantage.

TABLE 3.2 A relationship management system and the management of relationships

Markets	Structural features	Possible/probable power relations	Behaviour — Interpersonal	Behaviour — Organizational level
Client	A framework, which provides service guidance. Four management levels. A *relationship management system* is the main contribution, which supports cross-functional working and facilitates the subsequent levels. A *behavioural programme* provides a set of procedures to cover roles, functions and other activities. *Behavioural codes of conduct* comprise a set of memorable rules. *Line managers* model and oversee action and behaviour.	Inter-organizational relationships being conceptually developed to become more **cooperative**, hence in practice depending *interdependent*, practice depending upon relationship commitment levels in the dyad. Equality norms are significant for working, relying upon market forces and contracts to provide the overarching contextual hierarchy.	Reliant upon guidance from the relationship management system to frame behaviour. Discretion informs detailed behaviour and action, providing room for manoeuvre for individual initiative, creativity and problem solving. Tailoring of responses to programme and project context and client needs, yet within the system (not despite the system).	Management have four main functions: (i) invest in relationship management; (ii) design a system; (iii) implement the system; (iv) model the behaviour. There is need for iterative refinement and evolution. There is also potential to link to other operational systems at the front-end and for execution.
Suppliers	As above.	As above, albeit from the perspective of behaving as the client in relation to suppliers, and using equality norms rather than market power.	As above.	As above in the context of procurement and supply chain management.
Staff (employees and contract staff)	Development of relational contracts to be more inclusive, encouraging the development of social capital and staff identification with the employer.	Enhancement of the relational contract of employees, interpersonal relationships – greater **cooperation**.	Support from management and mutual support to enhance performance and job satisfaction.	Commitment and investment from senior management, commitment and investment from HRM, commitment from line managers.
Recruitment	Development of reputation through the industrial network, and brand reputational value in the labour market.	A reputation for a highly **cooperative** and satisfying domesticated market for employees. *Interdependence* prevails, contract staff used at minimal levels.	Close relationships through the industrial network and friendship groups with existing staff.	Management of corporate brand and market reputation.

In concluding this analysis, the last point raised deserves embellishment. Relationship management is potentially an organizational core competence or dynamic capability that informs the way in which programmes and projects are conducted internally (Davies and Brady, 2000). Inter-organizationally, with its origins in relationship marketing, it provides a competitive capability in the marketplace with clients and from supply chains (cf. Möller, 2006). Relationship management is a neglected area. Short termism focuses upon minimizing investment and overheads at the 'corporate centre', and taking costs out of projects at the operational level tends to dominate business consideration even though this increases risks at the project level where risk management is a dominant occupation. The outcome is a minimal service on the margins of meeting project requirements and risk induction of project failure. A medium and long-term view around relationship value changes the terms for competition to develop capabilities to add value and improve performance.

Relationship management as currently conceived falls short of a detailed focus at the level of behaviour and actions. This has been a major contribution to knowledge, not simply for project businesses and operations, but for management. Explicit linkage to organizational behaviour through behavioural programmes and codes of behavioural conduct add rigor. Setting the relationship management discourse in the context of organizational and project capabilities also sets it into the management fields of core competencies and dynamic capabilities to improve performance and enhance market position. The following *recommendations* are put forward for relationship management derived from relationship marketing:

A. Further research into internal relationship management, especially drilling down into behavioural programmes and codes;
B. Applied research into project contexts, especially for the set up of internal project teams and for TMOs;
C. Expounding the types of relationship and refining the means of management and researching the benefits.

Practice falls short of adoption of coherent a relationship management approach and system, thus invoking the following *recommendations*:

1. Management to pay greater heed to the way relationships are conducted at strategic and tactical levels both internally and in the marketplace;
2. Management to consider the adoption of robust relationship management principles that go beyond relational contracting and individual responsibility towards a systematic approach;
3. Explore opportunities to harness relationship management to improve internal integration and extend opportunities for adding value in the marketplace.

Management in practice has made strides along certain lines and the lessons learned for practical development for relationship management, particularly through relational contracting, implementing behavioural programmes, and using codes of conduct.

4

EMOTIONAL INTELLIGENCE AND RELATIONSHIP MANAGEMENT

Introduction

Emotional intelligence is a concept that has risen to become extremely popular, especially among business leaders with whom it resonates. It is not without controversy; the concept and theoretical underpinnings remain contested. Many theorists that prefer to disaggregate and isolate factors find emotional intelligence particularly problematic, whereas others are prepared to adopt a more inclusive approach even if it induces some conceptual 'messiness' at times. There is no single body of agreed theory among proponents, yet overall, it embodies an approach to relationship management for groups, teams and senior management. It is nested more at the level of individual behaviour and behavioural programmes rather than strategic systems, and therefore emotional intelligence is complementary to relationship management from marketing that has been discussed.

Emotional intelligence in the workplace is about harnessing our emotions to improve our performance individually and in teams. It was once thought that IQ provided a good indicator of career suitability and performance later in life. This has not been borne out in practice. Enhancing learning can increase our IQ by only 7–10 per cent, and IQ remains fairly constant after 25 years of age (Gardner, 1983). IQ is variously said to contribute 10 per cent (Sternberg, 1999), 15–25 per cent (Schmidt and Hunter, 1998) and 25 per cent of work performance (Hunter and Hunter, 1984). Emotional intelligence can improve and affect the success of the individual by up to 50 per cent (Goleman, 1998a). Whether in a few decades we will be looking back and questioning emotional intelligence in similar ways remains to be seen. Emotions are sensory and meaningful elements of knowing and managing (Ropo and Sauer, 2008). As a rule, people retain about 10 per cent of what they are taught, and 'rational thinking' informs only about 20 per cent of behaviour; therefore, emotional intelligence and its use in work group would appear to be important, but this is where the controversy starts.

There are two main schools of thought about emotional intelligence. There is trait theory, which is primarily based in socio-biology, attributing emotional intelligence to inherited factors, which change little over a lifetime. There are the ability-based models of emotional intelligence, which state that we are born with certain abilities, but can learn and enhance our emotional intelligence. It is this school of thought that has been popularized and is the most attractive from a management perspective. The two poles measure rather different things and thus are hard to compare directly and each may have some validity on their own terms. Overall, emotional intelligence remains a 'work in progress', yet is gaining traction in research and practice. It is beginning to be taken seriously in project business and project management.

The aims of this chapter are to:

A. Examine the theorization of emotional intelligence and its applicability to practice, including the range of different models of emotional intelligence;
B. Explore the link between emotional intelligence and relationship management, both within emotional intelligence theory and in connection with group emotional intelligence as a strategic organizational capability, including the interface between a relationship management system and the behavioural programme level;
C. Examine the strengths and weaknesses of emotional intelligence in theory and application in the management of project businesses and for the management of projects (MoP).

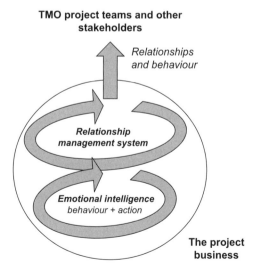

FIGURE 4.1 Emotional intelligence and the relationship management system

A main message of the chapter is therefore about the significant and growing contribution that emotional intelligence is perceived to be making to effective performance of managers and project businesses. The perceived contribution to functional and project teams is a further message, that is, group emotional intelligence. For the contribution to be at a team level, the project business needs to develop and embed support measures in routines to guide team action and behaviour at the programme and project levels. As routines are typically the partial product of recent and past practices (Parmigiani and Howard-Grenville, 2011), transference from the programme to project level need not be a considerable challenge.

Locating the management of relationships diagrammatically has been provided in the two preceding chapters, and Figure 4.1 does so for emotional intelligence and relationship management.

Emotional intelligence in theory and practice

The experience of work is saturated with feeling (Ashforth and Humphrey, 1995: 98). Feelings are spontaneous and emergent, emanating from relationships and sense making (Andersen, 2013; cf. Weick, 1995). There is an increasing focus upon emotions at work to the extent that understanding and harnessing them contributes to achieving organizational goals (e.g. Ashworth and Humphrey, 1995; Fineman, 2010; Andersen, 2013).

Emotional intelligence is a socio-psychological construct and offers one means to harness emotions to potentially good effect. Psychology is rooted in five personality dimensions, conscientiousness, extraversion, agreeableness, emotional stability and openness to experience, and in the six emotional categories of anger, fear, joy, love, sadness and surprise. Emotional intelligence has grown out of interpersonal skills. It forms one of the recognized intelligence types (Gardner, 1983). It is a development from the skill sets of managing emotions in a social context, what Thornlike (1920) termed *social intelligence* (Love et al., 2011). Emotion is socially contagious and thus affects the quality and impact of interactions. It is through interaction and relationships that the social dynamic is introduced in organizational psychology and in that way has become anchored in *organizational behaviour*, and hence in management.

Emotional intelligence therefore seems to be a continuation of management imposing its will on aspects of employee life (Hughes, 2010). While employees have workplace rights, workplaces are not generally run as democracies. All management models, systems and procedures, instructions and other frames of reference can enhance or restrict the room for manoeurve. There is nothing intrinsically oppressive or emancipating in managers harnessing emotions at work. It is *how* it is done that matters. On the positive front, emotional maturity has been perceived as a competence (McMurry, 1951). Emotional attachment and organizational identity help to improve performance (e.g. Prati et al., 2009).

But is there an intelligence that can be harnessed? Salovey and Mayer (1989) first formalized emotional intelligence as a measurement instrument, and they subsequently developed their definition as:

> . . . the ability to perceive accurately, appraise, and express emotion; the ability to access and/or generate feelings when they facilitate thought; the ability to understand emotions and emotional knowledge; and the ability to regulate emotions to promote emotional and intellectual growth.
>
> (Mayer and Salovey, 1997: 10)

Emotional intelligence therefore involves the ability to monitor our emotions and others, to discriminate among them and use them to guide thinking and actions. Linked to emotional intelligence and the ability to increase motivation and staff morale is transformational leadership (e.g. Burns, 1978; Bass, 1985; Goleman et al., 2002), which is an emotionally laden construct with its roots in charismatic leadership (Weber, 1947). Therefore claims in favour of emotional intelligence in organizations essentially cover three applied areas:

1. The *individual* applying emotional intelligence to his or her work, facilitated indirectly by conducive management and directly by personal development programmes that enhance performance through the effective use of emotions.
2. The *organization* applying emotional intelligence in groups, teams and functions, facilitated by personal development programmes, group emotional intelligence training and the introduction of guidance that constitutes a behavioural programme.
3. The *leader* applying a combination of innate and learned emotional intelligence to the leadership role to improve performance through motivation, morale raising initiatives and empathetic leadership, which falls into the conceptual category of transformational leadership.

The effects are to internally improve performance of the organization or project business. Customers and clients are keenly interested in performance of their suppliers and have also started to take an active interest in emotional intelligence. For example, in their construction related study, Butcher and Sheehan (2010) found that clients perceived first tier suppliers – the main contractor acting in the systems integrator role – that apply emotional intelligence to be a 'major differentiator', demonstrating higher levels of management commitment to their programmes, which was evident in levels of engagement and the propensity to listen. Those without the emotional commitment treated client programmes as income streams – an inward focus of organizational self-interest rather than a more outward client and service focus. This confirms other work, particularly the role of leadership in developing appropriate mindsets and action. Emotional intelligence is claimed to improve project leadership performance (Butler and Chinowsky, 2006; Clarke 2010), supporting the findings of previous work on leadership over the last 30 years (Walker, 2011). Clarke (2010) found team trust and commitment were built faster where project leadership exhibited high levels of emotional intelligence, yet interpersonal relationships were not strengthened by emotional intelligence, suggesting that emotional intelligence is complementary to relationship management expounded in **Chapter 3.** Other studies show that a deep understanding of the expectations and issues behind the surface appearance of requirements documentation is important for project managers as well as other management towards inducing successful outcomes project (e.g. Jepsen and Eskerod, 2009; Hobbs and Smyth, 2012; Boot-Handford and Smyth, 2013).

There are four main models of emotional intelligence, three of which are ability-based and one is a trait model (Petrides and Furnham, 2001). Three ability-based models are highlighted, that of the Salovey and Mayer model, the Bar-On model and the Goleman and Boyatzis mixed model (Bar-On et al., 2006). The strengths and weaknesses of each ability-based model are presented in Table 4.1.

The trait-based model of emotional intelligence is described as being located at the lower levels of personality, based on innate characteristics. It is defined as: . . . *a constellation of behavioral dispositions and self-perceptions concerning one's ability to recognize, process, and utilize emotion-laden information* (Petrides et al., 2004: 278).

The trait aspect allows measurement through self-reporting, yet it is theorized as largely non-cognitive (e.g. Petrides and Furnham, 2001) and thus exhibits a weak link with cognitive intelligence and the ability to manage emotions. One trait measurement model is the 'trait emotional intelligence questionnaire' (TEIQue) (Petrides, 2009). Some results using this model are reported later, however, this is the least adopted model from an organizational viewpoint because it does not leave any direct role for and is thus less attractive to management. Nor does it leave for any linkage to relationship management. Cartwright and Pappas (2008: 151; cf. O'Connor and Little, 2003) contrasted the 'scientific' and 'popular' versions of emotional intelligence. While Goleman (1995, 1998a) provided a major impetus to popularization, many of the tests and measures used and based upon personality traits have led to the conclusion that trait and ability emotional intelligence are two separate constructs.

The Mayer and Salovey (1997) model contains a mix of ability and some trait elements. The model employs the Mayer–Salovey–Caruso 'emotional intelligence test' (MSCEIT) (Mayer et al., 2000). MSCEIT is constructed and scores are calculated upon a similar basis to traditional intelligence tests. As it scores responses against prescribed 'correct' answers, there is a tendency to value conformity rather than diversity (Roberts et al., 2001), although this can be seen as beneficial for alignment within an organizational culture and for linkage to a relationship management system.

Bar-On (1997) defines emotional intelligence as sets of non-cognitive capabilities, competencies, and skills that influence the ability to cope with environmental demands and pressures. The Bar-On model incorporates more than just 'abilities' and claims emotional intelligence can be developed and improved. The model consists of five broad categories with fifteen subcategories. The five main categories are: (i) intrapersonal emotional skill, (ii) interpersonal emotional skill, (iii) adaptability, (iv) ability to manage stress, and (v) general mood. This model is commonly measured using the 'emotional quotient inventory' (EQ-i).

TABLE 4.1 Strengths and weaknesses of the ability-based emotional intelligence models

Model	Strength	Weaknesses
Salovey and Mayer model	Empirically proven (unlike other models) not to represent conventional personality traits. Seen as more representative of a cognitive intelligence than other models. (O'Connor and Little, 2003). Its measurement is objective (Mayer et al., 2000).	Criticized for not constituting being a cognitive intelligence but a 'learned skill' (Landy, 2005). Poor predictive validity of workforce performance (Bradberry and Su, 2006). Ambiguity over what constitutes a correct (emotionally intelligent) response during objective measures (Pérez et al., 2005). Confirmed lack of cultural variation sensitivity (Salovey, 2006). Empirically confirmed measurement gender bias (Salovey, 2006; Day and Carroll, 2004). Weak correlation with the other two EI models (Van Rooy et al., 2005).
Bar-On model	EI develops with age and can be developed via training and therapy. Emotional and cognitive intelligence considered to contribute equally to a person's general intelligence, thus indicating an individual's chances of succeeding in life (Bar-On, 1997).	Criticism that the model has little to do with emotion or intelligence. Measures overlap with existing personality traits (Matthews et al., 2002). Limitations of self-report measurement (e.g. Zeidner et al., 2004).
Goleman and Boyatzis model	Assertion that EI competencies can enhance human performance (especially in at work context) (Goleman, 1998a). Plentiful studies verifying the predictive validity of EI and work performance (Goleman, 1998a; Watkin, 2000). Advocated as more important than IQ in determining life success. EI competencies can be learnt at any age (Goleman, 1998a). Proficiency in all 18 competencies is not needed (Druskat and Druskat, 2006).	Criticized for being existing personality characteristics (Davies et al., 1998). Criticized for not constituting a cognitive intelligence (Matthews et al., 2002). The model is not conceptual (Brackett and Mayer, 2003). Limitations of self-report measurement (e.g. Zeidner et al., 2004). Criticism that performance enhancements are anecdotal and lack empirical research (Matthews et al., 2002).

Source: Adapted from Hobbs and Smyth (2012).

The Goleman and Boyatzis mixed model consists of four main categories: (i) self-awareness, (ii) social awareness, (iii) self-management and (iv) social skills (Boyatzis et al., 2000; Goleman et al., 2002). It is the last two categories that are closely associated with ability and learning on an individual basis, and associated with group emotional intelligence and relationship management in an organizational setting. Boyatzis et al. (2000) put forward the 'emotional competence inventory' (ECI) as a method of measurement for this model. Druskat and Wolff (2001) initiated research into effective performing teams using group emotional competencies and formulated 'emotionally competent group' (ECG) norms that improve the performance of groups by facilitating group trust and efficacy in networks (Wolff et al., 2006). Elfenbein (2006) also studied the effect of emotional intelligence on team performance. Mount (2006) and Müller and Turner (2010) concentrated on how emotional intelligence competencies improve the performance of project managers. Further, factors predicting success among project managers have been found to be 69 per cent emotional competencies and only 31 per cent factors related to business expertise (Mount, 2005, cited in Pryke and Smyth, 2006: 87). Druskat and Druskat (2006) proposed the following adaptation of the Goleman and Boyatzis model for group emotional intelligence pertaining to projects (Figure 4.2).

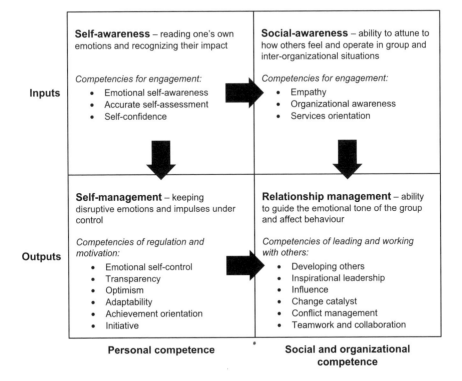

FIGURE 4.2   The Goleman and Boyatzis model applied to team emotional intelligence and organizational relationship management

Source: Adapted and developed from Druskat and Druskat, 2006.

Goleman developed a total of eighteen competencies (Goleman, 1995; Goleman 1998a; Goleman et al., 2002; see Figure 4.2). Cherniss (2001) and Druskat and Druskat (2006) argued that the higher the emotional intelligence of an individual, the greater the potential to adhere to and develop these competencies, coming through undirected learning and supplemented by directed learning. Collaborative working provides the link between group behaviour and performance (Goleman, 1998a; Druskat and Druskat, 2006; Wolff et al., 2006). Whereas relational contracting may facilitate collaborate working, emotional intelligence is a bottom-up behavioural means to develop collaborative working, emanating from within the firm.

The Goleman and Boyatzis model (Boyatzis et al., 2000; Goleman et al., 2002) provides the prime source for this chapter as more research has been conducted with this model for group emotional intelligence in general (e.g. Elfenbein, 2006) and explored in projects and their teams (e.g. Druskat and Druskat, 2006; Sunindijo et al., 2007; Hobbs and Smyth, 2012; cf. Lindebaum, 2009; Lindebaum and Cassell, 2012).

Extensive claims have been made for emotional intelligence, leadership being one noted area. It was Goleman (1998b) who proposed that high levels of emotional intelligence were attributed to effective leadership. Some research findings have confirmed initial claims (e.g. Miller, 1999; George, 2000; Palmer et al., 2001; Prati et al., 2003) supported by empirical investigation (e.g. Watkin, 2000; Palmer et al., 2001; Gardner and Stough, 2002). However, the challenges and criticism of emotional intelligence as a coherent theorization have been numerous too. These range from the reinvention of old ideas (Walker, 2011), lack of internal theoretical rigor, external critiques from other viewpoints, challenges to the methodology and methods employed (cf. Jordan et al., 2003; Daus and Ashkanasy, 2005). A fundamental challenge is to argue whether 'emotional intelligence' is indeed a kind of intelligence (Daus and Ashkanasy, 2005; Landy, 2005). The defense is that the construct is conceived psychometrically in accord with intelligence (e.g. Mayer and Salovey, 1993; Mayer et al., 1999; Brackett et al., 2004), building upon and aligning with related theorization (e.g. Ekman, 1973; Buck, 1976; Palfai and Salovey, 1993). The reliability and validity of measures were traditionally tested (e.g. Mayer et al., 2000; cf. Cronbach and Meehl, 1955). Emotional intelligence measures predict the emergence of effective leadership, specifically transformational leadership (e.g. Prati et al., 2003).

Several critics have challenged the claims that emotional intelligence improves employee and leadership performance (e.g. Jordan et al., 2002; Matthews et al., 2002; Day and Carroll, 2004; Zeidner et al., 2004; Landy, 2005). Lindebaum (2009) specifically highlighted the construction industry, claiming emotional intelligence is applied in the characteristic of an aggressive management style. This highlights that emotional intelligence is indeed benign; it depends how it is used. An outward focus or social orientation is one important factor of influence to avoid using emotional intelligence for control, manipulation, bullying and other forms of zealous self-interest.

Empathy, defined as the phenomenon that connects two otherwise isolated individuals to each other, is a critical variable necessary for understanding other people (Kenny and Albright, 1987). Empathy plays an important role to encourage emotional affirmation and emotional contagion (e.g. Coke et al., 1978; McBane, 1995). *Commitment* as a construct figures strongly in emotional intelligence in organizational contexts where personal and organizational goals are aligned (Goleman, 1998a). Evidence of commitment through attitude, effort and financial investment are further signs of the intent to use emotional intelligence in positive ways. Coupled with investment and other forms of commitment, emotional ties and bonds are the most likely means of personal and organizational alignment. Goleman labels those acting out of self-interest as *disaffected people*, which is rather strong as self-interested motivations can be neutral or coincidently aligned on occasions. Disaffection arises where individuals and groups are isolated (Douglas, 1999) or pursue interests at the expense of their employer and/or client. Self-interest can be a response to unhealthy management practices and a *toxic organization* (Frost, 2003), typically evident where negative emotions are accumulating to induce a spiral of blame, shame and adversarial relations related to power play and posturing.

Good leadership helps induce a social orientation, commitment, and shape the environment to form close interpersonal and organizational ties. Goleman et al. (2001) states that emotional intelligence has a role here, emotional intelligence being found to be twice as important as technical skills. Rosete and Ciarrochi (2005) found in their research that emotional intelligence, and particularly the ability to perceive emotions, was an important factor in predicting leadership effectiveness. Barling et al. (2000) looked at 49 managers and found that high emotional intelligence scores were associated with three of four transformational leadership factors. The factors were *idealized influence, inspirational motivation* and *individualized consideration. Intellectual stimulation* was more reliant upon cognitive than emotional abilities. Others have found complementary results (e.g. Dulewicz and Higgs, 2000; Higgs and Aitken, 2003). However, there are tensions and conflicts around leadership under the emotional intelligence banner. This becomes clear when examining it from a broader relational perspective. *Relational leadership theory* (Uhl-Bein, 2006) charts the move away from leadership as a concept of 'entity' focusing upon individuals and their leadership attributes per se towards conceptualizing leadership in context as a process of social construction. Uhl-Bein reflects upon relational leadership as a social influence for coordination and change. This view chimes with relationship management and has overlap with relationship management within emotional intelligence. However, trait theories of emotional intelligence are totally focused upon attributes, whereas the ability-based models of emotional intelligence that emphasize transformational leadership tend to recoil back into the entity-based conception. This may suit analysis of emotional intelligence at the individual level, but leadership is always relationally located. The logical direction of group emotional intelligence gives a different trajectory and it is argued points to the relational leadership agenda. This agenda is still to be developed in the emotional intelligence arena.

Leaders have an important implementation role modeling and mentoring as part of their social influence, yet more significantly identifying and developing organizational routines to support emotional intelligence, embed the routines and roll them out across different business units, and thus establish emotional intelligence as a core competency (cf. Prahalad and Hamel, 1990) and as an organizational capability (cf. Davies and Brady, 2000) to support other key project business and project functions. The evidence in project settings is currently partial and varied. The findings related to emotional intelligence research on leadership and management in a large construction and development project business are presented in Fact Box 4.1.

FACT BOX 4.1 EMOTIONAL INTELLIGENCE AND LEADERSHIP IN LARGE CONSTRUCTION AND DEVELOPMENT PROJECT BUSINESS

Across the management of a large national construction contractor around 30 per cent were aware of the concept of emotional intelligence. In a survey, they were asked to rank issues by importance. The development of swift trust in teams was seen as most critical, and second equal behind that were managing one's own emotions and leading others towards shared goals. Relationship development in teams in ways that withstand constant change were the next most important factors.

Amongst top performers, the most critical issues were perceived to be self-management with optimism, and social awareness including a service orientation, both scoring an average of 4.8 on a 1–6 scale. Relationship management issues were ranked fourth (4.4 average score).

Amongst the management roles, the chief executive scored lowest for emotional intelligence, followed by other board members and divisional directors. Department and project managers scored highest. This might be a function of generational issues, whereby technical capabilities were the prime route to senior positions or it could be that the project business does not value emotional and relationship abilities. Certainly, this project business is seen to be on a par with peers by market capitalization and performance.

Another interpretation is that the project business is failing to take responsibility for its own destiny regarding soft management skills. In support of this view, the survey found 9.7 per cent of initiatives and related support through the emergence of systems, routines and norms could be attributed to senior management, 26 per cent were directly attributed to individuals taking responsibility and 63.3 per cent were non-attributed in the survey.

Source: Pegram (2007).

Leaders and managers with high emotional intelligence may develop clan cultures, inducing inclusiveness that can prove defensive and inward looking (Ouchi, 1980; Douglas, 1999) – a negative form of relational leadership (cf. Uhl-Bein, 2006). This defeats the benefits to be derived from emotional intelligence and relationship management. There is growing albeit contested evidence that emotional intelligence supports leadership performance towards goal accomplishment at a tactical task level (Carmeli, 2003) and empathy for others (Sosik and Megerian, 1999; Henisz et al., 2012). It contributes to employee sense making by supporting the creation of narrative and locating team members in the organization (Ravasi and Schultz, 2006).

Lindebaum and Cartwright (2010) found some linkage between trait emotional intelligence and leadership. Lindebaum and Cassell (2012) examined how UK construction project managers make sense of emotional intelligence. They concluded that there are enduring, albeit changing, characteristics of the industry and the sense making processes of project managers renders the construct of limited utility. On the one hand, firms have been seeking individuals with exceptional management and leadership skills to improve interpersonal relationships skills (Dulaimi, 2005), the quality of which has been associated with the performance of projects (e.g. Bryman et al., 1987). Dulaimi and Langford (1999: 263) stated that industry performance improvement *can only be achieved through proper understanding of the dynamic role of its main resource – its people.* On the other hand, conflicts are pervasive, influenced by aggressive management styles (cf. Loosemore et al., 2003), fierce competition, tight profit margins and adversarial relationships (Holt et al., 2000; Smithers and Walker, 2000), encapsulated within a male-dominated culture (Fielden et al., 2000; Loosemore et al., 2003). Lindebaum and Cassell (2012) cited previous work to encapsulate their observations:

> The management style of many in contracting companies is based upon the street fighting man. Banter and joking, usually at the expense of others, is used for point scoring when things are on a reasonably even keel. If that fails or the pressure is great, verbal abuse and shouting are the weapons to instil fear and maintain power in the office corridor.
>
> (Smyth, 2000: 12–13)

There have been a series of advocates for emotional intelligence in this industry (e.g. Smyth, 2004; Songer and Walker, 2004; Mo et al., 2006), specifically (i) as a remedy for the blame and conflict culture in construction (Smyth, 2004); (ii) as a management tool to foster collaborations in construction (Songer and Walker, 2004); (iii) as a vitally important selection criterion for future generations of construction project managers (Butler and Chinowsky, 2006); (iv) as an intrinsically important element in engineering education (Riemer, 2003); and (v) assist project management scrutiny and channel attention to issues requiring immediate attention (Frijda, 1988). These needs and the relevance of emotional intelligence may vary across project sectors by intensity, yet there does appear to be a role, backed up by more recent empirical fieldwork (e.g. Hobbs and Smyth, 2012; Boot-Handford and Smyth, 2013).

Group emotional intelligence and project teams

Team performance depends upon interpersonal relationships (Caruso and Salovey, 2004). Teams consistently outperform individuals working in parallel (Baiden and Price, 2011).

Group emotional intelligence has pertinence for project businesses in several ways. As in most organizations, departments and group functions provide one forum for organizational behaviour. Specific for project businesses are the following:

1. The project team pertaining to the project business.
2. The temporary multi-organizational project team (TMO) (Cherns and Bryant, 1984).
3. The decision-making unit (DMU), comprising TMO decision-makers and decision-makers from the project business (cf. Figure 3.7), such as commercial and operational directors, key account managers, supply chain managers, and other technical and management roles as required (Smyth, 2000).
4. The wider project coalition of stakeholders (Winch, 2002; Figure 3.7).

Decision-making in these four requires effective management, arguably supported by emotional intelligence. Meetings vary in size and dynamics. For example, in a four-person group discussion, two people do over 70 per cent of talking, while three people do 86 per cent of the talking in a six-person group and 77 per cent of the talking in an eight-person group (Shaw, 1981). Emotional intelligence in chairing decision-making meetings can help break the pattern of dominance by extroversion and power play, turning to known specialists and those who have spoken little to invite them to make additional and informed contributions.

Based upon the analysis, there are good grounds to believe emotional intelligence makes the difference between an average team and an outstanding team, with emotionally intelligent team leaders (i) encouraging the use of emotional intelligence skills; (ii) motivating team members; (iii) drawing out the best performance from the members; (iv) developing trust, a sense of team identity and efficacy (appropriate, useful, effective, valuable behaviour and action); and (v) developing an outward focus in the respective employer organizations, the client and the broader network of suppliers and influencers (cf. Druskat and Druskat, 2006). Personal and team habits are the behavioural norms from which emerge the beginnings of informal routines (Parmigiani and Howard-Grenville, 2011),

TABLE 4.2 Behavioural norms for group emotional intelligence

	Norms of personal contribution	Norms to create awareness of emotions	Norms to regulate emotions
Member	Interpersonal understanding	Interpersonal understanding plus perspective taking (awareness of emotions in context)	Use awareness and feedback for confronting members who break norms
	Confronting members who break norms	Perspective taking	Caring behaviour
	Caring behaviour		
Group	Personal and team self-evaluation	Team self-evaluation plus feedback to create group perspective taking (reflection of group behaviour and underlying emotions in context) and performance measurement	Creating resources for working with emotions
	Creating resources for working with emotions		Creating an optimistic environment
	Creating an optimistic environment		Proactive problem solving plus anticipation with preventative action
	Proactive problem solving		
External group	Organizational Awareness	Organizational awareness	Building external relationships
	Building external relationships		

providing the raw material for core competency and capability development for group emotional intelligence. Table 4.2 sets out some of the main features for group emotional intelligence.

It is difficult to assess the emotional intelligence with which project managers and others who go on to work in project businesses commence their careers. An annual survey of master's level students has been conducted for self-awareness (Fact Box 4.2); however, this is partial concerning emotional competencies, and self-awareness and awareness of others can be used to manipulate and exert power.

FACT BOX 4.2 INDICATORS OF EMOTIONAL AWARENESS AMONG PROJECT BUSINESS ENTRANTS

Over a seven-year period, commencing 2007, cohorts of master's students have been asked to participate in the test related to reading emotions in others (adapted from Baron-Cohen, 2004). Overall, 480 students have taken part. They have been classified according to their professional and working background.

The task is to recognize emotions in the eyes of others across 18 separate images. The eyes are said to provide a good source for reading emotions because variation between different cultures is less than other factors, such as body language and tone of voice.

The rank order with the highest awareness are structural engineers, closely followed by architects and non-cognates (other educational and professional backgrounds), with mechanical and electrical engineers and project managers not far behind. Following up the rear were those with prior background or education in general contracting, civil engineering and from suppliers.

An interesting point is the reclassifying of results as 'professional' and 'non-professional'. The professions scored better as might be expected, but the score was higher if those who selected themselves as coming from a project management background are included in the professionals. This can be read as counterbalancing the large number of civil engineers who typically score lower and/or as evidence of the growing professionalization of project management.

Having a high score or the ability to be aware of the emotions of others does not make someone a better manager. It depends if they put their understanding to good use. It can be used to exert power and take advantage of others, for example through influence motivated by self-interest, manipulation, or identifying whom to bully.

Civil engineers do not have unreasonable scores, but they do need to pay particular attention to over-emphasizing a technical and task orientation in conducting their work and complementing their technical skills through the proactive development of their interpersonal skill sets to improve their performance.

Emotions are heterogeneous, and more significantly, are mobilized heterogeneously. In the study reported in Fact Box 4.2, architects were shown to have a good level of emotional intelligence entering the profession, at least as far as awareness is concerned. Yet, others have reported that they use their emotional skills in narrow ways (Gifford at al., 2000; Volker, 2010), the implication being that they are weaker in the social skills quadrant of the Goleman and Boyatzis model (Boyatzis et al., 2000; Goleman et al., 2002) and for relationship management (Duskat and Druskat, 2006).

Applying the trait model (Petrides and Furnham, 2001), different management levels were compared, and gender differences were considered in a project-related business (Fact Box 4.3). The findings are related to one project business in one project sector, raising the issue of sectoral context versus generality. How much does context matter? Andersen (2010) developed a model based upon inputs and outputs, personal and factual factors, which have been developed into a matrix to tease out some of the likely implications for project operations (Figure 4.3).

FACT BOX 4.3 EMOTIONAL INTELLIGENCE ACROSS MANAGEMENT LEVELS AND BY GENDER

A global financial and management consultancy, which undertakes many of its commissions as projects, was investigated using the trait model of Petrides and Furnham (2001). A total of 128 responses were received from senior, middle and junior management categories. The results were compared against responses from global population of 1676 individuals (Petrides, 2009). The 128 managers surveyed had significantly higher trait emotional intelligence scores. This reflects the observation that effective managers require high levels of emotional intelligence in their roles. It was found that different management levels showed no overall significance between them.

At a more nuanced level, there were differences between the ability of managers to assess their emotional intelligence. Senior and middle managers were quite accurate in their predictions of their total emotional intelligence, whereas junior managers on the whole overestimated their emotional intelligence.

Gender has been a long-standing issue in assessing emotional intelligence (e.g. Petrides and Furnham, 2001). Are females more self-deprecating? It was found that men tended to underestimate their emotional intelligence whilst women tended towards a bias of overestimation of their emotional capabilities. There was no significant relationship by gender between the traits of *well-being, self-control* and *sociability* within the trait model. On the other hand, *emotionality* scores were higher for women, implying greater relationship sensitivity to events in context. It was also found that women were numerically underrepresented in senior management (27.3 per cent), and overrepresented in junior management positions (72.7 per cent). The numerical split was even in the middle management roles (49.4 per cent males, and 50.6 per cent females). It may follow that being able to accurately self-estimate emotional capabilities is a factor of reaching managerial seniority and that female overestimation may be a negative factor rather than a socially generated gender issue.

Source: Sfeir et al. (2014).

Personal inputs	Service quality enhanced by emotional intelligence	Service and technical quality enhanced by emotional intelligence
Factual inputs	Technical quality enhanced by service content informed by emotional intelligence	Technical quality mediated by emotional intelligence
	Personal outputs	**Factual outputs**

FIGURE 4.3 Emotional intelligence and operational context

Figure 4.3 assumes that emotional intelligence is present at the personal and interpersonal level. The factual elements relate to external factors to the individual (and team). Given the project management focus and task orientation that has traditionally pervaded projects, then the factual content in terms of inputs and outputs are largely technical or perceived as such. Thus, a combination of factual inputs and outputs yields a matrix position where emotional intelligence is arguably least needed. This is most appropriate to the integrated provider of specialist solutions, that is, subcontractors and suppliers (Davies et al., 2007). Emotional intelligence enhances any business provider and thus the factual inputs-personal outputs combination enhances provision. Personal inputs and factual outputs are arguably optimal and also point towards the systems integrator role (Davies et al., 2007), where a reliance on 'soft' management skills is greater. The top right position is where the systems integrator role conceptually is located and the reliance upon the soft management inputs is greatest. However, the factors singled out by Andersen (2010) echo the prevalence of management to leave relationships to individual responsibility. Conceptually, a relationship management system and behavioural approach may blur matters in time as greater interdependency emerges.

In construction and based upon the work of Faulkner et al. (1989) and Love et al. (2010), the activities where a construction manager would benefit from emotional intelligence are identified as:

1. *Tasks* – conferring, preparing contracts and negotiating revisions, directing and supervising workers.
2. *Skills* – instructing, listening, making judgments and decision-making, negotiation.
3. *Characteristics* – dependability, leadership, self-control, stress tolerance, cooperation, innovation, adaptability/flexibility, initiative.

Managers with high levels of emotional intelligence have been found to positively influence the performance of construction businesses through transformational leadership behaviour (Butler and Chinowsky, 2006) and for leadership among project managers project (Sunindijo et al., 2007). Emotional intelligence provides a personal resource for coping with stress at work, although a wider body of work suggests that stress levels and a lack of management support building negative emotions among project managers (Love et al., 2011). However, the main point to draw out from these observations and findings is that leadership is not independent of functions, thus systems and behaviour within the organization, but rather that leadership and management have the management of organizational behaviour as a prime responsibility and thus prescriptively could or normatively should be more proactive in management and taking greater responsibility for the destiny of the project businesses they manage. Leaders are enablers of social coordination, change, and influence (Uhl-Bein, 2006). There are two facets to this, first the internal management and second the inter-organizational management. Relational leadership and group emotional intelligence will benefit from further conceptual and empirical development.

Relational leadership reflects the general trend on the ground for shared or distributed leadership (e.g. Ancona et al., 2007), yet this more decentralized leadership form should not be confused with leaving matters to individual responsibility, indeed the converse; the more authority is delegated and empowerment employed, the more sound parameters from an influential social framework are needed. Client personnel, especially those in the DMU, improve performance by exhibiting a range of personality attributes, including flexibility, tolerance for ambiguity, particularly empathy and the ability to read cues from clients and their representatives (Fitzsimmons and Fitzsimmons, 2011). This enables the influence rather than being the influence per se.

Clients are taking an increasing interest in behavioural issues – they are taking the lead where the project businesses have yet to do so. One major infrastructure client used 'climate assessment', providing an opportunity to analyze the results alongside a study into emotional intelligence on a major programme (Fact Box 4.4). The application of ability-based emotional intelligence, as part of personal development programmes for key management and operational staff or as part of a project business behavioural programme is likely to improve the possibility of employees forming an increased sense of personal identity, which improves organizational behaviour (Damasio, 2000; Uhl-Bein, 2006), as well as increasing the potential for social identity. *Identification* is the process by which members of a group increasingly feel they belong and demonstrate high levels of *affective commitment* (Davis and Walker, 2009). Identification is a key part of developing deep relationships and supports a social orientation with a client or customer focus.

FACT BOX 4.4 COLLABORATIVE BEHAVIOUR AND EMOTIONAL INTELLIGENCE ON A MAJOR INFRASTRUCTURE PROGRAMME

A major rail infrastructure client was employing a climate assessment tool or CAT by surveying their staff. The findings were ambivalent regarding the collaboration of programme partners although they were reasonably high across the whole team.

Climate assessment tool item	Range of scores (%)	Average score (%)
Perception that client and contractors work well together	65–77	68.50
Perception that the client and contractor will adopt a win-win approach (looking for mutual benefits)	61–73	70.00
Perception there is a good level of trust across the project team	56–83	68.75
Belief that project members know for what they are accountable	67–77	71.00
Feeling that project members are inspired by delivery team senior managers	63–69	66.50
Perception there is not a blame culture in the project team	61–70	65.00
Confidence the project will be delivered within programme	56–75	65.00
Belief that present work practices will overcome any future problems	61–73	69.00
Levels of understanding of each other's needs	67–73	70.50

Several different types of meeting were filmed across the programme and emotional competencies identified using body language and behavioural cues as the means of interpretation. These are presented in the table below, expressed as the average emotional competencies by organization per meeting.

Meeting	Organization	Empathy	Transparency	Optimism	Teamwork and collaboration	Self-confidence	Conflict management	Inspirational leadership	Achievement orientation
Technical queries progress 1	Main contractor	-1	-1	-1	1	-1	0	1	1
	Client	0	0	0	0	-1	0	0	0
Technical queries progress 2	Main contractor	1	0	0	-1	-1	0	1	0
Concourse meeting 1	Main contractor	0	0	1	1	0	1	-1	0
	Client	0	-1	-2	2	2	1	1	1
Concourse meeting 2	Main contractor	0	1	1	-1	0	-1	-1	0
	Client	0	-2	-3	3	1	-2	0	2
Suburban train shed 1	Main contractor	1	1	1	1	2	0	0	1
	Client	1	1	1	0	1	0	2	1
Suburban train shed 2	Main contractor	1	2	0	0	0	0	0	0
	Client	1	0	0	0	0	0	1	1
Suburban train shed 3	Main contractor	1	0	0	0	2	0	1	1
	Client	1	0	-1	0	0	0	2	1
Board meeting 1	Main contractor	1	1	0	1	-2	0	0	2
	Client	2	1	0	2	2	0	1	1
Board meeting 2	Main contractor	1	2	1	1	1	0	2	3
	Client	1	1	1	2	2	0	2	2
	Communications contractor	1	0	0	0	0	0	0	0
Weekly consultant review 1	Consultant engineer	1	0	0	2	0	0	1	1
	Client	2	0	0	3	1	0	2	2
Weekly consultant review 2	Consultant engineer	1	0	0	1	1	0	1	0
	Client	1	0	0	-1	3	0	1	0
Weekly consultant review 3	Main contractor	1	1	-1	1	0	0	2	0
	Consultant engineer	0	-1	0	1	1	0	1	0
	Client	1	2	0	2	3	0	1	2

(Continued)

FACT BOX 4.4 (Continued)

Weekly communi-cations 1	Communications contractor	−1	−1	1	1	0	−3	−2	1
	Client	0	−1	0	−1	0	−1	−1	1
Weekly communi-cations 2	Communications contractor	1	−1	0	0	−1	0	−2	−1
	Client	1	−1	−1	1	1	0	1	2

A large number of both low and negative scores were evident in the technical progress queries and were notable for the apparent lack of self-confidence displayed by both the client and main contractor members. The main contractor demonstrated some leadership, collaborative and achievement competencies and took personal responsibility for addressing important issues, suggesting innovative solutions. Yet, meetings were also characterized by a lack of optimism, for example, discussing the likelihood of past problems re-occurring and over the failure of a representative from another contractor to comply with agreed action. The client failed to show positive leadership. The concourse meetings also exhibited a distinct lack of optimism among client members.

The main contractor members demonstrated a lack of leadership, constraining their ability to persuade and influence. The three suburban train shed meetings demonstrated inspirational leadership from the client project manager and empathy was in evidence. The meetings displayed high levels of the achievement orientation competency, particularly during a safety review and to improve site security following a reported theft.

Weekly consultant reviews exhibited a lack of transparency amongst the consultant members. Developing win-win strategies in client-contractor relationships and low trust levels were a concern regarding the engineering consultant.

Source: Hobbs and Smyth (2012).

Emotions and the application of emotional intelligence among staff is not only important for reasons internal to the organization such as competence development, job satisfaction and performance, it is also important at the interface with clients and other stakeholders. The emotional reaction of clients affects their perceived satisfaction (e.g. Westbrook and Oliver, 1991; Liljander and Strandvik, 1997; Porath et al., 2011). The response from the project business is important in client management. Thus, handling any tension or dissatisfaction influences client perception, that is affecting perception in the light of information about events and improved understanding. It can help develop a sense of mutual identification between individuals at the interface with organizational stakeholders, notably clients, consultants and suppliers.

How emotional intelligence is implemented depends upon multiple factors. The project business strategy, the approach to relationship management, the choice of an emotional intelligence model, selectivity on what aspects to concentrate to develop capabilities that make a difference in the marketplace are all factors. What is chosen forms the basis of a training, personal development and/or behavioural programme. Building upon Table 4.2, although far from comprehensive, a few additional emotional abilities and regulative guidance can be used to develop systematic capabilities – see Table 4.3.

TABLE 4.3 Points of emotional abilities and regulative guidance for development

---

1. **Reflective regulation of emotions to promote emotional and intellectual growth**

    - Ability to stay open to pleasant and unpleasant feelings

    - Ability to reflectively engage/detach from an emotion depending on how it is judged for being informative or for utility

    - Ability to reflectively monitor emotions in relation to oneself and others

    - Ability to manage emotion in oneself and others by moderating negative emotions and enhancing pleasant ones without repressing or exaggerating information they may convey

2. **Understanding and analyzing emotions; employing emotional knowledge**

    - Ability to label emotions and recognize relations among the words and emotions themselves

    - Ability to interpret the meanings emotions convey regarding relationships

    - Ability to understand complex feelings: simultaneous feelings and blends of feelings

    - Ability to recognize likely transitions among emotions

3. **Emotional facilitation of thinking**

    - Emotions prioritize thinking by directing attention to important information

    - Emotions are sufficiently vivid and available that they can be generated as aids to judgement and memory concerning experience and events

    - Emotional mood swings change the individual's perspective from optimistic to pessimistic, encouraging consideration of multiple points of view

    - Emotional states differentially encourage specific problem-solving approaches

4. **Perception, appraisal and expression of emotion**

    - Ability to identify emotion in one's physical states, feelings and thoughts

    - Ability to identify emotions in other people, designs, artwork etc., through language, sound, appearance and behaviour

    - Ability to express emotions accurately and to express needs related to those feelings

    - Ability to discriminate between accurate and inaccurate, or honest versus dishonest expressions of feeling

---

Conclusion

The concept *relationship management* has to be treated with care. Its roots in relationship marketing have given it a strategic role at the level of organizational behaviour, systems and procedures, cascading down to inform micro-level conduct. The concept of relationship management in emotional intelligence is confined to a sub-component of emotional intelligence, specifically within the Goleman and Boyatzis model in the social skills quadrant (Boyatzis et al., 2000; Goleman et al., 2002), which becomes relationship management within group emotional intelligence (Druskat and Druskat, 2006). The applied operational level for the concept of relationship management within emotional intelligence is at the behavoural level, informing interaction, interpersonal and group skills in managing the social context through formal and informal routines.

This conceptual clarification is less important than the compatibility of the two concepts and in that regard, relationship management from the marketing domain is compatible with that derived from emotional intelligence. Indeed, emotional intelligence can be nested under relationship management principles and systems to provide a finer grain of analysis and understanding around norms and behaviour within a project business and for project management.

For management, the strength of the emotional intelligence concept is that it offers an easy point of entry for improving relationship management. It does not need any changes to the current structure and processes. It can be introduced without strategic announcement, rapidly creating interest and buy-in from staff. It is not a low cost option as there is a price tag to the use of any proprietary assessment test and will quickly need additional human resource management (HRM) capability for training, personal development and behaviour programmes, whether this is bought in or developed in-house. The main weakness as a stand-alone initiative is that it is indirect, anticipating influence on behaviour and action rather than directly guiding it at the applied and operational level.

Integration with a relationship management system is a clearer path. The relationship management system is implemented as a first stage with emotional intelligence in mind as a second stage and alignment of the two on the ground becomes part of the iterative refinement of a relationship management system largely on a bottom-up basis of identification for change with monitoring and sanction top-down. The interfaces are numerous, individual and group behaviour interfacing with any behavioural programme and behavioural code of conduct.

For staff, the main strength of emotional intelligence is that it provides individual focus and a personal development component. This also benefits management as this aspect, consistently implemented, conveys care and offers nurture. While a relationship management system has a strong top-down aspect to implementation and can appear more coercive, emotional intelligence appears more bottom-up, although in many respects, it is far more invasive. Emotional intelligence addresses an issue of relationship management, which is to conceptually avoid getting down to the detailed outworking at relationship level and what it can look like on the ground.

For researchers, the theoretical basis of emotional intelligence remains a contested field. There is more work being done on the brain and how this informs under-standing of intelligence. This may contribute to greater depth of understanding of the psychological workings. This risks neglecting the social aspects and how this affects organizational behaviour, at a more detailed level linkage to organiza-tional culture and linkage to the presence and levels of social identification with organizations. A thorny issue for researchers is the range of emotional intelligence models. The ability and trait models are arguably different constructs and thus have different purpose. The ability models are in competition conceptually and at an applied level for share of this growing consultant market. This is unlikely to be a resolved in the foreseeable future. The Goleman and Boyatzis mixed model arguably has more current pertinence in project markets, not for any intrinsic or conceptual reason, but because more work has been carried out on group emo-tional intelligence.

The chapter aims have been to address emotional intelligence and its applica-bility to practice, especially in groups and teams. Different models of emotional intelligence have been introduced, the Goleman and Boyatzis model being reviewed and developed in the context of group emotional intelligence. The link between emotional intelligence and relationship management from **Chapter 3** has been explored and thus the way in which emotional intelligence can be developed on a stand-alone basis or in combination to develop staff and capabilities to support the project business. Development in terms of norms, behavioural programmes has been investigated too. Finally, the strengths and weaknesses of emotional intel-ligence in theory and MoP practice have been considered. The development of emotional intelligence at project level has to be instigated from the 'corporate centre' and in that sense is conceptually prior to any particular project, yet informs the way in which projects are conducted. The project strategy has to be carefully formulated on a project-by-project basis as each TMO means that engagement with other organizations may involve other organizations that do not have rela-tionship management strategy and an investment programme in emotional intel-ligence. Alliances and informal ways of collaborative working may help, but otherwise the project business needs to be firm about establishing norms for operation at the front-end for implementation across the TMO in terms of pro-cedures and behaviours to inform actions of coordination and decision-making.

An important message is about how emotional intelligence is being and can be developed both theoretically and in practice to examine and extend collabora-tive working and by implication the potential for development, which accords with the growing management interest in organizational behaviour. There have been a number of theory–practice issues addressed during the course of this chapter, and these are reviewed in summary terms for the substantive issues specifically addressed.

SI no. 1: *Organizational Behaviour* is part of the process in addressing inte-grated management and the delivery of integrated solutions. Emotional intelligence contrasts with the structural approaches, and thus the emphasis on processes and behavioural dimensions is a significant contribution to how project working is conducted and also the scope for improving organizational behaviour. From the viewpoint of staff and other organizations working in and with the project business, the climate or atmosphere generated is likely to be more positive; however, emotional intelligence is benign as it depends *how* it is used and thus the application, for example in a behavioural programme, and under a relationship management systems, it is more likely to engender positive and aligned behaviour. The outworking in practice remains a work in progress.

SI no. 2: *Relationship Management Theory* as derived from its marketing roots is conceptually different to relationship management conceived within group emotional intelligence, however the two are compatible, operating at different levels where a behavioural programme can become part of or nested within a relationship management system. In this way a theory–practice issue is addressed at several operational levels.

SI no. 3: *Socio–Psychological Issues* of intuitive as well as cognitive behaviour are addressed in the chapter. Norms comprise an important part of setting the parameters for group emotional intelligence. These become norms for functional activity including project management. They become norms to guide DMUs and TMOs on a project-by-project basis.

SI no. 4: *Conceptual and Applied Hierarchical Integration* commences with investment at the level of portfolio management and within HRM. Programme and project management become the main focus for operation implementation, to which this chapter has contributed. Compliance is required, yet emotional intelligence contributes more directly and overtly to personal development than relational contracting and relationship management systems.

SI no. 7: *The Task Orientation* is a predominantly inwards focus. Emotional intelligence can be seen to reinforce the inwards focus although not the task. Group emotional intelligence engenders an opening for an outwards focus to develop with a much greater emphasis upon people and their interrelationships.

SI no. 8: *Relational Contracting* is not directly addressed in this chapter, but indirectly, group emotional intelligence is a force acting the other way, that is internally bottom-up to meet the externally driven and top-down relational contracting drivers at the level of programmes and projects.

SI no. 9: *Systems Integration* includes the human dimension and emotional intelligence that can make a significant contribution from the behavioural level to systems integration with relationship management and through behavioural programmes and codes of conduct, helping to consider this theory-practice issue.

SI no. 10: *Market Functioning* highlighted the potential to move and arguably increase the need to move away from survival mode to build capabilities and competencies. At the level of organizational behaviour, emotional intelligence and group emotional intelligence offer the potential to form core competencies and/ or dynamic capabilities that yield competitive advantage.

The chapter therefore contributes both to the current level of understanding of research and practice concerning emotional intelligence as well as exploring some signposts for normative and prescriptive development. Building upon these knowledge contributions, the primary *recommendations* of further research is to extend the investigation of emotional intelligence in project businesses and teams in several ways:

A. Using a range of emotional intelligence models, particularly for examining group emotional intelligence in greater depth and within which underpinning group norms require greater attention.
B. The way in which levels of emotion intelligence affect psychological contracts in project teams
C. Research into the linkage between emotional intelligence, relational leadership and social identification

Although there is enormous scope for research in this field, the above seem particularly pertinent for the understanding of emotional intelligence in connection with the broader scope of relationship management and MoP.

Recommendations for practice are for management to consider:

1. Adopting emotional intelligence and specifically group emotional intelligence as a means to develop relationship management in a comprehensive and rich way
2. Allocate investment to commence development of interpersonal relationships at the HRM-operational interface, and in relation to behavioural development, programmes and behavioural codes of conduct as part of concerted management of organizational behaviour
3. Emotional intelligence development, focusing upon front-end management strategy in order to inform TMO formation and conduct

Emotional intelligence starts with the individual. It moves into the sphere of interpersonal relations and then into both organizational and inter-organizational levels through group emotional intelligence. It does not directly tackle how relationships are formed and what underpins them. Trust is an important part of interpersonal relationship formation and team relations. This is the topic for the next chapter, drilling down to a finer grain of detail analysis and understanding.

5

TRUST AND RELATIONSHIP MANAGEMENT

Introduction

Trust has received considerable attention for the last 30 years or more in management and the last 20 years on projects (e.g. Bennett and Jayes, 1995; Egan, 1998; Meng, 2012). Trust is an attribute of relationships. If trust is present, how does it contribute to relationship management? Trust is seen as important in group emotional intelligence and relationship marketing/management in project environments (e.g. Smyth and Thompson, 2005; Druskat and Druskat, 2006). It has also been seen as an important part of relational contracting (e.g. Williamson, 1993). Yet how trust is formed, its status in relationships, its impact upon behaviour and the extent to which it can be managed is still to be fully developed.

There are two related issues about the significance of trust that can be addressed straight away. The first is about prior factors to the formation of trust. There is a considerable body of theoretical and empirical work that has sought to identify antecedents to trust (e.g. Wong et al., 2000; Dirks and Ferrin, 2002; Bijlsma, 2003). If there are antecedents, it begs the question as to why trust has received so much attention. One substantive problem is the failure to identify any consistent set of antecedents. Therefore trust may instead be ontological and thus without antecedents. Any factors of influence are therefore contextual conditions, which help to explain variance especially in project environments (Smyth and Thompson, 2005; Smyth, 2008a; cf. Butler, 1991).

The second issue is whether trust is foundational to relationship formation and sustenance, thus an ontological factor of significance. There are two conceptual camps in this respect. There has been a strong case in favour of trust as foundational (e.g. McAllister, 1995; Robinson, 1996; Smyth, 2008a; Gustafsson et al., 2010). The foundational and ontological nature of trust as an essential component of strong and enduring relationships lends increased importance to the generally agreed position of trust as significant in relationships formation and behaviour. Where trust is foundational, interactions between parties develop and potentially deepen relationships, within which the iterative formation of trust forms part of the dynamics in self-reinforcing ways, and conversely reinforcing in a corrosive way where trust is thin, misplaced or distrust is present. The second camp sees it as important but not essential in relationships, especially commercial ones and in institutional settings. In this view, relationships are less stable and subject to greater behavioural variation over successive interaction. At institutional levels, trust may not be seen as foundational between actors, but institutional stability lends greater certainty. This does not mean trust is necessarily present or at high levels. The existence of trust at institutional level is monitored on an annual basis for government, business and other organizations on a global basis (Edelman, 2013). From over 31,000 respondents, 48 per cent of scandals are perceived as attributable to corporate corruption on the one hand and the bonus and compensation organizational culture on the other hand. This suggests societies and businesses have been encouraging and creating the type of culture that is eroding trust in the marketplace and in the way management operate (cf. Kramer, 2009). However, presence of trust is growing across institutions, moving away from a negative position of distrust. Engineering and technological industries show the highest sectoral trust levels, whereas finance, banks and media are at the bottom. Specialists, experts and peers are most trusted in business, whereas the chief executive is the least trusted. Only 19 per cent of business leaders are perceived to take ethical and moral decisions, and only 18 per cent are thought to consistently tell the truth.

Institutional trust is higher than trust in leadership, a gap of approximately 30 per cent (Edelman, 2013), which accords with the findings of Zaheer et al. (1998), where organizational trust is not an aggregate of interpersonal trust of any one time due to lagged effects between the two levels. The main lesson is that people do not believe the recently prevalent values are sufficient and are looking for indications of change from the bottom-up (Edelman, 2013). Behaviour is a key indicator for trust, and thus close attention needs to be paid to management behaviour. This also raises the issues of whether management do and can manage trust in both organizational relations, and hence, inter-organizational ones.

The existence of trust in project businesses would be expected to have waned in the post-2008 downturn. The demise of relational contracting in some sectors is certainly one factor. For example, construction in the United Kingdom is one sector where price drivers have been to the fore among clients and relational contracting has been reduced. A small empirical snapshot of major project businesses related a slightly different and nuanced story (Table 5.1). Interviewees were asked how important trust is in their relationships with other parties. The respondents were therefore considering other parties as clients, suppliers and/or to a degree other external stakeholders depending upon their role. The interviewees said that collaborative practices have informally helped the maintenance of good strike rates in securing contracts and increased price leverage in supply chains rather

TABLE 5.1 A self-reporting snapshot of trust levels in relationships with clients, suppliers and other external stakeholders

Main contractor	Level of trust by role (%)				
	Board members	Marketing and business development managers	Project managers	Other	Total
UKCo		17%	100%	−50%	33%
EUCo	0%	80%	0%	50%	55%
AntCo		100%	50%	100%	88%
EuroCo	100%	67%	100%	75%	83%

than relying on market forces per se (cf. Smyth, 2013a). Perceived importance is not necessarily translated into practice. Yet the overall percentages for trust against each company are a reflection of how well these companies are performing in terms of securing work and market share.

Trust is intangible. It is sensed and observed indirectly through behaviour, which includes verbal communication. Trust is not the same as nor should be conflated with open communication (Smyth, 2008a). Communication helps facilitate information flows (e.g. Carson et al., 2003). Effective communication can have a reinforcing effect on trust development too, especially where self-interested trust is built upon with social motivation. Trust develops according to the predispositions of those involved and the operational context, of which communication is a small part of the picture, albeit one means through which evidence is sensed and assessed.

The aims of this chapter are to:

A. Examine the theorization of trust and its applicability to practice.
B. Explore the link between trust, its management and relationship management, thus, how trust can be developed as part of a set of management capabilities for effective operation on projects and in relation to market performance.
C. Consider the strengths and weaknesses of trust in theory and application in the management of project businesses and projects.

A main position adopted is that trust is foundational to effective relationships, both interpersonal and organizational, making a significant contribution to the effective performance of managers and teams both on an interpersonal and team level. For the contribution to be at a team level, the project business manages trust development by creating the supportive conditions and routines to guide and embed effective relationship development in teams and for guiding interorganizational action and behaviour.

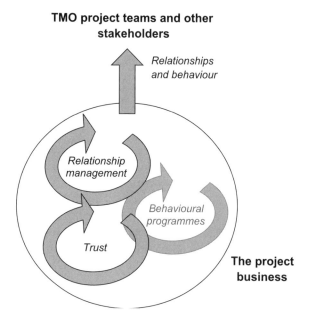

FIGURE 5.1 Trust and the relationship management system

Locating trust within the management of a project business is depicted in Figure 5.1. To take trust into the marketplace as intent to form and sustain collaborative and cooperative relationships of effective performance for both the project business and for the benefit of clients and other external stakeholders requires development of the conditions and behaviour internally. The argument here is that governance is insufficient, even if trust forms or is the central part of the governance structure and content. Trusting behaviour is modelled from the top, supported by investment and is organizationally embedded at all levels of operation. This includes transference into the project team through programme management and into each temporary multi-organizational project team (TMO). This can be achieved in a number of ways, including building upon relationship management principles and behavioural programmes such as offered by group emotional intelligence.

Trust in theory and practice

Scoping and defining trust

The character of an individual influences the disposition to trust, partly from innate characteristics and partly from the experiences that may render a person more willing to trust. Thus, trust is manifested as an attitude (Luhmann, 1979; Flores and Solomon, 1998). As an attitude, trust informs action to become a social dynamic in relationships. It is intangible (Ganesan, 1994; Fukuyama, 1995;

McAllister, 1995; Misztal, 1996), being indirectly observed as evidence in behaviour towards another or others (Moorman et al., 1993; Currall and Judge, 1995; Mayer et al., 1995; Smyth and Thompson, 2005). Trust is typically evaluated intuitively (e.g. Sitkin and Roth, 1993; Das and Teng, 2004; Tuomela and Tuomela, 2005), involving iterative intuitive assessments, especially in the early stages of relationship formation, although a cognitive element may increase over time (Gustafsson et al., 2010). It is the absence of trust that is more conscious than its presence (Dibben, 2004). Trust is foundational to an enduring relationship and only has meaning embedded in a relationship or set of group and organizational relationships. As such, it involves more than one party and can be two-sided or multi-faceted.

Trust is essential for high-quality workplace relations (e.g. Ferrin et al., 2006; Bernerth and Walker, 2009), task performance (e.g. Dirks and Ferrin, 2002; Colquitt et al., 2007), collaboration (Gulati and Nickerson, 2008), and its presence helps to mitigate deviant behaviour (Rotter, 1980). Trust takes time to build interpersonally and for it to induce inter-organizational trust because there are multiple interpersonal relationships in B2B relationships (e.g. Gulati, 1995), affected by the inter-organizational and network settings.

One-sided trust can enable collaboration, yet on occasions may lead to the other party taking advantage of trust exhibited by the other party, even being deceitful (cf. the Iago–Othello relationship). However, this raises the issue as to whether the person trusting the other party made inaccurate assessments and thus, whether the trust was *misplaced* in the first place. Contrary evidence of *distrust* may not have been available in a timely way. Misplaced trust is retrospective, providing learning opportunities to read behavioural signs, yet, can be used to be over-defensive in the future. There are no guarantees with trust, hence a degree of relational risk (O'Neill, 2002), that is where there are unknowns and uncertainties, and where complexity inhibits reliance upon rational calculation.

As relationships develop, the proportion of cognitive assessment may increase (Gustafsson et al., 2010), but the intuitive component of iterative assessment still remains a strong component of relationship assessment. The intuitive elements are derived from experience and habit:

> One way of classifying learning is cognitive (head knowledge and learning), experiential or affective ('university of life' and 'gut feel' which includes emotional engagement), and psycho-motor learning (repetitive in the sense of physically learning to ride a bike or management coaching – learning by doing again and again).
>
> (Smyth et al., 2010: 120)

There is an over-emphasis upon the cognitive across a great deal of the literature both theoretically and when conducting empirical investigation.

Trust is a moral concept, which is important for economics and governance (**Chapter 11**), yet trust is neutral, serving what is around in practice (Baier, 1994). Trust therefore has a self-fulfilling role in research and practice (Ferraro et al.,

2005), indeed, the creation and erosion of social capital as an organizational asset (Nahapiet et al., 2005). People act as reflections of each other, one party seeing aspects of themselves through others, hence creating the social desire for interaction and work. Ghoshal and Rocha (2006) point out that actions comprise more than self-interest. Self-love may lead us to do socially orientated and sometimes sacrificial acts. Even though these acts may make us knowingly feel of value or increase our self-worth in some way, this can never be pure self-interest because cognitive calculation would not lead us into these acts alone.

Many theorists claim trust does not occur in the market (e.g. Korczynski, 2000), while others change their mind or are skeptical (cf. Williamson 1975, 1985, 1993). Dasgupta (1988) represents those that take the contrary view, that is, not only can trust be present, but it is a necessity for the market to function. Too little trust will lead to market failure. Kramer (2009) has recently reasserted this view.

How can trust be defined? Barney and Hansen define trust in economic relations as *an attribute of a relationship between exchange partners* (1994: 2). More detail is provided in the market exchange in the following passage: *Your client's interest in you is based on their belief that your actions will reflect a high level of consideration for their interests. They must believe that you will act with their best interests at heart* (Dawson, 2000: 20).

The belief implies some uncertainty. At the level of a probability statement, confidence is needed, but beyond that, trust underpins positive assessment of future considered actions. This shifts the ground towards a management perspective or a component of organizational behaviour. It is in this literature that the term *vulnerable* repeatedly arises as an aid to definition. An element of vulnerability has been said to be present in applying a degree of trust in any interpersonal or inter-organizational relationship (e.g. Deutsch, 1958; Zand, 1972; Gambetta, 1988). This has culminated in much quoted definitions (e.g. Mayer et al., 1995; Rousseau et al., 1998), for example:

> . . . the willingness of a party to be vulnerable to the actions of another party based on the expectation that the other will perform a particular action important to the trustor, irrespective of the ability to monitor or control that other party.
>
> (Mayer et al., 1995: 712)

Mayer et al. (1995) are criticized for reducing trust to a dyadic relation of trustor-trustee, whereas trust is more than interpersonal covering combinations of social groups and inter-organizational relationships (cf. Wekselberg, 1996). Others criticize the exclusion of the influence of power and authority ascribed to roles and in the market (e.g. Husted, 1998; cf. Dasgupta, 1988; Korczynski, 2000).

There is a balance to be struck between the aspect of belief as cited above (Dawson, 2000) and vulnerability. Both belief and vulnerability are present in project environments. First, *vulnerability* is echoed in the definition pertaining to projects. The definition is looking forwards: *Trust is a disposition and attitude concerning the willingness to rely upon the actions of or be vulnerable towards another party, under circumstances of contractual and social obligations, with the potential for collaboration* (Edkins and Smyth, 2006: 84).

The extent of reliance and vulnerability is small at any one time (e.g. Gil et al., 2011). This reliance simultaneously reduces risk associated with vulnerability and mitigates risk as relationships develop. This contrasts with one view that trust is defined in terms of risk (e.g. Kramer, 1999; Schoorman et al., 2007; cf. Williamson, 1993). One party is no worse off by making reasonable assessments to trust (cf. misplaced trust) – it conflates the factors of risk (including relational risks) with the vulnerability. Trust affirmed reduces relational risk and lowers other perceived risks. Relationships are more efficient than economic factors in driving performance (Clegg et al., 2011). Projects look forward, they envisage performance to achieve the 'future perfect' (Pitsis et al., 2003). Trust as it looks forward requires a degree of vulnerability so to do (cf. Good, 1988).

Second, a predisposition coupled with a current assessment leads to a *belief* or *conviction* (Zaheer et al., 1998), as provided by this scoping definition:

> Trust is a current conviction that another party is willing to take individual and organisational interests into account within the context and under possible events. Trust is intuitively, sometimes part-cognitively, assessed concerning the other party from recent past performance and longer term reputation through the lens of personal history hence experiential disposition to trust, coupled with organisational capability (cultural, systemic and procedural path dependency) to accommodate trusting relations. The presence of a trusted party (i) reduces perceived (interpreted or 'subjective') risk, (ii) renders the relationship, organisational and project context more conducive to further (real or 'objective') risk reduction, and (iii) creates organisational and project opportunities to improve the service and content quality.
>
> (Smyth et al., 2010: 121)

A current conviction can be defined as the sense of who the other party or parties are, that is, the essence of who they are as beings or organizational entities as well as an assessment of their reputation and performance to date. This initial assessment is typically intuitive with some cognition component and provides the basis for the current conviction. Future contact provides further evidence of both the individual parties and the organisation. Iterative assessments will include greater cognitively assessed evidence, increasing confidence and allowing trust to move to a higher level.

Frameworks

Numerous frameworks of the examination of trust have been developed. Four norms were proposed for developing trust in relational contracting, namely, solidarity, mutual gains (win-win), flexibility and conflict solution (Macneil, 1980), although the link between the economics, contracts and management is partial. Trust is seen as part of the contract and governance under relational contracting. Three forms of B2B governance have been identified (Macneil, 1980; Williamson, 1985, 1993): (i) classical contract law, governance being primarily based upon authority or power; (ii) neo-classical contract law, governance being primarily based upon price and associated incentives; (iii) relational contracting, governance being primarily based upon norms of trust in the cognitive and thus calculative sense. These forms have been applied to project environments (e.g. Olsen et al., 2005; Müller, 2011; **Chapter 2**).

Too much governance is claimed to reduce trust, whereby unhealthy levels of accountability send the contrary message (e.g. Kadefors et al., 2001; Turner and Müller, 2004; Smyth, 2008a; Müller, 2011; cf. O'Neill, 2002). Conversely, too little trust raises non-recoverable transaction costs through legalism and cost escalation derived from adverse behaviour (e.g. Gustafsson et al., 2010). It can also induce fear. A more plural approach to governance is increasingly recognized (Müller, 2011). Trust is claimed to lower transaction costs (e.g. Barney and Hansen, 1994) and induce collaborative practices in projects (e.g. Anvuur and Kumaraswamy, 2008).

Thus, contracts have a greater social dimension (Macneil, 1980, 2000) and are located in a broader social setting of causality, comprising social relations that are based on issues beyond utility (Granovetter, 1985) and self-interest (e.g. Ghoshal and Rocha, 2006). Actions cannot be boiled down to transactional self-interest no matter how large a dose of causal reductionism is applied. As an internal critique of mechanistic transaction cost analysis (TCA), Lyons and Mehta (1997) developed a social orientation that extends beyond self-interested trust and offers scope beyond learning derived from serial transactions to achieve enhanced win-win outcomes. A social orientation has been in management ascendancy in addressing governance (e.g. Macneil, 1980, 2000), corporate and social responsibility (e.g. Solomon and Solomon, 2004), social capital (e.g. Nahapiet and Ghoshal, 1998), services and the co-creation of value (Prahalad and Ramaswamy, 2004; Vargo and Lusch, 2004).

This has a relationship to profit. Self-interested trust on the supply side is largely orientated towards meeting needs or in project terms satisfying the minimum requirements set out in the documentation. The expectation is for an average rate of return for the project sector. A social orientation in general and socially inter-ested trust in particular looks towards meeting desires above and beyond meeting minimum requirements, that is, adding value. The expectation is for an above average rate of return or reputation leading to increased market share. This brings together the belief as to what is possible for client and project business respectively with the necessary vulnerability on both sides to commit to a social orientation to improve performance and hence the benefits delivered and growth achieved.

The act of setting out on the path of meeting requirements is the tendency to account for action in terms of cost and contract to manage the risk and deliver to requirements. When issues arise, the provider manages cost and contract in ways that can lead to delays, increases in transaction costs and adversarial relations, whereby the project business becomes a potential or actual liability to the client. The act of setting out on a more socially orientated path is the tendency to be responsive and provide a service with added value, whereby the project business becomes an asset to the client. Travelling on the latter path, social capital is built up at the project business–client interface and in the market through reputation and brand, which is underpinned by trust (Smyth et al., 2010).

Trust was a highly ranked perceived need among main construction contactors prior to the main development of collaborative approaches of relational contracting according to a specialist management consultant survey of the UK industry (Leading Edge, 1994). Trust is important because it is sought among managers and its absence leads to negative outcomes (e.g. Bennis, 1999; Dirks and Skarlicki, 2004). Relational contracts between employer and employee are supposedly governed by trust, yet research does not always bear this out. Hierarchy and control are conceptually inherent to leadership and management, while recognizing trends over successive decades to decentralize power and responsibility for operational management within many sectors and locations of business conduct. Research has shown that around 22 per cent (126 responses) of facilities management staff distrust their leaders and perceive they have suffered honour violations (Keyton and Smith, 2009; cf. Edelman, 2013). These data are based upon perceptions derived from intuitive assessments and thus carry subjectivity, and it is on this basis that relationships are formed and largely evolve, especially in the formative stages – a form of interpretative sense making (Weick, 1995).

Berneth and Walker (2009) found that trust in the firm did not depend upon the propensity of managers to trust, but it depended upon the employees. There are several important implications, and there are tensions between them:

- Managers can rely upon authority (power) and thus lines of management even where this leads to violations of trust and honour.
- Managers have responsibility to model trusting behaviour because the propensity of employees to trust them and other colleagues in the organizational context is influenced by the way they are treated by their senior management and line managers. It is the managers who create the conditions for trust.
- The importance of influencing employee propensity and encouraging trusting relationship is dependent upon the extent to which trust is managed as a competency and as part of relationship management.

Doney and Canon (1997) proposed *capability*, *prediction* and *intentionality* as their frame of constructs, which is reasonably pertinent to markets, organizations and projects, yet errs too much on the cognitive-cum-calculative. Rousseau et al. (1998) proposed a framework of *calculus*-based trust (cognition), *relational* and *institution*-based trust (organizational), the third element combining aspects of the first two to form a critical mass. It is linked to psychological contracts. There is a strong cognitive element and the less tangible aspects are very focused upon the interpersonal and personal-organizational dimension via relational contracts. The inter-organizational is inadequately covered. The definition of trust by Mayer et al. (1995) has been quoted, and they developed a framework of trustworthiness, based upon *ability*, *integrity* and *benevolence*. This framework is focused upon interpersonal trust informed by the characteristics of individuals and their predisposition or propensity to trust.

This is restricting for management of the organization and context, and it assumes causal antecedents. In a project context, Wood et al. (2002) in an early project-related study found six dimensions in contracting, namely *honesty and openness in communications, promise-keeping, fairness/reasonableness, mutuality/reciprocity, values/ethics* and *reputation*. This has a stronger organizational and inter-organizational focus, albeit being set in the relational contracting context of partnering.

A framework that provides a sharp focus for proactive management and the potential to develop into an organizational capability (cf. Davies and Brady, 2000) aligns with the aims and objectives of relationship management. Butler and Cantrell (1984) proposed a five element framework of *integrity, competence, consistency, loyalty* and *openness,* which was later developed into the *conditions of trust* (Butler, 1991), which have been researched as both antecedents and contextual (Smyth, 2008a). Projects are contextual and this is developed further as part of a broader framework later. A broader framework is apt for the attributes and dynamics of markets, organizations and projects. Thus, a more inclusive framework is needed for the organizational context and the dynamics of relationships in a project setting. However, projects are temporal, indeed inherently temporary. This imposes particular demands that need to be accounted for first.

The issue is that trust can take a while to build, but distrust rapidly spreads (Elangovan and Shapiro, 1998; Jones and George, 1998; Kramer, 2009). Attention has been given to accelerating the time taken to build trust, *swift trust*. The extensive use of outsourcing and temporary sets of relationships in business led to challenging the assumption that trust takes time to build (Meyerson et al., 1996). TMOs need to build collaboration quickly. It has been argued that there has been an over-reliance upon relational contracting, for example through partnering, and governance. TMOs have relied in part on prior organizational and inter-organizational trust, reputation and strength of systems and procedures. Yet, this assumes strong systems and support from the 'corporate centre' and a coherent programme management in the respective organizations, which are frequently weak in regard to projects (e.g. Roberts et al., 2012). Tuomela and Tuomela (2005) focus upon the norms necessary to build trust and cooperation, namely (i) positional norms for personal action and behaviour around role, function and tasks; (ii) group norms to set standards and undertake tasks; (iii) situational norms to link individuals and teams through developing an ethos and principles for action; (iv) and an attitudinal norms that permit room for manoeuvre to take initiative and problem solving yet non-threatening to the other norms in content or by prior sanction.

Whether norms are put in place depends upon the conceptual positions as to whether trust is seen as foundational to forming and developing relationships and whether management has the will to act to induce and manage trust (e.g. Smyth et al., 2010). Norms take time to instil, relationship management providing the support to build trust rapidly. *Commitment* is a recurrent feature of relationship building and management (see **Chapters 2, 3** and **4**). This starts with management strategy, a systematic approach and tactical support. Trust formation first occurs at the inter-personal level before it can be reflected at an organizational level, remembering that customers and clients see the other party in interaction and interpersonal relationships as representative of the organization whom they represent (Porath et al., 2011; cf. Zaheer et al., 1998). Keh and Xie (2009: 739) found B2B relationships to be more sustainable, where customers having *deep trust in their providers tend to continue the relationship*. There is now widespread agreement that trust is considered an important component of effective and valuable relationships, especially in project environments (Kadefors, 2004; Lau and Rowlinson, 2009; Smyth et al., 2010; Gil et al., 2011).

One broad framework that has been employed on a series of studies and having seven components is set out in Table 5.2. The elements are the characteristics and components of trust, the obligations and conditions of trust, the levels and operational basis and finally the market for trust. One of the methodological problems of researching trust is that it is an intangible concept and intuitively assessed and therefore any self-reporting can only assess the cognitive aspect, and even so may lean more to confidence and the more calculative definitions at the expense of the intuitive. Thus questions are largely couched in ways that avoid directly addressing trust as the prime clause – Table 5.3 sets out the issues surveyed in the two most researched elements of the framework, namely the characteristics of trust and the conditions of trust.

TABLE 5.2 A project framework of trust

Trust element	Description and comments
Characteristics of trust	Utilizing the work of Lyons and Mehta (1997), who distinguish between uncertainties and the risk of opportunism by separating out confidence in the abilities of the other party and trust in their behaviour. The former does not need much trust or only 'calculative trust' (confidence) because there is a reasonable probability of the outcome. Behaviour is relational and the degree of confidence may be low especially without inter-organizational trust through strong systems and procedures, including relationship management. Lyons and Mehta point out as economists that the discipline recognizes instrumental behaviour, largely overlooking value-based, experiential or affect-based and traditional or habit-based behaviour. They incorporate a sociological dimension and form *socially orientated trust* in addition to *self-interested trust*. A social orientation need not be selfish, using self-interested trust as a springboard to enhance mutuality such as the classic win–win outcome. Socially orientated trust goes further, looking to the interests of the other party, including reciprocity, which in a business setting must provide the means to make a profit (e.g. Edkins and Smyth, 2006; Smyth, 2008). It has the distinct advantage, whereby financial control and profit is not the end, but satisfying clients and other internal and external stakeholders (excluding owners/shareholders) is the end point. Management conducted with business acumen is the means and a successful outcome for the supplier is profit and growth.

Components of trust	Comprises of a family of related concepts (Edkins and Smyth, 2006) and picks up the distinction between trust and confidence. Confidence comes from consistently meeting expectations, which in the language of trust is divided into hope and faith. Faith is more closely related to the difficulty of adding value and being innovative covering those things that are believed possible but have not been seen in this project context previously, whereas hope comprises less ambitious expectations of things known to be possible but not guaranteed (Smyth, 2008). As expectations are met, trust is mediated by greater probability and builds confidence, allowing trust to move to a higher level.
Social obligations of trust	Forms part of normative commitment (Meyer and Allen, 1991). Relational contracting implies some social obligations that are met through greater commitment. At a more proactive level, project business norms and socio-psychological contracts help form obligations as to how people treat each other, namely dignity based upon norms of equality and respect earned based upon norms of equity (Tuomela and Tuomela, 2005; Smyth, 2008). This covers relationships within organizations and interpersonal ones in dyads. For example, respect was found to be present between the client and excellent performing contractors (Butcher and Sheehan, 2010). Further 10 employee performance measures have been established in the UK construction industry to monitor respect for people (Glenigan Constructing Insight et al., 2011).
Conditions of trust	The conditions are contextual and contingent, which are derived from Butler (1991) and applied to projects as conditions of input intent – integrity, receptivity, loyalty, discretion and openness – and output abilities – consistency, promise fulfilment, fairness, competence and availability (Smyth and Thompson, 2005). As conditions, they provide fertile ground in which trust can develop and thus provide dimensions which management can nurture, for example to inform behaviour through programmes and codes of conduct.
Levels of trust	Considers differences within the organizational hierarchy (Janowicz-Panjaitan and Noorderhaven, 2009). For example, it has been found that senior and junior levels of management experience higher trust formation with others, but middle management have much lower levels (Smyth and Pilcher, 2008), probably because they are most commonly stretched, feel unsupported because of weak systems and the default to individual responsibility is prevalent in project organizations (cf. Roberts et al., 2012; Smyth, 2013a).

(Continued)

TABLE 5.2 (Continued)

Trust element	Description and comments
Operational trust	Focuses upon how trust influences product and service value. Trust is conceived and embedded as an organizational and project competency (cf. Davies and Brady, 2000; Brady and Davies, 2004). It forms part of social capital and hence value formation (Pryke and Smyth, 2006).
Trust in the marketplace	Sako (1992) has focused upon trust in terms of whether norms of obligations are used to draw organizations together and form relational bonds or whether organizations are kept at arm's length. Another marketplace focus has been the extent of dependency set out by Campbell (1995) – independent, interdependent and dependent depending upon permutations of dyadic competitive, command and cooperative approaches.

TABLE 5.3 Questions for research on the characteristics and conditions of trust

Trust element	Questions	Underlying trust concept	Descriptors for evaluation: • Selecting the closest descriptor for characteristics • Ranking for conditions
Characteristics of trust	Which of the following most accurately describes your assessment of the basis of those representing ABC Organization relationship with you?	Distrust	*Opportunism* – decisions and actions based upon their self-interest that in some cases may be detrimental to overall effective and efficient operations.
		Message of distrust	*Accountability* – decisions and actions that put their concerns about line management or stakeholder interests above overall effective and efficient operations.
		Neutrality	*Indifference* – decisions and actions do not appear to be in the best interests of operations nor in favour of any or both parties; they offer the path of least resistance.
		Self-interested trust	*Win-win* – willingness to be vulnerable towards you, trusting that your decisions and actions will be positive to overall effective and efficient operations, yielding short-term mutual advantage.

		Socially orientated trust	*Sacrificial* – willingness to 'go the extra mile' to help and support you, trusting that your decisions and actions will be positive to the overall effective and efficient operations, yielding long-term mutual advantage.
Conditions of trust	To what extent are the following conditions present in your relationship with the representatives of ABC Organization?	Intention dimension – inputs	Integrity, receptivity, loyalty, discretion and openness.
		Ability dimension – outputs	Consistency, promise-fulfillment, fairness, competence and availability.

Five separate studies have been undertaken using this framework. The context for each study has been different and the specific relationship details do not permit precise comparison, but an aggregation is presented for over 500 relationship perceptions, reported over an eight-year period, providing a good indication for the characteristics of trust (Table 5.2). The following additional points are made:

- Overall trust relationships are weak for construction organizations and projects, although different patterns may not be replicated for other project sectors.
- Underlying the figures presented (Table 5.4), self-interested trust are twice those of socially orientated trust, demonstrating the scope for an increased social orientation where beneficial in practice. Clients are poor at developing a social orientation, frequently relying upon market power and supplier dependency when addressing thorny issues.
- Internal relationships are marginally stronger than dyadic, offering support for the claim that inter-organizational relationships cannot be stronger than those in the respective organizations (Smyth, 2008a), the proposition originally derived from studies about loyalty (Reichheld, 1996).
- Relationships are two-way, but the project suppliers tend to perceive each relationship to be stronger than clients in the dyadic relationships.
- Relational contracts and partnerships, such as PPP-type (where PPP stands for public private partnership) projects do not have a substantive positive effect upon trust generation (Teicher et al., 2006). The quantity and cost management consultants are poor at trust development and management.
- The highest rated relationships are internal to the client and the client-professional consultant relationship is the strongest dyadic relationship.

TABLE 5.4 The summative characteristics of trust across five research projects

Relationship type		Strength (%)	Rank
Internal to the organization	Contractor	23.0	3
	Contractor and SPV	12.5	=5
	clients	24.5	1
Dyadic	Professions and client	23.7	2
	Contractor and public client	12.5	=5
	Contractor and public client	22.5	4

Sources: Developed from data reported in Smyth (2005); Edkins and Smyth (2006); Smyth and Pilcher (2008); Ayres and Smyth (2010); Schofield and Smyth (2012).

TABLE 5.5 The summative conditions of trust across five research projects

Relationship type		Intention dimension (rank)					Ability dimension (rank)				
		Integrity	*Receptivity*	*Loyalty*	*Discretion*	*Openness*	*Consistency*	*Promise-fulfillment*	*Fairness*	*Competence*	*Availability*
Internal	Contractor	=2	5	1	=2	4	2	5	3	1	4
	client	2	3	5	1	4	1	4	3	2	5
Dyadic	Professions and client	2	3	5	4	1	4	3	5	1	2
	Average rank	1	4=	4=	2	3	2	5	3=	1	3=

Sources: Developed from data reported in Smyth (2005); Edkins and Smyth (2006); Smyth and Pilcher (2008); Ayres and Smyth (2010); Schofield and Smyth (2012).

The same approach was adopted for the conditions of trust, which incorporates the summative results for four of the research studies (Table 5.5). The following additional points are made:

- Overall the conditions of trust are reasonable, given that these were not proactively managed with the exception of competence.
- In terms of the inputs of intent, contractor receptivity is weakest explaining the low loyalty to contractors from clients and the professions, but high loyalty displayed to them was perhaps due to dependencies.
- Competence is high in terms of ability, necessary to meet minimum requirements.

- Promise-fulfillment is weakest, especially among contractors, which suggests high levels of self-interest, opportunism and a failure to deliver satisfaction to staff, clients and other stakeholders. It is linked to the problems of poor receptivity in terms of intent, but shows an anomalous position with integrity, which is high. It is suggested that integrity operates at the level of interpersonal relationships and individuals taking responsibility, while promise-fulfillment is an organizational problem, and therefore resides with management.

The characteristics and conditions of trust are the two elements of the framework most consistently investigated in project research and could be said to be the most pertinent to relationship management as they are the easiest to transfer and translate into management principles to guide behaviour through a programme and code or set of procedures. Each sub-element can become a guiding principle; for example for a social orientation and promise-fulfillment, these can be operationalized as norms of performance evaluation (e.g. Gustafsson et al., 2010) and reflective practice (Schön, 1983). It is sometimes easier to identify the consequences of the absence of trust, that is, distrust. Therefore, reflective practices such as, 'is this action being led by a social orientation and what might the consequences of self-interest be?' and 'is this decision compromising our ability to fulfill a promise of non-contractual commitment to add value?' contribute to improvement and avoid blame. These types of questions routinely applied can provide useful guidance and coupled with one or two conditions of trust can form the basis for a behavioural code of conduct concerning trust management.

It is clear from the research evidence that there is minimal evidence of systematic relationship management for managing trust specifically. The prevalence of relational contracting, such as partnering and supply chain management, which emphasizes the role of trust may indirectly encourage trust development but does not proactively develop it through informal or formal routines. Too much is expected and too much power is ascribed to economic forces, legal contracts and overarching forms of governance. The research into trust and presented by others points towards proactive intervention and, as argued, achieving the difficult balance between control and room for manoeuvre can actually provide guidelines in which more initiative, innovation, creativity and problem solving occurs. It is not an easy management task, but then most of those are already being carried out.

In addition to evidence on the characteristics and conditions of trust, an additional word on the components of trust provides a useful link to a business model and earning logic. The components of trust focuses upon expectations (hope and faith) about achieving goals. Goals provide a key part of a business strategy as can trust. While issues of procurement have been elevated from departmental or functional processes to the boardroom, such as partnering, supply chain management and lean production, likewise tactical and behavioural issues, such as trust and confidence, can be elevated to strategic consideration.

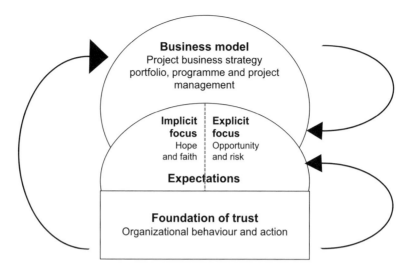

FIGURE 5.2 Trust and the business relationship

Source: Adapted from Gustafsson et al., 2010.

Implementation and application

Trust is foundational to relationship formation and development and is closely related to the expectations of business models, which act back to moderate expectations and organizational behaviour (Figure 5.2).

Gustafsson et al. (2010) found that in an analysis of 120 project deliveries, the more often the project manager evaluated company performance from the customer perspective (and verified it), the more satisfied the customer was. Projects with weak or negative margins for the project business tended to have lower customer satisfaction. Customers who were satisfied and paid high margins describe the supplier in the following positive terms: solutions fitted the requirements, there was easy communication, good cooperation, and good follow-up on issues post-completion. Whereas customers who were not satisfied described the supplier contrarily and believed the supplier had incompetency among its staff. These findings indirectly showed that trust impacted profitability and customer satisfaction. Further research findings are set out in Fact Boxes 5.1 and 5.2.

A common answer to a lack of satisfaction is often the demand to put in place a system of greater accountability about task and cost with more gateways to pass through, whereas increased accountability beyond reasonable or healthy levels has the opposite effect of telling others they are not trusted, encouraging (i) the taking of unprofessional decisions to meet the criteria of evaluation rather than satisfy the purpose for which the project is wanted, that is deliver benefits; (ii) increased transaction and other administrative costs without adding value; (iii) greater bureaucracy, legalism and adversarial behaviour. Accountability increases social distance. As Blois explained . . . *trust evolves through the process of a growth of knowledge and understanding of the people with whom we interact plus the actual experience of working with them* (1999: 206).

FACT BOX 5.1 TRUST OFFSHORE

Offshore engineering project teams are dispersed. Corporate support and guidance for highly complex projects are not provided face-to-face, amplifying the operational vulnerabilities and need for trust. The broader coalition including the decision-making unit (DMU) is virtual. Building trust and repair of any violations is difficult, further complicated by the presence of multi-cultural team membership.

So it was found in four global engineering teams examined on offshore sites in North and South America, Europe and the Indian sub-continent. It was found that such engineering teams have high trust needs, arising from physical dislocation and cultural diversity. The onshore and offshore teams within the DMUs were each co-located yet divided into 'in-group' and 'out-group' components, creating an asymmetry of trust amongst the subgroups. It was also found that centralized communication and technology acted to mediate common ground, yet, trust violations proved difficult to repair in these social spaces, although humour and self-reflection helped.

A separate research investigation of offshore projects in IT found that expertize did not have any decisive effect upon project success, yet levels of trust did matter, especially in regard to knowledge transfer, liaison and quality of communication. Communication and technology are again mediators, but these are precursors to knowledge transfer and close liaison, trust informing the understanding and social contract between the parties.

Sources: Adapted from Jarvenpaa and Leidner (1999); Westner and Strahringer (2010); Jarvenpaa and Keating (2012).

FACT BOX 5.2 THE VALUE OF DYADIC TRUST IN INDUSTRIAL NETWORKS

CROL© survey data from the Project-Based Institute (PBI) and interview data from 333 interviews from clients and suppliers involved in large international projects were analyzed, demonstrating that project businesses who invest in nurturing relationships or have a culture and norms that foster trusting behaviour have higher rates of profit than those that do not. Four different types of response were identified as to how customers saw their suppliers: (i) the supplier is attuned and can be turned to in order to meet business needs; (ii) the supplier is a reliable provider and installer of project components and packages; (iii) the supplier is one of many component suppliers; and (iv) the supplier will resolve emergent problems. These segments also proved instructive concerning procurement decisions. The biggest customer group was segment 'iii', representing 47 per cent of the customers, yet only represented 7 per cent of sales. Segment 'ii' represented 26 per cent of customers, yet represented 53 per cent of sales. Therefore, segment 'ii' has the most repeat business and the largest projects.

(Continued)

FACT BOX 5.2 (Continued)

The customers were all more or less equally satisfied. The difference was one of expectations related to trust. The customers in segments 'i' and 'iv' trusted the selected suppliers and the expectation of them were reasonably high, especially for quality and after sales service. The suppliers were considered in terms of giving useful advice on how to improve the performance of the installation; having the expertise to say which parts and components to use, which is a reason for buying sub-supplier parts from the supplier; having the latest and best knowledge regarding for example engines and power production; taking into consideration the customer's business; and paying attention to the general state of the installation, which is a reason to buy maintenance services from the supplier.

These customers expected high commitment and service levels and were reliant upon the supplier as part of their operational business model. Poor delivery delayed start up and poor service disrupted production and thus lost the business revenue. These suppliers who were trusted were considered an asset to the customer, whereas those that were not trusted due to reliability issues, legalism and poor service were considered a liability to the customers.

Customers in the other segments took contrary views and were less dependent and more transactional, yet their expectations were much lower and their expectations were that suppliers met minimum requirements rather than sought added value.

The suppliers who were most successful at meeting these expectations pursued various combinations of the following relationship management principles: (a) made commitments to nurture the relationships; (b) were responsive to emergent problems rather than resorting to cost and contract issues at the first consideration; (c) employed a routine of self-evaluation of team performance and sought ways for improvement, especially in the face of difficulties, rather than attribute blame; (d) generally employed principles of reflective practice.

Where self-evaluation was conducted, both margin and repeat business were higher.

Source: Adapted from Smyth et al. (2010).

If any accountability system is needed, it is a relationship management one, which has a greater emphasis upon developing rather than monitoring relationships and behaviour. Context was empirically found to change trust (Pinto et al., 2009), thus any system must give not only room for manoeuvre but flexibility for context, and for tailoring services to customer or client need.

Identification is based upon trust (Kramer and Wei, 1999). It builds from a discrete work setting and is stimulated by episodes, and events provide a catalyst around which subsequent confirmatory experience is necessary. A deeper sense of belonging and identification can develop long-term, often signified when people talk about the organization in terms of 'we' (Rousseau, 1998). Identification enables norms to be mobilized quickly, behaviours to be aligned, and it takes systems for granted. While it can build in rigidities this way, it is dynamic and it indeed informs incremental evolution and refinement of norms, behaviour and systematic routines. It enables a deep sense of trust and confidence in another party, whether individual or organizational, but it takes longer to engender than the formation and development of relationships. It is problematic for project teams unless high levels of consistency and continuity are in place.

The front-end is the place to start building trust. A systematic approach and procedures from the programme level articulate the link between the 'corporate centre' and its business model strategies, investment portfolio and earning logic for developing systems, organizational and project capabilities. The necessary management actions are to put in place to accommodate customer needs and fulfill promises. Such routines facilitate trust, and trust facilitates these and other routines for delivery (cf. Bradach and Eccles, 1989), especially at the tactical and operational level of implementation (Rousseau et al., 1998; Zaheer et al., 1998).

The findings of Lui et al. (2006) are particularly instructive during project execution. They found in the Hong Kong construction sector trust leads to improved credibility and the willingness to commit to investing in specific relational assets, that is investment in social capital. Contrary to previous research, they also found that where these investments had been made, there was a greater application of coercion particularly at the organizational level. These findings are in accord with the application of relationship management principles, or comprehensive relationship management systems, and with nested relationship-based programmes such as a behavioural code of conduct. These principles, systems and procedures guide specific behaviour and require compliance to the principles or system. Therefore they embody greater coercion or control by management. For example, Smith et al. (2009) showed that intentional misreporting is less prevalent where project managers are expected to strictly follow the rules.

These findings resonate with those of Zaheer et al. (1998), who found the inter-organizational level drives the exchange while reducing costs of negotiation and lowering conflict, while interpersonal trust facilitates relationship development, boundary spanning and aiding institutionalization, that is, structuring and embedding routines. Therefore, relational contracting helps frame an exchange, but it is interpersonal behaviour that provides the means on the ground. Thus, there is a need for an organizational link between the project business function and the project operations to facilitate trust from the front-end, which a relationship management system achieves to link inter-organizational behaviour with interpersonal behaviour. Zaheer et al. (1998) also found that inter-organizational level can work well even where interpersonal trust is low. The argument here is that the appropriate alliance can be put in place at the exchange level with senior management and procurement with the appropriate relational contract and governance, but it will not automatically affect operations, especially in projects where execution and delivery are (i) socially and sometimes physically dislocated from the 'corporate centre', (ii) there are weak systems between the project business and project team, (iii) projects teams are often TMOs and thus are influenced by several organizational norms and routines. Management therefore needs to focus on the means for interpersonal trust building.

Recent research has examined the link between trust and emotional intelligence on infrastructure projects between client and contractors. Overall, trust helped to establish relationships coupled with self-awareness in emotional intelligence, yet indicators of social awareness and management were weak, suggesting that project team collaboration and performance desired by the client was not being effectively developed through emotional intelligence. Self-management returned especially low scores, which also inhibits the development of interpersonal trust. This would appear to underscore the need for relationship, behavioural and trust management programmes from the project business through programme management (Fact Box 5.3).

FACT BOX 5.3 TRUST AND EMOTIONAL INTELLIGENCE ON A MAJOR INFRASTRUCTURE UPGRADE PROJECT

Delivering value for money on projects in the UK rail industry and the focus upon collaborative working in the industry advocated in the McNulty Report (2011) provided the research context. The research examined the management of a large multi-billion pound upgrade project. The relationships were dyadic between the client and main contractors responsible for delivery.

A total of 18 questions were asked, derived from the Goleman and Boyatzis model (Boyatzis et al., 2000; Goleman et al., 2002). The resultant scores are (i) self-awareness, 0.93; (ii) self-management, 0.68; (iii) social awareness, 0.73; (iv) social skills/relationship management, 0.74. The highest score is for self-awareness, although awareness can be used for good or bad, that is, to build a social orientation or pursue opportunism with guile at either extreme. Trust was interrogated against five elements of the trust framework (Smyth, 2008a), namely characteristics, components, social obligations, conditions of trust and trust in the marketplace. The percentage trust scores are related to the emotional intelligence scores in the table below.

Averages	Contractor ratings of the client	Relationship to emotional intelligence scores	Client ratings of the contractor	Relationship to emotional intelligence scores
Characteristics of trust	27	0.56	33	0.68
Components of trust	90	1.86	68	1.40
Social obligations of trust	80	1.65	74	1.52
Conditions of trust	87	1.78	77	1.58
Trust in the marketplace	50	1.03	50	1.03

Examining the interplay between trust and EI shows some interesting findings:

- The client is stronger at establishing a trusting relationship, but weaker maintaining and developing the relationship in terms of harnessing the use of emotional intelligence – temporal contracts mean contractors have to quickly make an impact, whilst the client arguably can more easily take a long-term view about building relationships;
- The contractor has a greater social orientation than the client;
- Self-awareness is not being used to improve self-management;
- Self-awareness is not being translated into social awareness and social management.

Source: Adapted from Boot-Handford and Smyth (2013).

The oil and gas industry employing project managing contractors in the systems integrator role have repeatedly failed to manage cost, a 40 per cent overrun being the average, which appears to have a root cause in management rather than budget and price issues alone, which Merrow (2011) apportions to the contractors neither trusting the owners nor other contractors with which they are working, whereas *successful megaprojects require an extraordinary degree of trust, cooperation, and communication between the business sponsoring the project and the technical functions developing and executing the project* (Merrow, 2011: 82).

Conclusion

At one level, effective relationship management mitigates the need for trust as it embeds norms and routines. However, drilling down through the system to behavioural programmes and codes to the tactical level of behaviour, a comprehensive system incorporates this level and is necessary to complete a comprehensive approach to collaborative working and integrated operations. The tactical level of trust operation is where norms are established providing the raw material for effective relational contracting, developing emotional intelligence, building other types of routine bottom-up that are embedded into a system of relationships and aid incremental development. At another level, trust is a key part of relationship management. Trust is no panacea as there are no guarantees and it can be misplaced. It carries relational risk, but where present, the gains can offset instances of misplaced trust and distrust.

Trust is valuable social capital to be nurtured and actively managed. The chapter has identified conceptual and practical issues between the organizational and the interpersonal levels in two ways. First is the issue between the project business and the project and the second is the gap between organizational trust and interpersonal trust. This is where two things come together to address the issues. Although the organizational and interpersonal are insufficiently 'joined up' in many project businesses, the supplier or the customer perceives the representatives and the organization to be largely one and the same, so the image of service and extent of integrated service is considerably influenced by the extent to which trust is facilitated and managed.

Trust is therefore managed directly or indirectly enabled by a systematic relationship approach to develop it, and a trust framework can alight upon the elements and convert these into guiding principles to form norms or more specifically frame action and behaviour. The framework reported upon most in this chapter has a number of elements that can be unpacked to form a code or reflective and evaluative behavioural practice. The characteristics of trust and the conditions of trust offer a good point of entry at this tactical level. Therefore the chapter has examined the theorization of trust and its applicability in practice. It has proceeded by developing a link between trust and relationship management, and how trust can be developed as part of a set of management capabilities for effective operation on projects and in relation to market performance. Managing trust is far from straight forward – trust remains intangible and evidence is largely sensed and observed through behaviour. Consistent vigilance is needed in managing trust. Consistency is twofold, both in terms of regularity of evaluation of its management and applying one framework or model to avoiding getting into conceptually contested areas of consideration in practice.

Trust is foundational to effective relationships, whether they are interpersonal and inter-organizational. Therefore trust makes a significant contribution to the effective performance of management, teams and hence operations. For the contribution to be at a team level, the project business needs to manage trust development by creating the supportive conditions and routines that are spread across the project business as part of programme management and embedded in the project organization. While there can and needs to be some reliance on trust building and swift trust, greater reliance can be placed on the routines established at programme level to inform all projects. The purpose is to provide routines to guide relationship development to improve the service experience, improve client and staff satisfaction, thus to improve performance and profitability. The chapter has therefore contributed to considering a number of issues covering theory and practice. Those pertinent to this chapter are summarized below.

SI no. 1: *Organizational Behaviour* has a normative management aim of moving closer towards *integrated management*. Trust has been a prescriptive and a conceptually normative part of the discourse on projects and project management for over 20 years, but much of it has been seen through the theoretical lens of relational contracting, specifically partnering, supply chain management and other alliances. Trust development within the organizations is dynamic, proactivity below the levels of relational contracting and governance being necessary prior to it being effective in the marketplace – a conceptual issue considered here and linked to the themes of foregoing chapters on strategy, systems and behaviour.

SI no. 2: *Relationship Management Theory* includes trust, and a bottom-up contribution from the tactical relationship level is made through proactive management of trust, applying norms and behavioural measures, an applied linkage to emotional intelligence also being possible.

SI no. 3: *Socio-psychological Issues* both populate and articulate relationships, and trust is foundational to relationship formation and development. It thus contributes towards the effective performance by moderating defensive predispositions and enhancing positive ones at the interpersonal level, forming social and psychological contracts between the interpersonal and organizational levels, and helping to form norms. These are particularly important within project management with the temporary and multi-organizational dimension of project teams.

SI no. 4: *Conceptual and Applied Hierarchical Integration* pertains to relationship management and programme management. Habits, group norms and actions inform trust and are part of trust in support of other performance issues. Senior management model and monitor to affect action down the hierarchy.

SI no. 5: *Conceptual and Applied Horizontal Integration* is provided by the pivotal role of management of projects (MoP), particularly at the front-end to connect programme management to execution at a tactical level for trust formation in preparation for and during execution.

SI no. 8: *Relational Contracting* places trust in a central role, particularly through contracts and governance measures, but the claims made for trust to be invoked by these measures are exaggerated and the induction of collaborative working is unreliable without proactive management of relationships and trust within respective organizations.

The main *recommendations* for future research are:

A. Further examination of the interpersonal and inter-organizational interface for trust development, especially in project businesses.
B. Further research as to the extent to which the behaviour of individuals are representative of organizations compared to the perceptions of clients, especially introducing small group and team dimensions into the analysis, and whether DMU members are more significant than other representatives. Contract staff compared to employees offer a further dimension.
C. Investigation as to how exerted market and organizational power affects particular conceptual components in the framework and their robustness as norms and code elements.

The transition from the presence of trusting relations to its proactive management has yet to be fully articulated. Flowing from this comes the principle *recommendations* for practice:

1. Management to elevate trust to a strategic focus in formal routines of a relationship management system.
2. Monitor trust levels applying a framework. Collect and collate performance data to compare teams with high and low levels and thus assess the financial

benefits in cost and profit terms, and within the evaluation of social capital worth in the organization.

3. Introduce norms and behavioural elements on an annual incremental basis to facilitate trust development.

Norms are pivotal for articulating trust and embedding measures to induce trust. Trust is informed by norms, trust embodies norms interrelated through the choice of theoretical lens and framework and helps form other norms for effective collaboration and performance both internally and in the marketplace. Norms therefore deserve further attention in the consideration of relationship management, and this is the focus for the next chapter that considers organizational culture.

6

ORGANIZATIONAL CULTURE

Introduction

Organizational culture is another thorny concept. In management, it is seen as an enabler or a constraint. If the formal systems, their coordinating mechanisms and formal routines, are aligned with the shared values, norms and informal routines of the organization, then effective operations follow. If the formal systems are in conflict with the rest of the culture and resultant informal routines, then constraints and barriers to effective working tend to result. In practice, managers say that something is 'part of the culture' as if there is nothing to be done about it or managers and leaders make claims about changing the culture as if it is in their total control. There is some truth in both these positions, but they are too simplistic. There is an intangible side to culture that is influential and constantly renegotiated. There is also a tangible side of artifacts including the formal systems (Schein, 1990, 1996).

Relationship management, whatever the combination of formal and informal routines in context, is part of the culture both as a reflection of and a contributor towards it. Non-conforming and unaligned action and behaviour is a product of human agency. There are patterns of dissonance and dislocation of action and behaviour from the prescribed organizational strategy and tactics, systems and procedures; there are cultural factors inside the organization, and sometimes emanating from outside the organization. These are disruptive to effective performance. Culture can be influenced and controlled to a degree, especially through formal measures, for example application of the management of projects (MoP) provides a more strategic and considered approach to structuring the organizational culture by virtue of the formal activities at the front-end. Organizational culture has relative autonomy, yet depends upon management. Autonomy may be asserted in the face of a change management programme, actions subverting and renegotiating or simply ignoring the terms. Management can destroy a culture through restructuring, the loss proving greater than the gain. Organizational culture has a tendency to give rise to unexpected consequences to management measures where the measures have been insufficiently thought through or its unfolding is unforeseen or under-estimated. Organizational culture is therefore a factor and force to be reckoned with in research and management practice.

Against this background, the following issues will be explored in this chapter:

A. Organizational culture as a force in and for management in relation to relationship management and MoP in theory and practice.
B. Alignment of key constructs and principles associated with organizational culture up and down the hierarchy, across programmes and horizontally along project lifecycles.
C. Recognition of constraints and barriers posed by organizational culture for management coordination mechanisms across organizational and inter-organizational boundaries.

Therefore, the chapter considers issues to help to assess what organizational culture contributes to relationship management in project businesses. A main message is therefore about the significant contribution that a 'healthy' aligned organizational culture makes to the effective performance of managers and teams, and for facilitating the interface between the 'corporate centre' and the temporary organizational project teams. Contributions in teams require project businesses to

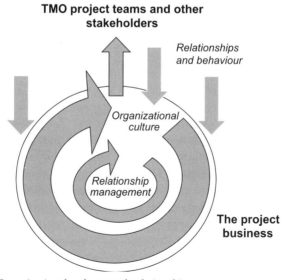

FIGURE 6.1 Organizational culture and relationship management

embed coordinating mechanisms and support measures in routines to guide team action and behaviour in order to ensure effective service consistency and continuity between projects. These routines are not simply designed and imposed top-down as they have typically emerged in partial form from past practices (Parmigiani and Howard-Grenville, 2011) and therefore are likely to be a reasonable fit to the whole organizational culture of the project business including their project teams. The linguistic roots of culture relate to cultivate, and therefore, one way of looking at organizational culture is to provide the conditions for organic and healthy growth. The location of organizational culture is indicated in Figure 6.1.

Organizational culture in theory and practice

Organization and culture

Culture is not as amorphous as sometimes assumed for *culture reaches from strategy and systematic processes to the norms and assumptions, including the intuitive and habitual* (Roberts et al., 2012: 77). As with theories and concepts reviewed in previous chapters, there are varied theories and models of organizational culture and therefore different definitions. Culture determines a specific *way of being*, which legitimizes social institutions as relationships and conventions between people. Hence, institutions are self-defined and self-reinforced. Culture is the social space of ideologies, discourses and practices and social organization in order to understand how established order and convention make their existence accountable (Tansey, 2004).

A general and 'common sense' statement is about *the way things are done around here*, a definition originally derived from Deal and Kennedy (1982). Culture is a pattern of beliefs and expectations that are shared among members, which generate norms that powerfully shape behaviour (Schwartz and Davies, 1981). Culture puts flesh on the skeletal structure of the firm (cf. Mintzberg, 1989). Schein defines culture in a group this way:

> . . . a pattern of shared basic assumptions that was learned by a group as it solved its problems of external adaptation and internal integration, that has worked well enough to be considered valid and, therefore, to be taught to new members as the correct way to perceive, think, and feel in relation to those problems.
>
> (1996: 17)

Others put different emphases, for example Cameron and Quinn (2006) are more interested in organizational culture as the source of competitive advantage and thus the role of leadership in relation to culture becomes of greater significance: *An organization's culture is reflected by what is valued, the dominant leadership styles, the language and symbols, the procedures and routines, and the definition of success that makes an organization unique* (Cameron and Quinn, 2006: 17).

Others look at organizational culture in relation to the wider societal culture at national or regional level or through some other unit of analysis (e.g. Hofstede and Hofstede, 2005). Organizational culture is fluid, sometimes iteratively evolving and sometimes dynamic at times of flux, but it always evolves in an open system of time and space (e.g. Douglas, 1999; Hofstede and Hofstede, 2005; cf. Hodgson and Cicmil, 2007; Henisz et al., 2012). Culture is about difference and similarity – the sameness or similarity of *shared* values and beliefs expressed in behaviour and action and the *distinctiveness* of the combination that helps lend an identity to the organization and the service delivered (Appiah, 2005; Fitzsimmons and Fitzsimmons, 2011).

Culture is guided and steered. Those in authority have most influence, but culture cannot be controlled (Parker and Bradley, 2000). Formal systems and procedures, the formal routines of an organization, help to invoke compliance, and function to effect when mutually aligned with systems and procedures.

Four models of organizational culture are reviewed. This is far from comprehensive, yet provides a sense of the range of conceptual views. The four selected are the following:

- The Hofstede model, comparing organizations across national cultures (e.g. Hofstede and Hofstede, 2005);
- The Schein model of organizational culture (Schein, 1990, 1996);
- The Cameron and Quinn model, called the 'competing values framework' (Cameron and Quinn, 2006);
- The Douglas model, a grid-group typology from what has been termed 'cultural theory' (Thompson et al., 1990; Douglas, 1994).

The Hofstede model assumes all societies and organizations face the same problems and it is only the solutions that differ. Universal dimensions are claimed to measure the different solutions and outcomes in terms of culture. The differences are considered at national level; therefore, the Hofstede model compares organizational and national cultures. Organizationally, it addresses the question why an organization with the same strategies and systems across the globe has different national characteristics in branch offices. The model aids the identification of boundaries and differences between different cultures. Culture is the learned and shared patterns of thinking, feeling and acting. It distinguishes one group from another. Practices can be observed from outside the organization, yet meanings are only known to those inside the organization (Hofstede and Hofstede, 2005). The dimensions of the model are power distance, uncertainty avoidance, individualism/collectivism, masculinity/femininity and time orientation (Table 6.1). The model is popular in project management research especially for comparative purposes, but the unit of comparison is largely at the international or regional level rather than the organizational level. This renders the model one step removed for assessing the contribution of relationship management.

TABLE 6.1 Measurement dimensions of the Hofstede model

Dimension	Summary description
Power distance	Concerns the relation to authority with a focus upon responsibility versus discipline. The focus is between being proactive and adopting initiatives or responding to guidance and control from others. Those that exert authority tend to use psychological distance or keeping people at 'arm's length'.
Uncertainty avoidance	Deals with uncertainty and ambiguity, including emotional and relational uncertainties. The focus is upon innovation versus precision. Uncertainty avoidance does not automatically imply risk aversion; the requirement is stability.
Individualism/ collectivism	Concerns the relationship between individuals and society in general, and employees and the employer in particular. The focus is upon management mobility versus employee commitment, between self-interest and precedence to relationships and goals.
Masculinity/ femininity	Considers the values (not gender), to some extent reflecting upon 'hard' and 'soft' issues. The focus is on a mass production mentality versus service. In construction this is closely reflected in the inwards focus of a task orientation versus a social orientation.
Time orientation	Concerns change over time. The focus is the long-term versus the short-term horizon and thus whether an organization is 'fire-fighting' or assessing root causes, making investments or squeezing out costs and profit.

The Schein model (Schein, 1990; 1996) has general application, drilling down to provide a clinical analysis of an organizational culture at three levels:

1. Artifacts – observable aspects of an organization, including behaviour, verbal and non-verbal communication, the use of space within an office, the written procedures, manuals, and the organizational structure.
2. Espoused values – stated beliefs and aims, the strategic and tactical goals as explicit elements of a culture. There may be some misalignment between espoused values and artifacts because of inconsistencies in articulating values through physical artifacts and implementable systems and procedures. In addition, not everything espoused by management reflects the core values; for example top management may state, *relationships are a top priority*, but fail to carry this through in practice.
3. Basic assumptions – the most representative of the pervading culture. These values are not written down nor stated as they are based upon assumptions that develop unconsciously, largely go unchallenged and are typically taken-for-granted in the context yet inform how people behave.

The purpose is not to classify different cultures but identify the character and attributes of the prevailing culture and organizational sub-cultures of misunderstanding and conflict.

The Cameron and Quinn model or 'competing values framework' assesses organizational culture and management skills. It is a matrix structure covering flexibility and discretion versus stability and control, integration and internal focus versus differentiation through an external focus to induce four positions that drive the culture:

a) Clan – a flexible integrated approach that is structured around stability, loyalty, with concern for cohesion and morale, modelling behaviour and mentoring, teamwork and participation;

b) Adhocracy – a flexible differentiated approach that is dynamic and entrepreneurial with concern for creativity, innovation and visionary leadership;

c) Hierarchy – a controlled integrated approach that is structured with systematic governance and procedures with concern for stability, predictability, and efficiency;

d) Market – a controlled differentiated approach that is results-orientated with concern for achieving stretch goals and targets, and taking corrective action as needed.

It has the particular aim of pursuing cultural coherence and competitive advantage. It implies that integration and differentiation are mutually exclusive, although high levels of differentiation can require drawing upon a range of threshold and core competencies that are integrated to meet demands from the marketplace. The competitive advantage focus lends strength for this model, but it also carries a major weakness. There is some difficulty of addressing relationship management as contributing to forming organizational culture and to it being a product of the culture when the model itself is both an input and output. Evaluation is better carried out using a model that is not dependent upon organizations where the rationale is competitive advantage.

The Douglas grid-group model is intentionally parsimonious (Douglas, 1999), evolving through several iterations (Thompson et al., 1990). Grid is about structure, while group is about processes that lead to the degree of incorporation into a group, producing four positions:

1. Fatalism – towards high structure and weak incorporation, carrying assumptions of capriciousness and resilience with the consequential outcomes of being passive where possible and otherwise reactive, risk averse, and resistant to learning;

2. Competitive individualism – towards minimal structure and weak incorporation, carrying assumptions of having a benign nature with the consequential outcomes of being proactive, risk taking, and open to experience, experimenting and learning;

3. Hierarchy – high structure with strong incorporation, carrying assumptions of a tolerant yet perverse nature with consequential outcomes of being proactive yet risk averse, trying to control the parameters of operation, and willingness to learn within the bounds of perceived risk and operational parameters;

4. Egalitarian – towards minimal structure with strong incorporation, carrying assumptions of ephemerality and concern for change with consequential outcomes of being reactive and risk averse, preference for incremental development and systematic control. Within an organization, this can work effectively where there are also mechanisms to induce an outward facing approach with strong procedures and compliance requirements attached. Else, egalitarians can become enclaves in relation to other groups.

The aim of the model is to define sources of cultural bias defined as shared values and beliefs, social relations which are the patterns of interpersonal relations, and a way of life comprising a viable combination of cultural bias and social relations. Groups or organizations can have a primary cultural position and subcultures. People and subgroups iteratively negotiate the culture through decision-making, behaviour and other actions. The model is presented in Figure 6.2.

Douglas (1994) pays particular attention to risks. Many project businesses do yet tend to see risks as things, whereas in contrast her comments on risks as social constructs are instructive:

> When risk enters . . . it becomes a menacing thing, like a flood, an earthquake, or a thrown brick. But it is not a thing; it is a way of thinking, and a highly artificial contrivance at that.
>
> (Douglas, 1994: 46)

Culture refers to a form of moral commitment, enabling a group or organization to pursue social activity and collaboration due to the shared norms and values

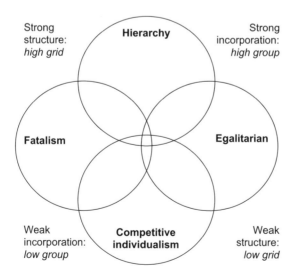

FIGURE 6.2 Dynamism of the grid-group model

Sources: Adapted from Auch and Smyth, 2010.

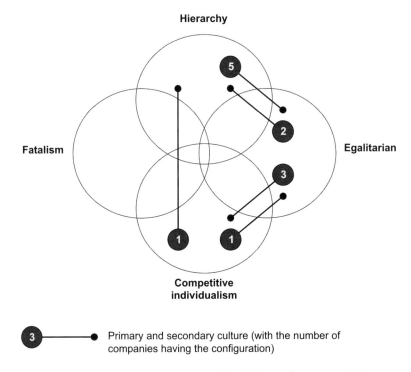

FIGURE 6.3   Map of project businesses research and the grid-group model

Sources: Auch and Smyth, 2010; Roberts et al., 2012; Smyth and Kusuma, 2013.

(Douglas, 2003), which includes a project as an activity and a partnership or temporary multi-organizational project team (TMO), where there is a need to find ways of working together in undertaking complex work that extends beyond conceptualization of risks and governance (Fabianski, 2014).

A general advantage of this model is its ethnographic origins and application in different contexts. It is appropriate for comparing different project businesses, and a number of project business research studies have been conducted using it. The results are mapped onto the model – see Figure 6.3.

There is a spread across three of the four positions, but hierarchy and egalitarian positions dominate. Hierarchy displays the following additional tendencies: vertical coordination and integration, relational contractual norms with governance using authority. Hierarchy displays norms and behaviours of commitment and engagement, honesty and professionalism, confidence or 'calculative trust' based upon high levels of embeddedness from systems and procedures to norms, especially to ensure consistency over project lifecycles and continuity in a programme. Therefore relationship management requires a robust system, supported by consistent management commitment to embed the necessary norms. Egalitarian attributes were the second most frequently occurring organizational culture from the organizational research. This displays horizontal coordination and integration, relational contractual norms with governance based upon trust with a similar set of norms. Here senior management need to ensure robust top-down design and implementation of relationship management as a complementary and enabling force to the horizontal coordination.

Research has also found that project businesses tend to rely primarily upon artifacts and to some extent espoused values. A great deal of operational responsibility is left to individuals, and this is where the underlying basic assumptions tend to come into play, these being variable due to the diversity of people. Thus there is tension between the espoused values and conduct on the ground in line with the Schein model of underlying assumptions (Schein, 1990, 1996; Fact Box 6.1). Further, effective culture is not a simplistic choice between

---

FACT BOX 6.1 EMBEDDING PRACTICES

Research has shown that a number of project businesses are highly reliant upon artifacts for the operational level of the project business and at the project level. This is for several reasons. The lack of cross-functional integration results in the reliance of the management from one function upon the implementation of strategies and policies from other functions, supported by individuals and teams independently taking responsibility. The result is a lack of embedded policies and associated behaviours at a deep level.

For example, a subcontractor who undertakes serial contracts for a range of main contractors is required to tailor the approach project-by-project, yet the experiences vary considerably between projects for the same main contractor. This is a function of weak systems between most main contractors and their site management, allowing project managers scope to develop temporary organizational subcultures for particular projects. The subcontractor perception is that this is a commonplace yet an unnecessary feature of working for each contractor. It tends to lead to increased costs in bid stages for a contract and confusion about compliance during execution. It also constrains their ability to develop systems of choice for integration.

A further example comes from a North American-owned international contractor with a hierarchical organizational culture that had developed a centralized, top-down system between its head office and projects, placing strong reliance upon espoused values and artifacts implemented top-down through policies, systems and procedures. Implementation and embedding practices had a greater emphasis upon horizontal working relying upon the secondary egalitarian culture, but implementation and adherence was uneven because the firm was perceived as being somewhat passive and behaviour was largely reactive at the project level.

Sources: Kelsey et al. (2010); Roberts et al. (2012).

control and collaboration. A study of two megaprojects discussed how cultures contribute to the project's success. Cross-team relationships, cooperation, trust, the contrast between good and bad relationships affected project outcomes. The project with poor relationships suffered from lack of information distribution and design agreement whereas the other project excelled in strengthening relationships, but failed to allow power to be used to enable responsibility being taken. Complex projects and the relationships within them are too complex to apply one consistent solution of control or cooperation (van Marrewijk, 2005). This confirms that control through a top-down relationship management system provides an important prescription for horizontal collaborative working on the ground.

A study focusing upon megaproject TMOs found that over the duration of a project lifecycle, regardless of the starting points that each separate organization brought to the team, the temporary organizational culture migrated increasingly towards hierarchy as the dominant or primary TMO and decision-making unit (DMU) culture (Fabianski, 2014). The front-end is traditionally conceived as a rational process conducted to take account of the context, but this research found that the context drives the sense making of how the front-end emerges, evolves, which is far removed from a rational, functional and planned view. Projects should be seen from the temporary organization perspective where organization emerges (cf. Løwendahl, 1995).

Norms and culture

At the detailed level of norms, management control versus collaboration can combine directives of compliance with cooperative conduct to achieve integration. Dress code and 'right behaviours' provide norms of conformity to provide reassurance (Goffman, 2005). The Gantt chart, for example, is an artifact that has the underlying aim of inducing habits to manage time (Geraldi and Lechter, 2012). People therefore learn to adopt certain social rules and habits in order to lend legitimacy to a role (Goffman, 1959). Adoption at the level of artifacts, such as dress code or a procedure, is high. Internalization of norms and behaviour is more challenging (Brown and Phua, 2011). Combining artifacts and associated embedded norms prove effective. Sharing tacit knowledge is a case in point where embedding is needed to induce it as a norm. Tacit knowledge used by TMO members is an inexpensive means to resolve issues, yet it is an unreliable source until its development and mobilization becomes an organizational norm (e.g. Lindkvist, 2011; Hoegl et al., 2011). Coordination is conducted through established norms and social interactions for projects rather than formal routines (Bechky, 2006; cf. Whyte and Levitt, 2011). Leadership has a role in encouraging adoption, yet embedding means building it into habits of operational processes, monitoring and reflective practice, continuing professional development, human resource management (HRM) and annual reviews, and so on.

There are two types of norms that influence organizational culture (cf. Clark, 1978):

1. *Norms of equality* – revolve around protection and care. They are needs based, hence conduct concerns communal action and a sense of belonging. Positive communal norms will encourage a social orientation and collaborative relationships driven by task and goal achievement.
2. *Norms of equity* – revolve around merit and proportional exchange (Kurtzberg and Medvec, 1999). Positive exchange norms are goal oriented and encourage self-interest in dyadic relations and among staff under the employment contract.

These are norms of distributive justice, based upon the existing culture and social systems to engender cooperation. There are also norms of procedural justice, which are pertinent to projects because new social structures are created, such as the TMO project team, which proceeds to form norms in contextual ways and draws upon the influences of its institutional-cum-organizational setting (Kadefors, 1995; Hodgson and Cicmil, 2007; Morris and Geraldi, 2011; Henisz et al., 2012). The issue then becomes how much of an influence does the setting have from the respective organizations taking part. For many projects, the weak systems and support between any one project business and project leave high levels of autonomy to the TMO and its team members to act in ways that are legitimized as contextually appropriate but, in practice, also have a great deal to do with habits and personal comfort zones of the key personnel, which may not induce norms that serve the employers or the clients towards optimal levels (Smyth, 2015; cf. Bresnen et al., 2004).

The formation of informal routines therefore occurs at an individual level, derived from TMO members bringing their previous working experience, sometimes relationships through being in the same network or being appointed by a DMU member of project manager of the TMO (cf. Engwall, 2003; Bayer and Gann, 2006). The experience embodies the existing habits and comfort zones, some of which may be ineffective at the new operational level, causing so-called behavioural blockages (Cheung et al., 2003; Crespin-Mazet and Portier, 2010).

Relational contracts and governance forms do not control the norms and behaviours. They are one influence only. They will face the same sets of issues and may be in conflict with norms at an operational level. Relational contracts refer to norms of obligation and cooperation that aim to guide behaviour (Macneil, 1980). People trust those who share common values, the culture of shared worlds (Rousseau et al., 1998), and promote a sense of shared social identity and have an emotional bond. Different aspects of socio-psychological contracts come to the fore in different cultures (Rousseau and Schalk, 2000). Staff assess the actions of managers and colleagues against their beliefs and what they think to be fair (Cropanzano et al., 2003; Porath et al., 2011) in the context of their role at work and in general with acknowledgement of the espoused and perceived values of the organization and/or TMO. This will be the case regardless of any contract imposed from a client.

Teams comprise likeminded and not so likeminded people (DeFillippi et al., 2006; Bredin and Söderlund, 2011). Norms are self-fulfilling, contributing to or blocking relationship management. For example, a norm of pursuing self-interest has a reinforcing effect upon staff and a norm pursuing a social orientation is similarly affirming, supported by social capital that accrues in value with use (Ferraro et al., 2005; Nahapiet et al., 2005). There can be tension and vying for position, negotiation and renegotiation of norms between different groups, for example between the primary and secondary cultures in the Douglas model (see Figure 6.2).

International businesses and projects pose particular issues. International project businesses that fail to understand the culture and norms they are working in can have a dramatic effect upon time, cost and quality criteria (e.g. Scott, 2008, 2012; Ruuska et al., 2009), although the problems are frequently presented in technical terms for reasons of accountability and legitimacy. The prevailing organizational culture is affected by the regional and national cultures (e.g. Hofstede and Hofstede, 2005; Auch and Smyth, 2010). The approach to virtual and geographically dispersed teams is frequently proposed as strong local leadership and empowerment (e.g. Hoegl et al., 2011); however, this is part of the problem concerning service consistency and continuity in project delivery. A strong relationship management system may pose problems too. International operations will require regional adaptions to the cultural context.

Creating an identity is important to induce a sense of belonging to those in the group by virtue of a contract rather than self-selection. A sense of belonging in turn induces identification. This is problematic for temporary teams, although many are not as temporary as sometimes supposed (Winch, 2013). Identity and identification have strong links with culture. Personal identity occurs in relation to others (e.g. Mead, 1934; Erikson, 1968; Ashforth and Mael, 1989). Personal identities can be shared in organizational settings, creating forms of solidarity and inclining a party to do something to support another where there is a sense of shared identity (Appiah, 2005). Where personal identities begin to become mutual, the shared identification is commencing the formation of social identity (e.g. Stryker, 1968; Tajfel, 1974; Ashforth and Mael, 1989). A social identity may induce tension because similarities that lead to identification may mark differences from the wider organizational culture unless (i) the values, beliefs, behaviour and actions are largely shared and the differences are of intensity rather than kind; (ii) any differences are not in conflict; or (iii) the level of identification is organizational. It is thought identification is unusual in project industries as brands to help support identification are weak and adversarial behaviour can be present, but this is partly a function of the lack of investment and inconsistent service provision. Professions associated with project businesses tend to induce higher levels of identification among staff and from clients. This is because professional codes of conduct create a sense of identity across each profession (Wallace, 1995), and the creative professions such as architects induce a shared set of values around design approaches and resultant branding (Smyth and Kioussi, 2011a, 2011b). Social identities and identification with other parties and organizations have a powerful effect upon behaviour, inducing conformity through self-selection (e.g. Hogg and Terry, 2000). Identification relies upon sense making (Weick, 1995) and heuristics to intuitively evaluate the extent of shared values and beliefs, and cognitively evaluate the extent of shared behaviour and action (Söderlund et al., 2008; Vaagaasar, 2011). However, a strong identity with the project business can cause tensions in a TMO and formation of a shared belonging for projects with reasonably long project lifecycles. This is not insignificant as Brown and Phua (2011) argue that identities are a key performance issue.

The norms of the organizations comprising TMO membership are important, especially those of the main project business or contractor. Moderate adaptation is acceptable and can have a positive effect on subsequent negotiations, while substantial adaptation is seen as a threat towards group distinctiveness or the emergence of a sense of belonging. Insecurity and being overstretched, especially at the beginning of a project can induce tension and adversity in the team. Incivility and aggression are norms that violate dignity and respect (cf. Porath et al., 2011), which will constrain the emergence of an identity. Relationships are strongest where an identity emerges. The emergence of an identity cannot be controlled although fertile conditions can be created, for example by applying behavioural codes based upon the conditions of trust (**Chapter 5**).

Control can also have a role, for example cooperation or coercion for making promises and threats as bargaining ploys during conflict. Trust is enhanced or is on the wane (Lui et al., 2006). If relationship failure results, new measures are evoked, typically formal ones of cost penalties and legal sanction. Where project businesses pursue project delivery against the minimal or value added requirements, that point is soon reached for two reasons. First, anything outside of meeting the original requirements tends to be treated as a *deviation* and thus to be rejected if possible (Smyth, 2013b), that is located outside the norms of operation. Second, the levels of social capital committed tend to be lower, leaving less room for pursuit within the TMO norms; indeed the range of norms employed will be narrower as well as the investment in each component of social capital, for example relationship management, group emotional intelligence and trust development. Investment in trust development has been empirically found to provide means to mediate between organizations and over contested issues to delay the initial shift to informal coercion and then the shift to formal coercion through sanction (Lui et al., 2006). Where project businesses pursue project delivery against added value criteria, there is more room for manoeuvre. First, these businesses will have mobilized greater levels of social capital. The norms will have a social orientation, which restrains transactions costs arising from conflicts and their risk of escalation. Second, it gives them flexibility to develop a system approach, and they will be more committed to resolving breakdowns or potential shortcomings of integration.

Yet much of the literature and management practice has concentrated upon structural solutions, such as co-locating project teams (e.g. Bresnen and Marshall, 2002; Briscoe et al., 2004; Lakemond and Berggren, 2006). Measures such as co-location structure the micro level, just as governance does at the organizational macro level. Measures such as co-location overlook how relationships are formed and influenced during the early stages of development by role and attendant expectation (Gabarro, 1987; Janowicz-Panjaitan and Noorderhaven, 2009; cf. Goffman, 1959) and the potential shift in cultural position over project lifecycles (Fabianski, 2014). Once projects obtain the go ahead, the TMOs tend to define the social boundaries of the project and transition to a culture that works in terms of the project context (cf. Lundin and Söderholm, 1995).

It is not the economics of transaction costs, the legal contract nor governance that determines a project culture, although they are all influential, nor is it necessarily the respective employer organizations in the TMO, it is what norms are perceived to be necessary and whether those norms serve the project depending upon intent and conduct: *Cultural norms are, after all, constituted not only by what they affirm and revere, but also what they exclude, reject, scorn despise and ridicule* (Appiah, 2005: 139).

The lack of conformity and compliance among staff and groups is commonplace in project businesses. There are various reasons for this. One reason is that people fail to form habits that align with organizational systems and procedures. They can fail to form habits that bring out their own excellence. These include habits *to give of themselves; the habit of supporting, encouraging and developing themselves and others through feedback; and the habit of excellence in the shared task or endeavour* (Nahapiet et al., 2005: 9). Developing such habits can form elements of a behavioural code of practice for spreading and embedding over the business. A behavioural code is also designed to generate additional new habits. The London 2012 Olympics programme included an infrastructure package of roads and bridges, and the project management organization developed *a temporary culture around a few 'disciples' and 'principles'* (CH2M Hill, 2013). *A little yellow book* was used for guidance and was closely aligned to a behavioural code of conduct. A code and new habits also form a basis for or part of a wider community of practice across the industrial network of suppliers, referrers and influencers, and clients (cf. Wenger, 1998). Therefore communities of practice induce coordinating mechanisms and routines from recent influences and past practices, which become established as current practices in a new project, network or organizational setting. Another reason for a lack of conformity and compliance is where staff distance themselves from the prevailing organizational culture. The consequence is that this prohibits shared identity developing. The organization may have inadvertently colluded with this due to their personnel and resource allocation policies. As Appiah puts it, *the autonomous agent has distanced himself from social influences and conventions, and conducts himself according to principles that he has himself ratified through critical reflection. Behold the citizen as a one-person ethics committee* (2005: 38).

Management arguably needs to be more invasive and impose controls where project business staff and project team members prefer to operate inside their typical comfort zone (Lindebaum and Cartwright, 2010). The project business that leaves management to individual responsibility is certainly encouraging such disunity, where much of what is shared is business jargon such as 'correct behaviours' and 'business drivers' that disguise the differences of meaning and informed action (cf. Smyth and Kusuma, 2013).

This might read as if culture is insufficiently structured. The systems may be but culture needs to leave room for manoeuvre. There needs to be social space where structuring yields *causes* for action and agency yields *reasons* for action – two different yet related things. Agency is qualified. We shape our lives at work, yet *others shape our shaping* (Appiah, 2005: 156).

How is the sense of shared identity recognized by others? Evidence of conformity to norms and informal routines, perceived to be part of a team (even as a specialist), going the extra mile and even stereotyping (founded or unfounded) help give a sense of identification by one person to others (e.g. TMO members) or to an organization (and its members). When a person sees that others recognize their identification, it has a further reinforcing role. Identities are multiple and overlapping (e.g. employer organization and TMO), context sensitive and can be transient (Appiah, 2005). Projects contribute to the shaping of our identity, but they are not fundamentally shaping our identity in a profound way because they are temporary and relationships may be transient. They provide reason for action, but insufficiently anchor the individual in the norms, formal and informal routines, especially where there are weak links between projects and the organization. A relationship management system, behavioural programmes and trust building strengthen the link and make connection with the employer to help projects make a bigger contribution to a shared set of values and sense of belonging (**Chapters 3, 4** and **5**).

Silence cannot be interpreted as compliance or agreement (cf. Gilligan, 1982). Silence can be a signal of fear of the consequences of asymmetrical power in organizations. This is rendered even more severe where management themselves employ an approach of silent control in the hierarchy, where there is less reliance upon formal processes and being seen to fit in through osmotic internalization is a main method employed in the social contract. Park and Keil (2009) investigated organizational silence, in particular individual reluctance to report bad news on IT projects. They showed how the combination of organizational structures, policies, managerial practices, and degree of demographic dissimilarity between the hierarchies create a climate of silence, which then impacts upon the willingness of individuals to undertake comprehensive reporting. Managerial practices, especially managers responding negatively to bad news, were found to be most influential, followed by structures and policies that foster centralized decision-making and lack formal mechanisms for upward feedback. This is a matter of spreading and embedding norms that affect individual behaviour. Butcher and Sheehan (2010: 42) found in the construction industry that norms of integrity, transparency and a desire to learn were important for *an ingrained culture of relationship building* and were valued by clients in appointing a contractor.

Leadership and culture

Institutional systems and procedures guide behaviour, cognitive dissonance acting as a means to highlight errant behaviour (Henisz et al., 2012). Luhmann (1979) has said that decentralization (delegation and empowerment) is supposedly an emancipatory attribute yet is ambiguous in practice as conformity to goals is still required (cf. **Chapter 3**). Andersen put it this way from the employer perspective: *how to take responsibility as an organization for ensuring that each individual employee takes responsibility for her own inclusion into the organization, which is always in the process of becoming something else* (2013: 46).

A framework is needed, otherwise control is exerted through favouritism or through silent control and manipulation, which Andersen (2013) says induces the *trembling organization*. This is a leadership issue. Employee and TMO members follow leaders and align their behaviour according to their perceptions of the leaders (Meindl, 1995). Positive perceptions are provided by what has come to be termed authentic leadership (Luthans and Avolio, 2003). There are close links between authentic leadership and the transformational leadership of emotional intelligence (cf. **Chapter 4**). Authentic leadership requires high levels of self-awareness and social awareness and the application of self-efficacy of positive optimism and confidence, and hope (Clapp-Smith et al., 2009), which relate to emotional intelligence and trust management. Competence for individual and/or organizational performance can be described as follows:

$$\text{Competence} = f(\text{Knowledge} + \text{Skills} + \text{Behaviour}) \times \text{Experience}$$

In cultural and relationship terms the function (f) is largely a matter of how people are guided through informal and formal routines. Relationship management has a considerable substantive role through the implementation of a system and the established and emergent norms help induce the informal routines on projects. The management issue from the cultural perspective is to initially assess whether the current cultural configuration is conducive to accommodating a relationship management approach as part of its continual flux and renegotiation. Relationship management and policies to articulate the system at a tactical level is a leadership and management issue, not just in terms of deciding to develop a system, but a leadership approach that drives implementation and monitoring compliance.

Leadership and management are already embedded in a culture, so the range of theoretical options, norms to be chosen and behaviours to be applied will be narrowed by their current sense and knowledge of organizational culture (cf. Pels and Saren, 2005). Leadership has a certain independence from the culture because a new leader or leadership team can introduce new emphases. Claims from leadership that they will change the organizational culture are spurious. They are neither completely removed from the prevailing culture, even through selection process in the labour market, and are not in control of the culture.

Relational leadership emerges from practices through interactions. While other leadership theories emphasize the leader, their traits and approach in ways that see leadership as an entity, relational leadership is less an entity and is located in the relational contexts (Uhl-Bein, 2006). It resonates strongly in this way with organizational culture. Transformational and authentic leadership are less embedded in relationships and informed by roles because these theories are reliant on attributes, for example trait or ability through the emotional intelligence lens. Attributes are stable and hence leadership is perceived as stable, whereas relational leadership is less stable and thus is conceptually more akin to the coordination mechanisms and routines that emerge from practice (cf. Parmigiani and Howard-Grenville, 2011; Jarzabkowski et al., 2012).

There is also a cultural propensity for informal and *ad hoc* arrangements in project businesses (Chambers et al., 2009) and more so at the level of the project. These will persist to some extent, and the room for manoeuvre within a prescribed system will continue and can be fruitful sources of norms and behaviour as part of the evolving culture, being harnessed for spreading and embedding across the organizational culture as part of a routine. Routines that work are cultivated and fine-tuned over time (Vaagaasar, 2011). They provide the raw material for a behavioural programme or behavioural code. An ethnographic study of the film industry found temporary organizations for films negotiate and routinize work patterns rather than being 'developed' ephemerally or imposed top-down (Bechky, 2006). Where programme management exists, relationship management provides a substantive mechanism to provide formal guidance where the project level per se is unable to generate the coordination.

The strategic management decision is about where the project business wants to compete in the changing marketplace and how they will compete. Adoption of relationship management strategies, systems and behaviour redefines, renegotiates and refines the culture. In terms of cultural theory the lines of operation become more horizontal and less reliant upon hierarchical control day-to-day, and leaders have to release control for them to evolve. This in turn refines the organizational identity, the type of language used (Fiol, 2002), and thus the sense making employed by staff and representatives of other organizations as to what extent social and organizational identification is present. This will suit some staff, suppliers and clients and less so others, much of which will occur through self-selection rather than any strategic or tactical action. The leadership and management role is subsequently to monitor the evolution and ensure that the substance remains aligned with the prevailing culture.

HRM is an important function in shaping the organizational culture, but it is not to be overemphasized in this respect. It has a leadership role in this respect to induce engagement. As Bredin and Söderlund (2011) point out, effective HRM is about employee engagement and interaction rather than the staff passively receiving top-down guidance and direction.

Roles allocated within temporary teams frequently lack clarity and thus involve unnecessary stress (Keith, 1978). Teamwork tends to place excessive demands upon time allocated for tasks (Perlow, 1999). Hobday (2000) draws attention to the consequence of weak links between the 'corporate centre' and projects upon training and staff development. This echoes work on the long-term effects of flexible teamwork on the individual (Sennett, 1998; Bredin and Söderlund, 2011). These factors tend to lead to appointment of people who are known by the DMU members (Saxenian, 1996), rather than people that will adhere to relationship management, programme management and HRM strategy. Project managers can be disconnected from the long-term goals of the firm (Engwall, 2003). HRM leadership needs to ensure alignment rather than allow project teams and DMU members to appoint people that have experience by fit with their personal identity rather than the organizational identity.

Conclusion

Organizational culture is about the difference of one organization to another in terms of the totality of how things are done. It is also about the similarity through shared values and beliefs, behaviours and action expressed through formal systems and procedures and informal mechanisms that form the organizational routines. The formal side of systematic integration is frequently weak in project businesses, especially between the project business and individual projects, leaving TMOs with scope to develop a subculture or an organizational culture with a high degree of independence. This might reflect the other organizations involved and the project goals, but the analysis has also shown how this frequently serves individual agendas of project managers.

Culture and the norms that steer action and behaviour on the ground arise from the formal management routines in the project business and for project management. The team needs room for manoeuvre to accommodate the diversity of membership, the needs of the project and to meet the goals of benefits delivery. The room for manoeuvre is framed by the culture. It was argued that teams adding value have more scope to be flexible, for example to accommodate emergent, and thus develop social capital, for example capabilities including relationship management, in self-reinforcing ways.

The analysis has also shown that organizational culture is stratified from the organization through to the individual. Sometimes this is analyzed in terms of climate or atmosphere, while this chapter has focused upon norms as this is helpful to connect to routines and behaviour and effectively links with relationship management in the context of organizational culture. The stratified approach underscores that value of a relationship management approach to the structuring and evolution of organizational culture at the various levels from the systems level for integration, behavioural programmes, behavioural codes of conduct down to the tactical alignment of individual behaviour. The role of identity was also considered as a cultural reinforcement, yet noting potential tensions between the project business and TMOs. Overall, relationship management plays an important role in project businesses and for projects, analyzed through the lens of organizational culture.

Therefore a series of aims and objectives have been achieved. Organizational culture as a force in and for management in relation to relationship management has been analyzed. Culture is formed for a TMO but precedes any project and thus links closely with MoP in theory and practice and with management from the 'corporate centre'. Alignment of key constructs and principles associated with organizational culture up and down the hierarchy, across programmes and horizontally along project lifecycles have been addressed, especially systems, norms and forms of behaviour. Recognition of constraints and barriers posed by organizational culture for management coordination mechanisms across organizational and inter-organizational boundaries has been considered. These operate at organizational, team and individual levels.

Therefore the chapter considered issues to help to assess what organizational culture contributes to relationship management in project businesses. A main message has been how a robust and aligned organizational culture makes an effective contribution to the performance of managers and teams, and for facilitating the interface with other organizations. This is constantly in flux and subject to renegotiation as culture unfolds. Therefore a primary management role is to harness the complementary aspects and manage out the non-aligned activity. Spreading and embedding appropriate measures requires close attention to processes, especially the informal routines and errant behaviour and acts of violation.

SI no. 1: *Organizational Behaviour* is closely connected to culture. Culture is potentially a force for integration or fragmented action inducing degrees of disintegration of management and service delivery. The influence of behaviour from the organization to individual level has been investigated, and it has been found that a relationship management system can contribute as it cascades through the levels to aid integration.

SI no. 2: *Relationship Management Theory* interfaces with organizational culture through the formal and informal routines of relationship management.

SI no. 3: *Socio-psychological Issues* are important for the way in which these are formed and develop are powerful influences in establishing norms and routines. People do not behave rationally all the time, unaligned behaviour, occasional errant behaviour and violations are all present due to social distance and weak identity unless formal routines intervene.

SI no. 4: *Conceptual and Applied Hierarchical Integration* was addressed through control and some coercion top-down was necessary to improve behavioural alignment and integration through a systematic approach. This is not necessarily in conflict with informal processes, and room for manoeuvre indeed frames this type of behaviour and action.

SI no. 5: *Conceptual and Applied Horizontal Integration* starts at the front-end of project lifecycles. There are cultural tensions between the organizational culture of the project team and the emergent cultures in any project team and TMO. Relationships are dealt with directly through guiding team and individual behaviour.

SI no. 8: *Relational Contracting* was found wanting as a crude way of approaching the structuring of projects through cost, legal and governance issues, which underplay the richness of organizational culture and therefore the complexity of management and leadership to steer the culture in aligned and contributory ways.

SI no. 9: *Systems Integration* extends beyond dovetailed artifacts and interface articulation, the analysis focusing upon the softest of issues, organizational culture.

The main contribution of this chapter has been to consider organizational culture and relationship management. They have a mutual contribution to make to each other and so inform the management of projects and vice versa. It is a stratified process or recognition and management of issues from the organizational level to the behavioural, from the 'corporate centre' to the project. One of the most important aspects is to align systems and procedures as well as encourage behavioural compliance. Analyzing these issues makes several important contributions to knowledge and practice. It moves analysis away from both structural solutions to dynamic issues and from simplistic mechanistic ones to a richer understanding that will yield greater satisfaction for clients and staff, despite and in certain ways because of the greater levels of direction and control introduced through relationship management. Mechanisms can be formed and implemented top-down, yet frequently emerge and iteratively evolve from practice where the management role is to identify, nurture and shape them coherently (cf. Jarzab-kowski et al., 2012).

However, there is still considerable scope for a richer understanding of the dynamics through additional research into organizational culture. This includes research *recommendations* into:

A. The interplay through the levels of operation and culture, for decision-making and particularly the key and pivotal roles of DMU and TMO members at the individual level.
B. A more detailed analysis between functional departments and between project functions and the interface between department and project functions.
C. The tendency towards hierarchy at the project level was noted, but more extensive research will reveal the pervasiveness of this trend.

Practitioners tend to veer towards organizational culture being used to explain factors beyond management control on the one hand and culture as something leadership can change with apparent ease. The following *recommendations* for practice are proposed:

1. Adopt a realistic position in management to influence through formal and informal routines.
2. Guide individual behaviour and actively align systems and behaviour as a rich and rewarding dimension for managing project business performance.
3. One place to start is the introduction and development of relationship management approach, a set of principles and arguably a robust formal system.

Organizational behaviour flows from the organizational culture. Behaviour is important for informing how systems operate on the ground. Systems guide and shape future action. This provide the focus for the next chapter.

7

ORGANIZATIONAL BEHAVIOUR AND SYSTEMS INTEGRATION

Introduction

This chapter is closely linked to and builds on the previous chapter at a more detailed level. Organizational behaviour is part of and arises from organizational culture. Organizational behaviour is therefore both causal in the formation and an effect of culture. Thus, the extent of its coherence or incoherence is reflected in both organizational culture and behaviour. Culture was considered in terms of consequential formal and informal routines in **Chapter 6.** Organizational behaviour comprises the behaviour articulating formal routines and the behaviour constituting informal routines. In **Chapter 1,** systems were defined as drawing together functions and their subsystems with the aim of integrating the totality. Integration was addressed through sets of procedures that are called coordinating mechanisms. These are mid-level procedures that are dynamic comprising for example behavioural programmes, which are relatively stable and guide practice (Jarzabkowski et al., 2012: 907). Some procedures are lower-level routines that help induce consistent behaviour (Parmigiani and Howard-Grenville, 2011) for example through behavioural codes of conduct as part of a system.

Relationships also feed into the system and have both coordinating and routinized roles. To the extent that systems, their coordinating mechanisms and routines are effective as inputs, they yield capabilities and support competencies as organizational outputs in project businesses and teams that can be decisive in the marketplace for delivering value and realizing profit, that is, performance outputs. The formal routines of systems and sets of procedures and rules require compliant behaviour. Some systems have strong behavioural components, for example health and safety systems and relationship management systems. It is common in the project management research to focus upon functional systems and subsystems to refine content and integrate with other functions and systems. That may be the conceptual 'ideal' or idealistic position. The practice is that many project businesses do not have integrated systems and have inadequate interfaces for dyadic and stakeholder management (e.g. Smyth, 2015; Zou et al., 2014). These facets have increasingly been studied, yet there is scope for further understanding and explanation through research, and there is plenty of scope for development of integrated practice.

This chapter aims to explore these issues, particularly in relation to how organizational behaviour and systems interface with relationship management principles structured as a formal system or informal routines at conceptual and applied levels. The previous chapter pointed towards the amount of non-compliant and errant behaviour, yet is tolerated, arguably for short-term cost reasons. The other side of the coin is to consider the benefits and disadvantages in addressing compliance to achieve greater functional and service integration. To begin to explore this area, the role of relationship management in project businesses and for projects, the chapter proposes to address the following:

A.   The way in which organizational behaviour and related systems are articulated across project businesses and the implications for the business, suppliers and clients.
B.   The opportunities and constraints faced by management at the interface of organizational behaviour, especially informal routines, and systems for integration.
C.   The strengths and weaknesses of management in developing integration and the effects on the business in the long and short run.

A tension in the role of organizational behaviour and the theoretical promise of integration compared to practice. Relationship management is arguably a missing piece

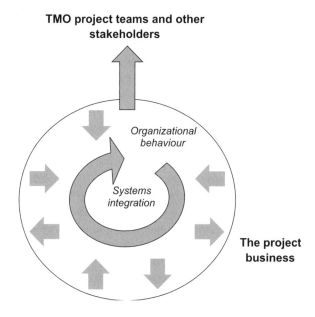

FIGURE 7.1   Organizational behaviour and systems integration

for addressing this theory–practice dissonance. Enhancing or adopting relationship management as part of organizational behaviour is a systems component and is nested in behavioural issues. Thus, adoption tends towards functionalist self-reinforcement, which management prescribes for improvement yet conceptually becomes more difficult to evaluate without dynamic observation rather than snapshot evidence. In other words, enhancement or adoption implies a strategic choice, giving rise to justifying the perceived need, which is further justified with each iteration and round of experience. The interaction between organizational behaviour and systems integration is depicted in Figure 7.1. The purpose of relationship management is to align these aspects and thus can be mapped over the figure as a regulatory and facilitative function, yet is itself part of the system and thus systems integration.

Organizational behaviour and systems

It has been said that systems thinking explains everything but predicts little (Handy, 1996). How a system works may help to understand and explain how processes operate. They are predicated upon the logic of the system, and the levels of congruence and disruption depend to a large extent upon whether the system is conceived as closed or the extent to which it is open. Yet all systems are open systems in practice. It is how the system is designed and emerges from practice. Designed inputs are configured, emergent practices are identified and shaped by management and operated on the ground to help induce consistent outcomes. Behaviour can be compliant or a disruptive component. Therefore, systems, their procedures in the form of coordinating mechanisms and routines, are relatively stable, practice always emerging to renegotiate and reshape aspects and the interpretation of meaning behind the systems (Parmigiani and Howard-Grenville, 2011; Jarzabkowski et al., 2012). Management wishes to see high degrees of compliance and behavioural consistency in order to be able to predict outcomes. However, the problems do not always reside with non-compliance and errant individual behaviour. The problems are frequently the way management has partially structured its systems, the lack of cross-functional integration and the primary focus upon systems as processing technical and financial matters from the business to the execution level. One missing functional piece has been the management of projects (MoP), yet the part that makes all this work and adds value is people and the relationships between them, which emerge from practice and which are guided by a relationship management system. This remains the uncomfortable and largely uncharted area. It is uncomfortable for cost reasons, for reasons of invasiveness and perceived dictatorial control of social and personal conduct, yet is central to value creation, benefits delivery and profit making. This book has argued that relationship management remains a poorly considered subsystem input and provides a means to guide behaviour.

It has been put like this:

> Interfaces occur between independent and semi-independent functions. Functional interfaces occur both within the project business and between

the project business and project. These are hierarchical interfaces and are not especially time bound. The project business–project interface is typically poorly structured, with weak systems and relationship management for top-down management support. The main issue raised here is about the quality of management. Functional interfaces also occur horizontally along project lifecycles from the front-end, through execution to post-project stages.

(Smyth, 2015: 35)

There is a misconception that because projects are unique, management cannot be standardized and routinized, including the management of organizational behaviour. Project management bodies of knowledge, methods, tools and techniques are trying to apply standard routines and compliant processes. However the scope of standardization tends to be narrowly focused upon specific elements of execution. Project management tools and techniques are largely embellishments of common sense. It is the other factors that arguably lead to time and cost overruns; not the control mechanisms of project management inappropriately applied – the overruns occur despite appropriate application. Managing the other factors requires sets of project and organizational capabilities (Davies and Brady, 2000; Brady and Davies, 2004). These constitute specific routines in dynamic application and practice.

It is the capabilities and competencies, of both technical and soft management types at threshold levels that provide inputs to regulate other factors, more so to manage quality and the provision of added value solutions that are conceptually referred to as core competencies and dynamic capabilities. These competencies and capabilities take many forms, and have been effectively rolled out over successive megaprojects (e.g. Davies et al., 2009; Brady and Davies, 2010). Project businesses are able to put in place 'economies of repetition' through capabilities, routines and learning processes that can lead to delivering 'repeatable solutions' (Davies and Brady, 2000). It opens up opportunities for replication of a business model (Winter and Szulanski, 2001; Jonsson and Foss, 2011). Replication is, however, far more than the standardization and exploitation of a business model, and much more than project management tools and techniques. Winter and Szulanski (2001) argue that it is a specific type of strategy that, in addition to an exploitation regime, also involves a subtle exploration phase. They have identified several key elements of a replication strategy: knowledge transfer, the role of a central organization, the core information necessary. However, on what types of production and types of project to which this is suited remains underdeveloped. Barriers and difficulties exist for such strategies related to cost control and investment minimization, organizational rigidities and other factors as investigated in the design and construction of renewable diesel refineries (Ruuska and Brady, 2011).

Repeatable solutions can be developed from the project level (Brady and Davies, 2004) and transferred onto other projects through a process of spreading and embedding by key personnel at programme management systems. Repeatable solutions can also emanate from the organizational level from strategic learning and implementation (Davies and Brady, 2000) systematically implemented through P³M processes. There are probably a series of factors that are necessary to effectively roll out such an approach across a series of projects. The exemplars, such as T5 at London Heathrow Airport, the London Olympics programme 2012 and Cross Rail in the United Kingdom are all projects and programmes that have shared a strong collaborative approach with incentives that are or have been client driven – a form of coercive approach by clients albeit a collaborative one. Where those external drivers do not exist, the capabilities need to emanate from and reside in the project business – perhaps a form of coercive approach by project businesses albeit a collaborative relationship management approach internally generated and taken out into the marketplace. These can be designed or more likely emerge in partial form from recent and existing practices to be shaped and nurtured by management (cf. Parmigiani and Howard-Grenville, 2011; Jarzabkowski et al., 2012).

The tensions along a continuum of individual responsibility-management facilitation-management coercion are apparent. At the extremes, the views can be expressed as follows: according to Bredin and Söderlund (2011: 53), *the orga-nizational context is critical for the relationships and, thereby, also for the management of the relationships*, and according to Andersen (2013: 2–3), *organizations increasingly colonize employees' freedom, identity and subjectivity*.

The dynamics of management in projects need to be addressed to facilitate integration, and whose interests are being served. Integration and aligned organizational behaviour are in the client interests. It is in staff interests of the temporary multi-organizational project team (TMO) to provide greater security as a basis for improved problem solving, to ease stress, innovation and the co-creation of value. The area most in doubt is the tension between the short-term cost concerns and profit realization among senior management and the long-term interests of business growth and profitability. Project businesses frequently struggle with inappropriate and fragmented systems as part of taken-for-granted thinking (Smyth, 2013a, 2014), yet the fragmentation is frequently where the choice has been made not to invest in systems of integration – a functionalist outworking in practice.

Organizational behaviour emanates from the prevailing state of affairs, but what is it? Organizational behaviour in management is a substantial field of knowledge and research; it has been given proportionately marginal attention in project business, although rebalancing is underway. A systems approach to integration is well established, yet still growing in the project literature (Morris et al., 2011). The systems integration interface with organizational behaviour in project businesses is underdeveloped in research and practice. Organizational behaviour, for example, has been described as: *The human side of work . . . It is this people-centred orientation that is taken as organizational behavior* (Greenberg and Baron, 2003: 2) and . . . *the impact that individuals, groups, and structure have on behavior within organizations* (Robbins, 2009: 44).

The literature tends to over-emphasize the degree to which management determines organizational behaviour, but in practice, interaction is problematic with loose coupling between behaviour and outcomes. In general, good decision-making comes from good behaviour, much of which flows from good habits (Nahapiet et al., 2005) and vice versa, although some variance exists, yet are habits individual or part of informal routines? Relationship management endeavours to provide formal means to guide otherwise informal and individual action into formal and informal routines. They arise from habits and become part of future habits with management nurture and development (cf. Parmigiani and Howard-Grenville, 2011).

The interactive and reflexive dynamic has been partly addressed through a contingency approach to organizational behaviour. A contingency approach emanating from the work of March and Simon (1958) tries to accommodate changing conditions, which leads to the evolution of cultural artifacts, such as contract forms, and new norms. It can lead to the reappraisal of strategic criteria and the renegotiating of decisions under conditions of rapid or dramatic change. This shows the extent of a normative element in management theorization and in project management practice (O'Leary and Williams, 2008; Morris and Geraldi, 2011). Not only does the project forecast what things will look like – the future perfect (e.g. Pitsis et al., 2003) – management is casting forward to support successful outcomes, through for example planning, budgeting, and risk management; but it is also recognizing the open-ended aspect – adopting a contingency approach to anticipate risk and manage emergent factors to add value (cf. Smyth, 2013b).

From a transactional viewpoint, Williamson (1971) argues in favour of fiat, for example in decision-making, because it is efficient – making progress and reducing perceived uncertainty – yet ineffective by accelerating decisions ahead of time and invoking either higher costs due to lock-in to previous decisions with sunk costs or compromise to the value delivered to the client. The transactional efficiency argument over effectiveness also tends to be self-reinforcing up the hierarchy, concentrating more decision-making power with finance departments based upon the information asymmetry of quantitative measure of operational effectiveness (cf. Milgrom and Roberts, 1992). In many project businesses, costs are seen as expenditure that do not affect technical and service quality if reduced, although this argument is eroded, often corrosive, in service provision (Grönroos, 2000; Smyth and Lecoeuvre, 2014).

Systems that are open in practice are traditionally over-structured in design in respect of the issues addressed, yet partial and under-considered for certain facets. Emergent routines and their impact are frequently overlooked (cf. Parmigiani and Howard-Grenville, 2011). Structuring is nonetheless necessary for management to consider design, alignment with strategy and operations on the ground, including emergent practices and their incorporation and fine-tuning or rejection. Informal routines are the raw material for emergent practices and their subsequent formalization. Informal routines are more difficult to identify, define and articulate, some of which will have been in existence for a long time and have become part of the taken-for-granted way of doing things, yet may not necessarily lead to coordinated activity and behaviour. The tendency is to over-determine the formal system as if it were 'closed' rather than effectively manage the interface in relation to the informal ways of doing things. It is aligned behaviour with the formal systems that proves effective. In project businesses, there are always non-routine and new emergent informal routines at the project level. As Gann and Salter (2000) argue, project businesses need to harness and reproduce their technological capabilities when they integrate or link non-routine project processes and routine business processes. Emergent informal routines in TMOs can be imported from the TMO to improve performance and develop new capabilities and can be exported from the parent organization to improve project performance. Strong systems based upon robust and consistent organizational behaviour are needed to operationalize this two-way exchange. This leads on to addressing how to manage the interaction between temporary actions and repetitive business practices (Acha et al., 2005).

Systems are increasingly being seen as broader structures and processes that are part of a wider and diverse set of organizational actors that are in constant flux and interplay in project teams, supply networks, and institutional influencers. These are ecosystems (e.g. Grabher, 2002, 2004), which are considerably reliant upon informal albeit sometimes tight-knit informal routines. Informal routines can be articulated for project businesses using analytical methods of social network analysis (Pryke, 2012) to examine the significance of linkages or ties. It has been put this way:

> In addition to the need for a certain level of standardisation, the companies involved in the establishment of an industrial ecosystem need manoeuvrabil-ity to be able to adapt to local variations and to develop successful industrial ecosystems on a regular basis. This also requires flexibility in the business model . . .
>
> (Tsvetkova and Gustafsson, 2012: 249)

The issue with the growing literature on business models and earning logic (e.g. Romme, 2003, Wikström et al., 2009) is that they can be conceived and rationalized as highly mechanical, whereas they are or can be flexible, adaptable and emergent within the ecosystem of the project working environment. As recently stated, the role of a business model is to define *the manner by which the enterprise delivers value to customers, entices customers to pay for value, and converts those payments to profit* (Teece, 2010: 172). If this is retained as the prime focus, then the systems do not become too rigid on the one hand and nor too flexible on the other hand, whereby behaviour enhances value and profit is permitted to endure even if non-compliant with the systems design.

The project is thus part of an open system (Ackoff, 1981; Walker, 2007; Smyth and Pryke, 2008) and making this work is a challenge of integration. Manoeuvre is not always functional. As discussed in **Chapter 6,** the relative autonomy of the project from any parent organization of the TMO also gives room for behav-ioural manoeuvre that is misaligned with parameters of value and profit set out by Teece (2010). The interface management is critical (e.g. Merrow, 2011; Smyth and Kusuma, 2013), and the associated project routines are needed for efficiency and capability development (Ahola and Davies, 2012; cf. Nelson and Winter, 1982; Stinchcombe and Heimer, 1985). They are needed as an interface to programme management to front-load decision-making and problem solving (Crespin-Mazit and Portier, 2010; cf. Morris, 1994) and to articulate and manage the relatively enduring relationships spanning project lifecycles (Bygballe et al., 2010).

Therefore, a way of depicting behaviour and systems is needed to address the complexity of the project business and project management setting. There is no single way to do this, one way being to link it back to the analysis on culture. Figure 7.2 maps the characteristics from the cultural position using the grid-group model.

Bringing together organizational behaviour and systems integration at the operational level means alignment of processes and tasks. Task conduct involves behaviour and action. Systems require coordinated flow. Inconsistent behaviour and action thwart systems flow, and such behaviour can emerge from norms bottom-up and become endemic habits. The need for alignment and coherence between behaviour at task level and the system has been achieved in part through traditional project management tools, yet this constitutes a small part of the total picture (see Figure 7.2). Effective relationships, as the undermanaged and sensitive area of projects, improve the support structures and systems necessary for effective coordination.

This aligns with other work that has found that integration occurred through three mechanisms on R&D-production relation project teams: the systems integrator role of the organization, the team level and the individual (Nihtilä, 1999). Although there was no relationship management reported in the findings, the integrator role was dependent upon the two other levels. At the team level, cross-functional working was found to be important, and there was also dependence upon the operation of individuals. The effectiveness of individuals was dependent upon project managers with experience being available, who had credibility with other individual actors or decision-makers. Personal attributes and determination were identified as important too. Where the team and individual support is enhanced in systematic ways, this will contribute to integration and avoid behaviour based upon the comfort zones of project managers (**Chapter 6**).

There are more interpretative approaches to the understanding of organizational behaviour. Following Weick (1995), the sense making approach considers how both practitioners and researchers come to understand what is happening on the ground. Sense making informs action and behaviour in context and in response to events as a type of sense giving (Polanyi, 1967). Sense making can occur at an individual and group or team level. While it will take account of the norms, systems and procedures believed to be significant, how it does so is largely dependent upon human agency taking into account both objective and subjective issues. This is an accurate reflection of what occurs and avoids many of the pitfalls of rationalistic over-determined approaches, however, the shortfall is that there is little or no guidance as to what managers do and perhaps should do and

High grid *strong structure*	**Isolated fatalism** Systems designed with an inward looking perspective which can take different forms depending upon whether considered at the project, functional or project business level: • Project business as an inward looking entity with minimal but potentially well-integrated systems; • Low levels of cross-functional integration in the project business where subcultures of isolation or silos exist; • Low levels of integration of project teams with the business; • Low tolerance to external forces and emergent issues; • Eventual fate for this type of organization is entropy or being takeover without a large shock to the system, for example new management, which introduces restructuring and change management. Organizational behaviour is defensive, passive and lacks tolerance for risk, having the following tendencies: • Reversion to disciplinary backgrounds and past experience to inform behaviour; • Narrow focus upon task and goals set by disciplinary expertise and informed by predispositions. Relationship management: • If present only as a defensive risk averse measure; • Based upon informal routines. Individual behaviour: • Tendency toward passivity; • Meeting the minimum requirements; • Insecurity and a sense of being threatened; • Resistance to any proposed repositioning such as restructuring and change management programmes.	**Hierarchy** Systems designed top down with the following tendencies: • Implement and operate in mechanistic and rigid ways; • Low levels of cross-functional integration in the project business; • Low levels of integration along project lifecycles, especially where projects operate relatively autonomously and thus the system is weak at the business-project interface; • Low tolerance to emergent issues over project lifecycles; • Lack of bottom-up refinement and evolution of the systems and induction of project capabilities to enhance integration across the business. Organizational behaviour either controlled top down or perceived by management to be controlled top down with the following tendencies: • Poor structuring and compliance requirements compromise implementation behaviourally; • Weak cross-functional and business-project systems drive individual behaviour towards isolated fatalism and/or individualism. Relationship management: • Absence is a reflection of the perception that more is effectively managed and under control than is the case; • Short-term tactical goals and low cost structures are functionally self-reinforcing; • Formal or informal systems are regulated with control perceived to be having more effect than is behaviourally the case; • Over-formalised structures restrict room for manoeuvre incurring rigidity, stifling innovation and service provision. Individual behaviour: • Where demands for compliance are high, value is added through interpersonal relationships, guided by individuals also taking responsibility, leading to strong relationships and a personal identity with the business and project goals; • Where an effective relationship management is in place, value is added through interpersonal relationships and systems lead to strong organizational relationships, potentially inter-organizational relationships and an organizational identity with the employer and/or project; • Where compliance is weaker fatalism emerges and errant behaviour disrupts value creation, constraining profitability and capability development.
Low grid *weak structure*	**Competitive individualism** Lack of formal systems with the following tendencies: • A reliance upon informal systems; • Internal market, careerism and use of power to informally coordinate actions; • Low levels of vertical and cross-functional integration in the project business; • Very weak interface between the business and projects. • Low levels of integration along project lifecycles; • Innovation, bottom-up refinement and	**Egalitarian** Systems are designed by agreement with the following tendencies: • Emergence is slow and refinement is incremental, a conservative approach adopted to implementation; • High levels of cross-functional integration in the project business with possible weak top-down oversight; • Potentially strong integration along project lifecycles; • Service flexibility in the face of emergent issues over project lifecycles, providing structures and processes are not challenged in ways that are perceived to raise risk to

FIGURE 7.2   *(Continued overleaf)*

Low group	High group
evolution of the systems and induction of project capabilities is the outcome of individuals and teams taking responsibility. Organizational behaviour is largely left to individual responsibility: • Incentivizing of individuals and teams through career rewards based upon perceived merit and favouritism of a selected few; • Pay and bonus schemes that are hard to fairly apportion on a merit basis. Relationship management: • Present to the extent that the market and clients demand a formal or informal system. • Absent by preference. Individual behaviour: • Low level of demand for compliance; • High reliance upon networking and social acceptance; • Sponsorship and favouritism, justified in terms of merit; • Maverick behaviour with positive outcomes rewarded where carried out by favoured individuals; • Silent control applied based around norms and behaviours that are to be absorbed through osmosis.	unacceptable levels; • Bottom-up refinement and evolution of the systems and induction of project capabilities to enhance integration across the business. Organizational behaviour complies with strong group norms and routines with the following tendencies: • Norms and behaviour can be restrictive, especially for creativity, innovation and problem solving unless part of the established norms; • Where norms and behaviour are not transferred into TMOs, either relatively autonomous subculture emerges or strong hierarchy is adopted from the organizational of another TMO member. Relationship management: • Absence is a reflection of the perception that the business, groups and teams currently effectively manage and control operations for the long-term, which is perceived to be self-reinforcing; • Formal or informal systems are strongly regulated through group norms and compliant low-risk behaviour. Individual behaviour: • Demands for compliance are high, value being added through interpersonal relationships, guided by individuals taking responsibility and are supported by the relationships and a sense of collective identity with the business and project goals; • Where an effective relationship management is in place, organizational relationships are reinforced; • Hierarchy demands will be made and may emerge where egalitarian management is perceived as too weak and slow, especially on projects working to tight time frames.
Low group *weak incorporation*	**High group** *strong incorporation*

FIGURE 7.2 Mapping organizational behaviour and systems integration onto the grid-group model

how compliance maps out in practice through sense making and other forms of interpretation. Researchers tend to focus upon the particular rather than establishing patterns out of interpretation that aid general management practice (Smyth and Morris, 2007).

Integration is only as good as the understanding of the value to be delivered. This does not start with a system but by the ability to listen and understand the needs at a deep level (Volker, 2010; Smyth, 2015). The understanding is therefore the result of individual and group sense making. Inducing shared understanding of goals, requirements (including added value intentions) and responsibilities can improve output quality in 'virtual teams' (Schepers et al., 2011) that share some of the same attributes as project teams, especially project teams working remotely. An internal survey of an international project business indicated that only 49 per cent of staff thought that the board of directors provides a clear sense of direction (unpublished Company Survey Report, 2009). This suggests that the problem with sense making in practice may reside less with teams and its members and more with management ability to convey on what grounds people should be making sense of things and encouragement and as to what shared beliefs and values are needed. Considered this way, sense making has an important role in helping to shape personal and social identity, which is a key to the development of strong relationships and informal routines of integration of people in order to integrate activities (cf. **Chapter 4**).

Combining the rational approach and the more interpretative one, it would further suggest that interpretative sense making is especially valuable at the strategic level for management as a process to inform strategic direction and intent, which is conveyed consistently to staff and project team members working remotely in 'virtual teams'. This strategically aids differentiation in a competitive marketplace. The interpretative approach gives scope for choosing precise action and unfolding behaviour. It is here that precision is needed to steer activities and align strategic aims with tactical behaviour on the ground. The implication is that a relationship management system provides the overarching approach to help link organizational behaviour with other systems as part of integration. Systematic guidance then informs behavioural programmes. Particular behaviours within programmes, and behavioural codes of conduct provide the detailed relationship goals.

The interpretative strategic sense making and the rational prescriptive action work together to not only spread the way things are done and specifically link organizational behaviour with systems integration but also to embed aligned and integrated behaviour. *Organizational embeddedness* is necessary for systematic working, so that formal and informal routines are mutually reinforcing. *Temporal embeddedness* creates mechanisms to shape action (Jones and Lichtenstein, 2008), which relates to programme management and project lifecycles where emergent practices are routinized as embedded processes. *Social embeddedness* guides interpersonal relations (Granovetter, 1985), providing hierarchical means or mechanisms from the programme to project level. Temporal and social embeddedness are therefore mechanisms for coordinating TMOs at the organizational and individual levels respectively (Jones and Lichtenstein, 2008). Temporal embeddedness takes three forms (Clark, 1985):

1. *Entrainment-based pacing* – daily and seasonal rhythms for organizing (Ancona and Chong, 1996). Organizational culture, strategic content and business models shape this level. Relationship management is present to the extent that it is embodied within strategic thinking and implementation.
2. *Chronological pacing* – coordination within a timeframe. Systems and formal routines govern action at this level. Relationship management is guided by specific relationships management routines at this level.
3. *Event-based pacing* – context for coordination routines (Söderholm, 2008). This is encapsulated in the task focus that dominates many project business

operations (Nandhakumar and Jones, 2001). Relationship management largely resides in team and individual responsibility, except where behavioural programmes and codes of conduct are governed by a relationship management system.

Social embeddedness takes two forms (Nahapiet and Ghoshal, 1998):

1. *Relational embeddedness* – relational ties, social identification and social dependencies that lead to organizational bonds and interdependencies.
2. *Structural embeddedness* – arises out of strong interpersonal and inter-organizational ties (Granovetter, 1973), with structuring that creates stability in social conduct (Giddens, 1979; Pryke, 2012).

Embedding capabilities, coordinating mechanisms and routines is seldom merely a top-down process as they typically emerge in nascent form from practice, and the management role is to use this as a basis for spreading and embedding such practices (cf. Parmigiani and Howard-Grenville, 2011; Jarzabkowski et al., 2012).

The importance of linking organizational behaviour and systems integration is highlighted *in absentia*. Merrow (2011) highlights the needs for systematically organized work in oil and gas projects, yet finds a lack of continuity to be an issue. Half of all project leaders are changed in a project lifecycle. This seldom involves one person, taking key team members with them. Across a range of projects success rates fell from 55 per cent to 13 per cent where there was leadership change over the project lifecycle. There are always other factors, but the leadership change exacerbates problems and compounds the issues to be addressed. Changes of leadership are seldom to do with the project, but are related to new projects coming on stream and other factors (Smyth, 2015). Continuity of understanding, knowledge, issues and action are lost and value is leaked when this occurs. The open system is open for the wrong reasons – value and benefit leakage coupled with increased costs and overruns. Thus, reliance upon individual sense making and tacit knowledge on projects are important attributes requiring structured and systematic handovers using shared norms and procedures and explicit knowledge transfer, else the same personnel are best retained for the short term benefit of the client and project. It may not be to the short-term business benefit but will be to the long-term business benefit through reputational and repeat business opportunities and accrued social capital (Smyth, 2015; cf. Gustafsson et al., 2010).

Project managers have increasingly found the project management is insufficient. For example, stage-gates have not been found to be useful for structuring activities (Collins et al., 2009). They need strong support from the corporate centre through integrated P^{3}M. Project managers are also finding that a network approach is required. For example, social network analysis is being used to coordinate and integrate activities (Pryke, 2012). It is the supply chain that requires integration against value criteria, rather than ease of management and risk minimization criteria (Smyth, 2015; see also for example Davies et al., 2007; Pryke 2012). Sydow and Windeler (1998) argue that network relationships are stable and provide the basis to develop key dynamic for integration and value delivery.

Relationship management has input in supply chains, integrating other providers (e.g. Davies, 2004; Davies et al., 2007). In many ways, competition is about the value proposition of entire supply chains competing against each other (Morledge et al., 2009; Pryke, 2012; cf. Gripsrud et al., 2006) and how well the main contractor plays the systems integrator role. Any shortfall in systems integration removes the customer or client a step from the value creation process. Distance tends to lead to value leakage. Conversely, serial transactions between the main contractor and suppliers give room for effective relationships to develop to improve systems integration (Martinsuo and Ahola, 2010).

Weak systems and relationship guidance lead to management leaving behaviour largely to individual responsibility. Individual behaviour will be guided by a range of stimuli including the systems and procedures in place and the norms of expectation that dominate in the firm. These are therefore partly perceived cognitively and partly sensed. There will be other factors from work, the work setting and external context, and personal influences in terms of experience and predispositions. These stimuli affect the feelings, the beliefs and attitude of the individual in ways that help to shape their behaviour (Spooncer, 1992). Most individuals seek some sense of significance from work as it constitutes a major part of their life and also in the context of relationship management feeds into personal identity. Four underpinning or core behavioural norms can be identified that are major drivers to seek a sense of significance and towards a personal identity. These are not necessarily positive, Table 7.1 setting out the norms and dominant behaviour types that emanate from the norms and go on to inform specific behaviour patterns.

While the weak systems between project businesses and projects have been raised, this affects individual behaviour, and thus the degree of compliance. Work connected to integrated teams, especially relational integration in value networks has highlighted the problems of fragmentation organizationally (e.g. Kumaraswamy and Rahman, 2006), but attention has been drawn to the need for common attitudes to support common practices for integration (Anvuur and Kumaraswamy, 2011). Baiden and Price (2011) have recently returned to the project assumption derived from other research that integrated teams lead to integrated delivery through collaborative working. They found a strong connection but not an automatic one. Effective teamwork comprised six key elements, namely, team identity, shared vision, communications, collaboration and participation, issue negotiation and resolution, reflection and self-assessment. This is the raw material of integration for teamwork. This makes a strong contribution to effective working to deliver integrated solutions, but there are other additional factors needed to ensure integrated project delivery. Behavioural issues are suggested as one, supported by the preceding analysis.

TABLE 7.1 Individual behaviour

Behavioural norms	Dominant behaviour types	Embedded behaviour	Ability/inability to cope
Pride	Unhealthy performance orientation	Over-estimation of self-importance, justified by seeking and securing above average achievement levels. High levels of self-control with high levels of accountability (ungrounded targets and overdependence upon incentives). Task drivers to fore.	Ability to perform based upon strong personal drivers. Arrogance leading to a tendency to break down under extreme pressure. Inability to effectively relate to others and set realistic targets for others.
	Blame	Over-estimation of self-importance, known to be undeserved but is justified by perceived poor performance of others. High propensity to be defensive and protective. Avoidance of taking responsibility where possible.	Fight of flight personal strategy and tactics. Tendency to point to and blame others. Ability to relate to and use others to provide a personal line of defence.
	Confidence	Realistic self-assessment. High levels of self-control with an outward focus. Concern for excellence achieved with healthy levels of performance.	Ability to behave proportionately to own and others strengths and weaknesses. Ability for good anticipation and proactive response.
	Humility	Realistic self-assessment and assessment of others. High levels of self-control with an outward focus. Concern for well-being of others.	Ability to behave proportionately to own and others strengths and weaknesses. Active and reactive to emergent events in positive ways. Ability to work with others and share praise and rewards.
Fear	Unhealthy appearance orientation	High concern to look good. People pleasers. Promote images and behaviours to look good and seek attention.	Concern for doing the wrong thing and not fitting in leads to adopting low risk strategy and tactics of inertia and minimalism.
	Shame	Double mindedness. Fear of being blamed. False humility.	Concern of not being good enough, being made the victim, leading to passivity, some levels of confusion and inaction.

Sources: Adapted and developed from McGee (1998); Smyth (2004).

Furthermore, attitudes and behaviour cannot be assumed to be aligned merely because they were on the previous project with the same client, contract type and team membership. People are like blocks of rubber, they change under pressure yet go back to their old shape once left alone (Markham, 1987; Smyth, 2000), hence the need for systems, including or especially a relationship management system. In the UK construction industry, at the time that collaborative working practices and integrated teams were at their height, it was reported that only 60 per cent of respondents said they worked in integrated teams and those that did were working for large project organizations (Constructing Excellence, 2009). Hartmann et al. (2010) on the Rijskwaterstaat (RWS) highways contract in the Netherlands indicated that organizations in the pilot project had difficulties moving beyond past behavioural patterns. Project members of the contractor continued to act passively and to wait for instructions, whereas RWS staff tended to dominate project meetings and to direct the work of the contractor. In a parallel UK highways project, contractual and relational capability building was inadequately addressed. Behavioural compliance to improve integration remains a neglected issue. Researchers and practitioners have placed more emphasis upon structures and structuring at an economic, contractual and management level rather than activity on the ground. This applies to interpersonal and organizational behaviour.

Conclusion

Organizational behaviour builds from the bottom-up to feed into the formation of norms and organizational culture (**Chapter 6**) to provide informal coherence that feeds into formal routines. The extent of coherence therefore supports systems and their integration for internal working and external working with other organizations in the network and in TMOs. The extent of coherence is not totally dependent upon formal systems as informal processes work very well where there is a stable environment. Project businesses do not exhibit these features and therefore investment into systems integration are important for successful integration for all project businesses and especially for those operating as systems integrators in the marketplace. Behaviour articulated through systems is part of the coherence for project businesses, yet is a neglected area.

Relationship management is one of the potential areas of systems investment and in this way, relationship management is both supporting integration across other subsystems but is part of systems integration itself. This begs the question as to why it is a neglected area of theorization and especially practice and whether this matters. It will not matter when and where clients are price driven. Price will undoubtedly remain a prime driver, yet increasing requirements and complexity of projects, especially in the upper market tiers of project size, are increasingly significant. The project businesses that are most attuned to how trends are developing and develop their project business capabilities accordingly will be best placed to compete and grow.

This chapter has addressed the behaviour and integration issues in terms of the way in which organizational behaviour and systems are articulated across project businesses and the implications for the business, suppliers and clients. It has considered the opportunities and constraints faced in interface management, especially systems for integration and organizational behaviour. It has further explored some of the strengths and weaknesses of management in managing behaviour and its consequences for developing integration. Short-term considerations are frequently to the fore, led by self-interest rather than the long-term interests of clients, stakeholders and, ironically, the project businesses.

The chapter has unpacked the integration issue and causes by incoherent behaviour both at an individual and organizational level. The theoretical promise of integration is frequently compromised or thwarted in practice. Existing patterns tend to be sustained as the outcomes serve to reinforce existing behaviour functionally providing the same assumptions and taken-for-granted thinking exists within management. The presence or absence of relationship management acts in the same way. Therefore, any claim that there may be a rapid shift in the way things are practiced is unlikely as there are a number of resistances and patterns of behaviour that act as constraints. However, there is evidence of changes in thinking and practices that have an earning logic and have yielded benefits behind and will sustain change among providers that have found market segments and are erecting barriers to entry (Smyth, 2015). This chapter has contributed to such thinking and future informed action by addressing the following theory–practice issues.

SI no. 1: *Organizational Behaviour* has provided a central theme and several types of behaviour have been addressed, including errant individual and non-compliant interpersonal behaviour, disparate individual and unaligned organizational behaviour with strategy and integration and selective behaviour that is compliant with systems and as part of relationship systems.

SI no. 2: *Relationship Management Theory* has been addressed as a means to support systems integration, yet as part of systems and hence systems integration for adding value in project delivery.

SIs no. 4 and **5:** *Conceptual and Applied Hierarchical* and *Horizontal Integration* has been indirectly considered as integrated systems operate in both directions. Relationship management helps to link the two dimensions, especially behaviour between the programme and project management levels.

SI no. 6: *The Project Preoccupation,* especially at the execution stage, at the expense of other management considerations is unsustainable once behaviours and relationships are taken seriously as key dimensions of project management and delivering with a service focus.

SI no. 9: *Systems Integration* occurs through well-designed and articulated systems, but their effectiveness is dependent upon behaviour patterns and action that are aligned with the strategies and systems. Embedding aligned social behaviour is therefore a management issue that goes beyond developing structures and individuals taking responsibility.

SI no. 10: _Market Functioning_ is also a central feature of this chapter. While the chapter has not concentrated on some of the key debates of integration around project and organizational capabilities (Davies and Brady, 2000; Brady and Davies, 2004), it has pointed to the role of behaviour as an important part feeding into that picture.

The main contribution has been to begin to examine behaviour at a finer grain of analysis than is normally carried out for projects and project businesses. This has been conducted in ways that avoid formulaic models, such as game theory, where rules are conceptualized for analysis rather than necessarily being an accurate reflection of reality. In addition, organizational behaviour as an interface with systems integration has begun to be developed.

There are a number of areas deserving further investigation, including:

A. The extent of diverse behaviour among TMO members and how these form routines at a detailed level, particularly the extent of divergent behaviour among project team members and how these constrain the formation of effective norms and routines.
B. The role of the main contractor or systems integrator in the TMO for setting norms, defining systems and mechanisms of integration, and the role of experienced project managers in facilitating or blocking appropriate behaviour.
C. The extent to which the systems integrator project business defines and establishes systems with interfaces to accommodate variety and diversity of other organizational systems interfaces within the supply chain and among other TMO membership.
D. The role of leadership in shaping organization behaviour at the project level, focusing functional and dysfunctional roles and the correspondence of these – whether strengths have corresponding weaknesses and vice versa.

There are several areas pertinent for management practice:

1. Invest in a relationship management system that is linked to and helps integrate other systems.
2. Develop a relationship management system aligned to a theoretical and conceptual approach, such as relational contracting, relationship management from relationship marketing, emotional intelligence, trust management, organizational culture and behaviour.
3. Establish protocols for the introduction and related negotiation to systematically establish conceptual principles, norms and procedures for relationship management into a TMO upon formation.
4. Management to address behaviour and the establishment of coherence in organizational behaviour in project businesses and on projects.
5. Management to incorporate relationship management as a system into organizational behaviour and as a part of systems integration.

6. Develop programmes and codes of behavioural compliance that are aligned to strategy with interfaces for internal and external integration.

This chapter has considered organizational behaviour and systems integration. One important component of effectiveness in these areas is a specific type of organizational behaviour, namely decision-making. It is often singled out as a separate topic due to its significance in business and for project businesses. As an important part of organizational behaviour, it provides the focus for the next chapter.

8

PROJECT BUSINESS AND PROJECT DECISION-MAKING

Introduction

One particular type of organizational behaviour is decision-making. Decisions are the means to translate ideas and directions into applied processes and actions. Decisions aim to improve performance from the strategic board level down to operational levels. Decisions are therefore part of the formal routines of systems and procedures. They are taken using available information and as events unfold, driven by both management needs and operational timeframes. As such, they are known to be needed, planned in advance, made and then implemented. Yet, manifested risks and emergent requirements are unknown in advance, decisions needing to be taken in reaction to events in which emergent problems are embedded.

Decision-makers are managers. They may act as autonomous agents or in groups within complex organizational systems and sets of procedures. Meetings are frequently forum for decision-making. Some decisions are primarily strategic, others tactical with strategic implications, for example project feedback loops to reproduce and enhance strategy and system design. Other decisions are tactical and operational, while many are linked to issues of accountability, legitimacy of the project, and the balance of power, legal and institutional requirements. Each has an important role, but the combined effect can be to shift the project management horizon away from the main purposes of delivering project benefits within time–cost–quality/ scope towards the management means rather than the end.

Therefore, plenty of scope arises to explore decision-making in project environments, which will be carried out with the following in mind:

A. The way in which decision-making is informed by and conducted across project businesses and for projects.

B. The opportunities and constraints faced by management from organizational behaviour and the impact upon decision-making, including relationship management at both scales.
C. The strengths and weaknesses of management in decision-making and the effects on the project business.

The chapter communicates the complex issues residing from organizational behaviour to decision-making and the extent to which this is well managed in the light of previous chapters and the focus upon relationship management. Further, decision-making is nested in procedural and behavioural issues affected by individual agency, especially where project management is conducted in the absence of or separately from a relationship management system.

Those making decisions, whether as individuals or teams, are accountable through the coordinating methods and procedures, typically involving recorded documentation. The criteria used in taking decisions, how these were applied is opaque beyond the decision-making unit (DMU). It has been noted that traditional notions of managerial control are eroded in this way and indeed are or can be somewhat illusory (Kahneman and Lovallo, 1993).

Decision-making in theory and practice

Decisions are taken at all business levels from strategy to operational levels. DMUs may have constant or stable membership according to role, some changing membership, for example over a project lifecycle. The precise membership for a type of decision-making meeting may change over time. A project DMU may include some senior management with responsibilities for the project within the 'corporate centre' both on the project business side and among within the owner and sponsor roles within the client body. Therefore, the DMU is not synonymous with the project temporary multi-organizational project team (TMO), nor synonymous with the project coalition (Winch, 2002). This is depicted in Figure 3.7. In Figure 8.1, membership is added, each role being represented by a solid circle. It can be seen that some DMU members are located in the 'corporate centre' of the project business, while others are located in the project team and are DMU members.

There are a number of ways to cut the conceptual cake for decision-making. Broadly, there are two main dimensions of consideration:

1. Rational-intuitive dimension:

    a. Rational and cognitive process of expressing or determining outcome preferences, dependent upon information availability;
    b. Subjective and intuitive process of assessment and judgment to reach outcomes that uses information, experience, organizational norms, individual values and beliefs.

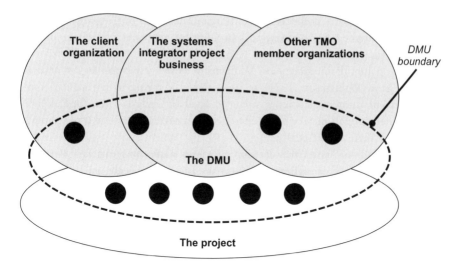

FIGURE 8.1   The project decision-making unit membership

2.   Causal dimension:

   a.   Decisions largely made deductively, rationally and/or intuitively, which
        are generally communicated and implemented top-down, coming from a
        single decision-maker or group;
   b.   Decisions largely made inductively from information and/or judgment in
        context and largely made in groups and teams.

Rational approaches to decision-making

Decisions try to determine direction and shape activities. The deliberate intent
and enactment derived from managerial and organizational cognition for rational
decision-making relates to the project management information approach
(Winch, 2002). Economics, behavioural economics and game theory stress
rationality. Particular types of decision-making or sets of decisions occur around
negotiation and bargaining in the market, particularly pertaining to the allocation of costs. This is also referred to as haggling in the economics literature,
especially regarding transaction cost analysis (TCA). Economics and game theory
empirical analysis is idealized, based upon simplified assumptions, but the
assumption that rationality is pervasive is rarely suspended. Incomplete contracts
and information asymmetry are two elements retrospectively introduced where
assumptions of availability and completeness of information are unsustainable
(cf. Williamson, 1975; Milgrom and Roberts, 1992). The Nash bargaining
matrix – win-win, win-lose, lose-win and lose-lose outcomes – introduced
game theory, but TCA tends to conflate the individual and the individual
organization in analysis. As Gibbons (2010; cf. Cyert and March, 1992) points

out, people have goals, collectivities and organizations do not, leading to defective analysis applied to organizations. In addition, rent-seeking behaviour can lead to inefficient outcomes on the terms of the TCA and game theorization. Recognizing inbuilt inefficiencies, Williamson noted it persists as a source of financial gain (Williamson, 1971) as an example of trying to rationalize competing sets of interest at a more nuanced level of analysis. The fundamental issues of determination around limited sets of criteria is to make the models work rather than reality persist.

Raiffa (1968) proposed the decision processes comprises four key elements, namely the degree of centralization, legitimacy and trust, diversity of information sources used, and the speed in reaching conclusion and taking actions. There is a need to rationally manage uncertainty by gathering information, assessing the viable options, applying experimentation, and action, identifying the number of possible events occurring, their chronological arrangement in regard to the information and choices, assessing the possible consequences of each alternative option, and risk assessment that particular uncertain events will incur. At the project level, constancy or purpose is important, Prasad (1996) finding that collaboration, commitment, communication, compromise, consensus and continuous improvement to be necessary ingredients.

These are based upon a behavioural approach to rational choice (Simon, 1955). Raiffa acknowledges, for example, that there is need to see how people actually behave rather than the normative view of how they *ought* to behave. This leads to the identification of biases and errors in decision-making, which are a departure from the rational outcome. This raises the question as to what leads to the biases and how misjudgments are made? Bounded rationality restricts decision-makers' effectiveness (Simon, 1955, 1979), which includes recognizing psychological limits and expressing subjective assessments. The result is that decision-makers draw upon affective interpretations and perceptions derived from culture, its norms and other contextual factors. Kahneman and Tversky (1986) claimed linearly derived single choices could not be assumed as pervasive and that variability in preferences prevails in practice. Tversky and Kahneman (1974) therefore developed the rational choice model further to include heuristics using 'rules of thumb' to make judgments under uncertainty. This brings order where there is uncertainty and complexity. They and others identified a number of heuristic principles that decision-makers and decision-making bodies rely upon to reduce task complexity and simplify decision-making:

1. Availability, representative and confirmation heuristics (Tversky and Kahneman, 1974) – probability assessments and assessments confirming biases with decision-makers tending to give extra weight to small data sets and prominent information, anchored to initial perceptions framed within the bounds of rationality;
2. Congruence heuristics (Baron et al., 1988) – reliance upon tried and tested solutions;

3. Positive test strategy (Klayman and Ha, 1987) – a type of hypothesis testing and confirmation bias, and anchoring decisions in these biases despite contrary information;
4. Prototype heuristics (Kahneman, 2003) – harnessing a systematic approach for innovative substitution and development;
5. Social heuristics (Beamish and Biggart, 2012) – a normative approach to resolve practical problems in social and institutional settings.

Heuristics are informed by prevailing norms, which provide part of the basis for decision-making. Heuristics try to fill the gap between decisions and values informed by experience, thus recognizing further levels of uncertainty and complexity to decision problems, processes and practice. This edges the analysis further from a purely rational and cognitive approach to reliance upon interpretation based upon intuition and affective learning. Social heuristics is a collective sense-making device and a precept of judgment (Beamish and Biggart, 2012). Heuristics can be applied at the organizational level (Scott, 2012). While sense making involves a degree of rational processing, there is typically a high degree of interpretation involved, arising from the organizational norms, individual experience and disposition. This shifts the ground substantially away from the rationalistic viewpoint towards the subjective approach at both the personal and organizational level of addressing decision-making. Interpretation and sense making may occur at the DMU level, especially affected by the context, norms and shared values, at meetings of DMU members where a mix of organizational and personal sense making is applied according to weighted power from the hierarchy and roles.

The analysis accords with the critique of rational decisional decision-making on its own terms, emanating for example from March and Simon (1958), Klein and Meckling (1958), Tversky and Kahneman (1974) and Cyert and March (1992) and extends beyond this to embrace interpretative criteria applied in practice, which are widely recognized when addressing particularly thorny issues, such as *wicked problems* that are unresolvable through the application of logic and rationality alone (Rittel and Webber, 1973) and unknown unknowns called *unk unks* (Wideman, 1992) that go beyond the contextual boundaries and the cognitive realm at any one time (Winch, 2010). Rational decision-making is rendered impotent in these instances.

Subjective approaches to decision-making

Others have developed approaches to decision-making, which place emphasis upon subjectivity and intuitive assessments. Intuitive assessments and evaluation draws upon values and beliefs of the individual, and taken-for-granted thinking and habits in the organization. The matters for decision and the context are weighed up utilizing these influential factors, yet they are seldom articulated, and there may be low levels of awareness of their influence among practitioners.

Weick (1995: 635) developed the term and concept of *sense making* where *reality is an ongoing accomplishment that emerges from efforts to create order*. Sense making is helpful where there is a lack of information and uncertainty and is even more helpful where there is ambiguity, that is where there is sufficient information to understand the options but yet insufficient to make decisions (Pich et al., 2002; Ward and Chapman, 2003; Hällgren and Maaninen-Olsson, 2005). Sense has to be made of the information and a choice made as to a preferred path. Choices and outcomes are also informed by explicit factors such as organizational strategy or project goals, project risk and learning, the behavioural preference of individuals. Formal and informal team relationships help bridge the intuitive and cognitive, and a relationship management approach helps improve the ability to make effective judgments.

Decision-making processes are described as an activity to set and regulate norms (Vickers, 1965), informed by other individual and organizational norms and procedures. Applying tacit knowledge, underlying assumptions and norms in sense making to establish the processes and outcomes demonstrate the limits to known artifacts and processes (Weick, 1995; Winch and Maytorena, 2011). Another way of looking at sense making is through the lens of complexity. Sense making is a device to simplify the complex world or bundle complexity into sets of general categories and rules of thumb. Interpreting complexity also involves ambiguity. Different individual actors will have different perspectives on the complex issues, informed by the disciplines and dispositions of those involved. The different disciplines add a further layer of criticism to the dominance of rationality because the professional and disciplinary domains of expertise induce a contested decision-making arena. Yet decision-making involving experts is effective, albeit bounded by discipline and experience. Effectiveness arises from collective or project team judgments on grounds that the combined expertise extends beyond the discipline boundaries (Volker, 2010).

Retrospectively interpretative decision-making may not always be effective. Subsequently, decision-making processes can be used to disguise this type of 'failure' in order to protect project legitimacy. Accountability mechanisms can also be subverted to legalistically serve legitimation, for example stage gate approvals, inspections and surveillance, sometimes litigation and arbitration with the results presented in ways to reinforce legitimacy (e.g. Clegg et al., 2002).

Decisions are needed when the next action is neither obvious nor automatic. Ambiguity and complexity provide amplified examples of these conditions. These types of decision, where interpretation is needed are frequently reliant upon inductive analysis. Information emerges, bringing sufficient information to the fore to apply other sense-making criteria to arrive at an informed, yet subjective, judgment.

Deductive and inductive approaches to decision-making

Decisions are not always deduced from the purpose of the project – delivery of a bundle of valued benefits. The end is frequently replaced by the means, which comes to act as the surrogate for the benefits. This is embodied legally in the contract and in project management by time, cost and quality. Sometimes, time, cost, quality issues are themselves displaced in decision-making at two levels: (i) internally by the reproduction of power relations, short-term financial issues, project risk, and systems and procedures of accountability (cf. Tansey, 2004; Andersen, 2013) and (ii) externally by the legitimacy of the project derived from political and wider institutional considerations (cf. Flyvbjerg et al., 2003).

Decision-making in traditional organizations is mostly deductive and top-down, made by individuals or executive groups. Project management methodologies are deductive artifacts of guidance as are many decisions guided by the tools and techniques of project management. They work well where there is a reasonable degree of routinization, but tend to be less relevant or even break down where uniqueness and issues of information availability prevail. They embody a rational approach, allowing limited room for manoeuvre and sense making. Hierarchy and market solutions cannot be relied upon to induce cooperation and agreement mechanisms (Söderlund, 2011b). At a detailed level, it has been found that individuals tend to take a strategic perspective in arriving at decisions, whereas teams assess in the context of the physical and social spaces in which they operate (Schepers et al., 2011). Strategic decision-makers align the project business with its environment, informed by theories, concepts and models that most closely conform to their worldviews and ideologies (Pels and Saren, 2005). The project director–project manager relationship is critical (Merrow, 2011). Therefore, leaders who are most likely to be individual decision-makers or paired in a dyad will probably apply a great deal of sense-making skills for scanning and evaluating their environment to inform decisions. This comprises high degrees of intuitive assessment and strategic judgment (cf. **Chapter 7**).

Aesthetic leadership and decision-making combines sensory knowledge and felt meaning, thus feeling and intuition with procedural, informative decision-making (e.g. Welsch, 1996; Katz-Buonincontro, 2011; cf. Goffman, 1959). The roots are in the work of Plato and Kant. Similarly, transformative leadership seen through the lens of emotional intelligence tries to harness emotions to improve leadership and decision-making, but it is also about engagement with emotions in decision-making (e.g. Goleman, 1998b; Goleman et al., 2002). 'Gut feelings' is a colloquial term suggesting the interrelationship between feeling and physical self that refers to intuitive acts of decision-making, especially concerning moral judgments and ethical assessments in turbulent organizational environments. However, less is known about actual characteristics of decision-making behaviour itself and perceptions that guide particular choices or decisions in project businesses and project management.

There has been greater decentralization of decision-making (Brown and Eisenhardt, 1998). While top-down deductive decisions help bring certainty, the basis upon which they are made in projects may be inappropriate as many issues require inductive development and problem solving in-situ, the solutions being aligned with the project strategy, processes and benefits delivery as part of the outworking. Brady et al. (2012) argue that a trial-and-error approach works well where time is critical, citing the studies on T5 at London Heathrow Airport as evidence (e.g. Davies et al., 2009; Brady and Davies, 2010). Brady et al. (2012) argue scant attention has been given to the space between rational and soft decision-making. Christensen and Kreiner argued that project managers should embrace uncertainty rather than try to fight it (cited in Hällgren et al., 2012).

Andersen has gone a step further in the management literature on the legitimacy front, arguing that in practice a considerable amount of effort is put into making decisions in ways to look as if these are made in response to events and context, whereas a considerable amount is geared to predispositions and experiential comfort zones (Andersen, 2013). This type of interpretation can erode legitimacy in the broader context, especially externally, because it can compromise project benefits to serve personal comfort zones and career ambitions. Internally, this type of decision-making is a ritual of legitimacy to fit accountability criteria – a 'tick box' exercise. Another part of the picture is based upon explicit and tacit criteria that take into account a range of emotional and behavioural criteria at group and team levels. Emotional intelligence tries to bring the intuitive and cognitive together to improve self and group management (Druskat and Wolff, 2001; Druskat and Druskat, 2006; **Chapter 4**). Emotional intelligence can be harnessed for good or bad. It depends upon individual and group intent. The decision-making process as a ritual is most obvious when people come out of a meeting and then realize nothing was decided. This is termed *non-decision-making* (Bachrach and Baratz, 1973). This occurs where key DMU members do not want decisions made that might threaten their self-interest, for example in cliques, enclaves and for protecting internal empires. It also occurs where the aim is to exclude the interests of external stakeholders. Non-decision-making has a connection with heuristics whereby complexity and biases lead to an overestimation or underestimation of the decision-making process (cf. Kahneman and Frederick, 2002; Kahneman, 2003) whereby the outcome or inaction is or maybe out of proportion to the reality and limits scope the actual decision-making to 'safe' issues, thus manipulating the institutional outcome (Bachrach and Baratz, 1973). In other words, biases emanating from the application of heuristics lead to skewed or deceptive interpretations of conditions.

Skewed sense making, manipulation and outright deception occur on a continuum of the *mobilization of bias*. The bias continuum stretches from unintended bias, which is usually perceived retrospectively, to a more systematic mobilization that crosses ethical boundaries and may end up as infringing professional ethical standards and ultimately enters the criminal realm of fraud and corruption. The mobilization of bias seldom arises as a one-off event, but tends to incrementally be introduced so that DMU members come to normalize and legitimize the decision-making thinking and behaviour to support the bias. This is a type of manipulative sense making. Subjective decisions are more difficult to challenge because DMU members may be uncertain of their scope for action and appropriateness, especially over time as any members challenging decisions can be perceived as difficult and become marginalized. It is also difficult where bias moves to the extremes and DMU members retrospectively have been drawn so far, but wonder whether it is possible to make a challenge at a late stage, for example when crossing the line between lawful and unlawful activity. The most common form of unintended bias resides at the other end of the continuum. This is legalism and moralism, whereby excessive adherence to bureaucratic rules and procedures is constraining, raising cost and tending to lead to passivity and amoralism.

Relationship norms and explicit relationship principles provide a systematic means to support decision-making to guide behaviour and action. A relationship management system and/or behavioural programme can address the types of decision-making issues set out.

Relationship management in decision-making

Decision-making typically involves an intensification of interpersonal and social interaction. There are meeting and decision-making protocols in most organizations, mostly about structuring meetings and recording the events and decisions taken. Relationship management and associated behaviour can govern protocols. Relationships and relationship management provide means for effective outcomes. The advantage of underpinning relationship management principles is twofold. First, some of the principles, especially linked to informal routines, provide an additional set of norms against which individuals and groups can undertake sense making and come to judgments. Second, principles embodied in a relationship management system provide explicit guidance about coming to a decision and will inform the sense making. In this way, it adds an indirect set of rationality, not because further information is provided to directly make a rational decision, but because the relationships add a level of certainty. In this way relationship management is an additional source of information that provides confidence and reduces relational risk (Smyth and Thompson, 2005; cf. Winch, 2002).

Diverse teams may bring different angles to decision-making, yet this does not imply non-compliance and a lack of trust, indeed the opposite where there is a high propensity to trust (Bernerth and Walker, 2009). Decision-making meetings can be guided by behavioural codes of conduct. There is a plethora of guidance to be drawn upon from listening skills and reflection, reflective practice to enhance learning, emotional stock taking and ensuring all present have had ample opportunity to speak and contribute their expertise. Developing this point, 2–3 people make between 70–86 per cent of the total contribution in meetings (Shaw, 1981; **Chapter 4**). There are some good reasons for this but there are dysfunctional aspects. There is a tendency to continue on the same decision-making path even where bias is apparent and new information refutes or contradicts previous information (Whyte and Levitt, 2011). Diversity of contributions aids sense making and judgments, challenges biased selection of information and the incremental mobilization of bias. Failure to have balanced contributions can also lead to non-decision-making (Bachrach and Baratz, 1973). Passivity or silence cannot always be assumed to confer agreement with a dominant view (cf. Gilligan, 1982). The mobilization of bias, bullying and forms of silent control (Chapter 6) can all lead to abstinence among DMU members. Therefore norms of decision-making meetings can be developed to encourage reflective practice, for example the chair of the meeting asking those who are saying little or nothing whether they have other information or perspectives to contribute. This may be perceived as inefficiency in running meetings, but it is more effective and better decisions can save consequential costs flowing from marred decisions. Another example would be to consider what are the criteria for each decision and record these.

Having an outward focus, or more specifically a client and service focus, is not merely an attitude but an organizational norm once embedded into thinking. Having an outward focus facilitates good decision-making (Kahneman and Lovallo, 1993). Further, framing the context of decision-making within relationship management systems and procedures improves decision-making. Fostering and enabling engagement also help to build social and organizational identity. Heuristics can be built upon and build social capital.

TMOs are social spaces of high interdependencies that require rapid sense making and establishment of decision-making norms. They require intensive flows of rich and thick information and knowledge transfer. This cannot be established through decision-making meetings alone, and other fora are necessary for interchange, exchange and interplay. This has been described in project terms of establishing ground for commonality, information and knowledge trading zones, tacit knowledge sharing, co-location and studio-type environments (e.g. Bechky, 2006; Lindkvist, 2011; Smyth and Kioussi, 2011a; Kelly et al., 2013). Project managers maintain balance and retain commitment (cf. Jones et al., 2011). They are part of the TMO, yet their role in the broader DMU that straddles the project and the corporate centre (see Chapter 8) is significant in facilitating an outward focus and applying relationship management principles developed as an organizational capability by the project business.

Project personnel like to participate in decision-making. They often have freedom in controlling work processes (Bredin and Söderlund, 2011), but this relative autonomy does not always work to the advantage of clients, employer or other stakeholders (Wells and Smyth, 2011, Smyth, 2015; **Chapter 6**). Decentralized decision-making (Brown and Eisenhardt, 1998) and empowerment in project environments (Greasley et al., 2005; Tuuli and Rowlinson, 2010) helps interface management to resolve conflicts and misunderstandings (Merrow, 2011). Vaagaasar (2011) found project managers showed some reluctance to take decisions, deferring to other key decision-makers. Group decision-making may be more reassuring, yet requires investigation. Participative decision-making is important for trust building (Dirks and Ferrin, 2002), which lowers negotiation costs (Zaheer et al., 1998), however wider participation may have increased costs compared to other decision-making formats, which may also explain why little evidence is found to support the claim for lower costs. A high degree of self-determination (Spreitzer and Quinn, 2001) may result in misalignment with strategy and non-compliance with organizational norms. Yet large numbers are likely to increase bureaucracy and behavioural legalism in decision-making.

Decision-making and negotiation

A particular type of decision-making is seeking an agreement through bargaining and negotiation. The need to negotiate and bargain implies some misalignment, yet seeks to find some common ground or compromise that is acceptable or satisfactory. The skill is being able to assess what the zone of potential agreement is and within the range of options for securing the best agreement for the organization the negotiator is representing. This is depicted in Figure 8.2. Where the negotiations fall within the zone, there is scope for a collaborative outworking, especially where there are aligned organizational cultures and behaviour (Henisz et al., 2012). Negotiations do continue even where the parties are not within the bargaining zone. Should the negotiator be a skillful negotiator, using tactics of driving a hard bargain, manipulation, aggressive bullying, they may be successful in securing an agreement, but an agreement where the other party has regrets, a win-lose outcome in game theory terms. There may be relationship consequences and associated transaction costs that are incurred during the remainder of the project lifecycle. It will also damage reputation and the potential for working together again, including repeat business. Ideally both parties need to sense they have secured a reasonable or advantageous agreement, a win-win outcome within the acceptable range.

The application of emotional intelligence and dyadic trust management can assist in the context of developing win-win negotiations. Where the signs are that such an outcome cannot be achieved a useful tactic is to *grow the pie* (Kurtzberg and Medvec, 1999). This can be a matter of widening the scope of negotiations to gain sufficient trade-off content. This has some yet limited scope. A productive stance is to add value in other ways, say, the supplier staying firm on key issues but adding something else of value to the client. This is easiest where the project business has developed capabilities of differentiation. The cost of mobilizing an existing yet differential capability to add value is less than constructing a new set of resources or shaving some area of cost to an unreasonable level.

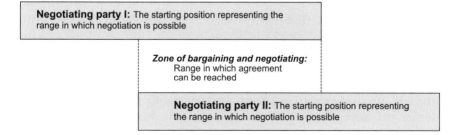

FIGURE 8.2   The zone of bargaining and negotiation

Decision-makers do not value the chance of future gains as highly as the chance to reduce future losses (Kahneman and Tversky, 1979), therefore in the negotiation context, one perceived path is to try to force the hand of the other party or be defensive rather than grow the pie. Therefore growing the pie can be a relationship-related principle in negotiation. In negotiation terms, this relates to the *best alternative to negotiated agreement* or BATNA, that is no agreement (Fisher and Ury, 1981). No agreement is psychologically bad for the negotiators. They will feel they have failed and may be told so on reporting back to their line management. The BATNA may be perceived as better than a compromised agreement that one party perceives they have lost or even that both parties have lost – a lose-lose outcome where both parties have strayed from the zone of bargaining and negotiation (Figure 8.2). The BATNA may be avoided by growing the pie. Market and transactional rigidities can be ameliorated through growing the pie. However, negotiating skill sets can induce new types of behavioural rigidities. For example, strong relationship commitment among team members can lead to the context being influential to the extent that strategic issues are overlooked (cf. Schepers et al., 2011). Strong relationships with high commitment levels are better able to tolerate errors and are more forgiving about transgressions (Jones et al., 2011).

In negotiation, the desire to preserve a relationship can be causal in compromise, being passive and loss of voice. Thus, one party may choose to be silent due to power being exerted by the other party or the perceived short term need to compromise the relationship in the interest of preserving it long-term. There is a paradox. On the one hand, raising an issue might prove to invoke adversarial behaviour in the other party, while the act of being silent and yielding to a compromise in the agreement may also compromise or diminish the relationship – a psychological issue in the ethics of care (Gilligan, 1982).

Conclusion

This chapter has considered decision-making. Norms and behaviour influence the outcomes of decisions and the management of relationships does or can have a significant mediating effect of enhancing alignment and overcoming dysfunctional attributes of decision-making. Rational and subjective approaches have been reviewed for the DMU and meetings at business and project levels and articulate the way that events are shaped. The context of relationships and their management, behavioural programmes and codes of conduct, linked to culture and norms, leadership and group emotional intelligence have been briefly reviewed. This has pointed to the scant amount of research and understanding of the effects of decision-making in the MoP in project management research.

An agenda has been scoped, covering the way in which decision-making is both informed and conducted across project businesses and for projects, and the opportunities and constraints faced by management at the interface of organizational behaviour and decision-making, particularly in reference to relationship management. The complexity organizational behaviour and its effects upon decision-making and the extent to which this is well-managed in the light of previous chapters has provided the primary focus. Decision-making nested in procedural and behavioural issues, especially within projects and project management is thus impoverished, especially when the analysis here is coupled with the weak systems operating in many project businesses, especially with the project interface.

A number of theory–practice issues have therefore been addressed out of the ten presented in **Chapter 1**. The issues addressed are summarized below:

SI no. 1: *Organizational Behaviour* at the micro level of decision-making is frequently considered in terms of rational models that influence practice too and economic and game theoretic propositions. These perspectives are useful, yet depict a limited range of process as conducted in practice. Therefore interpretative approaches with a subjective and emotional content have also been addressed, which provide the raw material for judgments and decisions derived from organizational norms, experience and affective learning and can further be enhanced applying relationship management principles to overcome practices such as the mobilization of bias. This offers a more comprehensive approach towards *integrated management.*

SI no. 2: *Relationship Management Theory* is useful in developing norms, addressing behavioural biases. It also helps create awareness that at one level introduces a greater level of cognition into sense making and to inform interpretative assessments. The rationality of complete information is an ideal that is too costly even if thought possible, thus reliance upon subjectivity and intuition or 'gut feel' will continue to take a prominent place with which relationship management supports the induction of effective outcomes. How relationship management theory is applied cannot be determined in advance as this is organizationally context specific.

SI no. 3: *Socio-psychological Issues* have been raised in several forms from heuristics, social heuristics, sense making and intuitive behaviour and judgment. It was stated at the outset in **Chapter 1** that people do not behave rationally all the time, and this chapter has built upon this by analyzing decision-making to help address the issues for practice. The role and functioning of relationships has remained underplayed in these contexts in research and practice.

SI no. 5: *Conceptual and Applied Horizontal Integration* has not provided a major theme of the chapter. Two points are brought out here. Decisions at the strategic front-end are most critical to setting up a project to achieve a successful outcome. During execution, the extent of systematic procedures and behaviour between the organization and TMO has been raised as having consequences over project lifecycles for both projects and the project organization.

SI no. 10: *Market Functioning* has not overtly been addressed, but the analysis provided through this chapter has indirectly reinforced the substantive shortcoming of structural and governance solutions to market operation in the project business.

The main contribution has to bring two areas of analysis together – relationship management and decision-making through the behavioural issues evident on the ground. Organizational behaviour and decision-making within it remains an under-developed research area with project management setting the stage for further research. There are several main *recommendations* for research therefore that flow from the analysis regarding project businesses and projects:

A. Attention should be given to two distinct areas of decision-making and the comparison between them:

    a. The project business, especially the programme level and the project level as to how their attributes differ, the significance of behavioural issues in decision outcomes;

    b. The strategic front-end and execution as to how their significance differs and whether behavioural characteristics differ and if so, why.

B. The limits of rational decision-making in project decision-making, including specifically in bargaining and negotiation contexts require further examination.

C. Investigation as to how norms inform decisions, how heuristics are formed and applied, how sense making is conducted around and during decision-making processes.

D. Investigation into the mobilization of bias and the extent of non-decision-making in project contexts.

There are several main recommendations for practice that flow from the analysis in this chapter:

1. Identify and set criteria for decisions ahead of discussion of the detailed issues to help make explicit and improve awareness the norms and issues informing interpretation, which will also indirectly address issues of bias, its mobilization and non-decision-making issues, permitting challenges to this type of thinking and related subversive norms before moving to decisions.

2. Differentiate between decision-making criteria of *means* – project management tools and techniques, time–cost–quality issues – and *end* – value issues of requirements met, benefits delivered and potential impact in use.

3. Introduce explicit norms and behavioural codes pertaining to decision-making. These may echo more general codes, yet are made more specific and 'translated' into the specificity of this behavioural context.

In summary, decision-making remains an area requiring further detailed investigation and analysis and further development on the ground. Relationship management and related norms and behaviour provide one fruitful way of progressing this significant area for research and practice. Many decision-making processes are perceived to be driven by rational issues of efficiency – an important area of consideration and pervading how meetings are managed, especially time managed – yet biases, rituals of non-decision-making and legitimizing macro-level accountability and micro-level self-interest that are unaligned with the project and client issues are major sources of inefficiency. Effectiveness is of equal importance driven by strategic project goals and organizational purpose. Detailed attention needs to be given to this because this is a key area of 'soft' management. As such, decision-making is a key part of service provision and derived service experience. It is also a forum for initiating the co-creation of value – not only a key source of value provision but also a major source for adding value. Service provision is a further significant topic. Relationship management is one primary means to enhance service provision. Therefore, service provision provides the focus for the next chapter.

9

TECHNICAL AND TECHNOLOGICAL TASK MANAGEMENT AND SERVICE PROVISION

Introduction

Project management has its operational roots in technology, forms of engineering and technical expertise, sometimes supported by institutes. The management of projects (MoP) also encompasses the strategic front-end, which is rooted in broader management issues. Yet the dominant belief system is technical and technological. There are project sectors located at the 'softer' end, and some do not necessarily see themselves as managing projects, for example events management, media campaigns, film making. Drilling down into project management using the tools and techniques to regulate time–cost–quality/scope leads to a focus upon *task management,* that is, 'getting the job done'. In other words, the focus tends to be the micro-level and less the wider implications, for example programme management, the project business portfolio and clients. The structuring of most project businesses echoes this perspective whereby the project is the primary or sole unit of consideration, and indeed, serves to reinforce the perspective (see also **Chapters 1** and **2**).

There is an incremental and increasing appreciation of a wider range of management factors in MoP, echoed in the growth of management-related, socio-psychological, economic and legal-based research and practice. The expansion of work and selective practice around capability development and new service models have been areas of rapid research growth, which are used to justify and articulate incremental change that has taken place, and through improved awareness begun to generate further management change. This shift is evident in the research in multiple forms, for example in extending the scope of the discipline (e.g. Morris and Hough, 1987; Morris, 1994), the waves of disciplinary foci (e.g. Morris et al., 2011; Morris and Geraldi, 2011), and theoretical approaches (e.g. Winch, 2002; Pryke and Smyth, 2006; Turner, 2006). Capability development (e.g. Davies and Brady, 2000; Brady and Davies, 2004) including partnering (e.g. Bresnen and Marshall, 2000), learning and knowledge management (e.g. Bresnen et al., 2004) are examples of conceptually pushing out the boundaries.

Relationship management is a 'soft' management issue, indeed a particular capability (**Chapter 3**). The derived experience from relationship management in the market is enhanced integration and service provision. Relationship management also affects technical content in two ways. First, quality is enhanced and hence value has been added. Second, relationship management has the potential to lever enhanced technical value from other sources through in supply chain management. Relationships management facilitates direct engagement with the client through collaborative working to co-create value inputs into the project that neither party could have achieved upon their own – the project business understanding and responding to client (latent) needs and the client understanding the options and potential. The co-creation at an applied level arises through joint innovation, creativity and problem solving.

Relationship management that is inter-organizational aims to bring together the actors or parties into close association, more so than relational contracting is able to do in practice (**Chapters 2** and **3**). The social distance between customer and supplier is perceived in neoclassical economic theory to emphasize the divide as essential (Walras, 1926; cf. Vargo and Lusch, 2008). Technical and technological tasks are conceptually firmly rooted in the production orientation, and production is perceptually separated from the demand side. In practice, the producer works, can or does work *with the consumer* and with *the consumer in mind*. For example, entertainers work *with the audience* and project managers undertake joint problem solving on a project *with the owner*, and the ergonomic design of a car or IT software package is or should be undertaken *with the user in mind*. Similarly, the consumer works *with the producers* to produce value, for example reflective feedback on a concept design, or a reader imagining the characters, scenes and interpreting a book, and the end user of an office finding the space can be used to effect in ways not originally specified or imagined.

This type of service provision is in line with recent theoretical developments, which conceives all activity as service provision (e.g. Vargo and Lusch, 2004, 2008; Prahalad and Ramaswamy, 2004). Production generates products that render services to the buyer, and many products are bundled into related service packages, such as aircraft production with associated maintenance, PFI and PPP-type projects (where PFI stands for project finance initiative and PPP for public private partnerships) with associated operational and facilities management services. In complex business-to-business (B2B) settings, co-creation occurs in two ways: (i) technical development and the service experience of working together to add value during execution, (ii) the impact of the project in use, the service being the flow of benefits. Relationship management enhances the service provision and helps to improve and maintain the follow of benefits in use.

These observations and trends in service provision are located in a much greater picture of the rapid development of services of recent decades. Services rose from providing 48.8 per cent of employment in 1965 across the ten leading nations to 73.7 per cent by 2005, a rise of nearly 25 per cent. According to subsequent research on how to view service provision, this would have been an understatement and service content continues to grow (Vargo and Lusch, 2004; Wölfl, 2005). Services now account for over 70 per cent of gross national product (GNP) in developed nations (Ostrom et al., 2010). Services are usually time-bound processes (Bitner et al., 2007) and sometimes are consumed as they are produced, for example theme park rides, a holiday or the service experienced during project delivery. Service provision is frequently bundled with technical and product content (e.g. Matthyssens and Vandenbempt, 1998; Normann, 2001; Alderman et al., 2003; Vargo and Lusch, 2004; Edvardsson et al., 2008).

This chapter will explore the technical and service dimensions of MoP, covering:

A. MoP and relationship management in regard to technical content and a service as separate attributes and as combined goods-service bundles associated with projects.
B. Explore relationship management in connection with the technical task–service management interface.
C. Recognition of opportunities and constraints of rethinking project management as technical and service provision across project businesses in general and specifically for the project business in the systems integrator role.

Focused consideration of the service provision is the main message. First, the project sectors that are more technically orientated such as IT and engineering-related projects have traditionally had service provision 'off the radar', and therefore, it is timely to address service provision. Second, those project sectors and businesses that perceive service provision as having equal weight benefit in the market through the co-creation of value, reputational benefit and sustainable growth.

Awareness of service provision is necessary. Project businesses believe they provide a better service than they do. For example, an employee survey of one of the largest international contractors showed that staff perception was that 91 per cent thought they provided a good service, whereas an investigation of clients showed their service was average and technically they were behind competitors (Chambers et al., 2009; Company Survey Report, 2009). This is an example of a project business that takes service provision seriously and employs some relationship management principles. The same survey evidence identifies the need to improve business management systems as only 34 per cent of employees perceived these to be adequate, too much being dependent upon a few champions taking individual responsibility.

Efficiency in terms of input–output ratios, pairing costs and minimizing investment are major causes of poor service provision leaving barely sufficient scope to meet minimal requirements. Effectiveness, driven by strategic project criteria from client and supplier organizational goals, is key to service provision and service experience, including the co-creation of value as a source of value and added value. Developing the service offer typically operates at four levels:

1. Nature of the *service concept* – project businesses develop marketing competencies and management capabilities to emphasize certain distinctive strengths.
2. Resource and organize the *service menu* – take generic capabilities and customize content and tailor services according to what clients value.
3. Develop *tailored services* – opportunities exist to 'tweak' configurations and learn from these to develop further core service competencies and dynamic capabilities for future application.
4. Manage *service communication and reputation* – to generate increased client and stakeholder awareness of the service benefits and link to relationship building via client identification in particular (see also **Chapter 4**).

Maintain a technical and technological focus, typically operating at the following levels:

1. The project as a *production concept* – project businesses traditionally focus upon the project as the primary unit of organization and delivery. Strengths perceived to be derived from specific technical and technological expertise are bundled as generic skills and capabilities rather than presented purely in terms of track record and assurance through financial standing.
2. Resource and organize to meet *minimum requirements* – meeting time, cost and prescribed scope and quality using project management methodologies and the tools and techniques for task management provide the point of departure for adding value.
3. Maximize *certainty* and minimize *risk* – manage scope at the front-end and develop response strategies to emergent requirements during execution where risk and uncertainty are increased.
4. Maintain low *transaction costs* – communicate on a 'need to know' basis to progress task management, minimize risk, apply budget control and cash flow management and employ the return on capital employed to invest in adding value.

Competitors have access to most technical or technical capabilities and thus conformance as a specified requirement is the baseline yet a zero sum competitive game, while service provision is conducted distinctly and thus differentiation is primary, requiring a greater outwards focus towards customers and service provision.

Technical provision and task management

Project businesses are experts and bring a range of specialist skills. Specialized skills and risk management encourage use of independent suppliers that understand the range of expertise. Integrating the supply and work packages is a service. Project businesses tend to think they are better at service provision than clients rate them. The reason is the management belief and project business orientation based upon technology and technical expertise. An expert view from the technical background and discipline *is* perceived as the service, yet only forms part of a service. From the client perspective, they receive added value across the majority of their procurement with an increasingly strong service component from suppliers. High levels of uniqueness, uncertainty and risk are looking extremely lame justifications as customized small batch and just in time production are increasingly the norm for many products. Added service value is increasingly demanded and dissatisfaction sets in if none is offered nor received. Suppliers defaulting against these criteria are perceived as poor, and those falling short of minimum standards as a liability to the customer. This analysis renders many project business a liability to their clients in current market conditions.

The technical aspects of production and service delivery no longer hold the dominant position in many markets (Sørensen, 2012). Project markets are no different, merely lagged in the pace of change. There remains scope for improvement from the production perspective, particularly through enhanced integration (**Chapter 7**). Butcher and Sheehan (2010: 41) recently reported from their findings client *annoyance at contractors who join their supply chain and try to dictate what should be important to the customer rather than listen*. The same research also found clients were looking for innovation and learning from first tier contractors as a way to add value beyond the specification within the technical and technological part of a project. As many technical capabilities are outsourced, relationship management becomes a key component for understanding the exact nature of client requirements, supplier capabilities and aligning the two. Technical knowledge remains a key component among systems integrator project businesses for they need to evaluate the technical requirements, technical package interfaces and quality in delivery. Hobday et al. (2005) address the scope for technical development and integration and how this has provided a basis from which a new service model has developed. This model is premised upon product–service integration to deliver integrated solutions (e.g. Davies et al., 2007).

Benefits flowing from the product or project, or unexpected benefits discovered in use, does not mean that the exchange was positive, even if the financial outcome was positive (cf. Lepak et al., 2007). Value for money for the content in use may be perceived to be poor, even if time, cost and quality are met. Further, some of the value generated in use may not be attributed to the supplier because the customer or client had to work hard to secure it. The client perceives the benefits as largely created and secured by their own hard work.

Value in use is assuming increasing importance not only for reasons of environmental sustainability but also from the viewpoint of total asset management and the derived value due to the organizational and financial benefits flowing from any project. Tensions between technical inputs and the desired outputs require a greater client focus and deep understanding of client core operations – a contrast to the tensions found with inward-focused, task-orientated project teams against business strategies with a wider organizational view. Maintenance of relationships between projects and the wider organization is essential if projects are to remain aligned to strategic direction and contribute to their delivery (Lycett et al., 2004).

The mainstream image of projects is essentially production orientated (Winter and Szczepanek, 2009). The basis for action is the one-off project task (Ekstedt et al., 1999) – the project and task preoccupation in project management. The operational tools of project management have largely been technically led in terms of their roots, for example, projects were typically organized around quantities. Gantt then realized that time was a more critical factor (Geraldi and Lechter, 2012). Time reinforces the micro-level production orientation in project management, conduct of tasks and their management. Quality is also technical, although MoP introduced scope as a more inclusive and strategic component of the iron triangle, time–cost–scope. The three primary dimensions of the production-orientated approach in project management are the following:

1. The technical content – discipline specific skills and expertise.
2. The technological content – any hardware and technological innovation.
3. The task management of injecting each aspect into the project.

These three aspects largely fall under 'what' rather than 'how': what expertise, what technology of innovative development, and what to do to manage the task to delivering the technical and technological content. Task management needs unpacking further. What is done might be to decide, for example to subcontract elements of the pyrotechnics for a product launch to a specialist provider in events management or a specialist mechanical and electrical subcontractor for a construction project. How that is then managed is the service component. Pyrotechnics raises multiple issues such as health and safety (H&S) involving the convention centre or exhibition venue, other subcontractors providing music, visuals and so on, as well as the audience. Managing interfaces is part of the service experience provided by the pyrotechnics business as a systems solution provider, for which their client, the events manager as systems integrator, is in receipt of that service experience. A mechanical and electrical subcontract for a construction project has to interface with other packages of the project on site that have been installed and are being installed at the same time. There is sometimes need for redesign and rework on site to ensure the physical interfaces have integrity. Managing organizational interfaces is the 'how' issue of service experience by the main contractor, both with the subcontractor but also with the client and their representatives. It is a complex flow of acts, episodes and sequences where relationships are key to integrating the management of 'how' in order to ensure the 'what' is integrated on the ground. It has performance and cost implications. The flow is not only across organizational interfaces, but emerges bottom-up from current practices that are harnessed to principles and concepts as well as being designed top-down from relationship management principles.

Where tasks are conducted independently or where weak systems give relative autonomy to project decision-making units (DMUs) and operatives, inefficiencies are more likely to occur. Managed interfaces and problem solving become assets. The same applies to relationships and their management over project lifecycles (Smyth, 2015).

Many project businesses say that the customer is only prepared to pay for the core solution – the technical and technology input. There are clients who genuinely are located in this *zone of indifference,* but they are the minority (Grönroos, 2000). It is the project business that needs to make the client appreciate the service benefits by demonstrating the indirect cost savings and enhanced problem solving in order to add and co-create technical value, and the long-term benefits across their programme. Systems integrators have colluded with clients in intensive price competition and failed to provide an alternative to clients that could benefit from an alternative approach based upon a deep understanding the client business.

Technical and technological task management comprises about 20 per cent of the impact from the client perspective (Leading Edge, 1998). Up to 35 per cent of client operating costs are due to quality issues, having to rework and adjust tasks because what has been delivered does not work as expected (Grönroos, 2000). This eats into profits of all parties. How projects are put to use is where delivered value begins to be manifested, where the benefits and impact for the client organization therefore begin to flow. Engagement with this dimension is addressed through (i) post-completion service, (ii) measuring the outcomes in benefits, and (iii) feedback and learning to develop the technical and technological inputs for the future. This could evolve iteratively and may feed into a shift from a task management preoccupation towards a bottom-up project ecology (cf. Ekstedt et al., 1999; Grabher and Ibert, 2011).

Service provision in theory and practice

Services are deeds, processes and performances (Zeithaml and Bitner, 1996). Adding service value can simply be improving the customer or client experience of what is being done or it can add new service features into existing ones (Grönroos, 2000). Service delivery is a creative process and differentiates providers (Fitzsimmons and Fitzsimmons, 2011). MoP *is* a service, especially for project businesses in the systems integrator role because these businesses are service providers. Services come in several forms: (a) the service 'product' of pre-packaged standard or routinized components, (b) technical operational issues that cannot be specified directly but may be embodied in an output specification, and (c) soft service specificity, such as legal advice or other one-off forms of information provision, consultancy and advisory issues. The scope of service provision can be subdivided into two outcomes that are present in all provision:

i)   The service configuration that yields a *service experience*, which tends to be overlooked when those responsible for delivery conduct provision through a technical lens of expertise;

ii) The service *value in use*, which concerns benefits delivery and is distinct from time–cost–quality.

These service outcomes have an ability to yield a profit to the systems and solutions providers, based upon business models understood through what has come to be known as the *service-dominant logic* (Vargo and Lusch, 2004). Both service experience and value in use are central considerations informing the approach to project configuration. These considerations impact any project and directly impact the project business through customer or client satisfaction, repeat business and hence strategic growth of the business to serve shareholders.

Client-side MoP is frequently considered, for example the work of Morris (e.g. Morris and Hough 1987; Morris, 1994, 2013) and Merrow (2011). Merrow underlines that the first stage gate is typically the weakest in most organizations at the front-end. Data from 14,000 oil and gas projects show a systematic relationship whereby the larger the project the poorer the preparation. It is also the case that the more remote the project geographic location, the greater the problem of team integration and the greater the likelihood of inadequate staff levels. For petroleum development mega-projects specifically, four out of five fail caused primarily by poor front-end planning and authorization (cf. stage gate 1), turnover in project leadership and their key team members (impact upon service consistency) and schedule aggressiveness (Merrow, 2011). This results from consistent poor decision-making. Merrow believes strong leaders employ a matrix approach, which draws in organizational stakeholders to enable integration and decision-making (cf. **Chapters 7** and **8**).

How the client side addresses the front-end and execution compared to the supply side is different. There is a lag, most importantly for the commencement of execution. This is depicted in Figure 9.1. Project businesses like to have early involvement to shape the project (e.g. Cova and Salle, 2011), but many are not proactive in engaging in project shaping or involved in shaping from a client-centric viewpoint. Client-side data stated that construction contractor and consultant expenditure on the operational activities only had 20 per cent impact upon the client although it represented 80 per cent of the costs, whereas in cost terms *the softer service issues only account for 20 per cent, yet may account for as much as 80 per cent of the impact upon the client* (Smyth, 2000: 41; Leading Edge, 1998). Recent research on four major international contractors confirms the imbalance, where service provision was reported upon as being 'off the radar' (Smyth, 2013a). However, it is the supply side that initiates service delivery, and co-creation is only

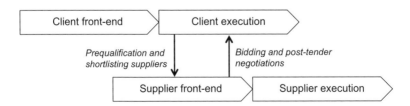

FIGURE 9.1   The inter-relationship of demand and supply side project lifecycles

possible with the appropriate level of engagement, especially applying a client and service orientation.

The project supply side is equally important to complete the picture. Different service concepts, and thus articulation at programme and project level, have distinct types of impact in the market and for particular clients: *Being customer oriented is not enough, the logic here implies learning, collaborating and co-creating value with the customer, and being adaptive to the customer's individual and dynamic needs* (Wikström et al., 2009: 116).

Rust and Zahorik (1993) state that the provision of service or production of a product offered for sale should be aimed at satisfying identified needs of the targeted customers. It has been stated:

> Contractors . . . do not understand owner's needs around creating operating assets. In my experience, contractors focus too narrowly on meeting targets on cost and schedule and attach little value to turnover sequencing and successful turnover of the asset to operations. These shortcomings should be expected given their orientation. Interestingly, construction organizations often appear more sensitive to the needs of turnover and commissioning than the engineering contractors.
>
> (Merrow, 2011: 302)

Construction contractors appear to be better than engineers, yet recent research shows that these majors also have got quite a way to go to change their orientation to a more service- and client-led approach (Smyth, 2013, cf. 2014). Relationship management can form an important component. Clients are not necessarily good at relationship management, many having reduced the perceived value of relationships with the systems integrator project business since the 2008 downturn. This occurred in the wake of reducing their in-house capabilities and the pursuit of lower prices (Merrow, 2011; Winch and Leiringer, 2013). The supply response has been to focus upon price and cost management – the reactive approach – or in some cases upon opportunities to support the client and add value within the price context or for additional payment – the proactive approach. Part of that support may be to make demands of the client side that unless they put adequate support in place, the contract price will increase, if not at the bid stage, certainly by the final account. The traditional assumptions are that services reside 'downstream' (Davies, 2004: 734), the logic of which is that it is always another organization that has this responsibility for service provision and the service experience. This is simply unrealistic.

There are trends towards *servitization* with the emergence of business models with differentiated earning logic (e.g. Romme, 2003; Davies, 2004; Vargo and Lusch, 2008; Wikström et al., 2009). The production orientated model or the goods-dominant logic (Vargo and Lusch, 2004) is primarily based upon input-output measures of efficiency rather that services of high value that are predesigned and iteratively developed and thus embody the technical value, the affective emotional service experience and flows of benefits including financial returns (Smyth, 2000; cf. **Chapter 4**).

The role of capabilities, particularly organizational capabilities, can make a significant contribution to a client and service focus (e.g. Davies and Brady, 2000). There are several reasons behind the significant contribution of organizational capabilities:

- Development of organizational capabilities may involve some technical aspects, for example derived from an innovation and technical service function, yet are most likely to be bundled into a set of services as well as technical attributes in project bids and delivery.
- Organizational capabilities offer consistency across the project business programmes, thus projects and for client programmes where there is repeat business. Consistency is a service. It is a rare project feature in most project markets because of the lack of integration systems at the project business–project interface.
- The presence of a new or emergent capability opens up further opportunities to enhance service configuration at programme and project levels, hence adding further value.
- Organizational capabilities that directly improve integration render a service to improve value propositions and execution.
- Enhanced MoP is an organizational capability when a systematic approach is applied.
- Relationship management is an organizational capability or core competency that adds service value as well as levering added and co-created value.
- Capabilities can invoke and induce new opportunities during a project and programme through learning and reflective practice that generates further capabilities for future projects once organizationally embedded.

The generation and development of organizational capabilities and the interplay between the project business and projects are schematically depicted in Figure 9.2, covering issues of variation, selection and retention. This is an evolutionary model and to an extent fits in with the open-ended and organic systems approach of project ecologies that span inter-organizational management issues (e.g. Grabher and Ibert, 2011; cf. Loch and Kavadias, 2011).

However, many project businesses close down service provision options. For example, the front-end is regularly 'skimped' in oil and gas. Merrow (2011) notes that the incentive to do so in the early stages of the project lifecycle is high because it typically comprises 3–5 per cent the total capital cost and is time consuming. The consequential cost implication for capital cost and loss of benefits delivered is likely to be far higher for the lack of front-end consideration. However, this is always intangible to project businesses that overlook the front-end. The consequential management of being brought to account against time–cost–quality, any adversity that arises, the disputes and legal costs are not attributed by senior

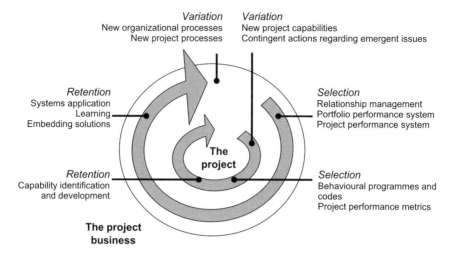

FIGURE 9.2 Stages of capability development at project business and project levels

Source: Adapted and developed from Loch and Kavadias, 2011.

DMU members to the lack of expenditure at the front-end. The disaffection of clients and therefore the loss of client lifetime revenue and hence value to the project business is unseen. For example, a hypothetical client has an annual spend of $900m of which 15 per cent is typically placed with each reasonably or marginally performing project business. If two contractors win 15 per cent each in year one, one performing well and the other having marginal performance, the long-term comparative impact is substantial. It might pan out in the way set out in Table 9.1. On a project-by-project basis, it appears inconsequential, but over a client lifetime, the good project business receives 2.5 times more business than the marginal project business. This has enormous implications for the two businesses in contrasting ways.

The extensive datasets of the oil and gas industry projects compiled by the consultancy firm IPA show less than 60 per cent of megaprojects are integrated during the development at the front-end (Merrow, 2011). Integration is not a project function; it is a project business function and thus must come through systems and programme management, mobilizing and lining up of the organizational capabilities to be used to develop integration. Leaving function and team integration to the commercial, operations and project director and project manager functions will tend to omit many of the strategic corporate level dimensions. Involving the corporate level will aid integration and/or highlight the lack of capabilities in a project business. Integrated teams are 60 per cent likely to be more proactive (Merrow, 2011). If protocols are in place for managed personnel flow, consistent service is far more likely to be delivered.

Integration is vertical and horizontal. Horizontally, it has also been noted above that technical issues associated with total asset management are typically not or insufficiently addressed from the viewpoint of integrated provision. This is the case even

TABLE 9.1 Comparison of revenue derived from client lifetime value to project businesses

Year	Comment	Good performing project business	Marginally performing project business
1	$900m annual spend: 15% placed with each project business	$ 135m	$ 135m
2	c.15% reduction in allocated work for the marginal project business	$ 135m	$ 115m
3	Ditto	$ 135m	$ 98m
4	Ditto	$ 135m	$ 84m
5	Ditto	$ 135m	$ 72m
6	Ditto	$ 135m	$ 61m
7	c.15% increase in allocated work for the good project business	$ 155m	$ 52m
8	Minimum threshold of project sum reached, so marginal project business receives no further contracts	$ 178m	
9	Maximum amount of work allocated to one project business at the upper limit	$ 205m	
10	Ditto	$ 200m	
Project business lifetime revenue or value calculated on a 10-year basis		**$1548m**	**$617m**

on PFI/PPP-type projects where the systems integrator retains concession responsibility for the assets. Lenders are largely resistant to technological innovation or development in the execution stage that may enhance operations in use, especially for facilities management related services. Lenders try to minimize perceived risk (e.g. Ive and Rintala, 2006). The work by Kumaraswamy and his colleagues has proposed a relationally integrated value network (RIVANS) model to enhance value propositions and delivery, extending beyond the limitations of structural integration and collaborative practices to include for example B2B cooperative networks, goal identification, personal and social identification between organizational members, norms to develop trust (e.g. Kumaraswamy et al., 2005; Anvuur and Kumaraswamy, 2008; Kumaraswamy and Anvuur, 2008; Kumaraswamy et al., 2010), which has been extended to include facilities and total asset management (Kumaraswamy et al., 2010). It has also been explicitly linked to relationship management (Zou et al., 2014).

A lack of integration on the supply side is critical. Clients have therefore increasingly made demands of project businesses about the level and type of commitment where project businesses have failed to take responsibility for improved integration. The level of integration on the client side is also critical. Project businesses need to start making the same sorts of demands of their clients because how clients manage the front-end and support execution affects the bottom line of a good project business. Suppliers are currently incurring increased costs, for example in oil and gas where clients are undermanned. Contractors throughout supply chains raise prices where a lack of resources and integration on the client side are perceived to increase risks and hence costs, up to 30 per cent on bid prices under certain conditions (Merrow, 2011).

'Soft' management support is therefore key to service provision, which links back to chapters on particular core competencies and capabilities. Social skills, such as those embodied in emotional intelligence, trust building and derived from relationship management, create a link between desired behaviour and personal identity according to Scott and Lane (2000). This has two important implications. First they say, social skills are important where the scope of operations expand as norms can become a less efficient regulator (cf. **Chapters 4** and **6**), and second social skills are a valuable service asset used to lever added value (**Chapters 3, 4** and **5**). Those that decide to develop enhanced service provision are typically different than those responsible at an operating level, hence the need for support processes and coordinating mechanisms (Janowicz-Panaitan and Noorderhaven, 2009). This includes programme coordinating mechanisms and project shaping mechanisms (Cova and Salle, 2011), which can be managed through a relationships management system or a set of procedures as part of other systems for integration (cf. Zou et al., 2014). These are seldom pre-given and stable, but also require shaping from and in practice (Jarzabkowski et al., 2012).

Early contractor involvement is seen as beneficial among most project businesses. The client tends to experience this as the contractor taking opportunity to shape the project to fit the project business rather than seeking to add value for the client. There has also been a move away from project planning as a perceived means to determine action and bring certainty towards a more flexible approach of monitoring and integration (Whyte and Levitt, 2011). Agile methods are flexible, yet rigorous application of agile approaches has largely failed to enhance service provision; for example IT project evidence shows that tailoring has been to accommodate the *comfort zones* of project managers rather than needs of the clients or project business (cf. Wells and Smyth, 2011).

One common constraint is that budgets are project specific. It is necessary to monitor and control cost, but this is insufficient. There is no financial incentive to capture learning from project problem solving, innovation, and other actions that are the raw material for building project capabilities for future roll out at the programme management level. There is a need for an additional budget head for such non-recoverable costs, that is, activity not charged against any project. While it might be seen to be open to some abuse in that funds might leak into the project budget, this also provides an incentive for project managers to develop initiatives to tap into this resource on a basis of reasonable accountability to justify so doing.

The role of the project manager and the leadership role they undertake in the TMO is key to project success. Hyvari (2006) found that leadership ability among project managers accounted for approximately 76 per cent of a project's success and its lack contributed approximately 67 per cent where there is project failure. A project manager lacking leadership skills can increase the unexpected transaction costs by 25 per cent (Levitt, 2007). The internal relationships project leaders have and generate are important to team performance induced through high levels of respect and admiration (Tansley and Newell, 2007).

In the health service, Suhonen and Paasivaara (2011a, 2011b) consider the importance of 'shared social capital' in projects and how motivation and well-being of those involved make a significant contribution to project performance. How can the value of social capital be assessed and relationships be measured? Management is increasingly grappling with the issues that are difficult to measure, relying upon their expert and informed judgment. Long-term benefits can be measured through performance measurement systems at the firm level (e.g. Deng and Smyth, 2013, 2014), and short-term key performance indicators (KPIs) make sense in the context of an integrated measurement system for programme and project performance.

Management is stretched, hence the tendency to adopt paths of least resistance in fast moving and stressful business environments. Short-term financial drivers emanating from project business owners compound the tendency. One of the greatest constraints on the development of effective governance and service provision has been *impatient capital*, whereby managers have sought to satisfy the demands of financial markets that demand low risk and high returns (Narayanan and DeFillippi, 2012). A case in point is provided in Fact Box 9.1.

Brady and Maylor (2010), reporting upon a poorly performing project organization found project managers were more concerned with technical expertise and accountability, particularly supplying the 'numbers' to line managers rather than attending to the project purpose. They commented: . . . *much attention was given to the prevailing 'technical' culture, where the focus was on technical excellence rather than meeting the needs of the business case* (2010: 789).

There is a strong incentive from the relationship management perspective to engage with improvement to service provision. Relational integration tends to induce higher levels of personal and social identification with the organization and teams (e.g. Anvuur and Kumaraswamy, 2008). Identification solicits emotional and ultimately social identification (e.g. Prati et al., 2009; cf. **Chapter 4**). Social, hence organizational, identity becomes an important motivating factor among staff towards maximizing the service experience acting back to strengthen ties. The resultant social capital derived from strong ties and relationship management creates a virtuous spiral of social capital between service provision and relationship management (Figure 9.3). Relationship management also spans into inter-organizational management. Strong social identity additionally encourages identification with clients and other TMO members from a service perspective (cf. Michalski and Helmig, 2008). There is a tension between organizational identity and project affinity (cf. Dainty et al., 2005), where the organization is the project business. Yet, this is only a problem in project businesses that have weak systems at the interface with their projects.

Research has highlighted the difficulty that systems integrators have in shifting from a technical to a customer-centric and service orientation (Kirsilä et al., 2007).

FACT BOX 9.1 OPERATIONAL FUNCTIONS AND SERVICE INCOHERENCE

A major international construction company identified the need to develop a centralized project function in the form of a project management office (PMO), as an important part of an evolving strategy to achieve corporate goals. The PMO was tasked with implementing the portfolio strategy, cascading down to the project strategy at a detailed level.

There emerged confusion between central operational functions of the PMO (cf. Aubry et al., 2008). It appeared there was a lack of coordinating mechanisms from the PMO function and possible ambiguity as to what should form part of the PMO. In addition, relationship management was absent, although there was general agreement about the importance of building relationships for pan project coordination and for project success. Trust was considered to be important by those responsible. The result was a difference of views about how to build relationships, which included being open and honest, maintaining direct contact, informal chats and coffee meetings and sharing ideas. The 'ownership' of relationships was unclear. Should an interpersonal relationship become a PMO-project relationship?

- 20 per cent stated 'no';
- 40 per cent said only indirectly;
- 40 per cent stated 'yes', but only at different project stages and under certain circumstances.

Conditional acceptance may have been about the individuals being involved at the stage in question and may have also been related to the disconnected functions along project lifecycles that the PMO was supposed to be addressing. There were different views as to whether managers at the project level should have direct access to senior management or have to go through the PMO.

In terms of protocols and procedures, central documents and guidance were typically ignored in general and at a project level.

Source: Developed from Fay (2012).

The same applies to supply chain management in regard to relationship management. If the focus is to lever and co-create value through collaboration, then, it has to be value that clients want. Pryke (2012) goes a step further saying that the management of standing supply chains is an additional and possibly more significant emphasis than programme and project management per se. This type of integration presents the challenge of not only managing relationships across functional but also organizational boundaries.

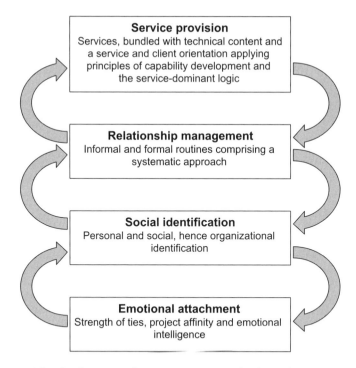

FIGURE 9.3 The development of service provision and relationship management

Configuring and managing service provision involves four elements:

1. Developing the *service concept* – what the project business will emphasize in provision based upon the organizational and project capabilities and what existing and target clients are known to value;
2. Developing the *service package* – configuring the concept and supporting the service experience with a robust system of procedures and managed behaviour;
3. Augmented *service offering* – tailored services marginally adjusting and/or in addition to the package to meet specific client and project needs;
4. Managing *communication, learning* and *image* – making full use of lessons learned on projects to enhance and develop new capabilities on future projects, seeking feedback on benefit delivered and hence value in use, and using relationship management principles to manage the image during the service experience, in business development and across industry and other networks (developed from Grönroos, 2000).

Internally, financial departments and functionaries remain a major constraint for internal and external relationship management. They tend to view costs through the lens of a production model. Cutting many costs 'behind a service' reduces support and hence service quality on projects (Smyth and Lecoeuvre, 2014).

Thus service development tends to be inappropriately externalized. While supply chain management theory advocates collaborative interventions to work together to induce and release value, in practice it has meant increasing demands and giving instruction for collaboration. Performance and improvement is then *thrown over the wall* to the next tier until social and organizational distance dissipates the result to a weak form of the intent (Smyth, 2006: 22; Mason 2008).

Relationship management between the main project business and its supply chain management is central to value leverage. Questions are being raised in the media, especially in global business about the integrity of supply chains, their ability to deliver value and act responsibly, whether it is in garment manufacture, oil and gas exploration, or IT project failure. Whether this signals a shift, whereby a greater number of products and services are re-defined as core and brought back in-house, remains to be seen. Nonetheless, relationship management is going to become more important than ever. Systems integration in procedural and technical terms is important and relationship management realizes the full potential for high performance, delivering value added projects and attendant services for clients and profitability for suppliers.

Human resource management (HRM) has a role in this process, although frequently marginalized as a project business function. It involves four core areas, namely flows, performance, involvement and development (Bredin and Söderlund, 2011). Flows are particularly pertinent to service provision. It considers the flow of people in the organization as part of resource allocation and links directly to the resource-based view of the firm concerning competitive advantage derived from how resources are allocated (Wernerfelt, 1984). Flows relate directly to relationship management as job rotation between projects and teams affect service consistency on projects and for client programmes. HRM conceptually affects the competencies of staff and thus indirectly the core competencies, such as relationship management in the project business, indeed it affects all organizational and project capabilities (cf. Davies and Brady, 2000; Brady and Davies, 2004).

Söderlund and his colleagues (Söderlund et al., 2008) found that (a) technical development, (b) time constraints, and (c) exploration of competence were all triggers to develop relationships, centering upon problem solving and intensification of activities. These were all developed on an interpersonal basis, that is, separately from any project business management. Yet project management businesses know that projects are time constrained, technically demanding and usually require diverse skills and competencies. They further found that the teams acted *variably in the same relationship* depending upon the mix of interests, expectations and characteristics of the individuals involved (Söderlund et al., 2008: 521). A focus upon client goals and project requirements was insufficient. This makes a strong case for relationship management.

Relationships management is far from easy. It is more than a matter of the detailed level of operation, which has been a focus of this chapter. Macro-level factors are important. Discontinuous demand results in difficulties developing relationships characterized by trust and commitment (Eloranta, 2007; Martinsuo and Ahola, 2010), reducing the probability of project success (Söderlund and Andersson, 1998). Relationship competencies take time to develop, hence relationship competencies are emergent (Vaagaasar, 2011). They can be tactically encouraged through behaviourally related concepts such as swift trust (Meyerson et al., 1996) or strategically orchestrated through relationship management systems. Relationship management provides a long-term conceptual framework, implemented as a system to address discontinuity of work and the establishment of both relationships and their attendant competencies.

Conclusion

The task management focus, underpinned by technical and technological expertise has been a primary focus of much project management research and practice. This approach feeds into project management as an execution function and a prevailing preoccupation with the project as the scale of management thinking and action. It therefore feeds into the production orientation or goods-dominant logic in the management literature.

Broader management scope has been introduced through MoP, and the third wave of project management is becoming more contextual in organizational and institutional terms (e.g. Morris et al., 2011; Morris, 2013). However, the focus remains on the project as the prime unit of analysis, albeit linked to the project business through programme and portfolio management. The service dimension in the sense of service provision with a client focus service provision largely remains absent in theorization and practice. It has been moving in that direction through influences from the resource-based view of core competencies, dynamic capabilities and, in particular, how these are translated into projects through project and organizational capabilities of innovation, integration, and solutions provision (e.g. Davies and Brady, 2000; Brady and Davies, 2005; Hobday et al., 2005). This is also rooted in the new service model and the service-dominant logic, located in the wider scheme of developing business models with their earning logic (Romme, 2003; Wikström et al., 2009, 2010).

Although the service-dominant logic has strong roots in marketing as well as production, relationship management has been evolving into an approach centred more upon information and dialogue as a means to lever as well as create value. This may partly be because the co-creation of value is collaborative, yet the heart of this remains relationship development and maintenance, which is only 'owned' and hence embedded in the firm through formal and informal means of relationship management. To bring this chapter firmly into the relationship management territory, the uncertainty and complexity of projects in their temporal and contextual setting demand more than MoP as it stands to achieve systems integration and delivery services with high-quality service experiences and project value in use. Relationship management offers one means. This could be read as a normative statement requiring management prescription. The main point is that the analysis of theory and practice evidence points to current substantive areas – an analysis of what *is* rather than what should be. There are many normative solutions as well as prescriptive routes to explore. Relationship management is one such possibility that conceptually seems to address the issue. This has been recognized in practice for a period of time. The triad of project customer or client service is strategy-systems-people (Leading Edge, 1994). Winter and Szczepanek (2009: 9) cite a practitioner, who says:

> It seems to me the project is much more about developing the internal service operation than about implementing a new IT system, and if we were to adopt this view of the project, then the whole approach would be very different, including how staff could get involved.

The issue is one of framing an approach to the management of projects and identifying the nature and scope of the problems as a precondition to later solving them (Schön, 1983; Winter and Szczepanek, 2009). The focus therefore moves from the project per se to a complimentary higher level of client and service focus (e.g. Normann, 2001; cf. Grönroos, 2000; Winter and Szczepanek, 2009; Zou et al., 2014), which counters the production orientation or incorporates it in the service-dominant logic (Vargo and Lusch, 2004).

At the operational level, this chapter has sought to consider how and to what extent MoP and relationship management connect to technical content, connect to service provision and to what extent these interconnect in theory and practice through bundling and systems integration. Recognition of opportunities and constraints of rethinking project management as technical and service provision across project businesses in general and specifically for the project business has been considered from the project business and client perspective.

It has been shown that many project sectors carry a technical focus informed by a production orientation. This poses multiple internal and external constraints to service provision at the operational level for in-house projects and more so in TMO project teams. The lack of internal integration at project business and team levels is prevalent, enforced and reinforced by serial factors such as investment and cost control regimes of financial departments. Yet, the demands from clients, their end users and the wider range of stakeholders up to society and environmental levels of consideration are been expressed through more sophisticated and complex demands. In other words, there are important factors that imply the current business models will not work for growth and success. Shareholders will be quick to embrace new models that deliver higher returns, especially once these are shown to be sustainable. This is the test for theory and conceptual models in practice. It is the management task to test them in robust ways.

A number of substantive issues have been addressed. These are set out in relation to the original ten issues presented in **Chapter 1.**

SI no. 1: *Organizational Behaviour* has only been indirectly dealt with as the foci as orientations are more about the underlying attitudes and values that are embedded as norms and part of taken-for-granted thinking, which then pervade behaviour. The attitudes should not be underestimated as to the barriers created to *integrated management*.

SI no. 2: *Relationship Management Theory* has not been extended, merely connected to the prevailing approaches to technical, task and service matters.

SI no. 3: *Socio-psychological Issues* have been addressed whereby taken for granted thinking and attitudes are embedded. Greater theory awareness is necessary among practitioners, and the chapter has tried to scope these complex issues at the theory–practice interface for technical and service content both at the project business and at operational levels in relation to relationship management and MoP.

SIs no. 4 and **5: *Conceptual and Applied Hierarchical*** and ***Horizontal Integration*** concerns having relationship management practices to articulate the programme and project lifecycle dimensions. Relationship management may not be the only means of coordination vertically and horizontally, but is a prime means and the focus of this book.

SI no. 6: *The Project Preoccupation* has been a central theme of this chapter whereby many project businesses think of the prime unit of analysis as the project. Supply side programme, client and service foci are overlooked because of the project preoccupation, hence addressing the theory–practice issue. Effective execution requires strategic front-end management, coupled with systems integration of which relationship management can form an important part. Technical content is frequently seen as the primary delivery focus for task conduct rather than service provision and task management at the micro level is an expression of the project preoccupation.

SI no. 7: *The Task Orientation* has also been a central theme of this chapter and is linked very closely to the project preoccupation. The traditional approach at the operational level has been found to encourage an *inwards focus*. There is an outwards focus covering a client and service orientation that can also be perceived through a broader lens, which will be conceptually developed further under the service-dominant logic – for further details see Smyth (2014).

SI no. 9: *Systems Integration* was considered in **Chapter 7** at a broader scale, this chapter drilling down to the task level. Project businesses have a considerable issue between the aims of project delivery and the outworking. Relationship management provides an important system on the palette of formal and informal routines available.

Eight of the ten issues are addressed to varying degrees in this chapter. A particular emphasis was placed upon **SIs 6, 7** and **9**. The original contribution has been to give consideration to the task management focus in connection to services and systems integration. A number of *recommendations* for further research flow from the analysis:

A. A detailed comparative investigation as to the extent to which the production orientation is embedded, and the extent to which it is confined to project sectors of technical and engineering expertise.

B. Detailed research into attitudes and barriers at operational level among key decisions makers and project team members about the understanding, existing and potential scope of service development in project sectors.
C. Further detailed research into systems integration and the lack of it around specific technical integration in bringing supply chains together and associated relational issues.

The following management *recommendations* are proposed:

1. Consideration of the extent and lack of integration around service provision at executive level, particularly the interfaces and interplay between finance, marketing and operational functions, hence leadership.
2. Development of informal routines and elements of a behavioural code that include service provision and particularly the improvement of the service experience.
3. Development of assessments and measures to evaluate the service experience and value in use of the project and its impact.

Structures, systems and processes can be devised, but it is their impact upon the ground that is decisive. In many project sectors, management at all levels is locked into a technical, technological and task management mindset that is part of a production-orientated approach and goods-dominant logic. This provides a limited set of business models from which to choose and thus compete in the market. This arguably will prove insufficient and competitively unsustainable the way project markets are unfolding. The client and service focus or service-dominant logic are needed to absorb and develop the technical and task elements to render them as service provision of enhanced performance and high value.

Service provision is unappreciated and undervalued by some clients, who will remain predominantly transactional, providing an important market segment in which some project businesses will continue to survive. For many clients, there has been a lack of quality and consistent service provision. There is a great deal of work to do to create new market segments of high value, which needs to be demonstrated rather than announced and claimed. This takes investment and project businesses prefer to be reactive followers rather than leaders. Clients are used to too many project businesses claiming more than they deliver, even in the top tier of national and international markets, so those that successfully transition are likely to emerge stronger than rivals.

This leads to concrete questions around roles and responsibilities, and conceptually around issues of ethical and moral standing, which will be considered in the next chapter as a matter of business reasoning rather than a bolt on optional extra, which is how much of the debate around business ethics is conducted.

10

MORAL MATTERS AND PROJECT BUSINESS

Introduction

In everyday life, the most important questions tend to be the moral ones. Morality is implicitly present and intuitively evaluated where explicit and cognitive assessments cannot be made. This is the case in management – the organizational values, strategic thinking, tactical response, behaviour and action that are 'good' – espoused through communication and informing decision-making. Moral issues are one of the main reasons why management intent and decisions are neither automatic nor mechanical. If they were, management would be unnecessary. Ethics is a subset of morality concerning compliance with shared norms, standards and regulatory regimes. Lay morality, including that of management, may be inconsistent. One person representing a project business may hold a different interpretation of the organizational values compared to another, leading to marginal inconsistency. Values are often transferred by osmosis more than through formal presentation – caught not taught – which gives individuals more scope to shape the values and prevailing moral tone with diverse nuance. People hold conflicting values, and organizations are containers of moral range especially in project businesses where contract specific project team members and weak systems at the project business–project interface induce social distance over which morality, values and culture have different standpoints. Morality, therefore, revolves around individual values and beliefs, organizational culture and core values, as well as relational and project contexts. The terms *core values* and *organizational values* are commonplace as short-hand for those held by key decision-makers, for an organization cannot have values itself; it is a receptacle for the values that others have that come to represent the organization over time.

The purpose of this chapter is to recognize the diverse and the heterogeneous nature of morality. It is inappropriate to advocate prescriptive options available to management. This does not mean that pluralism is necessarily best, but simply to recognize what is evident on the ground and across locational and organizational space. Management has to deal with the moral patterns and forces, which are different in time and space, displaying some incoherence and inconsistency at times.

In conceptual terms, for relational contracting, morality arises from good governance around price, authority and trust. The version of relationship management derived from relationship marketing is imbued with the implicit morality that people are generally pursuing 'good' within the organization and across organizational boundaries. Emotional intelligence seeks to bring together intelligence from cognitive and emotional human abilities for the general and personal 'good'. Trust as a moral concept, as noted by Baier (1994), is neutral as it serves the purposes or other moral principles that are around. Culture in its various forms comprises moral commitment shown in social practices of structuring, process, norms and values and risk, especially relational risk (Douglas, 2003). It refers to disapproved action and behaviour (Douglas, 1994). Decision-making carries forward the values derived from the relational and social landscape to make judgments that carry moral content in the sense of morality as encompassing both what is considered 'good' and 'bad'.

The chapter investigates the connection between relationship management across its various forms and the moral implications by beginning to explore:

A. The role of morality and ethics in management and relationship management that is frequently omitted or left implicit in theorization and practice.
B. The implementation of ethical and moral dimensions of relationship management, linked to formal or informal sets of routines.
C. The strengths of focusing upon morality and ethics in management and the constraints of moralism and amoralism in management.

The main message is that morality is inescapable whether theorization or management recognizes it or not. For some, this might challenge the notion of objectivity in research and rationality in management. Objectivity is present but not separate from values, for example interest in doing one piece of research in management of projects (MoP) rather than another piece is itself a value judgment as to what is important. Subjectivity is not necessarily devoid of reason and, therefore, irrational. Abstraction can separate notions and concepts out for ease of development, but they always come back together again on the ground. This has to be recognized, and thus the recognition of morality and attendant values as an essential part of MoP and relationship management indeed helps to bring them into sharper focus.

Social constructions

Much of what has occurred in economic and management research is to subsume issues of governance, social relations, trust and ethics and other key issues under the forces of the market and beneath the goals and purposes of management. This is merely the social perspective of the day. It offers one view but is not the only reality – considered as a 'natural law', it is without grounding. Social relations, governing and governance, and trust are broader than economic and management contexts and broader than the associated forces. Indeed, they predate both, as we know them. Therefore, it may be apposite to discuss the market and management under the governance lens, as part of social relations, and morality. Apart from aiding the understanding of what we can call the *moral economy* alongside the market economy, it will aid decision-making that improves both efficiency and effectiveness of market exchange and management.

Values and emotions have reasons attached, whereas science tends to try to take values out of reasoning, and the social research tends to remove reasoning from the values. Yet managers have *good reason to feel pleased* with those that help a project go well. A manager may say to a project manager, 'I have good reason to be angry because you deliberately did not use the required project management methodology and the project is consequently failing'. Values inform culture, strategy, help articulate relationships, and are fundamental to tactical goals. They are therefore causal factors for research and drivers in practice, generating nascent relationships, coordinating mechanisms, routines and capabilities, all of which implicitly or explicitly embody moral content and intent. A feature of Adam Smith's (1759) work is that forms of organization, hence the structure and pro-cesses, encourage particular types of moral sentiment, whether good or bad. For example management structures and incentives that reward short-term collective performance on an individual basis encourage self-interest, whereas a firm orga-nized so that it rewards group, and team action is more outward focused, collegiate or set up as a trust owned by employees, encourages cooperative engagement to enhance performance. A trust may encourage egalitarian decision-making that is slow and costly, possibly ineffective, whereas a hierarchical organization may make efficient decisions that anticipate market trends that may prove highly effective. There are values behind such issues as to what is organizationally important and what is the view of staff, customers and stakeholders. In addition, there are other surface phenomena, such as whether a firm wishes to be a first mover (potentially high risk, high yield) or learn from the experience of others and be a first fol-lower (potentially above average risk and returns). These issues relate back to morals and provoke a moral sentiment too. Similarly, there are values behind non-decision-making and the fatalistic culture that resists change because 'it is not the way we do things around here'. Career self-interest, management inertia, moralism and bureaucratic legalism can all invoke negative emotional responses ranging from fear to unhealthy self-righteousness.

Empirical research suggests that there is a high degree of organizational adop-tion of ethical policies, but what is very variable is the extent to which the policies are enacted (Weaver et al., 1999). Even where morality and ethics are given a firm position in practice, it does not mean all is harmonious; far from it. Institu-tions and organizations engage in a war for legitimacy, which starts at the highest level of abstraction in the context of this book, namely culture (Tansey, 2004). This applies to project businesses and projects. It applies to academic research. Schools of academic thought and disciplines are institutional artifacts that are in conflict. For example, economists have tended to be vigorous at excluding subjectivity and values, especially those of the positivist persuasion. Some have also been advocates of management doing so too. This was the case with the Austrian School of economists. Friedman (1970) asserted that managers are amoral agents, and the only interest managers need be concerned with is the interests of shareholders. It is premised upon the view that markets are distinct and separate from morality. Thus, morality is separate from the operations of the firm. Yet, as part of the 'hidden hand', market mechanisms take account of the externally held moral views for it to continue working, expressed through the needs and desires of actors before they get to the market to demand and supply goods. The amoral view fails to recognize all exchanges require a degree of trust and the economy needs confidence at an aggregate level to continue to function. In more complex and intricate ways, the market is logically predicated upon a moral economy as much as on a market economy. This has yet to be extensively explored across stakeholder management.

A main function of management is to direct decisions according to values embodied in the strategy, processes, and configuration of multiple stakeholder interests at any point, not just shareholders. It is a social orientation and includes decision-making in client interests with a view to improving shareholder value (**Chapter 4**). Professional codes of practice, 'industry watchdogs' and other interventionist and regulatory measures all embody ethical principles. The customer or client, suppliers and other affected stakeholders all have and express to varying degrees their interests, which are underpinned by values and moral codes. There were moral concerns connected to the downturn in 2008 (e.g. Kramer, 2009), which has been described as essentially a 'moral crisis', meaning *the loss of the sense of responsibility that comes with the exercise of the management function* (Zollo and Freeman, 2010: 191). Serving markets, specifically ethically serving customers – the end purpose – became subservient to the incentive structures and packages – the means. In project markets, project management as the means can tend to obscure the end purpose of delivering benefits. It was Aristotle who long ago commented: *Where there are ends distinct from the actions, the results are by nature superior to the activities* (2004: 3).

Morality and ethics are integral and internal to the firm and its management. It can be argued that the extent to which morality has been excluded theoretically and the extent to which this has influenced practice has given rise to increased regulation. All regulation at one level can be seen as a failure of some acceptable or reasonable level or form of morality on the ground. Contrasting differences in moral management can be encapsulated in comparative views, the following three items reflecting points on a continuum: 'it is right to do what we like and can, it is only wrong if we are found out'; 'it is right to comply with rules and regulations, beyond which we will look after ourselves'; and 'the handshake is our word and bond'. All can work if the values are shared. The cost structures are different. Positions requiring high levels of accountability to ensure mutuality of interests are costly day-to-day. It is costly to defend against opportunism with guile. Costs are incrementally incurred, many of which are associated with defense against events that may not arise.

It is not necessarily the case that all immoral acts are conscious. Some are the result of ignorance and naivety and some lead on from amorality. The market economy is flexible enough to absorb high degrees of immorality. The issue is that the market economy needs to be sufficient morality at the aggregate level for it to continue to function without inducing a crisis – the moral economy being the other side of this same coin. This is a relative position as what constitutes acceptable morality in different cultures and for different types of exchange. A rigid set of moral market requirements is infringed more quickly than a lax one, but a lax one reaches the dysfunctional tipping point quicker as outcomes become less certain and costs rise, for example where corruption, dishonesty or misaligned incentives are widespread.

In the case of project business, morality can be consigned to risk management, especially to relational risk. This may be sufficient where conduct is rigid and risk is most tangible. It is not the case where much is disguised, especially where there is deceit, manipulation and opaque practice. Yet, high levels of morality can become self-righteous at an individual level, expressed as a form of moralism. In relationships, it can inhibit others being fully themselves and it curbs the expression of identity. The result is weaker ties and less cooperation. Organizationally, zealous management and the search for justice through very high levels of social obligations on the one hand (cf. informal routines) and bureaucratic procedures (cf. formal routines) on the other hand can stifle proactivity, hence creativity, innovation and problem solving. At organizational level, this shapes up as bureaucratic legalism. In relation to clients, it also tends to encourage an inwards focus on the supply side. It was raised early on in the book that relationship management can act as a constraint, imposing too many dictatorial requirements or encouraging an outward focus (see **Chapters 1, 2, 3** and especially **Chapter 4**). The management aim is to provide a framework to create greater room for manoeuvre, but in practice, getting the balance between the two is difficult and is the subject of constant adjustment and renegotiation as the working context changes.

Morality has a direct relation with social capital. Social capital is a means to enhance service experience and lever technical value. It is an asset of competitive advantage and can be gauged in similar ways to brand, although less effort has been put into this type of calculation. Social capital is used to mobilize organizational and project capabilities (**Chapter 7**) for innovation, problem resolution and adding value. Social capital is also a direct source of added service value in the way relationships are managed.

In **Chapter 5**, it was argued that trust is foundational to relationships (e.g. McAllister, 1995; **Chapter 5**). Hosmer (1995) in particular draws out some of the moral implications, starting with trust having an underlying and implicit moral duty attached. Linkage is made with expectations and the morality associated with social obligations and conditions of trust (e.g. Granovetter, 1985; Butler, 1991;

Sako, 1992). This serves to emphasize the importance of trust management. Inter-organizational trust can be high even where interpersonal trust is low (Zaheer et al., 1998). This can be for several contextual reasons:

- Trust derived from market reputation as well as relationships, especially where trust and confidence are seen as synonymous;
- Time lag between low trust arising at the interpersonal level and its effect inter-organizationally;
- Trust is eroded with one part of an organization yet remains robust in other parts or overall.

Inter-organizational trust can act back to have positive effects at the interpersonal level (Zaheer et al., 1998). A lack of trust, mistrust and distrust can erode whatever efforts there are to establish sound values and norms into a project business, into project teams and with clients. Self-interested trust is confined to the sphere of management and economics that sees self-interest as a prime or *the* prime motive despite considerable argument mustered in opposition from various perspectives (e.g. Smith, 1759; Kant, 1785; Etzioni, 1988; Rocha and Ghoshal, 2006) and empirical evidence (Kahneman et al., 1982).

Project constructions

Risk and uncertainty are social constructions; in other words, they are of our own making, and the project community has decided to give a great deal of attention to both. That does not mean there is not good reason to do so. Experience tells project managers that there are phenomena that present practical obstacles to progress. Uncertainty and risk help understand and manage these phenomena. One of the theory–practice issues presented in this book has been the preoccupation with projects, so much attention being given to projects because of the need to temporally manage project uncertainty and risk. Many of the issues touched upon in this book tackle that issue, namely systems integration, portfolio and programme management, organizational capabilities and relationship management. Effective MoP requires support from the project business. This begs the question as to what is the responsibility of management. The principle may be to take a long-term view, but that raises moral and ethical points as to whether current owners and thus shareholders should receive less today in the hope of something more in the medium to long term. At present, that point has yet to be reached, because most project businesses are still working with the mindset of project preoccupation with a task and technical focus rather than a consistent client and service focus, which raises a further ethical issue. Should the shareholders be looked after more than clients? Both have reasons to believe they should be served – balancing act of a trade off when performing at the level of meeting minimal requirements to yield minimal profits, but not where serving the client builds reputation and hence market share by adding value. Internal and inter-organizational fragmentation of effort and weak systems, historically high adversity and low trust levels with poor relationship management, and services that lack consistency on projects and continuity between projects are part of the minimum requirements picture. The explicit or implicit moral decision or position is clear − minimal investment, minimal cost and minimal requirements are met for survival and marginal growth. It is probable that the market is increasingly challenging that position with clients, and to some extent regulatory systems, demanding more complexity of content and higher service levels, posing the question as to whether these demands can consistently be met through the status quo. Perhaps ways will be found, but there are also opportunities for some project businesses to break ranks and increase short-term risks to become more competitive and grow long-term market share.

Social constructions are different from natural laws because they are of our own making. Taking uncertainty, there is only uncertainty and doubt, where certainty has preceded uncertainty (Gustafsson, 2002; cf. Wittgenstein, 1969). In other words, it only matters when we see an alternative which we would like to think is possible and explore in context. This raises the question about needing to know in advance or whether is reasonable to expect to know in advance. Is it morally questionable to impose perceived certainty where there is little? The chosen starting point has huge issues for pricing, for example lump sum or guaranteed maximum price contracts on the one hand and cost plus or target cost contracts on the other hand. A pragmatic position chimes with application of *strategy as practice* (e.g. Whittington, 1996), providing scope for adjustment. It also chimes with the practice perspective of how relationships, coordination and capabilities emerge, for example evident in the work of Parmigiani and Howard-Grenville (2011) and Jarzabkowski et al. (2012). Clegg et al. (2007) propose an ethics as practice research agenda with the aim of fostering ethically informed management, particularly around the impact of governance structures on the project-related behaviour. This can be taken forwards through formal agreements about rights and duties or through behavioral codes of conduct between actors developed bottom-up for example. Governance can frame pragmatism at an operational level; for example a great deal of partnering practice has developed in pragmatic ways:

> The normative and cognitive perspective on relational contracting asserts that increases in cooperation and reductions in opportunistic behaviour can occur due to the threat of non-pecuniary social sanction, even in the absence of a contractual obligation.
>
> (Henisz et al., 2012: 43)

There are indirect pecuniary incentives in the shape of repeat business and enhancement in client lifetime value (CLV). These are powerful incentives for ethical behaviour and good moral conduct. This is in line with arguments presented in other chapters − strong relationships and moral conduct make good business sense. Morality is not a matter of trade-offs as many economists would have it. Moral management and project management practice draw upon social capital as organizational assets that appreciates with use (e.g. Smyth, 2008a; Gustafsson et al., 2010). At the personal level, particularly in relation to identity, individuals tend to account for themselves in relation to the pursuit of goals that are perceived as 'good' (Brown and Phua, 2011; cf. Aristotle, 2004). Yet there is nothing automatic as people can choose to behave badly, and organizations can do so also, causing the social fabric to disintegrate and trust to decrease (Rotter, 1980; cf. Kramer, 2009).

Dasgupta in his argument that trust is a necessary part of all transactions writes *there must be some **cost** involved in honest behavior* (1988: 59). At face value, this might imply that dishonesty is cheaper, although it carries high transaction costs due to the high levels of accountability and bureaucracy it invokes. Further, accountability carries its own problems. O'Neill (2002) persuasively argues unhealthy levels of accountability lead to unprofessional action. Dishonesty tends to be expensive at an aggregate level as well as unfair, for example where corruption prevails. Dasgupta argues that incentive structures can drive honesty and dishonesty, trust and distrust, depending upon their strength and organizational support. Williamson (1993: 469) states: *because opportunistic agents will not self-reinforce open-ended promises to behave responsibly, efficient exchange will be realized only if dependencies are supported by credible commitment.*

Project operations tend to lack support, leaving social space for dishonesty and corruption at a general level. The lack of integration, the weak systems between the 'corporate centre' and the resultant dependence upon individuals taking responsibility for action specifically leaves the project business open to opportunistic behaviour at the expense of the client, other temporary multi-organizational project team (TMO) members and also the project business by its own staff. The fact that many project managers tailor project management methodologies to their own 'comfort zones' rather than client need, context, and alignment with the policies of the project business is a case in point (Wells and Smyth, 2011). Culture and organizational norms provide a more robust and least cost *check on opportunism* (Williamson, 1993: 476). The implication is that the culture is moral and influences ethical action. This is important yet sees culture as a regulator, whereas a culture and norms may not necessarily support what is considered 'good'. Social capital can indirectly act as a cultural regulator as well contributing to wealth creation by adding value in the exchange (cf. Nahapiet and Ghoshal, 1998).

Culture is heterogeneous in organizations and TMOs, being subject to constant re-negotiation (Douglas, 1999; cf. **Chapter 6**). Negotiation necessarily takes time and incurs costs. At a philosophical level, organizations embody different sets of moral values, which inform the negotiation. Moral and ethical behaviour is multi-dimensional and non-linear both organizationally and individually, even within the working assumptions of following a strategy or project plan, and pursuing what is 'good'. Where pursuit is also 'bad' or immoral to varying degrees, additional costs are incurred. Many economists and some management literature assume a static view of morality and ethical behaviour. An event does not necessarily carry a single fixed cost concerning a moral position. The actual unfolding is complex with competing views over positional content and nuance.

People wish to feel accepted, secure and significant in their role (McGee, 1998; Smyth, 2004). These factors help trust form, induce positive behaviour and provide a sense of personal identity derived from the workplace. Identity is important in developing strong relational ties. The moral constructs of dignity and respect are important contributory factors, in evidence through the actions and behaviours of people towards each other. Dignity is closely associated with who a person as a human being is, regardless of contextual performance. Respect is earned in context and is closely related to individual performance. Security comes from provision of essentials, such as shelter, from being nurtured and cared for and a sense of belonging. Significance closely relates to Table 7.1. Good performance that is noticed and merits reward socially and financially feeds the sense of significance. Table 7.1 refers to unhealthy appearance orientation, whereas a healthy one is based upon sincerity and integrity. Taking responsibility is the positive antidote to blame, but it requires management support in order to provide the secure basis for action. Finally, honour is the counterpart to shame. A sense of honour encourages proactive behaviour and action. Ironically, it is the area leadership tends to violate most (Keyton and Smith, 2009). Leaders use their position of power to often inadvertently infringe the organizational honour code (cf. Appiah, 2010).

At an aggregated level of transactions at the micro level of the moral economy, that is, in the segment or sector and with clients, the economic underpinning will be eroded where there are extensive behavioural patterns of disrespect and where honour codes in the network are ridden roughshod. This erodes security and the ability to build trust and confidence to support the economy. A cumulative lack of respect tends to filter down to undermine the dignity of the actors involved in the long run, which then erodes security, hence the sense of belonging and identity. People will tend to select themselves out of such contexts where possible or become increasingly passive with a loss of *voice* (cf. Gilligan, 1982). Such deference replaces genuine relationship with types of imposition such as bullying and abuse to motivate individuals and teams in a downward spiral of dysfunctional behaviour. These types of behaviour patterns erode trust and are counter to the principles of emotional intelligence (Smyth, 2004, 2008a). These factors are then aggregated to have a compounded and weakening effect upon the moral economy.

Organizational and institutional support to projects comes at additional cost and fair process tends to take longer, especially in decision-making (Henisz et al., 2012). Early in the project lifecycle, especially at the front-end, this may result in saving time and cost during execution. Less benefit is derived by taking longer during execution, however, the client is taking more interest as the project moves towards completion. Senior decision-making unit (DMU) members who are not part of the TMO on the client side become increasingly engaged again, and project directors and managers on the client side are concerned about reporting to the senior DMU members and ensuring the quality is being delivered in a timely way and within budget towards handover. This is the time when staff churn on the supply side can be highest as key people are moved onto new projects to secure their employment and careers. There are costs to reputation and CLV if repeat business suffers from a lack of organizational support during these stages. The mindset of project preoccupation will not see this cost. A client and service mindset is necessary to adequately perceive this perspective.

Good practice in developing and managing networks is the pursuit of *non-aggressive behaviour* not just in building positions of influence but managing standing supply chains in negotiation and for project execution (Pryke, 2012: 222). Is the network necessarily 'good'? There has been a tendency in research to see networks as a way forward, perhaps implicitly morally superior on ground of fairness. Project networks can be seen as less hierarchical and egalitarian, where market power is less pervasive. Markets are networks and power in the market informs their formation and influences broader institutional structuring. Further, individuals also structure networks in terms of hierarchical power along lines of individual strength of ties and nodes and also by market leverage and influence (Amin and Hausner, 1997; Pryke, 2012). There is a need to assess others individually and collectively whether relationships are interpersonal, inter-organizational or articulated around social networks. Networks are benign, it is how they are used and structured that is important. People act as 'moral watchdogs', classifying the actions of others for conformance to their beliefs and values, to those of the organization and operational goals. They assess actions against respect being shown and fairness in general conduct (Porath et al., 2011). A great deal of assessment is intuitive. Cognitive assessment tends to come to the fore where there is overt and intended dysfunctional practice, which in the extreme flouts standards, regulations and laws. Cognitive assessment leads to the identification of gaps in management that have moral implication in organizations and networks (Table 10.1). The implication is that management and key actors plug the gaps, but there is nothing automatic about this. Existing norms and organizational habits are

TABLE 10.1 Examples of potential management gaps in moral matters

Individual	Firm	Customer	Market and network
The absence of meaningful work and the presence of stressful work environments	Overemphasis upon the interests of shareholders	Adversarial behaviour	Under-emphasis upon the moral economy and an overemphasis on network power
Career politics	Overemphasis upon the interests of senior management	Dyadic self-interest and opportunism	Under-emphasis upon societal interests
Mobilization of bias and non-decision-making	Overemphasis upon organizational interests	Unhealthy dependency upon client due to market power	Under-emphasis upon social and environmental interests

insufficient regulators on which management can rely for they are part of taken-for-granted thinking and sometimes part of the problem. It requires moral investment and the mobilization of social capital.

A stronger contextual ethos is formed (cf. Clegg et al., 2007), rebuilding trust and building confidence. Self-interested trust builds the contextual ethos as the first steps, a virtuous spiral being reached where socially orientated trust develops. In the project business and project context, this is summarized in Figure 10.1, showing the interplay that trust has as a neutral concept but reinforcing as well as serving what is around.

Brien (1998) argues that direct approaches to instill ethical behaviour through codes of ethics and other policy-like measures often fail, and that self-regulating approaches at the professional level are more successful because they build a culture of trust. This finding challenges formal relationship management, implicitly favouring informal relationship management routines, building upon the emergent partiality of practice (cf. Parmigiani and Howard-Grenville, 2011; Jarzabkowski

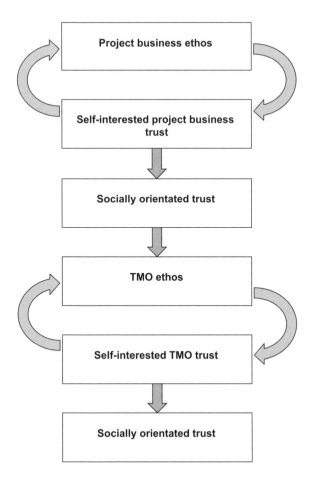

FIGURE 10.1   Trust and the interplay with moral matters

et al., 2012). The impact of morality held by project managers was investigated by Huang and Chang (2010), whereby project managers with absolute moral principles have a stronger tendency to discontinue a failing project than those with a relativist stance. Similarly, they showed project managers favouring least harm are more likely to discontinue projects than those low on idealism. This is a focus of arresting the 'bad' rather than promoting the 'good'. Other empirical evidence supports this view that it is easier to be against rather than for something. It shows that managers tend to secure ethical behaviour by punishing deviation, while employees show preferences for rewarding aligned conduct. Managers, according to employees, are generally weak at proactively scoping and guiding behaviour and action to meet prescribed goals. Further mentoring and coaching are considered better ways to establish sound means than one-way communication and dialogue. Formality is therefore needed to correct a lack of compliance, and advantage is secured where management form positive relationship systems.

Leadership is an important issue. There is a growing stream of literature on *authentic leadership* with the moral implication that there is too much 'unauthentic leadership', which suggests people are uncomfortable in the role and cannot be themselves (cf. Goffman, 1959). If individuals depart from their identity in leadership they are unable to lead effectively and organizational identity is consequently weakened. Unauthentic leadership can also imply the mobilization of bias, thus manipulation, deceit and even dishonesty. In these cases the lack of authenticity may have less to do with the leader, but it is unauthentic in relation to the strategy and broader organizational culture, hence posing a threat to organization identity.

The decentralized organization frequently advocates empowerment with high levels of motivated engagement of middle and junior management. While decentralization may help reduce project business costs, empowerment requires authority. Concern, especially where there are tendencies to apply blame or 'name-and-shame' tactics, will hold individuals back from accepting power and responsibility. They become more self-interested and defensive, being concerned for 'covering their backs' and satisfying accountability criteria. As Tuuli and Rowlinson (2010) point out, greater support is needed to achieve empowerment that is located in a broader organizational context, project environments amplifying the need because of the uncertainties and risks associated with operations.

In their study of trust, Keyton and Smith (2009) found that leaders violate honour more than others. This appears at the dyadic level too between the project business and clients. Appiah (2010) makes a convincing case for a focus upon honour and how the honour code for any society and cultural setting evolves and changes, until a trigger or tipping point is reached where a marked shift occurs. This can be applied to project markets. For example in construction, the mid-1990s saw a shift from adversarial relations to relational contracting influenced by partnering and supply chain management across many sectors and the Andrews project in the oil and gas industry in particular. Protecting the self-organizational interest gave way to collaborative working practices. Collaborative working practices emerged. The buoyant market up to 2008 saw prices rise and collaborative practices fall short of expectation as construction organizations failed to embed practices at a project businesses level. Responding at minimal levels on a project-by-project basis led to a rapid reappraisal of what was honourable. Price assumed increased prominence among clients, and alliance relations have been used to drive down prices in supply chains (Smyth, 2013a).

These moral matters are not abstract ideals, but contextually informed by the strategic goals of the organizations involved and grounded in the purposes and goals of projects. Honour is attached to the individuals in the relationships, but only makes sense linked to purpose. The goals of a project can be distorted, as noted, where the means become more important than the end and hence the moral and ethical issues become skewed in the process, inducing the greater possibility of failure for all parties.

The issues discussed therefore drill down to many of the practical issues discussed, including the consistency of service. For example, over half of the oil and gas megaprojects change their leader over the project lifecycle, most of which are unplanned. Where there is no leadership change, average project cost overruns are 11 per cent, whereas with leadership change, the average cost overrun is 30 per cent (Merrow, 2011). The empirical data are collected from the demand side perspective, yet equally apply to the supply side project business. The large cost difference is not just a matter as to how good a leader is, but is a function of the lack of systems integration and the considerable reliance upon tacit knowledge of project leaders (cf. Roberts et al., 2012), the informal relationships and individual responsibility taken by the leader that is not 'owned', hence embedded, nor managed by the project business. Merrow (2011: 181) describes it this way: *When the project leadership turns over, it seems to trigger a loss of memory among some functions and organizations that borders on total amnesia.* Churn, especially leadership turnover, also erodes trust and confidence in the DMU and TMO. These are the hidden costs applied, largely motivated by (i) putting forward the 'A-team' to secure the next project at the expense of the current one and the potential loss of client lifetime revenue (Smyth, 2015), (ii) keeping transaction costs low by applying efficiency drivers to minimize the costs of carrying staff between projects at the expense of service consistency and project profit, and (iii) keeping investment costs minimal by not investing in systems to integrate service provision.

The moral issues that flow are the following:

1. Clients and project businesses place too much responsibility upon project leaders and managers rather than support management systematically.
2. Project leader and management stress is high with a consequential loss of job satisfaction and increased risk of burnout (cf. Table 10.1).
3. Both the service experience and value provided to clients by project businesses and/or the support given to the project business by the client are compromised.
4. The project profitability and potential business growth are compromised, paradoxically, to increase short-term returns to shareholders through the

minimization of investment and cost, which at the extreme can be couched as a management dereliction of duty of failing to adequately inform shareholders of the consequences of short-term efficiency drivers (cf. Table 10.1).

At the level of the individual and where relationships are anchored, there has been ongoing debate around role and the effect this has on the individual and relates to issues of personal identity and authentic leadership. The issue boils down to whether people performing a role are not being themselves with the consequence that identity and authenticity are compromised. Goffman (1959) stated individuals act in ways acceptable to their audience and will 'self-distantiate' from their true self to complete the task to the satisfaction of their organizational audience. Berger and Luckmann (1967) in contrast say this is being true to self, merely playing to different strengths in different roles. Alignment of self to perform an expected role depends upon how aligned any individual is to the organization. This is partly resolved through the selection process where people tend to select themselves into environments in which they believe they will fit as well as organizations selecting people who they think to fit the role. At a more detailed level, the position adopted here for sake of clarity is that people are multi-faceted with diverse skill sets, characteristics and personality traits. This means they are able to perform a variety of roles. Providing there is reasonable alignment through the selection and self-selection process, leaders and other employees can perform a variety roles without compromising self and hence their identity.

Recalling **Chapter 2** on relational contracting, ethical issues are implicitly covered through governance, specifically price, authority and trust. There is an imbalance between these three, and thus, there is a different emphasis upon each. The position is that the market decides or only the shareholder interests are served. As noted in **Chapter 2,** the conceptualization of relational contracting generally and governance specifically is insufficient to coordinate and regulate collaboration and hence the extent to which morality is pursued is left to other spheres of management and within the project context specifically largely to individual and team responsibility. The market interests at the level of exchange are one-sided. Relational conduct cannot be ensured because there is weak ethical linkage to relational contracting, using the term ethical here to mean compliance with the conceptual demands.

Relationship management as derived from relationship marketing is proactive, starting within the firm, and is developed via formal and informal routines. It provides assurance for greater levels of internal and external integration aligned with client needs and project profitability. Commencing with a system, cascading down to behavioural programmes and action and behaviour guided by a behavioural code of conduct provide means (**Chapter 3**). The ethical requirements in terms of compliance to such a relationship management approach are much more demanding and prescriptive in terms of what is perceived as 'good'. A relationship management system should adhere closer to client requirements and prove more satisfying to staff. In principle, that makes this form of relationship management attractive from a moral standpoint, and from the viewpoint of contributing to the moral economy, and thus, the health of project markets. However, there are a series of problems with this view. The first is that there is much greater scope for misalignment of cultural norms, the business strategy, other systems and procedures. The second point is that it assumes rigorous implementation. Finally, it assumes that the theory is correct, which has yet to be adequately tested in project environments because adoption has been largely partial to date, many project businesses have incrementally and often implicitly adopted the principles and practices. Any ethical and moral benefits can only be tentatively supposed to date.

Interpersonal skill development and emotional intelligence are programmes being adopted by many firms, especially across North America. Group emotional intelligence is still a field in its infancy. Relationship management within emotional intelligence is therefore largely untested, yet it is sufficient to say that there is an underlying assumption across most of the literature that emotional intelligence is not only good but is put to 'good' use. While some caution was exercised in **Chapter 4,** this ethical position for emotional intelligence requires evaluation. As a theoretical approach, emotional intelligence is benign. It is how people use it that is important. The derived personal and group skill sets can be used to manipulate and exert power over others in unethical ways – increase the mobilization of bias, imposition of power and the use of opportunism with guile. There is nothing intrinsically morally 'good' about emotional intelligence per se.

Trust is foundational to relationship formation and development but is also benign in isolation (**Chapter 5**). The moral pertinence of trust is that it strengthens the prevailing ethical and moral environment while it is being shaped and re-negotiated. The management of trust is arguably a neglected area. There may be a normative call, but the position largely adopted in this book has been to consider theory and practice and in so far as there has been an extensive refocus upon and a widespread industry call for greater levels of trust and collaboration, the supply side have yet to respond seriously enough to adopt concepts and principles for trust management. The issue therefore emanates more from industry prescription, especially from the client side, than it does from normative theorization.

Culture as presented in **Chapter 6** embodies morality. Morality helps to shape an organizational culture and is most evident in the underlying assumptions, the organizational norms and espoused values. However, morality is heterogeneous. It tends to exhibit tensions and conflicts in organizational values and norms, between the systems and procedures that contribute in ways that can make some of the cultural phenomena more apparent, which provide pointers to management as to what requires attention.

The same does not hold true for decision-making, which tends to be a more limited activity in scope of involvement, yet amplifies the ethical issues at stake for any decision, especially for the reflective practitioner (**Chapter 7**). Decision-making is frequently where issues of governance, relationship management guidance, trust, emotional intelligence and cultural understanding come together according to their presence in the project business and TMO project teams. In this sense, the state of moral play, the ethical underpinnings are most under scrutiny in the social space of decision-making. Instrumental, experiential and value-based thinking come together in decision-making and non-decision-making. It is the place where honour is established, honour is lost, sometimes violated and where the honour code is established, iteratively redefined and evolves.

In analyzing these theoretical and conceptual approaches, whatever any one researcher or manager may think or prefer, practice is a melee. It might be thought that concepts of relationship management and trust necessarily imply a more rigorous and singular moral and ethical approach. That is not the case. Morality in this context does not come from 'on high', but is inextricably linked to practical purpose and goals, both by strategic intent and tactical action. As business environments are dynamic and fast moving, the purposes and goals shift over time and the morality and ethics will need to move in sympathy. This is not to argue for pluralism as an ideal or for moral migration through any relativist stance. There are other societal influences at work beyond the outworking of the market aggregated upon from particular exchanges and transactions, from the organizational behaviour and management intervention on the ground, which help frame society and the moral economy in any era. At the level of MoP and project businesses responsible for this management on the supply side, this is simply an analysis of what *is* rather than what ought to be.

Conclusion

'Moral matters' can be understood as a focus on a set of moral issues, which is the main focus of the chapter. It can be normative nomenclature, pointing towards what ought to be happening, which has provided a further secondary focus for this chapter. This secondary focus starts from the position that this makes business sense and feeds into the moral economy, which is necessary to support the market economy. It did not start with morality and ethics as something desirable to do as a 'bolt on extra'. My own research has taken calls from industry at face value, such as those calls for greater collaboration and trust, and the research has examined how seriously these are being taken in practice. The theory–practice issues set out in this book (**Chapter 1**) reflect this starting point. 'Moral matters' is therefore a description of issues that are in evidence and being analyzed. This has long been recognized, since Adam Smith (1759), through the last century (e.g. Perry, 1916), until now. Expunging morality and then reintroducing it through the back door is unhelpful in research and for setting the tone in practice: *For unfortunately economics like philosophy is a somewhat nomadic science and does not respect fences; with the result that it grazes quite shamelessly where moralists are wont to roam* (Perry, 1916: 444).

Project management similarly grazes across boundaries (e.g. Morris et al., 2011). Some of the most conceptual, interesting and practical challenges currently lie within the interstices requiring overlap and multidisciplinary consideration to address the issues. It is therefore surprising that there has been very minimal research on moral and ethical issues in project management. Perhaps, this is a reflection of industry interests and technical disciplines. It may also be a reflection of a broader stance in the management discipline, although ethical and moral matters have a bigger slice of the action here. It is also possible that project management conducted in sectors that do not give it that name, for example 'project management' as campaigns, event management, media production, and change management are more comfortable with the soft management issues in general and matters of morality and ethics. This is worth further examination, perhaps through comparative study.

The prime focus has been linking morality and ethics to aspects of relationship management, yet a further dimension is that morality is also part of the formation of social capital. Relationship management forms social capital and is reinforced by relational contracting, relationship marketing, emotional intelligence, trust and culture. The ethical dimensions of these theories and concepts inform how they are shaped on the ground, arising from the values management hold. These implicit and explicit moral aspects infuse the design of the systems and procedures in practice.

Therefore, this chapter has investigated relationship management in its various forms through an explicit lens for morality and ethics. This is in contrast to the frequently omitted or implicit theorization and practice of morality in project businesses and project management. The chapter went further to show that morality can make business sense and underpins the necessary requirements to support the market economy through the moral economy. The implementation of relationship management has ethical and moral dimensions connected with formal or informal sets of routines that have been addressed. The strengths of focusing upon morality and ethics in management and the constraints of moralism and amoralism in management have been explored.

The main message is that morality is inescapable in theory and practice. Values are embedded into both. Values and value judgments are not devoid of reason and indeed from a management perspective are essential ingredients to pursuit of what is perceived to be 'good', which includes being a 'good' manager. MoP benefits form broader support, of which moral matters form part. Relationships are a prime vehicle for the expression and exercise of such values.

Morality and ethics are frequently considered in terms of a trade-off with profit and other financial criteria in economics. They are frequently treated as a separate or specialized topic in the management literature, rendering morality and ethics an optional extra for consideration if desired and commercially viable. This is echoed in MoP and project management research. The contribution of this chapter has been to show that morality and ethics are embedded in project business and project theorization, and are embedded practice. The advantage of greater awareness is that it helps to enrich understanding and integrate practice more thoroughly and explicitly. Relationship management has an important role in this respect as part of social capital. The contribution to considering the theory–practice issues from **Chapter 1** is summarized below.

SI no. 1: *Organizational Behaviour* has provided the backcloth, whereby morals and ethics inform personal and organizational behaviour. The purposes and goals of the organization act back to influence the structuring and content of moral and ethical matters. Relationship management as social capital is a capability of organizational behaviour, which contributes towards integrated management with morality implicitly or explicitly embedded.

SI no. 2: *Relationship Management Theory* is imbued with moral matters, yet this aspect has received surprisingly little consideration in the management literature. Relationship management requires *coherent conceptual principles* for application, which have been explored in connection with the different approaches to relationship management, including relational contracting, relationship management derived from relationship marketing, emotional intelligence, culture and aspects of decision-making.

SI no. 3: *Socio-psychological Issues* have indirectly been considered in so much as management theory and practice tend to leave morality and ethics on the implicit level or even expunge them where influenced by traditional economics.

SI no. 8: *Relational Contracting* and its shortcomings in regard to relationship management have been further emphasized from the perspective of morality. The way in which collaboration and governance are treated is confirmed as narrow and compromised compared to the expectations in the marketplace and the social capital necessary to enhance integrated performance.

SI no. 9: *Systems Integration* is aided by moral matters as values come to the fore, helping to pinpoint areas where alignment is needed with organizational culture and behaviour, specifically the formal and informal routines of the project business and for project management.

SI no. 10: *Market Functioning* ranges from survival towards *competitive advantage,* moral matters feeding from the moral economy into the market economy. In other words, weight has been added to the understanding of economic working whereby behaviour at the level of transactions and exchange is aggregated to significantly affect the health of a sector and economy.

There is considerable scope for a richer understanding of moral matters, especially the dynamics in the formation, hence structuring, and the evolution of MoP and organizational behaviour in project businesses. The research *recommendations* include:

A. The interplay of moral and ethical influences embedded at the project business level with morality and ethical practices in TMO project teams for the member organizations.

B. Further work on the detailed formation and evolution of moral concepts on the ground, particularly commitment, honour and other social obligations. Their relationship to behavioural codes of practice where implemented requires investigation. Related and additionally, research into how trust serves commitment, honour and social obligations and the dynamics of moving from self-interested to socially orientated trust in practice requires further exploration and examination.

C. Comparative studies between project sectors that classify their activities as 'project management' and those that do not, particularly in relation to social capital management, ethics and relationship management.

The following *recommendations* are proposed for practice:

1. Adoption of a more explicit set of organizational values that are less geared to rhetorical positioning and are more explicitly related to moral and ethical principles.
2. Explicitly align organizational values to strategic intent, such as business strategy and annual plans, business models and how profit streams arise (earning logic), behavioural programmes, aligning formal and informal relationship management routines present and being developed to values. Each approach to relationship management implies certain moral options and explicit management choice from the 'moral menu'.
3. Make values part of performance assessment and integrate with performance measurement systems for corporate and project benchmarking. This is also included the assessment of clients, suppliers and other network members that can directly affect financial performance of the project businesses due to their approach to business ethics and morality. It is particularly important that these means and measures are discussed and integrated with financial practices as part of the awareness induction of service logistics in project businesses and for the accounting of social capital in project businesses.

One of the issues that has been raised at various points in the analysis to date is that projects are both increasingly complex with high levels of uncertainty and risk, and clients are becoming more demanding about the sets of requirements to be met, thus placing greater emphasis upon the bundled sets of capabilities necessary for effective execution. It has also been argued that some, perhaps many, project businesses have shown reluctance to proactively respond, tending to wait for clients to enshrine the step changes into project documentation as requirements and contractual clauses. In other words, project businesses have had preference for working with value added rather added value criteria. Thus, ethical requirements implicitly or explicitly attached to MoP and relationship management do or may make a positive contribution to social capital for meeting the growing complexity of projects and demands from clients.

What has yet to be extensively developed is the increasing use of the project as the *delivery channel* for an increasingly large chunk of economic activity (cf. **Chapter 1**). The project as a mainstream means of delivery for a wider range of operational activities than ever before introduces opportunities for increased learning and transferability of better practices between different types of project business and project operations. Moreover, it means that MoP becomes more important for the performance of national economies. The growing use of the project is the subject for the next chapter.

11

PROJECT PERVASIVENESS IN SOCIETY AND THE MANAGEMENT OF PROJECTS

Introduction

Project pervasiveness is underpinned by a number of features. The use of projects as the vehicle of operational means for conducting activities is on the increase. From the market management perspective of the supplier, the term for this is *delivery channel* (Smyth, 2015). The project business acting in the systems integrator role is thus the manager of the channel. The management applied to the delivery or execution activity is *project management*, which more recently has been broadened into the management of projects or MoP (Morris, 1994).

Many organizations have decided to bundle certain activities into a discrete set of activities, the bundle being called a programme or project. A programme may consist of a subset of activities, each of which is a project, that are linked because of the common way in which they are managed on the supply side or become linked in use upon completion on the demand side.

First, certain projects are conducted in-house with responsibility for execution. In-house delivery may be required because the necessary expertise is only to be found in-house and thus the project is merely a device for operational execution – internal delivery. Other projects are conducted in-house for reasons of separation – taking the operations 'off-line' – yet provide a degree of integration because the thinking and learning for creativity, innovation and problem solving, technical and service expertise are diverse and can be spread later across the organization. Some change management projects and programmes are like this for example (Lundin and Söderholm, 1995). Other in-house delivery is also reliant upon a broader supply context, for example R&D projects that are plugged into broader networks (Beamish and Biggart, 2012).

Second, many projects are not part of core operations and are sufficiently discrete that they can be outsourced, requiring diverse sets of specialist skills and expertise that can only be provided by specialist suppliers or subcontractors. The diversity of complex solutions and range of specialist integrated solutions providers required give rise to the additional role of the systems integrator (e.g. Davies et al., 2007).

Thus the project is a flexible medium that can be used for a number of different reasons, in different ways and contexts. Despite the relentless reporting of project failures across multiple areas of project business, the incidence of using projects as the operational means in-house and the outsourced delivery channel continues to grow apace (Wikström et al., 2010; Liinamaa, 2012). Estimates range between 25 per cent and 35 per cent of gross domestic product (GDP) in developed countries (McKeeman, 2002; EURAM SIG, 2012). There are several reasons why projects become a preferred mode of delivery:

- The project has been thought of as less bureaucratic and carries lower costs, while being operationally flexible (Bredin and Söderlund, 2011);
- Perceived cost control is critical and may override (added) value realization;
- Risk allocation 'off-line' when conducted in-house and via outsourcing in the market;
- The mobilization of specialist expertise (see above), whereby the project becomes a 'skill container' (Winch, 2013);
- Ease of complexity management for activities in fixed or restricted timescales for non-standard, thus unique, content, and on occasions, non-routinized management processes (Cherns and Bryant, 1984; Packendorff, 1995).

The aims are to explore:

A. The implications of more pervasive project application for MoP.
B. The implications of the broader use of the project as a delivery channel upon MoP and relationship management as inter-related systems.
C. The strengths and weaknesses of the project as a delivery channel in respect of relationship management and complexity.

The aim is to convey on the one hand that many espoused reasons for choosing the project as a delivery channel are not as straightforward as might appear, while on the other hand many project businesses remain passive in the face of the implications of the pervasive use of projects. There are some underlying assumptions that are less robust than supposed that are used to provide legitimacy of purpose in the market.

The pervasiveness of projects

Projects are time-bound and temporary activities conducted in temporary multi-organizational project teams (TMOs), supported by relatively stable project organizations (cf. Winch, 2013). The trend towards the greater use of projects has been referred to in many different ways. For example *projectization* is a term coined to signify turning organizational profit centres into dedicated project teams (Peters, 1992). *Projectification* similarly involves turning functions into project activities (Midler, 1995). *Projectivization* broadens matters further to cover societal activities as projects (Eksted et al., 1999). These terms provide indications of the pervasiveness of projects. The sheer diversity of activities organized as projects adds an extra layer to project complexity in terms of breadth and range. This has introduced projects to new social settings applying different forms of social capital within different settings of cultural configuration and organizational behaviour, which research has only begun to grapple with through the recognition of history and context (e.g. Engwall, 2003), and the concept of *project ecologies* (e.g. Grabher, 2002; Grabher and Ibert, 2011). Some, but less, attention has been given to the project as delivery channel (Smyth, 2015).

The pervasiveness of projects might be expected to facilitate extensive learning and knowledge transfer. Project businesses are best placed to effect such transfer, yet the tendency is to operate with an inward focus and project preoccupation (Lundin and Söderholm, 1995; Grabher and Ibert, 2011) reminiscent of the myopia once levelled as criticism of marketing management when it was driven by a production orientation (Levitt, 1960; **Chapter 9**).

The promise of reflective practice and learning from other project sectors and activities is the improvement of value propositions through greater systems integration. This has generally been limited due to keeping investment low and the focus at the project level (**Chapters 7** and **9**). MoP has placed considerable emphasis upon operational systems and functions. This too has faced restraints in practice due to the lack of cross-functional working and separate disconnected subsystems (Smyth, 2015; **Chapter 7**). It has been said that systems thinking explains everything but predicts little (Handy, 1996). In the context of social space within the built environment, Berman (1982) addressed modernism where society plans are perceived to systematically and inexorably move towards their goals. The linear conception of modernity is very much based upon the model of industrialization and flowline production. Berman went on to address postmodernism where change is in the air without solid direction, action is in flux and ideas emergent in the alchemy of distillation. He argued that what comes out of postmodernism is an emergent new order with new ways of thinking, hence new goals, plans and processes. What is now called *environmental sustainability* was proposed to be at the heart of the new order. If we suppose his analysis is right, environmental sustainability forms an important and increasingly necessary part simply for survival. It may not be the whole picture, but there are points for exploration at a societal level, including how 'production' is constituted and viewed. Projects provide temporary discrete units for processing activities. Projects also provide a means of accelerating activities, even if some precision is lost in the face of uncertainty and complexity. B2B clients are impatient to shoehorn solutions, even partial solutions, into their current activities to accelerate their activities. Systems that account for coordination and harnessing routines can help induce management capabilities to meet some of the major challenges projects pose.

Industrialization has seen an influx of variants and alternatives to the historical dominant flowline production system and its goods-dominant logic. Just-in-time, small batch and agile production are just a few variants, in part made possible by the digital revolution in flowline production. However, this is only part of a bigger shift to mass customization of production and tailoring of services. As fast as firms try to stabilize management routines and fix production content, change from multiple directions disrupts the pattern – firms are no longer 'firm' but flux. Indeed, coordinating mechanisms and routines typically lack stability and permanence and are part of iterative change, whereby cultural norms and systems are renegotiated and evolve respectively (cf. Parmigiani and Howard-Grenville, 2011; Jarzabkowski et al., 2012). Many drivers of change come from customers as exchange value is increasingly replaced with use value, and where customers and users alike increasingly co-create the services (of which products are simply a part) with producers and other stakeholders (Vargo and Lusch, 2004). Many of the changes come from institutional settings as the old economic, political and social models of doing things break down, need remoulding or simply need replacing as their useful lifecycle has run its course. Natural laws are stable, but social 'laws' are constructed and will change. They are not independent of society and act back to change society and themselves (Polanyi, 1946, 1952; Berger and Luckmann, 1967). Polanyi put it this way, using language as an analogy of how it helps articulate something to take it forward, yet constraints change until objections are found, which is what is happening in production:

> The circularity of the theory of the universe embodied in any particular language is manifested in an elementary fashion by the existence of a dictionary of the language. If you doubt, for example, that a particular English noun, verb, adjective has any meaning in English, an English dictionary dispels this doubt by a definition using other nouns, verbs, adjectives, the meaningfulness is not doubted for a moment.
>
> So long as each objection is defeated in its turn, its effect is to strengthen the fundamental convictions against which it was raised.
>
> (Polanyi, 1952: 222)

Real objections do emerge whereas the dictionary is only a record of the current state of play. So in recent times youth started to use 'wicked' as having the contrary meaning, that is, something 'wicked' is 'cool', 'exciting' and generally 'good'. There is nothing new about this. 'Awful' (full of awe) underwent the same transformation in the opposite direction to acquire its modern meaning. Language is a good illustration as to how we come to share and develop common understanding, forming rigidities that do incrementally shift, and at a tipping point induce a shift. More fundamentally shifts create a new worldview or paradigm. The shift from project management to MoP has been a wave, perhaps a shock wave rather than paradigm shift, and the third wave is more institutional, informed by socio-psychological content layered with ethnographic and ecological understanding (cf. Morris et al., 2011).

These societal changes change institutional structures and processes, change the way organizations are structured, operate and the way people act (cf. Giddens, 1979, 1981). The project and societal pervasiveness is one emergent trend. Society has some stability, and there are tensions over trying to establish and stabilize goals, but shifts occur. The production orientation with its inward focus is now destabilized, although the project business community is one of those trying to hold onto these vestiges with the technical, task and project preoccupation. This is paradoxical as the project as a delivery channel is part of the overall change underway. Pervasiveness has led to, it is suggested, a decisive shift towards services, service provision and a client and service orientation, especially among businesses that do not use the language of project management, including key account management (programmes), advertising campaigns (projects), change management (projects), event management (projects), mergers and acquisitions (projects), product launches, fashion design (projects) and global shows (programmes), films (projects) and TV programme making. The explicit use of labelling is more familiar for programme and project activity, such as oil and gas exploration, IT systems and software installations, construction, property development, and some new product development, which most closely are aligned to the paradox of being part of the change yet resist the change.

Projects therefore exist at the interface between modernity and postmodernism – the societal and organizational goal is set with the project as a renewed cherished artifact! Project management tries to make it an entirely modern affair by managing and eradicating the uncertainties, tries to stick to the timeframes and controlling costs. The bodies of knowledge emphasize these management goals, most especially Project Management Body of Knowledge (PMBoK®) (PMI, 2013). Clients and project managers alike tend to extol these virtues. Project businesses educate clients to think this way as they see their role as bringing certainty to the unknown and to the ambiguous (Smyth, 2015). However, it all overlooks one of the main reasons for having projects in which ambiguity and uncertainty, because all is not known in advance. If we take the tenets of flux and embrace non-linear thinking, use value and the pace of change that leads to reformulating and moderating goals within timeframes, then the potential of the project is to add value, increase benefits and improve impact (cf. Morris, 2013). That means co-creating, recognizing and responding to emergent demands, knowing that many benefits in use outweigh additional capital costs (perhaps defined in terms of range rather than fixed figures). This is a shift to joint working at the end user–sponsor–supplier interface, embracing ambiguity, working together to articulate and respond to emergent requirements and learning from projects in use. It is a move in execution from the emphasis on problem solving to creativity. It needs greater in-house expertise on the client side or among representatives and systems integrators to ensure that supply is carefully monitored, costs are reasonable, controlled and value is added and assessed.

Relationship management in its various forms is a possible step along this path, not because it is normatively and prescriptively useful, but because the analysis between the conceptual promises of theory and the outworking in practice firmly point to the need for greater organizational support, just in the same way that shortfalls in project management previously pointed to the need for strategic support at the front-end that MoP brought into awareness. To add further weight to this argument, relationship management is located at the interface between modernity and postmodernity in the project world. It articulates the continuing search for certainty yet embracing the emergent with creativity. It is located at the functional interfaces at organizational level. It carries its own shortcomings and rigidities with it – its language, the functionalist systems and procedures that are self-reinforcing. It is not a quick fix or long-term stable solution, merely a step along the way. Nor is it a linear path because clients will increasingly seek differentiated supply to which it is to respond.

Clients have been the instigators of many initiatives and innovations in the project world (e.g. Egan, 1998; Brady and Davies, 2010). Relationship management is probably one thing that clients cannot initiate. *Relationship management has to come from within the project business.* This is a normative and prescriptive statement, as there is will and agency. At an institutional level, adoption of relationship management could be the difference between occupying the postmodern ground of flux and change as society establishes a new order and becoming part of the new order. This is the promise for the project world to the extent that others have mapped previously whether it is the paradigm shift of Kuhn (1996), the weight of evidence tipping the scales (cf. Lakatos, 1970) or the social space of the environment (Berman, 1982).

A further paradox arises at this point. The argument has been that a shift in thinking and action is underway as part of a more general societal change, which is both driving forward the adoption of the project as a delivery channel and will stimulate the project management community itself to change. The project management community may be *reactive* to these changes as a whole, yet the trends suggest that project business management will become more *proactive* in the face of the changes. One of those changes may involve relationship management for some if not many project businesses. Reactivity and the current preoccupation with task have led to project management becoming an end in itself rather than the channel to fulfill the more significant project purpose – deliver benefits. The service logic, a client and network orientation, provide new means to focus upon the delivery of benefits. In a different context, Castells (1996) analyzed society as moving increasingly towards a network where the network is the scale of enactment and the project is the unit of operation.

Social capital and relationship management

A good deal of the corporate planning I have observed is like a ritual rain dance; it has no effect on the weather that follows, but those who engage in it think it does. Moreover, it seems to me that much of the advice and

instruction related to corporate planning is directed at improving the danc-
ing, not the weather.

(Mintzberg, 1994: 139)

The argument has placed considerable emphasis upon the 'corporate centre' as the
means of support for the project to improve effective performance, particularly
in the light of the changes and trends presented. Whether the support comes
direct from the centre, via portfolio and programme management is a matter of
strategy. Strategy and planning can end up a ritual, ineffective or compromised
in implementation or simply self-serving. Effective strategic planning works when
it makes a difference on the ground, yet the forethought, consistent implementation and consistency of action necessary to do so is a major challenge which too
often receive insufficient attention in the competing demands senior and middle
management face.

The greatest challenges arguably arise from those things that are most intangible,
cut across silo thinking and functional remits and are the most difficult to measure
in terms of impact upon performance. All aspects of social capital fall into this
category. Yet it is precisely social capital that is most likely to have greatest effect
in the future and aligns most clearly with the trends outlined above. There are
three simple reasons why this is the case:

1. Social capital is *an asset that appreciates with use*, contrary to physical capital that
    depreciates with use;
2. Social capital is inextricably linked to *service* provision and added service value;
3. Social capital is a means of *integration* by connecting up activity as well as facilitating
    systems integration.

Social capital needs support for development and operation, and this task
resides with the project business rather than the project level. Even on occasions
where capabilities develop or lessons are learned at the project level, they are
only tacitly transferred in the absence of management intervention. Consistent
transfer requires a system of processing and coordination. Social capital comprises
aspects of project learning and knowledge management, lean and agile processes,
collaborative practices from relational contracting, group emotional intelligence,
and trust and confidence building as well as relationship management. Social
capital is reinforcing and appreciates because it is used for its own development,
that is: (a) as a basis to develop a capability, and (b) to add to an existing project
business capability from the project level. The social capital may comprise capabilities developed at the project business level where effective and/or efficient
organizational systems and procedures improve performance in administration
and project execution. Relationship management is a case in point. It can take
several forms as discussed over the course of this book. In short, *relationship
management needs central support to be developed and maintained in order to provide
central support across and on projects.* As social capital relationships structure routines

and facilitate coordination that supports other systems, and indeed can be organized as a capability for integration.

Relationship management as social capital provides an important bridge between the centre and MoP and between the front-end and execution, as well as supporting feedback loops (Figure 11.1). One of the assumptions among client organizations and project businesses is that the project is a discrete and relatively autonomous activity. This will remain the case compared to highly routinized and standardized production and service activities, but the emergent market for projects of the size and complexity render this less and less the case on the supply side, both from the project business and from the network of providers (e.g. Håkansson and Snehota, 1995; Davies et al., 2007; cf. Castells, 1996). Project execution is not as autonomous as supposed and is increasingly dependent upon formal and informal systems that span organizational boundaries. The ability to work across the boundaries depends upon high levels of internal vertical and horizontal coordination. Projects are not as discrete as a delivery channel, but the support on the supply side is increasingly being seen as integrated operationally.

Projects are not as discrete in terms of risk as sometimes assumed. If the systems integrator, other suppliers and subcontractors fail or fall short the leakage of value and manifested risk come back to reside with the next tier in the supply chain and ultimately with clients. This issue was recognized and addressed in the construction of London Heathrow Airport T5 by the client (Davies et al., 2009; Brady and Davies, 2010). It was recognized to the cost of developers in the property crisis of the early 1980s with off-balance sheet finance and will probably become an increasingly issue around some PPP/PFI-type projects (where PPP stands for public private partnerships and PFI for project finance initiative) over the coming years.

Risk is largely seen in relation to finance, particularly cost and profit, rather than loss of benefits and thus use value. The risk is usually evaluated in relation to the bid price, hence budget. Rigorous cost control and accounting are absolutely

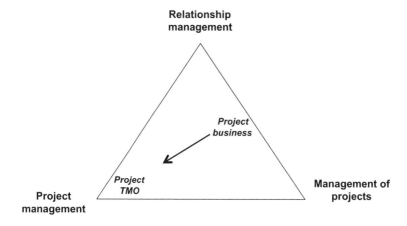

FIGURE 11.1 Relationship management and the management of projects

essential, however, the contract price and the outturn cost are typically very different. Thus the risk is evaluated against a fictitious construct. A range of project costs might be a better way forward, but only where these can be adequately assessed against (a) added value options and (b) risk probabilities and manifestations. In a sense, this is merely an extension of the conceptual view of risk as including positive as well as negative factors.

MoP includes the strategic front-end, which gives room for greater emphasis upon exploration, while project execution places greatest emphasis upon exploitation (cf. March, 1991). This ambidexterity combines greater effectiveness over pure efficiency criteria and the growing service focus would suggest that creativity and innovation will come more to the fore (e.g. Davies, 2004; Davies and Hobday, 2005; Hartmann et al., 2010). Social capital is oil in this mechanism for value creation and as means to both facilitate other value-creating processes. Social capital is a prime means to reinforce in society the project as the unit of operation, and the network is the scale of enactment.

Conclusion

This chapter has tried to link together a number of strands. In so doing, it has explored the implications of more pervasive project application for MoP, particularly through outsourcing whereby the project is used as a delivery channel that benefits from the application of MoP and relationship management as parts of interrelated systems. There are strengths and weaknesses of the project as a delivery channel in respect of relationship management and complexity, which is related to some of the prevailing assumptions that see the project largely in terms of a discrete bundle of activities that can be managed with relative autonomy with primary foci upon cost and risk management.

Choosing the project as a delivery channel is and will not be as straightforward as frequently assumed, a passive approach to the management of project businesses may prove less sustainable. The chapter has not aimed to add substantively to the addressing the theory–practice issues, but it has reinforced the coverage of the following issues:

SI no. 1: *Organizational Behaviour* – from the over-simplification of management behaviour towards *integrated management,* in particular the role of relationship management as part of social capital.

SI no. 2: *Relationship Management Theory* – from disparate theorization towards *coherent conceptual principles* for application by learning across different project sectors and developing in certain project businesses as means to manage the growing complexity of service and technical demands.

SIs no. 4, 5 and **9: *Integration*** – from project management towards *portfolio, programme and project management* (P³M) in the hierarchy; towards *integrated solutions over project lifecycles and programmes* horizontally; and towards managed integrated supply chains and clusters of knowledge services as well as technical capabilities respectively with social capital and relationship management as forces for and of integration.

SI no. 6: *The Project Preoccupation* – from a project centric view towards *a client and service focus.*

SI no. 10: *Market Functioning* – from survival towards *competitive advantage* in markets of growing complexity.

The chapter does not bring forward any new recommendations for research and practice, but amplifies some of those previously made, which are brought together in the final chapter. This chapter has therefore provided a precursor to the concluding chapter.

12

THE SOCIAL SPACE OF PROJECT CONDUCT

Introduction

Acceleration of life seems inexorable and always challenging. People may live longer, but life keeps speeding up and probably will continue to do so. Activities accelerate in time and space. The drive for acceleration makes the project an ideal vehicle. The resources are quickly mobilized, and it's very temporal nature in terms of delivery and in terms of organization yield flexibility.

This book has been less concerned with the time dimension. The focus has been on space, in particular the social space. In what ways can the *social space of conduct* be condensed in order to accelerate economic and time efficiency, but more significantly, how can the effectiveness of performance be improved? The *social space of conduct* can be broken down into the *social space of project business conduct* and the *social space of project conduct*, yet the most significant aspect for projects is the interplay of projects nested in the social space occupied by the project business as it faces out to its network and into the project. Projects are located in time and social place, sometimes in locational space. The social space of projects is a landscape of relationships, which hitherto has received scant consideration in project practice as well as theory. This is not a prescriptive or normative statement, but is supported by evidence. While the specific focus of relationship management as a means to address the social space of projects can indeed be read as both normative and prescriptive, the issues of theory and practice provide adequate evidence to argue the case because current research understanding and practice demonstrates that current approaches are insufficient in themselves. More support is necessary and relationship management provides one means, arguably with a strong supportive case as the techniques and tools of project management are only as good as the hands they are in, the relationships of projects in project businesses, teams and the industrial network. It is relationships that add value, both in the form of *value added* and *added value*, that is, meeting minimum requirements and enhancing the value for money in technical and service content.

If everyone is moving at the same pace across the social landscape, looking at other travellers on the same road gives no indication of movement. It is only the changing background that gives any sense of movement. Each project and its context are different, but the actors carry on in much the same way they think they have done. The rear mirror view of project management provides lessons that do not necessarily inform the future. Focusing upon the steering wheel and other tools for driving does not lead to the required destination. They are needed but are not the prime focus. Anticipating the road ahead gives a different view and the horizon up ahead gives rise to some sense for how best to navigate the road ahead. This is a collective or team activity for projects and therefore improvement in the performance of projects first requires the managed articulation and configuration of relationships. Individual and organizational development occurs in relationships and through relationships. Relationships are the foundation of development and *voice* is the barometer (Gilligan, 1982). Voice is two-way, and thus requires listening to evoke relational dialogue (cf. Ballantyne and Varey, 2006). Dialogue does not imply a more egalitarian approach, but a lack of it explicitly means a top-down hierarchical culture that pursues performance and profit by other means than relationships or despite relationships. Spanning boundaries and overcoming obstacles is less to do with project management theorization; it is to do with relationships, underpinned by ideas of the imagination, and applied in systems and with tools and techniques.

The book has explored a range of concepts and theoretical positions for relationship management in projects, including relational contracting, marketing-related relations, and cultural norms and organizational behaviour. Each theory and conceptual model has a different approach to relationship management. This offers considerable scope for differentiation of project management to tailor services to the diversity of market need. Some approaches may be better than others, but the decisive issue is how a chosen approach is taken up and adopted to serve certain types of client.

The main message is that none of the approaches to relationship management happen of their own accord. As with other project activities, it needs organizing. The project team is typically not the best setting in which to do this partly because the necessary relationships arise prior to execution and second because project teams have little time to organize their social space, frequently inadequately inheriting the prior relational space from business development, bid management and other MoP functions at the front end. The project business is best placed to instigate the management of relationships (cf. Figure 11.1; cf. Figure 3.1). Investment and commitment can emanate directly from the 'corporate centre' or be organized through portfolio and programme management.

The *main aim* of the book has therefore been to set out how theoretical developments and developments in practice for relationship management as applied to the management of projects. The book has tried to draw the threads together from organizational behaviour comprising discrete actions in separate and independently structured and organized functions for the meeting of minimum requirements at adequate or satisficing performance levels towards relationship management as an integral part of project business strategy and the management of projects at the operations level – see Figure 1.1. A distillation of some of the main objectives across the chapters and hence the issues covered are set out below:

- The development of a systematic and operational focus for *relationship management* in project businesses and projects.
- Relationships are dynamic and subject to change on an interpersonal level and in the organizational setting of project businesses, the nexus of TMO organizations, suppliers and other stakeholders.
- Relationships as a source of risk, and the mitigation of risk from their management through formal and informal routines.
- Provision of a consistent and added value service.
- Examine different relationship management theories and applications including the conceptual strengths and weaknesses, and the constraints of implementation:

  - Relational contracting, specifically its structuring, governance, and coordinating mechanisms for integration;
  - Relationship management as a system approach;
  - Emotional intelligence and group emotional intelligence as a behavioural programme;
  - Trust and its development and management;
  - Organizational culture and norms as a regulating process for relationships and behaviour.

- Organizational culture as a force in and for management in relation to relationship management and MoP in theory and practice.
- The articulation of organizational behaviour and systems across project businesses and the implications for the business, suppliers and clients.
- The articulation of decision-making in reference to relationship management.
- MoP and relationship management in regard to technical content and service as separate attributes yet particularly the combined goods-service bundle associated with projects with a focus upon task and service management interface, especially for the project business in the systems integrator role.
- The role of morality and ethics in management and relationship management linked to formal or informal sets of routines.
- The implications of more pervasive project application for MoP, the project as a delivery channel.

The above span several levels from the organizational culture, its systems and behavioural programmes through codes of behavioural conduct to informal routines and interpersonal behaviour. The objective is to provide a balance between guidance for action that requires compliance in order to yield consistency of action,

4444444444

yet is sufficiently accommodating to give the individual room for manoeuvre to be who they are and take initiative. This is a difficult balance and too much control can have a counter effect, yet the current position is frequently inconsistent service and value leakage for the client and lost profit for project businesses.

Contributions to knowledge

In exploring and examining the objectives, a number of theoretical and conceptual contributions to knowledge have been developed. The book has addressed several overarching theoretical issues:

1. *Effective relationships and proactive relationship management contribute to performance effectiveness and efficiency* – conceptually relationships are known to decrease transaction costs, although the claims are more extensive than evidence available. Efficiency provides a short-term motivation for the development of relationship management, yet it requires investment, especially in formal systems to develop and hence is unlikely to yield short-term returns. Long-term returns arise from effectiveness in value creation and delivery, particularly added service value, which is difficult to measure except from growth rate measures such as rate of growth, especially from repeat business, profit margins, and market share in segments of operation. Significantly, relationships and their management are both contributors to effective capability development and a source of capability development that adds value. The ability to build capabilities and differentiate services is an entry point for reputational growth and thus the securing of new business from clients. Capabilities are generic compared to project type or procurement route and will lead to diversification based upon track record in traditionally defined segments (cf. Smyth, 2015). Added value and the co-creation with other partners including the client and monitoring the benefits in use are key components for the continued development of relationship management to enhance performance effectiveness.
2. *Informal and formal relationship management contributes to integrated portfolio, programme and project management (P³M)* – the development of integrated solutions by specialist subcontractors and the systems integrator roles in project business and project delivery benefit from proactive relationship management to facilitate internal integration of their operations and as part of a network coordinating functions to facilitate integration across organizational boundaries. The extent of internal integration has an important role in managing the interfaces with other organizations on the demand and supply sides. Networks are becoming increasingly significant as outsourcing increases, and the sources for integrated added value do not necessarily accord with organizational boundaries, hence the increasing need for the effective systems integrator role.
3. *Structuring of formal relationship management contributes to the areas of guidance and control in organizational behaviour* – conducted in a relationship management system, cascading down to a behaviour programme and behavioural codes of

conduct that guide action and behaviour alongside informal relationship management to provide room for manoeuvre to take initiatives and play to interpersonal strengths. Formal relationship management is the only direct means. It cannot be managed by the client through market relations, namely relational contracting as subscribed by transaction cost management. Consistent relationship management is dependent upon proactive management of the project business and sourcing specialist project businesses at a time when project execution is more dependent upon networks.

4. *Development of informal relationship management contributes to the areas of guidance and influence in organizational behaviour* – managed via the organizational culture and guided by cultural norms, habits and informal routines that interface with other formal systems. This is largely an indirect process and is heavily reliant of a strong culture, awareness of norms and individuals and teams taking responsibility. This is easier to facilitate where there is a strong hierarchical organizational culture and where the project business already has strong differentiating capabilities beyond those required to meet minimum client requirements.

5. *Bringing together the management of projects and relationship management contributes to a systematic and organizationally coordinated approach* – social capital makes important contributions where in existence to MoP. Effective relationships help and are part of social capital formation. Social capital, including moral matters and ethical considerations provide considerable scope for service differentiation and adding value. The advantage of social capital in general is that it appreciates with use, yet its intangible nature makes it more difficult to instigate, manage and measure. The front-end strategic development of projects introduced an element of social capital into the prior stage to execution, hence MoP. In the same way that execution requires prior support that is now being extended into the 'back-end' of project management, MoP requires further support from the 'corporate centre' to maintain its significance. Portfolio and programme management feed into project management as part of the picture as does the development of organizational capabilities, one of which, potentially a key one, is relationship management.

The book has set out a structured approach to relationship management and demonstrated the need through the analysis of theory in relation to practice. This is necessary with the complexity and size of projects and the need for project businesses to effectively compete. A structured approach in summary entails: (i) working with perforated organizational boundaries and being outward facing, supported by internal and inter-organizational relationship management; (ii) organizational structures to facilitate top-down and bottom-up relationship management development and for cross-functional working to support systematic integration; (iii) formal routines that are facilitated by and include relationship management as part of 'hard' and 'soft' systems approach for managing internal and external factors of projects and project businesses to develop capabilities that constitute appreciating social capital of competitive advantage; and (iv) informal routines that support an ethical nurturing of each other to help mobilize norms and behaviours to promote for example trust development, group emotional intelligence, reflective practice and social identification.

Bringing together MoP and relationship management capability development with the two main conceptual roles of project businesses is set out in Figure 12.1. The figure shows the scope for effective relationship management by pointing towards the trajectory that project businesses are on.

Chapter 1 introduced some key issues for research and practice:

- To what extent are relationships managed by project businesses?
- In what ways are relationships managed at an operational level through systems in teams and by teams?
- What is the extent of the issue between the theoretical principles applied in practice and the theory?

Relationships are seen as important, and the operational focus upon them has markedly increased over the last 20 years, partly because of the greater awareness of their contribution and partly because of client-led initiatives of relational contracting. However, most project businesses espouse the value of relationships yet largely leave it to individual responsibility. Growing numbers of behavioural programmes, for example around health and safety (H&S), have not yet been connected up to create a more systematic approach. Researchers and practitioners alike tend to back off direct management of relationships, focusing on structures, issues and indirect processes. The substantive theory–practice issue thus remains considerable.

Drilling down to a finer grain of analysis, a number of specific research issues were identified in **Chapter 1,** ten in total. Each subsequent chapter has reviewed the extent to which these substantive issues have been addressed. A map of the

Organizational and project capabilities

	Front-end	Execution	Back-end
Systems integrator	From functional systems and procedures towards relationship management to *identify* technical and service value	From functional systems and procedures towards relationship management to *lever* technical and service value	From functional systems and towards relationship management to *monitoring* and *impact* of value created, and lessons learned
Integrated solution providers	From technical and task focus to integrated responses to *articulate* specialist solutions and their delivery	From technical and task focus to integrated responses to *configure* specialist solutions and their delivery	From technical and task focus to integrated responses to *monitoring* and *learning* from design and delivery

The management of projects

FIGURE 12.1   The management of projects and relationship management capabilities

outcome is presented in Figure 12.2. All the substantive issues have been addressed in more than one chapter. **SI no. 7** on the task orientation and management was addressed the least across the chapters, although the issue did comprise a considerable chunk of **Chapter 9.** The remainder received focused examination across a majority of the chapters.

The contribution to filling each substantive research issue is consolidated in the following commentary.

SI no. 1: *Organizational Behaviour* – provides the overarching construct within the management discipline under which action and behaviour in the project business and in projects is located. It covers culture and systems, group and team behaviour as well as interactions between those involved representing their respective organizations. Relationship management is a means to guide behaviour towards *integrated management*. The contributions made to addressing this substantive research issue are:

- Enhancing opportunities for the delivery of integrated solutions through improvements in *integrated management* through a more proactive approach to the management of organizational behaviour (**Chapter 3**).
- Emphasizing processes and behavioural dimensions for integrated project management (**Chapter 4**).
- Trust development within the organization (rather than in response to relational contracting) and then consistently taken into the marketplace (**Chapter 5**).
- Culture as a potential force for integration of management and service delivery or fragmented action that is actively influenced (not controlled) by management (**Chapter 6**).

SI no. / Chapters	2	3	4	5	6	7	8	9	10	11
SI no. 1: *Organizational Behaviour*		▓	▓	▓	▓	▓	▓	▓	▓	▓
SI no. 2: *Relationship Management Theory*		▓	▓	▓	▓	▓	▓	▓	▓	▓
SI no. 3: *Socio-psychological Issues*	▓		▓	▓	▓	▓	▓	▓	▓	
SI no. 4: *Conceptual and Applied Hierarchical Integration*	▓	▓	▓	▓	▓		▓	▓	▓	▓
SI no. 5: *Conceptual and Applied Horizontal Integration*	▓	▓		▓	▓	▓	▓	▓	▓	▓
SI no. 6: *The Project Preoccupation*	▓		▓	▓	▓	▓	▓	▓	▓	
SI no. 7: *The Task Orientation*	▓							▓		
SI no. 8: *Relational Contracting*	▓		▓	▓	▓	▓	▓	▓	▓	▓
SI no. 9: *Systems Integration*	▓	▓	▓		▓	▓		▓	▓	▓
SI no. 10: *Market Functioning*	▓	▓	▓		▓	▓	▓	▓	▓	▓

FIGURE 12.2 A map of filling the ten substantive issues of research

- Individual and interpersonal behaviour requires management attention to induce alignment with organizational behaviour, its strategy and systems (**Chapter 7**).
- Decision-making provides the raw material for judgments and decisions derived from organizational norms, experience and affective learning. This can further be enhanced applying relationship management principles, offering a more comprehensive approach towards *integrated management* (**Chapter 8**), which is broader and deeper than economic and game theoretic propositions informed by subjective and emotional content.
- Attitudes and values pervading behaviour are embedded as norms and taken for granted thinking. Effective management forms accumulative social capital (**Chapters 9** and **11**). Misaligned attitudes should not be underestimated as barriers to *integrated management*.
- Morals and ethics inform personal and organizational behaviour, and the purposes and goals of the organization act back to influence the structuring and content of moral and ethical matters. Relationship management and social capital are capabilities and assets respectively that are embedded in organizational behaviour which contribute towards *integrated management* (**Chapter 10**).

SI no. 2: *Relationship Management Theory* – its roots are in relationship marketing yet can take a number of conceptual forms aligned with other concepts and thus can be applied in different ways. It can be formally structured from a strategy, designed in systems with behavioural programmes and codes to guide specific action. Relationship management embodies the aim for *coherent conceptual principles* for application. The contributions made to addressing this substantive research issue are:

- Management has recognized the significance of relationships but have yet to fully articulate the need and develop the means of application (**Chapter 3**).
- Relationship management conceived as a system derived from roots in marketing, behaviour within group emotional intelligence, operating at compatible levels where a behavioural programme can become part of or nested within a relationship management system (**Chapter 4**).
- Trust is foundational, making a bottom-up contribution from the tactical relationship level to proactive behavioural management (**Chapter 5**).
- A formal or informal relationship management system can contribute as it cascades through the organizational levels to aid integration (**Chapter 6**).
- A means to support systems integration, yet as part of systems and hence systems integration for adding value in project delivery (**Chapter 7**).
- Relationship management contributes towards developing effective norms and addressing behavioural biases, harnessing of emotions and identification as important parts of guiding decision-making (**Chapter 8**).
- Connecting behaviour to the prevailing approaches to technical, task and service provision is not easily translated and implemented into the project specific environments (**Chapter 9**).

- Relationship management requires *coherent conceptual principles* that connect to morality and ethics to manage the growing complexity of service and technical demands that comprise part of coherence (**Chapters 10** and **11**).

SI no. 3: *Socio-psychological Issues* – combining cognition action and rational decision-making with *intuitive behaviour and judgment* to encompass the broader remit of MoP, institutional factors and issues of organizational behaviour. Evaluation, interpretation and other sense making activities are central to the management role for making judgments and assessments. Working towards considering this research issue has included:

- Market drivers, including relational contracting, are inadequate for inducing rationality and aligning intuitive behaviour. Socio-psychological issues injected into working relationships at a detailed level contribute to the effective extent of aligned *intuitive behaviour and judgment*, strengthened by relational contracting through contracts, routines and management action (**Chapter 2**).
- Norms help to set the parameters for group emotional intelligence in project management, to guide decision-making units (DMUs) and TMOs (**Chapter 4**).
- As trust is foundational to relationship formation and development. It contributes towards the effective performance and resolution through the reinforcement of socio-psychological contracts, which are important within the temporary and multi-organizational dimension of project teams (**Chapter 5**).
- Socio-psychological issues are powerful influences in establishing norms and routines. People do not behave rationally all the time, unaligned behaviour, occasional errant behaviour and violations are all present due to social distance and weak identity unless formal routines intervene (**Chapter 6**).
- Heuristics, social heuristics, sense making and intuitive behaviour contribute to assessments and decision-making undertaken through the roles relationships perform (**Chapter 8**).
- Embedded taken for granted thinking and attitudes are addressed through improved theory awareness among practitioners (**Chapter 9**).
- Management theory and practice tends to leave morality and ethics on the implicit level or even endeavour to expunge it where influenced by traditional economics, whereas the contrary position prevails on the ground (**Chapter 10**).

SI no. 4: *Conceptual and Applied Hierarchical Integration* – vertical coordination mechanisms of formal and informal routines for implementing relationship management through *portfolio, programme management* to *project management* (P³M) help structure habits, group norms and actions. Effective P³M provides a layered approach to integrated implementation from investment, through pan-project considerations at the 'corporate centre' to inform and steer project management. The contributions made to addressing this research issue are:

- The implementation of a robust system, designed and implemented top-down from the 'corporate centre' and/or through P³M, especially programme management (**Chapter 3**).
- Investment at the level of portfolio management and within human resource management (HRM). Programme and project management become the main focus for group emotional intelligence in operational functions and teams (**Chapter 4**).
- Habits, group norms and actions inform trust and are part of trust in support of other performance issues. Trust as part of relationship management helps the formation and mobilization of effective programme management (**Chapter 5**).
- Control and some coercion top-down are necessary to improve behavioural alignment and integration through a systematic approach. This is not necessarily in conflict with informal processes and the need for room for manoeuvre at individual and team levels (**Chapter 6**).
- Integrated systems operate in the hierarchy and relationship management helps to link the levels, especially behaviour between the programme and project management levels (**Chapter 7**).
- Relationship management practices help articulate *portfolio, programme and project management* (P³M) and supply chains and clusters along the project lifecycles (**Chapters 4, 5** and **9**).

SI no. 5: *Conceptual and Applied Horizontal Integration* – a series of functional systems for the development of integrated solutions including relationship management over project lifecycles and programmes. Going a step further than the advocacy of in-house cross-functional working, boundary spanning has become a pertinent issue, which includes routines wherein relationships are managed. The contributions made to this substantive issue are:

- Articulated through a robust relationship management system, helping to link a series of functional systems towards *integrated solutions.* Therefore other formal routines traditionally covering communication, technical systems and procedures are supplemented and enhanced by a 'soft' system of relationship management (**Chapter 3**).
- Trust is pivotal in MoP at the front-end to connect programme management to execution at a tactical level for trust formation in preparation for and during execution (**Chapter 5**).
- There are cultural tensions between the organizational culture and the emergent cultures in any TMO project team. Relationships are dealt with directly through guiding team and individual behaviour, which prescriptively should start at the front-end of project lifecycles (**Chapter 6**).
- Integrated systems operate horizontally and relationship management helping to link the functions and stages, especially behaviour between the front-end and execution (**Chapter 7**).

- Decisions at the strategic front-end are most critical to setting up a project to achieve successful outcomes; during execution, the extent of weak systems between the organization and the project team has consequences for both projects and the project organization (**Chapter 8**).

SI no. 6: *The Project Preoccupation* – practice and research have primarily focused upon the project as the prime unit of analysis and management in comparison to a complimentary *client and service focus*. Relationship management is an important component to addressing these issues to increase consistency and continuity, thus the analysis addressing this research issue includes:

- Relationship management system shifts the ground towards a broader view of service provision and client benefits through adding value and considering how project management is conducted from the front-end into the post-completion stages (**Chapter 3**).
- A greater *client focus* based upon collaborative working for single projects and project business programmes (**Chapters 2** and **11**).
- Raising the profile of and demand for compliance with a broader range of management issues during execution and delivering with a service focus (**Chapters 7** and **11**).
- Effective execution requires strategic front-end management, coupled with systems integration of which relationship management can form an important part. Task management at the micro-level is an expression of the project preoccupation. Technical content is frequently seen as the primary delivery focus for task conduct rather than service provision (**Chapter 9**).

SI no. 7: *The Task Orientation* – practice and research have primarily focused upon an *inwards focus*. An *outwards focus* exceeds traditional perceptions of managing clients, H&S, other regulatory issues, external stakeholders, and goes beyond technical expertise and experiential knowledge towards a deep understanding of the client and the benefits required with a complementary service approach. Working towards addressing this research issue has included:

- Relationship management shifting the ground towards a broader view of service provision and client benefits through adding value and considering how project management is conducted from the front-end into the post-completion stages (**Chapter 3**).
- Group emotional intelligence engendering a significant shift towards an outwards focus and thus away from a preoccupation with task and a much greater emphasis upon people and their interrelationships (**Chapter 4**).
- The traditional approach at the operational level encourages an inwards focus. There is an outwards focus covering a client and service orientation that can also be perceived through the lens of service provision and the concept of the service-dominant logic (**Chapter 9**).

SI no. 8: *Relational Contracting* – a market and procurement driven response that is deficient in terms of prompting *internal management to induce relationship management* in project practice. Few project businesses have used relational contracting as a basis to transition to relationship management. The contributions made to investigating this research issue are:

- Invoking the challenge towards developing relational capabilities that flow from the contract and governance based upon trust, which may shift ground towards *internally induced relationship management*. This has occurred on a limited basis in practice among certain project businesses, yet scope is present (**Chapters** 2 and **4**).
- Trust has a central role, particularly through governance measures, but the claims made for governance are too great and laden with the promotion of collaborative working that is unreliable without proactive management of relationships and trust within the respective organizations. (**Chapter 5**).
- The structuring of projects through cost, legal and governance issues underplays the richness of organizational culture, moral and ethical matters, and therefore the complexity of management and leadership to steer the culture in aligned and contributory ways (**Chapters 6** and **10**).

SI no. 9: *Systems Integration* – managed integrated supply chains and clusters of knowledge services as well as integrated soft systems linked to technical capabilities. Project businesses in the systems integrator role are positioned to integrate supply chains in all tiers, and identify, capture and co-create (added) value. Working towards assessing this research issue has included:

- A conceptually holistic approach to facilitate systems integration through relationships delivering value and from a relationship management system, linked with other subsystems (**Chapter 3**).
- A significant contribution at the behavioural level to systems integration through behavioural programmes and codes of conduct (**Chapter 4**).
- Artifacts and other soft issues form part of organizational culture, which has a subtle dynamic for renegotiating how these are used and sometimes structured; therefore, managing alignment is important (**Chapter 6**).
- Well-designed and articulated systems depend upon behaviour patterns and action aligned to the strategies and systems (**Chapters 7** and **10**).
- Relationship management provides an important system on the palette of formal and informal routines to address the considerable issue between the aims of project delivery and the outworking (**Chapter 9**).

SI no. 10: *Market Functioning* – focusing upon survival as a first step, then developing *competitive advantage* through increasing proactive capability development in relation to the complexity of demands. Analysis of this research included:

- Relationship management as constituting a source of social capital to improve performance in the market and being a means to develop dynamic capabilities of competitive advantage (**Chapter 3**).
- Seeking *competitive advantage* through relational contracting, although weak, invites greater proactivity, success being dependent upon addressing **SI no. 9** (**Chapter 2**).
- Building capabilities and competencies from emotional intelligence and group emotional intelligence in ways to yield competitive advantage (**Chapters 4 and 11**).
- The role of behaviour feeds into effective operations from the level of individual exchanges, contributing to a bigger picture of market performance morally and financially (**Chapters 7** and **10**).
- Indirect reinforcement of the shortcomings of structural and governance solutions to market operation in the project business (**Chapter 8**).

Future directions

Morris (2013) has highlighted value, context and impact as continuing issues for the future. There are several contributions related to this:

- *Value* means benefits configured at the front-end and delivered during execution. This book has demonstrated the central role that relationship management has in configuring and delivering value. The role has still to be fully appreciated and acted upon in most project businesses, at strategic, systems and behavioural levels in project businesses and for project operations.
- *Context* means all the specific features for the project and its environment that influence how the project strategy is formed at the front-end and implemented during execution. Context has causal influence and causal properties, which relationship management helps manage *both* as part of the context and also a prime means for managing the context, including relational risk with all stakeholders.
- *Impact* means the usefulness of any project for the client, stakeholders and society. The preoccupation of project management academics and practitioners with functions and task has neglected relationships as something to be managed for delivering service and 'product' benefits as well as for business profitability and providing rewarding work for employees.

All firms need to declare profits. Profit is the by-product of conducting other activities successfully. People and relationships are central to these activities and to value creation. Arguably social capital remains an underdeveloped frontier of management and profit generation. Most organizations do not know what the value of their human resources and social capital is. Organizations that foreclose on relationship management give themselves insufficient room for manoeuvre to grapple with the issues of social capital (PricewaterhouseCoopers, 2003). There remains a need for technical capabilities, effectiveness being dependent upon their management through relationships and people-related processes. Indeed, there is also an increasing need for human resource capabilities (Bredin and Söderlund, 2011), to which relationship management only serves to reinforce. Most working for their organization are unaware of their full capabilities. The reason for the lack of knowledge is the lack of support to explore and develop their capabilities. We need a new conception of people and their capabilities. This is more than harnessing learning and developing knowledge-based services. It is the totality of people working together in relationships.

Recommendations for research and practice

A number of recommendations have been proposed across the chapters and a consolidated summary is presented here. The recommendations have been listed under heading to give a cumulative and clustered sense of what has emerged. First, recommendations for further research are presented.

A. Research into the project business.

   a. A more detailed analysis between functional departments and between project functions and the interface between department and project functions.
   b. A detailed comparative investigation as to the extent to which the production orientation is embedded and the extent to which it is a function of research largely confined to project sectors of technical and engineering expertise.
   c. Further detailed research into systems integration and the lack of it around specific technical issues and relational issues.
   d. The interplay of moral and ethical influences embedded at the project business level with morality and ethical practices in TMO project teams for the member organizations.

B. A greater understanding as to how project businesses (explicitly and implicitly) formulate and implement relationship management from senior management to operations level.

   a. The interplay through the levels of operation and culture, for decision-making and particularly the key and pivotal roles of DMU and TMO members at the individual level.
   b. Investigation as to how norms inform decisions, how heuristics are formed and applied, how sense making is conducted around and during decision-making processes.
   c. Investigation into the mobilization of bias and the extent of non-decision-making in project contexts.

    d.   Further work on the detailed formation and evolution of moral concepts on the ground, particularly commitment, honour, any other prominent social obligations and their relationship to behavioural codes of practice where these are implemented. Related and additionally, research into how trust serves commitment, honour and social obligations and the dynamics of moving from self-interested to socially orientated trust in practice.

C.   Research into relationship management.

    a.   Research into the detailed influence and impact of social and psychological contracts internally and in the market relationships under relational contracting.

    b.   The influence of different organizational cultures, norms and informal routines remain a largely under-researched area in relational contracting.

D.   Research into the management of projects from a relationship management perspective.

    a.   The extent to which the systems integrator project business defines and establishes systems with interfaces to accommodate variety and diversity of other organizational systems interfaces within the supply chain and among other TMO membership.

    b.   Decision-making remains a neglected area overall, and attention should be given to two distinct areas and the comparison between them:
        i.   The project business, especially the programme level, and the project level as to how their attributes differ, the significance of behavioural issues in decision outcomes;
        ii.   The strategic front-end and execution as to how their significance differs and whether behavioural characteristics differ and if so why.

    c.   Detailed research into attitudes and barriers at operational level among key decision-makers and project team members about the understanding, existing and potential scope of service development in project sectors.

E.   Research into project management from a relationship management perspective.

    a.   The role of the main contractor or systems integrator in the TMO for setting norms, defining systems and mechanisms of integration, and the role of experienced project managers in facilitating or blocking the process with aligned and unaligned behaviour.

    b.   Research into relational contracting has still to unpack when and under what circumstances the tipping point is reached to invoke proactive relationship management. This involves investigating a range of different project types and contexts, including how relationships are structured both in respective organizations and in the dyadic relationships.

    c.   The cultural tendency towards hierarchy at the project level was noted, but more extensive research will reveal the pervasiveness of this trend.

d. The extent of diverse behaviour among TMO members and how these form routines at a detailed level, and the extent of divergent behaviour among project team members and how these constrain the formation of effective norms and routines.

e. The role of leadership in shaping organizational behaviour at the project level, focusing functional and dysfunctional roles and the correspondence of these – whether strengths have corresponding weaknesses and vice versa.

f. The limits of rational decision-making in project decision-making, including specifically in bargaining and negotiation contexts.

g. Comparative studies between project sectors that classify their activities as 'project management' and those that do not, particularly in relation to social capital management, ethics and relationship management.

Second, recommendations for practice are presented.

1. Investment:

   i. Consideration of the extent and lack of integration around service provision at executive level, particularly the interfaces and interplay between finance, marketing and operational functions, hence leadership.

   ii. Make values part of performance assessment and integrate with performance measurement systems for corporate and project benchmarking. This could or should also include the assessment of clients, suppliers and other network members that can directly affect the financial performance of the project business due to their approach to business ethics and morality. It is particularly important that these means and measures are discussed and integrated with financial practices as part of the awareness induction of service logistics in project businesses and for the accounting of social capital in project businesses.

   iii. Invest in a relationship management system that is linked to and helps integrate other systems.

2. Relationship management:

   i. Overreliance upon individuals and individualism versus control of behaviour and action is an important area of management about which greater awareness and practice experience can be exchanged for greater integration and systematic management.

   ii. Management to incorporate relationship management as a system into organizational behaviour and as a part of systems integration.

   iii. Management to address behaviour and the establishment of coherence in organizational behaviour in project businesses and on projects.

   iv. Develop programmes and codes of behavioural conduct that are aligned to strategy with interfaces for internal and external integration.

    v.   Adoption of more explicit sets of organizational values that are less geared to rhetorical positioning and are more explicitly related to moral and ethical principles.

    vi. Explicitly align organizational values to strategic intent, such as business strategy and annual plans, business models and their earning logic, behavioural programmes and to formal and informal relationship management routines present and being developed. Each approach to relationship management implies certain moral options and explicit management choice from the moral menu becomes the ethical requirements to comply with the relationship management strategy for the project business.

3.   Systems and procedure:

    i.   Adopt a realistic position in management and influence through formal and informal routines.

    ii. Introduction and development of a relationship management approach, set of principles and a robust formal system.

    iii. Guide individual behaviour and actively align systems and behaviour as a rich and rewarding aspect for project business performance.

    iv. Consideration of aligning behaviour, especially habitual behaviour that has developed into informal routines, closely to programme management and to project management where TMOs have to be swiftly established with a greater risk of misalignment in the temporal context.

    v.   Development of informal routines and elements of a behavioural code that includes service provision and particularly the improvement of the service experience.

    vi. Development of assessments and measures to evaluate the service experience and value in use of the project and its impact.

    vii. Identify and set criteria for decisions ahead of discussion of detailed issues to make explicit and improve awareness the norms and issues informing interpretation. This will also help indirectly address issues of bias, its mobilization and non-decision-making issues, permitting challenges to this type of thinking and related subversive norms before moving to decisions.

    viii. Introduce explicit norms and behavioural codes pertaining to decision-making. These may echo more general codes, yet are made more specific and 'translated' into the specificity of this behavioural context.

4.   Relationship management approaches:

    i.   Investigate opportunities and means to transition from relational contracting to relationship management in project businesses.

    ii. Develop a relationship management system aligned to a theoretical and conceptual approach, such as relational contracting, relationship management from relationship marketing, emotional intelligence, trust management, organizational culture and behaviour.

5. Relationship management in project management:

    i.   Establish protocols for the introduction and related negotiation to systematically establish conceptual principles, norms and procedures for relationship management into a TMO upon formation.
    ii. Differentiate between decision-making criteria of *means* – project management tools and techniques, time–cost–quality issues – and *end* – value issues of requirements being met, benefits delivered and potential impact in use.

Conclusion

The book has considered relationship management. It has addressed relationship management in terms of different theoretical frames of reference and attendant principles. It has addressed relationship management from the project business to the project level. It has addressed project lifecycles, thus embracing MoP, and has addressed inter-organizational relationship management. It has considered relationship management in terms of formal systems and informal processes.

Relationship management is more prevalent than appreciated for two reasons. It has been found to be present implicitly. It has found to be growing in explicit importance. The two aspects share the common attribute, that is, management tends to retreat from overt management of relationships at a fine grain of analysis, placing too much reliance upon individuals taking responsibility. For formal routines, there also tend to be a lack of robustness at the systems level and between the project business and its projects. Empirical evidence has been drawn upon or cited in support as well as the logic of the theory compared to practice on the ground.

As with much, if not most, research and analysis within the sphere of management, and certainly project management, there is an implied, if not explicit, normative and prescriptive component. In this book, the analysis and empirical evidence stand on their own terms yet point towards the normative and prescriptive elements, which become reinforced by trends in project markets that suggest that relationship management provides one avenue of performance enhancement to meet client and stakeholder demands.

Relationship management is inappropriate in all market segments, and where greater levels of integration are needed, it does not necessarily provide the main strategic direction for all project businesses, but it is likely to be the case that internal integration in the project business and external integration for delivery will require effective relationships. Thus, greater awareness is important for practitioners in order to make sound strategic decisions between options. In this respect, practitioners have yet to be adequately served by much of the research community, which has continued to distance itself from directly addressing relationships wherever possible. Relationships are an important part of the greater integration between organizational functions, and between 'hard' and 'soft' management issues.

Projects are temporal and social activities. Projects occupy social space more than they occupy locational space. How projects are conducted in that social space is a key aspect for the future effectiveness and hence of project performance in delivery and in use. Relationships are important, and their management is part of the management of projects as they effectively link the project business to the project in robust ways. This is an exciting work in progress in research and practice, and is necessary for producing efficient and effective projects.

REFERENCES

W. Aarseth and H.C. Sorhaug, 'Improving business performance in multi-company projects through "cooperative power": presentation of a collaborative tool model', *International Journal of Business Performance Management,* 11 (4), 2009, 364–382.

M.Y. Abolafia, *Making Markets: opportunism and restraint on Wall Street,* Cambridge: Harvard Business Press, 1996.

V. Acha, D.M. Gann and A.J. Salter, 'Episodic innovation: R&D strategies for project-based environments', *Industry and Innovation,* 12, 2005, 255–281.

R.L. Ackoff, *Creating the Corporate Future,* New York: Wiley, 1981.

K. Acquino, T.M. Tripp and R.J. Bies, 'Getting even or moving on? Power, procedural justice, and the types of offenses as predictors of revenge, forgiveness, reconciliation, and avoidance in organizations', *Journal of Applied Psychology,* 91 (3), 2006, 653–668.

C.R. Agnew, P.A.M. van Lange, C.E. Rusbult and C.A. Langston, 'Cognitive interdependence: commitment and the mental representation of close relationships', *Journal of Personality and Social Psychology,* 74 (4), 1997, 939–954.

T. Ahola and A. Davies, 'Insights to the governance of projects: analysis of *Organization Theory and Project Management: administering uncertainty in Norwegian offshore oil* by Stinchcombe and Heimer', *International Journal of Managing Projects in Business,* 5 (4), 2012, 661–679.

N. Alderman, C.J. Ivory, R. Vaughan, A. Thwaites and I.P. McLoughlin, 'The project management implications of new service-led projects: new issues and directions for research', *Paper presented at EURAM 2003,* 3rd–5th April, Milan, 2003.

M. Alshawi and I. Faraj, 'Integrated construction environments', *Construction Innovation,* 2, 2002, 33–51.

A. Amin and J. Hausner, 'Interactive governance and social complexity', pp. 1–31. *Beyond Market and Hierarchy: interactive governance and social complexity,* A. Amin and J. Hausner (eds.), Cheltenham: Edward Elgar, 1997.

D. Ancona and C.-L. Chong, 'Entrainment: pace, cycle, and rhythm in organizational behavior', *Research in Organizational Behavior,* 18, 1996, 251–284.

D. Ancona, T.W. Malone, W.J. Orlikowski and P.J. Senge, 'In praise of the incomplete leader', *Harvard Business Review,* February, 2007, 92–100.

E.S. Andersen, 'Toward a project management theory for renewal projects', *Project Management Journal,* 37, 2006, 15–30.

E.S. Andersen, 'Are we getting any better? Comparing project management in the years 2000 and 2008', *Project Management Journal,* 41 (4), 2010, 4–16.

N.Å. Andersen, *Managing Intensity and Play at Work: transient relationships,* Cheltenham: Edward Elgar, 2013.

N.A. Ankrah, D. Proverbs and Y. Debrah, 'Factors influencing the culture of a construction project organisation: an empirical investigation', *Engineering Construction and Architectural Management,* 16 (1), 2009, 26–47.

A.M. Anvuur and M.M. Kumaraswamy, 'Better collaboration through cooperation', *Collaborative Relationships in Construction,* H.J. Smyth and S.D. Pryke (eds.), Oxford: Wiley-Blackwell, 2008, pp. 107–128.

A.M. Anvuur and M.M. Kumaraswamy, 'Measurement and antecedents of cooperation in construction', *Journal of Construction Engineering and Management,* 138 (7), 2011, 797–810.

K.A. Appiah, *The Ethics of Identity,* Princeton, NJ: Princeton University Press, 2005.

K.A. Appiah, *The Honor Code: how moral revolutions happen,* London: W.W. Norton and Co., 2010.

Aristotle, *The Nicomachean Ethics,* translated by J.A.K. Thomson, London: Penguin, 2004.

B. Aritua, S. Male and D.A Bower, 'Defining the intelligent public sector construction procurement client', *Management, Procurement and Law,* 162 (MP0), 2009, 75–82.

K. Artto, A. Davies, J. Kujala and A. Prencipe, 'The project business: analytical framework and research opportunities', *The Oxford Handbook of Project Management,* P.W.G. Morris, J.K. Pinto and J. Söderlund (eds.), Oxford: Oxford University Press, 2011, pp. 133–153.

B.E. Ashforth and R.H. Humphrey, 'Emotions in the workplace: a reappraisal', *Human Relations,* 48, 1995, 97–125.

B.E. Ashforth and F. Mael, 'Social identity theory and the organization', *Academy of Management Review,* 14 (1), 1989, 20–39.

M. Aubry, B. Hobbs and D. Thuillier, 'Organisational project management: a historical approach to the study of PMOs', *International Journal of Project Management,* 26, 2008, 38–43.

F. Auch and H.J. Smyth, 'Cultural divergence in project firms: the case of a leading main contractor operating from multiple offices', *International Journal of Managing Projects in Business,* 3 (3), 2010, 443–461.

D. Ayres, and Smyth, H. J. 'Trust between clients and consultants in retail construction', *Proceedings of RICS Cobra 2010,* 2nd–3rd September, Paris, 2010.

P. Bachrach and M.S. Baratz, *Power and Poverty: theory and practice,* Oxford: Oxford University Press, 1973.

B. Baiden and A.D.F. Price, 'The effect of integration on project delivery team effectiveness', *International Journal of Project Management,* 29, 2011, 129–136.

A.C. Baier, *Moral Prejudices: essays on ethics,* Cambridge: Harvard Business Press, 1994.

D. Ballantyne and R.J. Varey, 'Introducing a dialogical orientation to the service-dominant logic of marketing', *The Service-Dominant Logic of Marketing: dialog, debate and directions,* R.F. Lusch and S.L Vargo (eds.), Armonk, NY: M.E. Sharpe, 2006, pp. 224–235.

Banwell Report, *The Placing and Management of Contracts for Building and Civil Engineering Works,* Ministry of Public Building and Works, London: HMSO, 1964.

J. Barling, F. Slater and E.K. Kelloway, 'Transformational leadership and emotional intelligence: an exploratory study', *Leadership & Organization Development Journal,* 21 (3), 2000, 157–161.

C.I. Barnard, *The Function of the Executive,* Cambridge, MA: Harvard University Press, 1968.

J.B. Barney, 'Firm resources and sustained competitive advantage', *Journal of Management,* 17, 1991, 99–120.

J.B. Barney and M.H. Hansen, 'Trustworthiness as a source of competitive advantage', *Strategic Management Journal,* 15 (2), 1994, 175–190.

R. Bar-On, *The Emotional Quotient Inventory (EQ-I),* Toronto: Multi-Health Systems, 1997.

R. Bar-On, R. Handley and S. Fund, 'The impact of emotional intelligence on performance', *Linking Emotional Intelligence and Performance at Work,* V.U. Druskat, F. Sala and J. Mount (eds.), Mahwah, NJ: Lawrence Erlbaum, 2006, pp. 3–19.

J. Baron, J. Beattie and J.C. Hershey, 'Heuristics and biases in diagnostic reasoning: congruence, information, and certainty', *Organizational Behavior and Human Decision Processes,* 42 (1), 1988, 88–110.

S. Baron-Cohen, *The Essential Difference: men, women and the extreme male brain,* London: Penguin, 2004.

S. Barrett and C. Fudge, *Policy and Action: essays on the implementation of public policy,* London: Methuen, 1981.

B.R. Barringer and J.S. Harrison, 'Walking a tightrope: creating value through interorganizational relationships', *Journal of Management,* 26 (3), 2000, 367–403.

B.M. Bass, *Leadership and Performance beyond Expectations,* New York: The Free Press, 1985.

S. Bayer and D.M. Gann, 'Balancing work: bidding strategies and workload dynamics in a project-based professional service organisation', *System Dynamics Review,* 22 (3), 2006, 185–211.

R. Bayliss, S.-O. Cheung, H.C.H. Suen and S.-P. Wong, 'Effective partnering tools in construction: a case study on MTRC TKE contract 604 in Hong Kong', *International Journal of Project Management,* 22, 2004, 253–263.

T.D. Beamish and N.W. Biggart, 'The role of heuristics in project-centred production networks: insights from the commercial construction industry', *The Engineering Project Organization Journal,* 2, 2012, 57–70.

B. Bechky, 'Gaffers, goffers, and grips: role-based coordination in temporary organizations', *Organization Science,* 17, 2006, 3–21.

M. Beer, B. Spector, P.R. Lawrence, O.N. Mills and R.E. Walton, *Managing Human Assets,* New York: Free Press, 1984.

J. Bennett and S. Jayes, *Trusting the Team: the best practice guide to partnering in construction,* Reading: Reading Construction Forum, 1995.

W. Bennis, 'Five competencies of new leaders', *Executive Excellence,* 16 (7), 1999, 4–5.

P. Berger and T. Luckmann, *The Social Construction of Reality: a treatise in the sociology of knowledge,* New York: Doubleday, 1967.

M. Berman, *All That is Solid Melts into Air: the experience of modernity,* 1988 edition, London: Penguin, 1982.

J.B. Bernerth and H.J. Walker, 'Propensity to trust and the impact on social exchange: an empirical investigation', *Journal of Leadership and Organizational Studies,* 15 (3), 2009, 217–226.

L. Berry, 'Relationship marketing', *Emerging Perspectives on Service Marketing,* L. Berry, G. Shostack and G. Upah (eds.), Chicago, Il: American Marketing Association, 1983, pp. 25–28.

W.G. Biemans, M.M. Brenčič and A. Malshe, 'Marketing-sales interface configurations in B2B firms', *Industrial Marketing Management,* 39, 2010, 183–194.

K.M. Bijlsma, 'Antecedents of trust in managers: a "bottom-up" approach', *Personnel Review,* 32, 2003, 638–664.

M.J. Bitner, A.L. Ostrom, F.N. Morgan, 'Service blueprinting: a practical technique for service innovation', Phoenix: Center for Services Leadership, Arizona State University Working Paper, 2007.

K.J. Blois, 'Trust in business to business relationships: an evaluation of its status', *Journal of Management Studies,* 36 (2), 1999, 197–215.

D. Boddy, D. Macbeth and B. Wagner, 'Implementing collaboration between organizations: an empirical study of supply chain partnering', *Journal of Management Studies,* 37 (7), 2000, 1003–1017.

N. Boot-Handford and H.J. Smyth, 'The interplay of emotional intelligence and trust in project relationships', *Proceedings of 7th Nordic Conference on Construction Economics and Organisation 2013,* Norwegian University of Science and Technology, 12th–14th June, Trondheim.

R.E. Boyatzis, D. Goleman and K.S. Rhee, 'Clustering competence in emotional intelligence', *The Handbook of Emotional Intelligence,* R. Bar-On, and J. Parker (eds.), San Francisco: Jossey-Bass, 2000, pp. 343–362.

M.A. Brackett and J.D. Mayer, 'Convergent, discriminant, and incremental validity of competing measures of emotional intelligence', *Personality and Social Psychology Bulletin,* 29 (9), 2003, pp. 1147–1158.

M.A. Brackett, P. Lopes, Z. Ivcevic, J.D. Mayer and P. Salovey, 'Integrating emotion and cognition: the role of emotional intelligence', *Motivation, Emotion, and Cognition: integrating perspectives on intellectual functioning,* D. Dai and R. Sternberg (eds.), Mahwah, NJ: Lawrence Erlbaum, 2004, pp. 175–194.

J.L. Bradach and R.G. Eccles, 'Price, authority and trust: from ideal types to plural forms', *Annual Review of Sociology,* 15, 1989, 97–118.

T.R. Bradberry and L.D. Su, 'Ability-versus skill-based assessment of emotional intelligence', *Psicothema,* 18, 2006, 59–66.

T. Brady and A. Davies, 'Building project capabilities: from exploratory to exploitative learning', *Organization Studies,* 25 (9), 2004, 1601–1621.

T. Brady and A. Davies, 'Learning to deliver a mega-project: the case of Heathrow Terminal 5', *Procuring Complex Performance: studies of innovation in product–service management,* N. Caldwell and M. Howard (eds.), Abingdon: Routledge, 2010, pp. 174–197.

T. Brady and H. Maylor, 'The improvement paradox in project contexts: a clue to the way forward?' *International Journal of Project Management,* 28, 2010, 787–795.

T. Brady, A. Davies and P. Nightingale, 'Dealing with uncertainty in complex projects: revisiting Klein and Meckling', *International Journal of Managing Projects in Business,* 5 (4), 2012, 718–736.

K. Bredin and J. Söderlund, 'HRM and project intensification in R&D based companies: a study of Volvo Car Corporation and AstraZeneca', *R&D Management,* 36 (5), 2006, 467–485.

K. Bredin and J. Söderlund, *Human Resource Management in Project-Based Organizations: the HR quadriad framework,* Basingstoke: Palgrave Macmillan, 2011.

M. Bresnen, 'Construction contracting in theory and practice: a case study', *Construction Management and Economics,* 9, 1991, 247–263.

M. Bresnen and N. Marshall, 'Partnering in construction: a critical review of issues, problems' and dilemmas', *Construction Management and Economics,* 18 (2), 2000, 229–237.

M. Bresnen and N. Marshall, 'The engineering or evolution of co-operation? A tale of two partnering projects', *International Journal of Project Management,* 20 (7), 2002, 497–505.

M. Bresnen and N. Marshall, 'Projects and partnerships: institutional processes and emergent practices', *The Oxford Handbook of Project Management,* P.W.G. Morris, J.K. Pinto and J. Söderlund (eds.), Oxford: Oxford University Press, 2011, pp. 154–174.

M. Bresnen, A. Goussevskaia and J. Swan, 'Embedding new management knowledge in project-based organizations', *Organization Studies,* 25 (9), 2004, 1535–1555.

M.B. Brewer, 'In-group bias in the minimal intergroup situation', *Psychological Bulletin,* 86, 1979, 307–324.

A. Brien, 'Professional ethics and the culture of trust', *Journal of Business Ethics,* 17 (4), 1998, 391–409.

G.H. Briscoe, A.R. Dainty, S.J. Millett and R.H. Neale, 'Client-led strategies for construction supply chain improvement', *Construction Management and Economics,* 22 (2), 2004, 193–201.

A.D. Brown and F.T.T. Phua, 'Subjectively construed identities and discourse: towards a research agenda for construction management', *Construction Management and Economics,* 29, 2011, 83–95.

S.L. Brown and K.M. Eisenhardt, *Competing on the Edge: strategy as structured chaos,* Boston, MA: Harvard Business School Press, 1998.

A. Bryman, M. Bresnen, J. Ford, A. Beardworth and T. Keil, 'Leader orientation and organisational transience', *Journal of Occupational Psychology,* 60, 1987, 15–19.

R. Buck, 'A test of nonverbal receiving ability: preliminary studies', *Human Communication and Research,* 2, 1976, 162–171.

J.M. Burns, *Leadership: transformational leadership, transactional leadership,* New York: Harper and Row, 1978.

T. Burns and G.M. Stalker, *The Management of Innovation,* London: Tavistock, 1961.

D.C.A. Butcher and M.J. Sheehan, 'Excellent contractor performance in the UK construction industry', *Engineering, Construction and Architectural Management,* 17, 2010, 35–45.

C.J. Butler and P.S. Chinowsky, 'Emotional intelligence and leadership behavior in construction executives', *ASCE Journal of Management in Engineering,* 22 (3), 2006, 119–125.

J.K. Butler, 'Toward understanding and measuring conditions of trust: evolution of conditions of trust inventory', *Journal of Management,* 17, 1991, 643–663.

J.K. Butler and R.S. Cantrell, 'A behavioural decision theory approach to modeling dyadic trust in superior and subordinates', *Psychological Reports,* 55, 1984, 19–28.

L.E. Bygballe, M. Jahre and A. Swärd, 'Partnering relationships in construction: a literature review', *Journal of Purchasing & Supply Management,* 16, 2010, 239–253.

K.S. Cameron and R.E. Quinn, *Diagnosing and Changing Organizational Culture,* San Francisco: Jossey-Bass, 2006.

N. Campbell, *An Interaction Approach to Organisation Buying Behaviour: relationship marketing for competitive advantage,* Oxford: Butterworth-Heinemann, 1995.

A. Carmeli, 'The relationship between emotional intelligence and work attitudes, behavior and outcomes: an examination among senior managers', *Journal of Managerial Psychology,* 18 (7/8), 2003, 788–814.

S.J. Carson, A. Madhok, R. Varman and G. John, 'Information processing moderators of the effectiveness of trust-based governance in interfirm R&D collaboration', *Organization Science,* 14 (1), 2003, 45–56.

S. Cartwright and C. Pappas, 'Emotional intelligence, its measurement and implications for the workplace', *International Journal of Management Reviews,* 10 (2), 2008, 149–171.

D.R. Caruso and P. Salovey, *The Emotionally Intelligent Manager: how to develop and use the four key emotional skills of leadership,* San Francisco: Jossey-Bass, 2004.

M. Castells, *The Rise of the Network Society,* Oxford: Blackwell, 1996.

CH2M Hill, 'Company presentation', *Cultural Impacts on Project Processes and Outputs: a research agenda,* ESRC Seminar Series, 12th December, London: University College London, 2013.

M. Chambers, T. Fitch, I. Keki and H.J. Smyth, 'Differences between customer experience and business development propositions: the case of a major contractor in the infrastructure market', *Proceedings of the ARCOM 2009,* 7th–9th September, Nottingham, 2009.

C. Cherniss, 'Emotional intelligence and organizational effectiveness', *The Emotionally Intelligent Workplace,* C. Cherniss and D. Goleman (eds.), San Francisco: Jossey-Bass, 2001, pp. 3–12.

A.B. Cherns and D.T. Bryant, 'Studying the client's role in construction management', *Construction Management and Economics,* 2, 1984, 177–184.

S.-O. Cheung, T.S. Ng, S.-P. Wong and H.C. Suen, 'Behavioral aspects in construction partnering', *International Journal of Project Management,* 21 (5), 2003, 333–343.

S.-O. Cheung, K.T.W. Yiu and P.S. Chim, 'How relational are construction contracts?' *Journal of Professional Issues in Engineering Education and Practice,* 132 (1), 2006, 48–59.

Y.K.F. Cheung and S. Rowlinson, 'Supply chain sustainability: a relationship management approach', *International Journal of Managing Projects in Business,* 4 (3), 2011, 480–497.

M. Christopher, A. Payne and D. Ballantyne, *Relationship Marketing: creating stakeholder value,* Oxford: Butterworth-Heinemann, 2002.

S. Cicmil and D. Hodgson, 'Making projects critical: an introduction', *Making Projects Critical,* S. Cicmil and D. Hodgson (eds.), New York: Palgrave Macmillan, 2006, pp. 1–25.

S. Cicmil and D. Marshall, 'Insights into collaboration at the project level: complexity, social interaction and procurement mechanisms', *Building Research & Information,* 33 (6), 2005, 523–535.

R. Clapp-Smith, G.R. Vogelgesang and J.B. Avey, 'Authentic leadership and positive psychological capital: the mediating role of trust at the group level of analysis', *Journal of Leadership & Organizational Studies,* 15 (3), 2009, 227–240.

K.B. Clark and S.C. Wheelwright, 'Organizing and leading "heavyweight" development teams', *California Management Review,* 34 (3), 1992, 9–28.

M.S. Clark, 'Reactions to a request for a benefit in communal and exchange relationships', *Dissertation Abstracts International,* 38 (10-B), 1978, 5089–5090.

P. Clark, 'A review of the theories of time and structure for organizational sociology', *Research in the Sociology of Organizations,* 4, 1985, 35–79.

N. Clarke, 'Emotional intelligence and its relationship to transformational leadership and key project management competencies', *Project Management Journal,* 41 (2), 2010, 5–20.

S.R. Clegg, T.S. Pitsis, T. Rura-Polley and M. Marosszeky, 'Governmentality matters: designing an alliance culture of inter-organizational collaboration for managing projects', *Organization Studies,* 23 (3), 2002, 317–337.

S.R. Clegg, M. Kornberger and C. Rhodes, 'Business ethics as practice', *British Journal of Management,* 18 (2), 2007, 107–122.

S.R. Clegg, B. Kjersti and T.S. Pitsis, 'Innovating the practice of normative control in management contractual relations', *The Oxford Handbook of Project Management,* P.W.G. Morris, J.K. Pinto and J. Söderlund (eds.), Oxford: Oxford University Press, 2011, pp. 410–437.

R.H. Coase, 'The nature of the firm', *Economica,* 4, 1937, 386–405.

R.H. Coase, 'Industrial organization: a proposal for research', *The Firm, the Market and the Law,* R.H. Coase (ed.), Chicago: University of Chicago Press, 1988, pp. 57–74.

J.S. Coke, C.D. Batson and K. McDavis, 'Empathic mediation of helping: a two-stage model', *Journal of Personality and Social Psychology,* 36 (7), 1978, 752.

J.S. Coleman, 'Social capital in the creation of human capital', *American Journal of Sociology,* 94, 1988, S95–S120.

S.T. Collins, A.A. Yassine and S.P. Borgatti, 'Evaluating product development systems using network analysis', *Systems Engineering,* 12 (1), 2009, 55–68.

J.A. Colquitt, B.A. Scott and J.A. LePine, 'Trust, trustworthiness, and trust propensity: a meta-analysis of their unique relationships with risk taking and job performance', *Journal of Applied Psychology,* 92, 2007, 909–927.

Company Survey Report, *Annual Employee Survey,* Unpublished Report, 2009.

Constructing Excellence, *Never Waste a Good Crisis: a review of progress since 'Rethinking Construction' and thoughts for our future,* www.constructingexcellence.org.uk/news/article. jsp?id=10886, 2009. Accessed 22nd August 2013.

E.L. Cook and D.E. Hancher, 'Partnering: contracting for the future', *ASCE Journal of Management in Engineering,* 6 (4), 1990, 431–446.

L. Cortina, V. Magley, J. Hunter Williams and R. Day Langhout, 'Incivility in the workplace: incidence and impact', *Journal of Occupational Health and Psychology,* 6 (January), 2001, 64–80.

B. Cova and R. Salle, 'Six points to merge project marketing into project management', *International Journal of Project Management,* 23, 2005, 354–359.

B. Cova and R. Salle, 'Shaping projects, building networks', *The Oxford Handbook of Project Management,* P.W.G. Morris, J.K. Pinto and J. Söderlund (eds.), Oxford: Oxford University Press, 2011, pp. 391–409.

B. Cova, P.N. Ghauri and R. Salle, *Project Marketing: beyond competitive bidding,* Chichester: John Wiley, 2002.

J.K. Crawford, 'The project management maturity model', *Information Systems Management,* 23, 2006, 50–58.

F. Crespin-Mazet and P. Portier, 'The reluctance of construction purchasers towards project partnering', *Journal of Purchasing & Supply Management,* 16, 2010, 230–238.

L. Cronbach and P. Meehl, 'Construct validity in psychological tests', *Psychological Bulletin,* 52 (4), 1955, 281–302.

R. Cropanzano, D.E. Rupp and Z.S. Byrne, 'The relationship of emotional exhaustion to work attitudes, job performance, and organizational citizenship behaviors', *Journal of Applied Psychology,* 88 (1), 2003, 160.

S.C. Currall and T.A. Judge, 'Measuring trust between organizational boundary role persons', *Organizational Behavior and Human Decision Processes,* 64 (2), 1995, 151–170.

R.M. Cyert and J.G. March, *A Behavioral Theory of the Firm,* Oxford: Blackwell, 1992.

F. Czerniawska, *The Intelligent Client: managing your management consultant,* London: Hodder & Stoughton Educational Division, 2002.

A.R.J. Dainty, A. Bryman, A.D.F. Price, K. Greasley, R. Soetanto and N. King, 'Project affinity: the role of emotional attachment in construction projects', *Construction Management and Economics,* 23 (3), 2005, 241–244.

D. Dalcher, 'The nature of project management: a reflection on *The Anatomy of Major Projects* by Morris and Hough', *International Journal of Managing Projects in Business,* 5 (4), 2012, 643–660.

A.R. Damasio, *The Feeling of What Happens: body and emotion in the making of consciousness,* London: Vintage, 2000.

T.K. Das and B.-S. Teng, 'Between trust and control: developing confidence in partner cooperation in alliances', *The Academy of Management Review,* 23, 1998, 491–512.

T.K. Das and B.-S. Teng, 'Trust, control, and risk in strategic alliances: an integrated framework', *Organization Studies,* 22 (2), 2001, 251–283.

T.K. Das and B.-S. Teng, 'The risk-based view of trust: a conceptual framework', *Journal of Business and Psychology,* 19 (1), 2004, 85–116.

P. Dasgupta, 'Trust as commodity', *Trust: making and breaking cooperative relations,* D. Gambetta (ed.), Oxford: Blackwell, 1988, pp. 49–72.

C.S. Daus and N.M. Ashkanasy, 'The case for the ability-based model of emotional intelligence in organizational behavior', *Journal of Organizational Behavior,* 26, 2005, 453–466.

A. Davies, 'Moving base into high-value integrated solutions: a value stream approach', *Industrial Corporate Change,* 13 (5), 2004, 727–756.

A. Davies and T. Brady, 'Organizational capabilities and learning in complex product systems: towards repeatable solutions', *Research Policy*, 29 (7–8), 2000, 931–953.

A. Davies and M. Hobday, *The Business of Projects: managing innovation in: complex products and systems*, Cambridge: Cambridge University Press, 2005.

A. Davies, T. Brady and M. Hobday, 'Organizing for solutions: systems seller vs. systems integrator', *Industrial Marketing Management*, 36, 2007, 183–193.

A. Davies, D.M. Gann and T. Douglas, 'Innovation in megaprojects: systems integration at London Heathrow Terminal 5', *California Management Review*, 51, 2009, 101–125.

P.R. Davis and D.H.T. Walker, 'Building capability in construction projects: a relationship-based approach', *Engineering, Construction and Architectural Management*, 16 (5), 2009, 475–489.

R. Dawson, *Developing Knowledge-Based Client Relationships: the future of professional services*, Oxford: Butterworth-Heinemann, 2000.

A. Day and S. Carroll, 'Using an ability-based measure of emotional intelligence to predict individual performance, group performance, and group citizenship behaviours', *Personality and Individuals Differences*, 36 (6), 2004, 1443–1458.

T.E. Deal and A.A. Kennedy, *Corporate Culture: the rites and rituals of corporate life*, Reading, MA: Addison-Wesley Publishing, 1982.

R.J. DeFillippi and M.B. Arthur, 'Paradox in project-based enterprises: the case of film-making', *California Management Review*, 40 (2), 1998, 1–15.

R.J. DeFillippi, M.B. Arthur and V. Lindsay, *Knowledge at Work: creative collaboration in the global economy*, Oxford: Blackwell, 2006.

F. Deng and H.J. Smyth, 'Contingency-based approach to firm performance in construction: critical review of empirical research', *ASCE Journal of Construction Engineering and Management*, 139 (10), 2013, http://dx.doi.org/10.1061(ASCE)CO.1943-7862.0000738.

F. Deng and H.J. Smyth, 'Nature of firm performance in construction', *ASCE Journal of Construction Engineering and Management*, 140 (2), 2014, http://dx.doi.org/10.1061(ASCE)CO.1943-7862.0000778.

M. Deutsch, 'Trust and suspicion', *Journal of Conflict Resolution*, 2, 1958, 265–279.

M.R. Dibben, 'Exploring the processual nature of trust and cooperation in organisations: a Whiteheadian analysis', *Philosophy of Management*, 4 (1), 2004, 25–39.

K.T. Dirks and D.L. Ferrin, 'Trust in leadership: meta-analytic findings and implications for research and practice', *Journal of Applied Psychology*, 87, 2002, 611–628.

K.T. Dirks and D.P. Skarlicki, 'Trust in leaders: existing research and emerging issues', *Trust and Distrust in Organizations: dilemmas and approaches*, R.M. Kramer and K.S. Cook (eds.), 2004, pp. 21–40. New York: The Russell Sage Foundation.

B. Donaldson and T. O'Toole, *Strategic Market Relationships: from strategy to implementation*, Chichester: Wiley, 2001.

P.M. Doney and J.P. Canon, 'An examination of the nature of trust in buyer–seller relationships', *The Journal of Marketing*, 61, 1997, 35–51.

M. Douglas, *Risk and Blame: essay on cultural theory*, London: Routledge, 1994.

M. Douglas, 'Four cultures: the evolution of a parsimonious model', *GeoJournal*, 47, 1999, 411–415.

M. Douglas, 'Being fair to hierarchists', *University of Pennsylvania Law Review*, 151 (4), 2003, 1349–1370.

H.L. Dreyfus and S.E. Dreyfus, 'Expertise in real world contexts', *Organization Studies*, 26 (5), 2005, 779–792.

V.U. Druskat and P. Druskat, 'Applying emotional intelligence in project working', *The Management of Complex Projects: a relationship approach*, S.D. Pryke and H.J. Smyth (eds.), Oxford: Blackwell Science, 2006, pp. 78–96.

V.U. Druskat and S.B. Wolff, 'Building the emotional intelligence of groups', *Harvard Business Review*, 79 (3), 2001, 90–91.

A. Dubois and L.-E. Gadde, 'Supply strategy and network effects-purchasing behaviour in the construction industry', *European Journal of Purchasing and Supply Management*, 6, 2000, 207–215.

S. Duck, *Personal Relationships 4: dissolving personal relationships*, New York: Academic Press, 1982.

M.F. Dulaimi, 'The influence of academic education and formal training on the project manager's behavior', *Journal of Construction Research*, 6, 2005, 179–193.

M.F. Dulaimi and D. Langford, 'Job behaviour of construction project mangers: determinants and assessment', *Journal of Construction Engineering and Management*, 125, 1999, 256–264.

V. Dulewicz and M. Higgs, 'Emotional intelligence: a review and evaluation study', *Journal of Managerial Psychology*, 15 (4), 2000, 341–372.

F.R. Dwyer, P.H. Schurr and S. Oh, 'Developing buyer–seller relationships', *Journal of Marketing*, 51 (2), 1987, 11–27.

J.H. Dyer and W. Chu, 'The role of trustworthiness in reducing transaction costs and improving performance: empirical evidence from the United States, Japan, and Korea', *Organization Science*, 14 (1), 2003, 57–68.

R. Eccles, 'The quasifirm in the construction industry', *Journal of Economic Behavior and Organization*, 2, 1981, 335–357.

Edelman, *The 13th annual Edelman Trust Barometer*, www.edelman.com/insights/intellectual-property/trust-2013/, 2013. Accessed 9th August 2013.

A.J. Edkins, J. Geraldi, P.W.G. Morris and A. Smith, 'Exploring the front-end of project management', *Engineering Project Organization Journal*, 3 (2), 2013, 71–85.

A.J. Edkins and H.J. Smyth, 'Contractual management in PPP projects: evaluation of legal versus relational contracting for service delivery', *ASCE Journal of Professional Issues in Engineering Education and Practice*, 132 (1), 2006, 82–93.

B. Edvardsson, M. Holmund and T. Strandvik, 'Initiation of business relationships in service-dominant settings', *Industrial Marketing Management*, 37 (3), 2008, 339–250.

Sir John Egan, *Rethinking Construction*, www.constructingexcellence.org.uk/pdf/rethinking%20construction/rethinking_construction_report.pdf, Department of the Environments Transport and Regions, London, 1998. Accessed 7th August 2013.

K.M. Eisenhardt and J.K. Martin, 'Dynamic capabilities: what are they?' *Strategic Management Journal*, 21, 2000, 1105–1121.

P. Ekman, *Darwin and Facial Expression: a century of research in review*, New York: Academic Press, 1973.

S. Ekman, *Authority and Autonomy: paradoxes of modern knowledge work*, Basingstoke: Palgrave Macmillan, 2012.

E. Eksted, R.A. Lundin, A. Söderholm and H. Wirdenius, *Neo-industrial Organising: renewal by action and knowledge formation in a project-intensive economy*, Malmö: Liber Abstrakt, 1999.

A.R. Elangovan and D.L. Shapiro, 'Betrayal of trust in organizations', *Academy of Management Review*, 23, 1998, 547–566.

H. Elfenbein, 'Team emotional intelligence: what it can mean and how it can affect performance', *Linking Emotional Intelligence and Performance at Work*, V.U. Druskat, F. Sala and J. Mount (eds.), Mahwah, NJ: Lawrence Erlbaum, 2006, pp. 165–184.

K. Eloranta, *Supplier Relationship Management in Networked Project Business*, Licentiate Thesis, Helsinki: Helsinki University of Technology, 2007.

J. Elster, 'Social norms and economic theory', *The Journal of Economic Perspectives*, 1989, 99–117.

M. Engwall, 'No project is an island: linking projects to history and context', *Research Policy,* 32, 2003, 789–808.

M. Engwall, 'PERT, Polaris, and the realities of project execution', *International Journal of Managing Projects in Business,* 5 (4), 2012, 595–616.

E.H. Erikson, *Identity: youth and crisis,* New York: Faber & Faber, 1968.

P.E. Eriksson and O. Pesämma, 'Modelling procurement effects on cooperation', *Construction Management and Economics,* 25, 2007, 893–901.

A. Etzioni, *The Moral Dimension: toward a new economics,* New York: Free Trade Press, 1988.

EURAM SIG, *Special Interest Group on Project Organizing,* http://euram2012.nl/userfiles/file/61%20%20Project%20Organising%20General%20Track%20bis.pdf. Accessed 5th April 2012.

C. Fabianski, *Complex Partnership for the Delivery of Urban Rail Infrastructure Project (URIP): how culture matters for the treatment of risk and uncertainty?* PhD, London: University College London, 2014.

A.C. Faulkner, J.H. Sargent and S.H. Wearne, 'Civil engineers' managerial roles and needs: report of survey', *Construction Management and Economics,* 7 (2), 1989, 155–174.

R. Faulkner and A. Anderson, 'Short-term projects and emergent careers: evidence from Hollywood', *American Journal of Science,* 92 (4), 1987, 879–909.

A. Fay, *Project Management Office: a relationship approach to the achievement of strategic objectives in project-based organizations,* MSc Dissertation, London: University College London, 2012.

F. Ferraro, J. Pfeiffer and R.I. Sutton, 'Economics language and assumptions: how theories can become self-fulfilling', *Academy of Management Review,* 30, 2005, 8–24.

D.L. Ferrin, K.T. Dirks and P.P. Shah, 'Direct and indirect effects on third-party relationships of interpersonal trust', *Journal of Applied Psychology,* 91, 2006, 870–883.

S.L. Fielden, M.J. Davidson, A.G. Gale and C.L. Davey, 'Women in construction: the untapped resource', *Construction Management and Economics,* 18, 2000, 113–121.

S. Fineman, *Understanding Emotion at Work,* London: Sage, 2003.

S. Fineman, 'Emotion in organizations: a critical turn', *Emotionalizing Organizations and Organizing Emotions,* B. Sieben and Å. Wettergren (eds.), London: Palgrave Macmillan, 2010, pp. 23–41.

C.M. Fiol, 'Capitalizing on paradox: the role of language in transforming organizational identities', *Organization Science,* 13 (6), 2002, 653–666.

R. Fisher and W.L. Ury, *Getting to Yes: negotiating agreement without giving in,* London: Penguin, 1981.

T. Fitch, I. Keki and H.J. Smyth, 'Power and perceptions in business development: the case of a major contractor and design consultancies in civil engineering influencer and referral markets', *ARCOM 2010 Conference,* 6th–8th September, Leeds, 2010.

J.A. Fitzsimmons and M.J. Fitzsimmons, *Service Management: operations, strategy, information technology,* New York: McGraw-Hill, 2011.

F. Flores and R.C. Solomon, 'Creating trust', *Business Ethics Quarterly,* 8, 1998, 205–232.

B. Flyvbjerg, N. Bruzelius and W. Rothengatter, *Mega Projects and Risk: an anatomy of ambition,* Cambridge: Cambridge University Press, 2003.

R. Foord, B. Armandi and C. Heaton, *Organization Theory: an interactive approach,* New York: Harper & Row, 1988.

D. Ford, L.-E. Gadde, H. Håkansson and I. Snehota, *Managing Business Relationships,* Chichester: Wiley, 2003.

J.D. Frame, *The New Project Management: tools for an age of rapid change, complexity, and other business realities,* Chichester: Wiley, 2002.

R.P. French Jr. and B.H. Raven, 'Legitimate power, coercive power and observability in social influence', *Sociometry,* 21 (2), 1958, 83–97.

M. Friedman, 'The social responsibility of business is to increase its profits', *The New York Times Magazine,* September 13, 1970.

N.H. Frijda, 'The laws of emotion', *American Psychologist,* 43, 1988, 349–358.

P.J. Frost, *Toxic Emotion at Work: how compassionate managers handle pain and conflict,* Boston, MA: Harvard Business School Press, 2003.

F. Fukuyama, *Trust: the social virtues and the creation of prosperity,* London: Penguin Books, 1995.

J.J. Gabarro, 'The development of working relationships', *The Handbook of Organizational Behavior,* J.W. Lorsch (ed.), Englewood Cliffs, NJ: Prentice-Hall, 1987, pp. 172–189.

L.-E. Gadde and A. Dubois, 'Partnering in the construction industry: problems and opportunities', *Journal of Purchasing and Supply Management,* 16, 2010, 254–263.

J.R. Galbraith, 'Organizational design: an information processing view', *Interfaces,* 4 (3), 1974, 28–36.

D. Gambetta, 'Can we trust trust?' *Trust: making and breaking of cooperative relations,* D. Gambetta (ed.), Oxford: Blackwell, 1988, pp. 213–238.

S. Ganesan, 'Determinants of long-term orientation in buyer–seller relationships', *Journal of Marketing,* 58 (2), 1994, 1–19.

D.M. Gann and A.J. Salter, 'Innovation in project-based, service-enhanced firms: the construction of complex products and systems', *Research Policy,* 29 (7), 2000, 955–972.

H. Gardner, *Frames of Mind: the theory of multiple intelligences,* New York: Basic Books, 1983.

L. Gardner and C. Stough, 'Examining the relationship between leadership and emotional intelligence in senior level managers', *Leadership and Organization Development Journal,* 23 (1/2), 2002, 68–78.

J. George, 'Emotions and leadership', *Human Relations,* 53 (8), 2000, 1027–1044.

J.G. Geraldi and T. Lechter, 'Gantt charts revisited: a critical analysis of its roots and implications to the management of projects today', *International Journal of Managing Projects in Business,* 5 (4), 2012, 578–594.

J.G. Geraldi, L. Lee-Kelley and E. Kutsch, 'The Titanic sunk, so what? Project manager response to unexpected events', *International Journal of Project Management,* 28, 2010, 547–558.

S. Ghoshal, 'Bad management theories are destroying good management practices', *Academy of Management Learning & Education,* 4 (1), 2005, 75–91.

S. Ghoshal and H.O. Rocha 'Beyond self-interest revisited', *Journal of Management Studies,* 43 (3), 2006, 585–619.

R. Gibbons, 'Transaction cost economics: past, present, and future?' *The Scandinavian Journal of Economics,* 112, 2010, 263–288.

A. Giddens, *Central Problems in Social Theory,* Los Angeles: University of California Press, 1979.

A. Giddens, 'Agency, institution, and time-space analysis', *Advances in Social Theory and Methodology,* K. Knorr-Cetina and A.V. Cicourel (eds.), 1981, pp. 161–174.

R. Gifford, D.W. Hine, W. Muller-Clemm, D.A.J. Reynolds and K.T. Shaw, 'Decoding modern architecture: a lens model approach for understanding the aesthetic differences of architects and laypersons', *Environment and Behavior,* 32 (2), 2000, 163–187.

N. Gil, J.K. Pinto and H.J. Smyth, 'Trust in relational contracting as a critical organizational attribute', *Oxford Handbook on the Management of Projects,* P.W.G. Morris, J.K. Pinto and J. Söderlund (eds.), Oxford: Oxford University Press, 2011, pp. 438–460.

C.G. Gilbert, 'Unbundling the structure of inertia: resource versus routine rigidity', *Academy of Management Journal,* 48, 2005, 741–763.

C. Gilligan, *A Different Voice,* Boston, MA: Harvard University Press, 1982.

J.H. Gittell, 'Supervisory span, relational coordination and flight departure performance: a reassessment of post bureaucracy theory', *Organization Science,* 12 (4), 2001, 468–483.

Glenigan Constructing Insight, Constructing Excellence in the Built Environment, and Department for Business, and Innovation, *UK Industry Performance Report Based on the UK Construction Industry Key Performance Indicators,* UK-KPI, London: www.constructingexcellence.org.uk/pdf/KPI_Report_2011.pdf, 2011. Accessed 9th August 2013.

E. Goffman, *Presentation of Self in Everyday Life,* Reading: Cox and Wyman, 1959.

E. Goffman, *Interaction Ritual: essays in face-to-face behavior,* New York: Pantheon, 2005.

D. Goleman, *Emotional Intelligence: why it can matter more than IQ,* London: Bloomsbury, 1995.

D. Goleman, *Working with Emotional Intelligence,* London: Bloomsbury, 1998a.

D. Goleman, 'What makes a leader?' *Harvard Business Review,* 82 (1), 1998b, 82–91.

D. Goleman, R.E. Boyatzis and A. McKee, 'Primal leadership: the hidden driver of great performance', *Harvard Business Review,* 79 (11), 2001, 42–53.

D. Goleman, R.E. Boyatzis and A. McKee, *The New Leaders: transforming the art of leadership,* Boston, MA: Harvard Business School Press, 2002.

D. Good, 'Individuals, interpersonal relations, and trust', *Trust: making and breaking cooperative relations,* D. Gambetta (ed.), Oxford: Basil Blackwell, 1988, pp. 31–48.

G. Grabher, 'The project ecology of advertising: tasks, talents and teams', *Regional Studies,* 36 (3), 2002, 245–262.

G. Grabher, 'Architecture of project-based learning: creating and sedimenting knowledge in project ecologies', *Organization Studies,* 25 (9), 2004, 1491–1514.

G. Grabher and O. Ibert, 'Project ecologies: a contextual view on temporary organizations', *The Oxford Handbook of Project Management,* P.W.G. Morris, J.K. Pinto and J. Söderlund (eds.), Oxford: Oxford University Press, 2011, pp. 175–198.

M.S. Granovetter, 'The strength of weak ties', *American Journal of Sociology,* 78, 1973, 1360–1380.

M.S. Granovetter, 'Economic action and social structure: the problem of embeddedness', *American Journal of Sociology,* 91, 1985, 481–510.

K. Greasley, A. Bryman, A.R.J. Dainty, A.D.F. Price, R. Soetanto and N. King, 'Employee perceptions of empowerment', *Employee Relations,* 27 (4), 2005, 354–368.

S.D. Green, *Making Sense of Construction Improvement: a critical review,* Chichester: Wiley-Blackwell, 2011.

S.D. Green, and P. McDermott, 'An inside-out approach to partnering', *Proceedings of the ESRC-EPSRC Workshop on Partnering in Construction,* Manchester: University of Salford, 1996.

S.D. Green and S. May, 'Re-engineering construction: going against the grain', *Building Research & Information,* 31 (2), 2003, 97–106.

S.D. Green, C. Harty, A.A. Elmualim, G. Larsen and C.C. Kao, 'On the discourse of construction competitiveness', *Building Research & Information,* 36, 2008, 426–435.

J. Greenberg and R.A. Baron, *Behavior in Organizations,* New Jersey: Prentice Hall, 2003.

G. Gripsrud, M. Jahre and G. Persson, 'Supply chain management: back to the future?' *International Journal of Physical Distribution and Logistics Management,* 36 (8), 2009, 643–659.

C. Grönroos, *Service Management and Marketing: customer management in service competition,* 2nd edition, Chichester: Wiley, 2000.

S.L. Gruneberg and G. Ive, *The Economics of the Modern Construction Firm,* Basingstoke: Macmillan, 2000.

R. Gulati, 'Does familiarity breed trust? The implications of repeated ties for contractual choice in alliances', *Academy of Management Journal,* 38 (1), 1995, 85–112.

R. Gulati and J.A. Nickerson, 'Interorganizational trust, governance choice, and exchange performance', *Organization Science,* 19 (5), 2008, 688–708.

E. Gummesson, *Total Relationship Marketing,* Oxford: Butterworth-Heinemann, 2000.

G.T. Gundlach, R.S. Achrol and J.T. Mentzer, 'The structure of commitment in exchange', *The Journal of Marketing,* 59, 1995, 78–92.

M. Gustafsson, *Between Before and After: studying project implementation real-time,* unpublished paper, Turku, Finland: Åbo Akademi University, 2002.

M. Gustafsson, H.J. Smyth, E. Ganskau and T. Arhippainen, 'Bridging strategic and operational issues for project business through managing trust', *International Journal of Managing Projects in Business,* 3 (3), 2010, 422–442.

C.J. Haberstroh, 'Organizational design and system analysis', *Handbook of Organizations,* J.G. March (ed.), Chicago: Rand McNally, 1965, pp. 1171–1212.

A. Hadjikhani, 'Project marketing and the management of discontinuity', *International Business Review,* 5 (3), 1996, 319–336.

H. Håkansson, *International Marketing and Purchasing of Industrial Goods,* London: Wiley, 1982.

H. Håkansson and I. Snehota, *Developing Relationships in Business Networks,* Boston: International Thomson Press, 1995.

M. Hällgren and E. Maaninen-Olsson, 'Deviations, ambiguity and uncertainty in a project-intensive organization', *Project Management Journal,* 36 (3), 2005, 17–26.

M. Hällgren, M. Jacobsson and A. Söderholm, 'Embracing the drifting environment: the legacy of a Scandinavian project literature classic', *International Journal of Managing Projects in Business,* 5 (4), 2012, 695–713.

G. Hamel and C.K. Prahalad, *Competing for the Future,* Boston: Harvard Business School Press, 1996.

C.B. Handy, *Gods of Management: the changing work of organizations,* Oxford: Oxford University Press, 1996.

C.B. Handy, *Understanding Organizations,* London: Penguin, 1997.

K.R. Harrigan, 'Joint ventures and competitive strategy', *Strategic Management Journal,* 9 (2), 1988, 141–158.

A. Hartmann, A. Davies and L. Frederiksen, 'Learning to deliver service-enhanced public infrastructure: balancing contractual and relational capabilities', *Construction Management and Economics,* 28 (11), 2010, 1165–1175.

K. Hartshorn, 'Humane workplace is a productive workplace', *National Productivity Review,* 16 (2), 1997, 1–7.

C. Harvey, *Secrets of the World's Top Sales Performers,* London: Century, Random, 1988.

B. Hedberg, G. Dahlgren, G. Hansson and N.-G. Olve, *Virtual Organizations and Beyond: discover imaginary systems,* Chichester: John Wiley & Sons, 1997.

J.B. Heide and G. John, 'Alliances in industrial purchasing: the determinants of joint action in buyer–seller relationships', *Journal of Marketing Research,* 27 (1), 1990, 24–36.

J.B. Heide and A. Miner, 'The shadow of the future: effects of anticipated interaction and frequency of contact on buyer–seller cooperation', *Academy of Management Journal,* 35 (2), 1992, 265–291.

C.E. Helfat, 'Know-how and asset complementarity and dynamic capability accumulation', *Strategic Management Journal,* 18 (5), 1997, 339–360.

C.E. Helfat and M.A. Peteraf, 'The dynamic resource-based view: capability lifecycles', *Strategic Management Journal,* 24, 2003, 997–1010.

A. Helkkula, C. Kelleher and M. Pihlström, 'Characterizing value as an experience: implications for service researchers and managers', *Journal of Service Research,* 15 (1), 2012, 59–75.

W.J. Henisz, R.E. Levitt and W.R. Scott, 'Towards a unified theory of project governance: economic sociology and psychological supports for relational contracting', *The Engineering Project Organization Journal,* 2, 2012, 37–55.

F. Herzberg, 'One more time: how do you motivate employees?' *Harvard Business Review,* 46, 1968, 53–62.

M. Higgs and P. Aitken, 'An exploration of the relationship between emotional intelligence and leadership potential', *Journal of Managerial Psychology,* 18 (8), 2003, 814–823.

S. Hobbs and H.J. Smyth, 'Emotional intelligence in engineering project teams', *Proceedings of the CIB Research to Practice Conference,* 26th–29th June, Montreal, 2012.

M. Hobday, 'The project-based organisation: an ideal form for managing complex products and systems?' *Research Policy,* 26, 2000, 689–710.

M. Hobday, A. Davies and A. Prencipe, 'Systems integration: a core capability of the modern corporation', *Industrial and Corporate Change,* 14 (6), 2005, 1109–1143.

D.E. Hodgson and S. Cicmil, 'The politics of standards in modern management: making the project a reality', *Journal of Management Studies,* 44 (3), 2007, 431–450.

M. Hoegl, M. Muethel and H.G. Gemunden, 'Leadership and teamwork in dispersed projects', *The Oxford Handbook of Project Management,* P.W.G. Morris, J.K. Pinto and J. Söderlund (eds.), Oxford: Oxford University Press, 2011, pp. 483–499.

G. Hofstede and G. Hofstede, *Cultures and Organisations: software of the mind,* London: McGraw-Hill, 2005.

M.A. Hogg and D.J. Terry, 'Social identity and self-categorization processes in organizational contexts', *Academy of Management Review,* 25 (1), 2000, 121–140.

E. Holmen and A.-C. Pedersen, 'How do suppliers strategise in relation to a contractor's supply network initiative?' *Journal of Purchasing & Supply Chain Management,* 16, 2010, 264–278.

G.D. Holt, P.E.D. Love and L.J. Nesan, 'Employee empowerment in construction: an implementation model for process improvement', *Team Performance Management: An International Journal,* 6, 2000, 47–51.

L.T. Hosmer, 'Trust: the connecting links between organizational theory and philosophical ethics', *Academy of Management Review,* 20 (2), 1995, 379–403.

C.L. Huang and B.G. Chang, 'The effects of managers' moral philosophy on project decision under agency problem conditions', *Journal of Business Ethics,* 94 (4), 2010, 595–611.

J. Hughes, 'Emotional intelligence: Elias, Foucault and the reflexive emotional self', *Foucault Studies,* 8, 2010, 28–52.

P.H. Hui, A. Davis-Blake and J.P. Broschak, 'Managing interdependence: the effects of outsourcing structure on the performance of complex projects', *Decision Sciences,* 39 (1), 2008, 5–31.

J.E. Hunter and R.F. Hunter, 'Validity and utility of alternative predictors of job performance', *Psychological Bulletin,* 96 (1), 1984, 72–98.

B.W. Husted, 'The ethical limits of trust in business relations', *Business Ethics Quarterly,* 8 (2), 1998, 233–248.

I. Hyvari, 'Project management effectiveness in project-oriented business organizations', *International Journal of Project Management,* 24, 2006, 216–225.

M. Imai, *Kaizen, the Key to Japan's Competitive Success,* New York: McGraw-Hill and Random House, 1986.

G. Ive and S.L. Gruneberg, *The Economics of the Modern Construction Sector,* Basingstoke: Macmillan, 2000.

G. Ive and K. Rintala, 'The economics of relationships', *Management of Complex Projects: a relationship approach,* S.D. Pryke and H.J. Smyth (eds.), Oxford: Blackwell, 2006, pp. 282–302.

B.B. Jackson, *Winning and Keeping Industrial Customers,* Lexington, KY: Lexington Books, 1985.

M. Jacobsson and A. Söderholm, 'Breaking out of the straightjacket of project research: in search of contribution', *International Journal of Managing Projects in Business*, 4, 2011, 378–388.

M. Janowicz-Panjaitan and N.G. Noorderhaven, 'Trust, calculation, and interorganizational learning of tacit knowledge: and interorganizational roles perspective', *Organization Studies*, 30 (10), 2009, 1021–1044.

S.L. Jarvenpaa and E. Keating, 'Global offshoring of engineering project teams: trust asymmetries across cultural borders', *The Engineering Project Organization Journal*, 2, 2012, 71–83.

S.L. Jarvenpaa and D.E. Leidner, 'Communication and trust in global virtual teams', *Organization Science*, 10 (6), 1999, 791–815.

P. Jarzabkowski, J.K. Lê and M. Feldman, 'Toward a theory of coordinating: creating coordinating mechanisms in practice', *Organization Science*, 23 (4), 2012, 907–927.

M.C. Jensen and W.H Meckling, 'Theory of the firm: managerial behavior, agency costs and ownership structure', *Journal of Financial Economics*, 3 (4), 1976, 305–360.

A.L. Jepsen and P. Eskerod, 'Stakeholder analysis in projects: challenges in using current guidelines in the real world', *International Journal of Project Management*, 27, 2009, 335–343.

C. Jones and B.B. Lichtenstein, 'Temporary inter-organizational projects: how temporal and social embeddedness enhance coordination and manage uncertainty', *The Oxford Handbook of Inter-Organizational Relations*, S. Cropper, M. Ebers, C. Huxham and P. Smith Ring (eds.), Oxford: Oxford University Press, 2008, pp. 231–255.

C. Jones, W. Hesterly and S. Borgatti, 'A general theory of network governance: exchange conditions and social mechanisms', *Academy of Management Review*, 22 (4), 1997, 911–945.

G.R. Jones and J.M. George, 'The experience and evolution of trust: implications for cooperation and teamwork', *Academy of Management Review*, 23, 1998, 531–546.

T. Jones, P.A. Dacin and S.F. Taylor, 'Relational damage and relationship repair: a new look at transgressions in service relationships', *Journal of Service Research*, 14 (3), 2011, 318–339.

A. Jonsson and N.J. Foss, 'International expansion through flexible replication: learning from the internationalization experience of IKEA', *Journal of International Business Studies*, 9, 2011, 1079–1102.

P.J. Jordan, N.M. Ashkanasy, C.E.J. Härtel and G.S. Hooper, 'Workgroup emotional intelligence: scale development and relationship to team process effectiveness and goal focus', *Human Resource Management Review*, 12 (2), 2002, 195–214.

P.J. Jordan, N.M. Ashkanasy and C.E.J. Härtel, 'The case for emotional intelligence in organizational research', *Academy of Management Review*, 28, 2003, 195–197.

A. Kadefors, 'Institutions in building projects: implications for flexibility and change', *Scandinavian Journal of Management*, 11 (4), 1995, 395–408.

A. Kadefors, 'Trust in project relationships: inside the black box', *International Journal of Project Management*, 22, 2004, 175–182.

A. Kadefors, C. Gerle and L. Nyberg, 'Trust and distrust in temporary client-contractor relations', *17th Annual IMP Conference*, 9th–11th September, Oslo, 2001.

D. Kahneman, 'A perspective on judgment and choice: mapping bounded rationality', *American Psychologist*, 58 (9), 2003, 697–720.

D. Kahneman and S. Frederick, 'Representativeness revisited: attribute substitution in intuitive judgment', *Heuristics and Biases: the psychology of intuitive judgment*, T. Thomas, D. Griffin and D. Kahneman (eds.), Cambridge: Cambridge University Press, 2002, pp. 49–81.

D. Kahneman and D. Lovallo, 'Timid choices and bold forecasts: a cognitive perspective on risk taking', *Management Science,* 39 (1), 1993, 17–31.

D. Kahneman and A. Tversky, 'Prospect theory: an analysis of decisions under risk', *Econometrica,* 47 (2), 1979, 237–251.

D. Kahneman and A. Tversky, 'Rational choice and the framing of decisions', *Journal of Business,* 59 (4), 1986, S251-S278.

D. Kahneman, A. Tversky and P. Slovic, *Judgment under Uncertainty: heuristics and biases,* Cambridge: Cambridge University Press, 1982.

I. Kant, *Grounding for the Metaphysics of Morals,* translated by J.W. Ellington, (1981 ed.), Indianapolis, IN: Hackett Publishing, 1785.

A. Kaplan, *Power in Perspective: power and conflict in organizations,* London: Tavistock, 1964.

J. Katz-Buonincontro, 'How might aesthetic knowing relate to leadership? A review of the literature', *International Journal of Education & the Arts,* 12, 2011, 1–18.

H.T. Keh and Y. Xie, 'Corporate reputation and customer behavioral intentions: the roles of trust, identification and commitment', *Industrial Marketing Management,* 38, 2009, 732–742.

P.M. Keith, 'Individual and organizational correlates of a temporary system', *Journal of Applied Behavioral Science,* 14 (2), 1978, 195–203.

N. Kelly, A.J. Edkins, H.J. Smyth and E. Konstantinou, 'Reinventing the role of the project manager in mobilising knowledge in construction', *International Journal of Managing Projects in Business,* 6 (4), 2013, 654–673.

J. Kelsey, P.W.G. Morris, A. Roberts. H.J. Smyth and A. Wilson, *Health & Safety, Benchmarking and Culture,* Unpublished Report, London: University College London, 2010.

M. Kempeners and H.W. Van der Hart, 'Designing account management organizations', *Journal of Business and Industrial Marketing,* 14, 1999, 310–327.

D.A. Kenny and L. Albright, 'Accuracy in interpersonal perception: a social relations analysis', *Psychological Bulletin,* 102 (3), 1987, 390–402.

J. Keyton and F.L. Smith, 'Distrust in leaders: dimensions, patterns, and emotional intensity', *Journal of Leadership & Organizational Studies,* 16 (1), 2009, 6–18.

S.F. King and T.F. Burgess, 'Understanding success and failure in customer relationship management', *Industrial Marketing Management,* 37, 2008, 421–431.

J. Kirsilä, M. Hellström and K. Wikström, 'Integration as a project management concept: a study of the commissioning process in industrial deliveries', *International Journal of Project Management,* 25, 2007, 714–721.

J. Klayman and Y.-W. Ha, 'Confirmation, disconfirmation, and information in hypothesis testing', *Psychological Review,* 94 (2), 1987, 211–288.

B.H. Klein and W.H. Meckling, 'Application of operations research to development decisions', *Operations Research,* 6, 1958, 352–363.

B. Kogut, 'Joint ventures: theoretical and empirical perspectives', *Strategic Management Journal,* 9 (4), 1988, 319–332.

A.K. Kohli and B.J. Jaworski, 'Market orientation: the construct, research propositions, and managerial implications', *Journal of Marketing,* 54, 1990, 1–18.

M. Korczynski, 'The political economy of trust', *Journal of Management Studies,* 37 (1), 2000, 1–21.

R.M. Kramer, 'Trust and distrust in organizations: emerging perspectives, enduring questions', *Annual Review of Psychology,* 50 (1), 1999, 569–598.

R.M. Kramer, 'Rethinking trust', *Harvard Business Review,* June, 2009, 69–77.

R.M. Kramer and J. Wei, 'Social uncertainty and the problem of trust in social groups: the social self in doubt', *The Psychology of the Social Self,* T.R. Tyler, R.M. Kramer and O.P. John (eds.), London: Lawrence Erlbaum, 1999, pp. 145–168.

K. Kreiner, *The Site Organization: a study of social relationships on construction sites,* Copenhagen: The Technical University of Denmark, 1976.

K. Kreiner, 'In search of relevance: project management in drifting environments', *Scandinavian Journal of Management,* 11 (4), 1995, 335–346.

K. Kreiner, 'Comments on challenging the rational project environment: the legacy and impact of Christensen and Kreiner's *Projektledning i en ofulständig värld*', *International Journal of Managing Projects in Business,* 5 (4), 2012, 714–717.

T. Kuhn, *The Structure of Scientific Revolutions,* Chicago: University of Chicago Press, 1996.

M.M. Kumaraswamy and A.M. Anvuur, 'Selecting sustainable teams for PPP projects', *Building and Environment,* 43 (6), 2008, 999–1009.

M.M. Kumaraswamy and M.M. Rahman, 'Applying teamworking models to projects', *The Management of Complex Projects: a relationship approach,* S.D. Pryke and H.J. Smyth (eds.), Oxford: Blackwell, 2006, pp. 164–186.

M.M. Kumaraswamy, F.Y. Ling, M.M. Rahman and S.T. Phng, 'Construction relationally integrated teams', *Journal of Construction Engineering and Management,* 131 (10), 2005, 1076–1086.

M.M. Kumaraswamy, A.M. Anvuur and H.J. Smyth, 'Pursuing "relational integration" and overall value through "RIVANS"', *Facilities,* 28 (13/14), 2010, 673–686.

T. Kurtzberg and V.H. Medvec, 'Can we negotiate and still be friends?' *Negotiation Journal,* 15 (4), 1999, 355–362.

I. Lakatos, 'Falsification and the methodology of scientific research programmes', *Criticism and the Growth of Knowledge,* I. Lakatos and A. Musgrave (eds.), London: Cambridge University Press, 1970, pp. 91–196.

N. Lakemond and C. Berggren, 'Co-locating NPD? The need for combining project focus and organizational integration', *Technovation,* 26, 2006, 807–819.

F.J. Landy, 'Some historical and scientific issues related to research on emotional intelligence', *Journal of Organizational Behavior,* 26 (4), 2005, 411–424.

E. Larson, 'Partnering on construction projects: a study of the relationship between partnering activities and project success', *IEEE Transactions on Engineering Management,* 44 (2), 1997, 188–195.

E. Lau and S. Rowlinson, 'Interpersonal trust and inter-firm trust in construction projects', *Construction Management and Economics,* 27, 2009, 539–554.

P.R. Lawrence and J.W. Lorsch, *Organization and Environment: managing differentiation and integration,* Boston, MA: Harvard University Press, 1967a.

P.R. Lawrence and J.W. Lorsch, 'Differentiation and integration in complex organizations', *Administrative Science Quarterly,* 12, 1967b, 1–30.

Leading Edge, *Capturing Clients in the 90s: a benchmark study of client preferences and procurement routes,* Welwyn: Leading Edge, 1994.

Leading Edge, *On the Edge, 9.1,* Hitchin: Leading Edge, 1998.

R. Leifer and D. Andre, 'Organizational/environmental interchange: a model of boundary spanning activity', *Academy of Management Review,* 3 (1), 1978, 40–50.

D.P. Lepak, K.G. Smith and M.S. Taylor, 'Value creation and value capture: a multilevel perspective', *Academy of Management Review,* 32, 2007, 180–194.

R.E. Levitt, 'CEM research for the next 50 years: maximizing economic, environmental, and societal value of the built environment', *Journal of Construction Engineering and Management,* 133 (9), 2007, 619–628.

R.E. Levitt, J. Thomsen, T.R. Christiansen, J.C. Kunz, Y. Jin and C. Nass, 'Simulating project work processes and organizations: toward a micro-contingency theory of organizational design', *Management Science,* 45 (11), 1999, 1479–1495.

T. Levitt, 'Marketing myopia', *Harvard Business Review,* 38 (July–August), 1960, 24–47.

T. Levitt, *The Marketing Imagination,* New York: Free Press, 1983.

R. J. Lewicki and B.B. Bunker, 'Developing and maintaining trust in work relationships', *Trust in Organizations: frontiers of theory and research,* R.M. Kramer and T.R. Tyler (eds.), Thousand Oaks, CA: Sage, 1996, pp. 115–139.

J. Liinamaa, *Integration in Project Business: mechanisms for integrating customers and the project network during the life-cycle of industrial projects,* PhD dissertation, Turku, Finland: Åbo Akademi University, 2012.

V. Liljander and T. Strandvik, 'Emotions in service satisfaction', *International Journal of Service Industry Management,* 8 (2), 1997, 148–169.

D. Lindebaum, 'Rhetoric or remedy? A critique on developing emotional intelligence', *Academy of Management Learning and Education,* 8 (2), 2009, 225–237.

D. Lindebaum and S. Cartwright, 'A critical examination of the relationship between emotional intelligence and transformational leadership', *Journal of Management Studies,* 47 (7), 2010, 1317–1342.

D. Lindebaum and C. Cassell, 'A contradiction in terms? Making sense of emotional intelligence in a construction management environment', *British Journal of Management,* 23, 2012, 65–79.

M. Linder, *Projecting Capitalism: a history of the internationalization of the construction industry,* Westport, CT: Greenwood Press, 1994.

L. Lindkvist, 'Knowledge integration in product development projects: a contingency framework', *The Oxford Handbook of Project Management,* P.W.G. Morris, J.K. Pinto and J. Söderlund (eds.), Oxford: Oxford University Press, 2011, pp. 464–482.

C. Loch and S. Kavadias, 'Implementing strategy through projects', *The Oxford Handbook of Project Management,* P.W.G. Morris, J.K. Pinto and J. Söderlund (eds.), Oxford: Oxford University Press, 2011, pp. 224–251.

M. Loosemore, A.R. Dainty and H. Lingard, *Human Resource Management in Construction Projects: strategic and operational approaches,* London: Taylor and Francis, 2003.

P.E.D. Love, P.R. Davis and D. Misty, 'Price competitive alliance projects: identification of success factors for public clients', *ASCE Journal of Construction Engineering and Management,* 136 (9), 2010, 947–956.

P.E.D. Love, D. Edwards and E. Wood, 'Loosening the Gordian knot: the role of emotional intelligence in construction', *Engineering, Construction and Architectural Management,* 18 (1), 2011, 50–65.

S. Lowe, N. Ellis, S. Purchase, M. Rod and K.-S. Hwang, 'Mapping alternatives: a commentary on Cova, B. et al. (2010). "Navigating between dyads and networks", *Industrial Marketing Management,* 41, 2012, 357–364.

B. Løwendahl, 'Organizing the Lillehammer Olympic Winter Games', *Scandinavian Journal of Management,* 11 (4), 1995, 347–362.

N. Luhmann, *Trust and Power,* Chichester: John Wiley and Sons, 1979.

N. Luhmann, 'Membership and motives in social systems', *Systems Research,* 13 (3), 1996, 341–348.

S.S. Lui, H.-Y. Ngo and A.H.Y. Hon, 'Coercive strategy in interfirm cooperation: mediating roles of interpersonal and interorganizational trust', *Journal of Business Research,* 59, 2006, 466–474.

R.A. Lundin and A. Söderholm, 'A theory of the temporary organization', *Scandinavian Journal of Management,* 11, 1995, 437–455.

F. Luthans and B.J. Avolio, 'Authentic leadership development', *Positive Organizational Scholarship,* R.E. Quinn (ed.), San Francisco, CA: Barrett-Koehler, 2003, pp. 241–261.

M. Lycett, A. Rassau and J. Danson, 'Programme management: a critical review', *International Journal of Project Management,* 22, 2004, 289–299.

B. Lyons and J. Mehta, 'Contracts, opportunism and trust: self-interest and social orientation', *Cambridge Journal of Economics,* 21, 1997, 239–257.

D.J. McAllister, 'Affect and cognition based trust as a foundation for interpersonal cooperation in organisations', *Academy of Management Review,* 38 (1), 1995, 24–59.

S. Macaulay, 'Non-contractual relations in business: a preliminary study', *American Sociological Review,* 28 (1), 1963, 55–67.

D.A. McBane, 'Empathy and the salesperson: a multidimensional perspective', *Psychology & Marketing,* 12 (4), 1995, 349–370.

M. McDonald, T. Millman and B. Rogers, 'Key account management: theory, practice and challenges', *Journal of Marketing Management,* 13, 1997, 737–757.

R.S. McGee, *The Search for Significance,* Nashville, TN: Word Publishing, 1998.

R.S. McKeeman, *Early Warning Sign of IT Project Failure,* IS SIG, Newtown, PA: PMI, 2002.

R.N. McMurry, 'The executive neurosis', *Harvard Business Review,* 30 (6), 1951, 33–47.

I.R. Macneil, *The New Social Contract: an inquiry into modern contractual relations.* New Haven, CT: Yale University Press, 1980.

I.R. Macneil, 'Relational contract theory: challenges and queries', *Northwestern University Law Review,* 94 (3), 2000, 877–908.

R. McNulty, *Realising the Potential of GB Rail: final independent report of the rail value for money study – main report,* http://assets.dft.gov.uk/publications/report-of-the-rail-vfm-study/realising-the-potential-of-gb-rail.pdf, 2011. Accessed June 2011.

T.W. Malone, 'Towards an interdisciplinary theory of coordination', *Proceedings of the 1st International Conference of Enterprise Integration Modeling Technologies,* South Carolina, June 8–12, 1991.

S. Manning, 'Embedding projects in multiple contexts: a structuration perspective', *International Journal of Project Management,* 26, 2008, 30–37.

J.G. March, 'Exploration and exploitation in organizational learning', *Organization Science,* 2 (1), 1991, 71–87.

J.G. March and H.A. Simon, *Organizations,* New York: Wiley, 1958.

C. Markham, *Practical Consulting,* London: Institute of Chartered Accountants in England and Wales, 1987.

M. Martinsuo and T. Ahola, 'Supplier integration in complex delivery projects: comparison between different buyer-supplier relationships', *International Journal of Project Management,* 28, 2010, 107–116.

J. Mason, 'Specialist contractors and partnering', *Collaborative Relationships in Construction: developing frameworks and networks,* H.J. Smyth and S.D. Pryke (eds.), Oxford: Wiley-Blackwell, 2008, pp. 27–41.

S. Masten, 'The organization of production: evidence from the aerospace industry', *Journal of Law and Economics,* 27, 1984, 403–417.

G. Matthews, M. Zeidner and R. Roberts, *Emotional Intelligence,* Cambridge, MA: MIT Press, 2002.

P. Matthyssens and K. Vandenbempt, 'Creating competitive advantage in industrial service', *Journal of Business and Industrial Marketing,* 13 (4/5), 1998, 339–355.

J.D. Mayer and P. Salovey, 'The intelligence of emotional intelligence', *Intelligence,* 17, 1993, 433–442.

J.D. Mayer and P. Salovey, 'What is emotional intelligence?' *Emotional Development and Emotional Intelligence: educational applications,* P. Salovey and D. Sluyter (eds.), New York: Basic Books, 1997, pp. 3–31.

J.D. Mayer, D.R. Caruso and P. Salovey, 'Emotional intelligence meets traditional standards for an intelligence', *Intelligence,* 27, 1999, 267–298.

J.D. Mayer, P. Salovey and D.R. Caruso, 'Selecting a measure of emotional intelligence', *The Handbook of Intelligence,* R. Sternberg (ed.), Cambridge: Cambridge University Press, 2000, pp. 320–342.

R.C. Mayer, J.H. Davis and F.D. Schoorman, 'An integrative model of trust', *Academy of Management Review,* 20, 1995, 709–734.

G.H. Mead, *Mind, Self and Society,* Chicago: University of Chicago Press, 1934.

J.R. Meindl, 'The romance of leadership as a follower-centric theory', *Leadership Quarterly,* 6, 1995, 329–341.

X. Meng, 'The effect of relationship management on project performance in construction', *International Journal of Project Management,* 30, 2012, 188–198.

E.W. Merrow, *Industrial Megaprojects: concepts, strategies and practices for success,* Hoboken, NJ: Wiley, 2011.

A.D. Meyer, A.S. Tsui and C.R. Hinings, 'Configurational approaches to organizational analysis', *The Academy of Management Journal,* 36 (6), 1993, 1175–1195.

J.P. Meyer and N.J. Allen, 'A three-component conceptualization of organizational commitment', *Human Resource Management Review,* 1 (1), 1991, pp. 61–89.

D. Meyerson, K.E. Weick and R.M. Kramer, 'Swift trust and temporary groups', *Trust in Organizations: frontiers of theory,* R.M. Kramer and T.R. Tyler (eds.), Beverly Hills, CA: Sage, 1996, pp. 166–195.

S. Michalski and B. Helmig, 'What do we know about the identity salience model of relationship marketing success? A review of the literature', *Journal of Relationship Marketing,* 7 (1), 2008, 45–63.

C. Midler, '"Projectification" of the firm: the Renault case', *Scandinavian Journal of Management,* 11 (4), 1995, 363–375.

R.E. Miles and C. Snow, 'Organizations: new concepts for new forms', *California Management Review,* 28 (3), 1986, 62–73.

P. Milgrom and J. Roberts, *Economics, Organization and Management,* Englewood Cliffs, NJ: Prentice-Hall, 1992.

D. Miller, 'Configurations revisited', *Strategic Management Journal,* 17 (7), 1996, 505–512.

M. Miller, 'Emotional intelligence helps managers succeed', *Credit Union Magazine,* 65 (7), 1999, 25–26.

R. Miller and D.R. Lessard, *The Strategic Management of Large Engineering Projects: shaping institutions, risks, and governance,* Cambridge, MA: MIT Press, 2000.

H. Mintzberg, *Mintzberg on Management: inside our strange world of organizations,* New York: Simon and Schuster, 1989.

H. Mintzberg, *Rise and Fall of Strategic Planning,* New York: Simon and Schuster, 1994.

B.A. Misztal, *Trust in Modern Societies: the search for the bases of social order,* Cambridge: Polity Press, 1996.

R.H. Mnookin, S.R. Peppet and A.S. Tulumello, *Beyond Winning,* Cambridge, MA: Harvard University Press, 2000.

Y. Mo, A. Dainty and A. Price, 'The relevance of EQ to construction project management education and practice: an investigative framework', *Proceedings of the 22nd Annual ARCOM Conference,* 4th–6th September, Birmingham, UK, 2006.

K. Möller, 'Role of competences in creating customer value: a value-creation logic approach', *Industrial Marketing Management,* 35, 2006, 913–924.

C. Moorman, R. Deshpande and G. Zaltman, 'Factors affecting trust in market research relationships', *Journal of Marketing,* 54, 1993, 81–101.

R.M. Morgan and S.D. Hunt, 'The commitment-trust theory of relationship marketing', *Journal of Marketing,* 58 (July), 1994, 20–38.

R. Morledge, A. Knight and M. Grada, 'The concept and development of supply chain management in the UK construction industry', *Construction Supply Chain Management: concepts and case studies,* S.D. Pryke (ed.), Oxford: Blackwell, 2009, pp. 23–41.

P.W.G. Morris, *The Management of Projects,* London: Thomas Telford, 1994.

P.W.G. Morris, 'Implementing strategy through project management: the importance of managing the project front end', *Making Essential Choices with Scant Information: front end decision-making in major projects,* T.M. Williams, K. Samset and K.J. Sunnevåg (eds.), Basingstoke: Palgrave Macmillan, 2009, pp. 39–67.

P.W.G. Morris, 'Research and the future of project management', *International Journal of Managing Projects in Business,* 2010, 3, 139–146.

P.W.G. Morris, *The Reconstruction of Project Management,* Chichester: Wiley-Blackwell, 2013.

P.W.G. Morris and J. Geraldi, 'Managing the institutional context for projects', *Project Management Journal,* 42, 6, 2011, 20–32.

P.W.G. Morris and G.H. Hough, *The Anatomy of Major Projects,* Chichester: John Wiley and Sons, 1987.

P.W.G. Morris and J.K. Pinto, 'Introduction', *The Wiley Guide to Managing Projects,* P.W.G. Morris and J.K. Pinto, (eds.), Hoboken, NJ: John Wiley and Sons, 2004, pp. xiii–xxiv.

P.W.G. Morris, J.K. Pinto and J. Söderlund, 'Towards the third wave of project management', *The Oxford Handbook of Project Management,* P.W.G. Morris, J.K. Pinto and J. Söderlund (eds.), Oxford: Oxford University Press, 2011, pp. 1–11.

J. Mount, 'The role of emotional intelligence in developing international business capability: EI provides traction', *Linking Emotional Intelligence and Performance at Work,* V.U. Druskat, F. Sala and J. Mount (eds.), Mahwah, NJ: Lawrence Erlbaum, 2006, pp. 97–124.

R. Müller, 'Project governance', *The Oxford Handbook of Project Management,* P.W.G. Morris, J.K. Pinto and J. Söderlund (eds.), Oxford: Oxford University Press, 2011, pp. 297–320.

R. Müller and R. Turner, 'Leadership competency profiles of successful project managers', *International Journal of Project Management,* 28 (5), 2010, 437–448.

J. Nahapiet and S. Ghoshal, 'Social capital, intellectual capital, and the organizational advantage', *Academy of Management Review,* 23 (2), 1998, 242–266.

J. Nahapiet, L. Gratton and H.O. Rocha, 'Knowledge and relationships: when cooperation is the norm', *European Management Review,* 2, 2005, 3–14.

J. Nandhakumar and M. Jones, 'Accounting for time: managing time in project-based teamworking', *Accounting, Organizations and Society,* 26, 2001, 193–214.

V.K. Narayanan and R. DeFillippi, 'The influence of strategic context on project management systems: a senior management perspective', *Project Governance: getting investment right,* T.M. Williams and K. Samset (eds.), Basingstoke: Palgrave Macmillan, 2012, pp. 3–45.

R. Nelson and S. Winter, *An Evolutionary Theory of Economic Change,* Cambridge, MA: Belknap Press, 1982.

D. Nicolini, 'In search of project chemistry', *Construction Management and Economics,* 20, 2002, 167–177.

J. Nihtilä, 'R&D-production integration in the early phases of new product development projects', *Journal of Engineering and Technology Management,* 16, 1999, 55–81.

T. Nishiguchi, *Strategic Industrial Sourcing: the Japanese advantage,* Oxford: Oxford University Press, 1994.

B. Nooteboom, H. Berger and N.G. Noorderhaven, 'Effects of trust and governance on relational risk', *Academy of Management Journal,* 40 (2), 1997, 308–338.

R. Normann, *Reframing Business: when the map changes the landscape,* Chichester: Wiley, 2001.

R. O'Connor, Jr. and I. Little, 'Revisiting the predictive validity of emotional intelligence: self-report versus ability-based measures', *Personality and Individual Differences,* 35 (8), 2003, 1893–1902.

T. O'Leary and T. Williams, 'Making a difference? Evaluating an innovative approach to the project management centre of excellence in a UK government department', *International Journal of Project Management,* 26 (5), 2008, 556–565.

B.E. Olsen, S.A. Haugland, E. Karlsen and G.J. Husøy, 'Governance of complex procure-ments in the oil and gas industry', *Journal of Purchasing and Supply Chain Management*, 11, 2005, 1–13.

E.M. Olsen, S.F. Slater and G.T.M. Hult, 'The performance implications of fit among busi-ness strategy, marketing organization structure, and strategic behavior', *Journal of Marketing*, 69, 2005, 49–65.

O. O'Neill, 'Lecture 1: spreading suspicion', *A Question of Trust*, Reith Lectures BBC 4, London: www.bbc.co.uk/radio4/reith2002/lectures.shtml, 2002. Accessed 6th August, 2013.

W.J. Orlikowski and J. Yates, 'It's about time: temporal structuring in organizations', *Orga-nization Science*, 13 (6), 2002, 684–700.

A. Ostrom, M. Bitner, S. Brown, K. Burkhard, M. Gaul, V. Smith-Daniels, H. Demirkan and E. Rabinovich, 'Moving forward and making a difference: research priorities for the science of service', *Journal of Service Research*, 13 (1), 2010, 4–36.

W.G. Ouchi, 'Markets, bureaucracies and clans', *Administrative Science Quarterly*, 25 (10), 1980, 129–141.

J. Packendorff, 'Inquiring into the temporary organization: new directions for project management research', *Scandinavian Journal of Management*, 11 (4), 1995, 319–333.

T.P. Palfai and P. Salovey, 'The influence of depressed and elated mood on deductive and inductive reasoning', *Imagination, Cognition and Personality*, 13, 1993, 57–71.

B. Palmer, M. Walls, Z. Burgess and C. Stough, 'Emotional intelligence and effective lead-ership', *Leadership and Organizational Development Journal*, 22 (1), 2001, 5–10.

C. Park and M. Keil, 'Organizational silence and whistle-blowing on IT projects: an inte-grated model', *Decision Sciences*, 40, (4), 2009, 901–918.

R. Parker and L. Bradley, 'Organisational culture in the public sector: evidence from six organisations', *International Journal of Public Sector Management*, 13 (2), 2000, 125–141.

A. Parmigiani and J. Howard-Grenville, 'Routines revisited: exploring the capabilities and practice perspectives', *The Academy of Management Annals*, 5 (1), 2011, 413–453.

A. Parmigiani and W. Mitchell, 'The hollow corporation revisited: can governance mecha-nisms substitute for technical expertise in managing buyer-supplier relationships?' *European Management Review*, 76, 2010, 46–70.

A. Payne, D. Ballantyne and M. Christopher, 'A stakeholder model to relationship market-ing strategy: the development and use of the "six markets" model', *European Journal of Marketing*, 39 (7/8), 2005, 855–871.

C. Pearson and C. Porath, *The Cost of Bad Behaviour: how incivility damages your business and what you can do about it*, London: Penguin, 2009.

L. Pegram, *Report on Emotional Intelligence*, London: Unpublished Report, 2007.

J. Pels and M. Saren, 'The 4Ps of relational marketing, perspectives, perceptions, paradoxes and paradigms: learnings from organizational theory and the strategy literature', *Journal of Relationship Marketing*, 4 (3/4), 2005, 59–84.

J.C. Pérez, K.V. Petrides and A. Furnham, 'Measuring trait emotional intelligence', *Inter-national Handbook of Emotional Intelligence*, R. Schulze and R.D. Roberts (eds.), 2005, Cambridge, MA: Hogrefe & Huber, pp.123–143.

L.A. Perlow, 'The time famine: toward a sociology of work time', *Administrative Science Quarterly*, 44 (1), 1999, 57–81.

R.B. Perry, 'Economic value and moral value', *The Quarterly Journal of Economics*, 30 (3), 1916, 443–485.

T.H. Peters, *Liberation Management: necessary disorganization for the nano-second nineties*, Basingstoke: Palgrave Macmillan, 1992.

K.V. Petrides, 'Psychometric properties of the trait emotional intelligence questionnaire (TEIQue)', *Assessing Emotional Intelligence,* C. Stough, D. Saklofske and J. Parker (eds.), New York: Springer Publishing, 2009, pp. 85–101.

K.V. Petrides and A. Furnham, 'Trait emotional intelligence: psychometric investigation with reference to established trait taxonomies', *European Journal of Personality,* 15 (6), 2001, 425–448.

K.V. Petrides, N. Frederickson and A. Furnham,' The role of trait emotional intelligence in academic performance and deviant behavior at school', *Personality and Individual Differences,* 36, 2004, 277–293.

M.T. Pich, C.H. Loch and A. De Meyer, 'On uncertainty, ambiguity, and complexity in project management', *Management Science,* 48 (8), 2002, 1008–1023.

J.K. Pinto and D.P. Slevin, 'Critical success factors across the project life cycle', *Project Management Journal,* 19 (3), 1988, 67–75.

J.K. Pinto, D.P. Slevin and B. English, 'Trust in projects: an empirical assessment of owner/contractor relationships', *International Journal of Project Management,* 27, 2009, 638–648.

T. Pitsis, S. Clegg, M. Marosszeky and T. Rura-Polley, 'Constructing the Olympic dream: a future perfect strategy of project management', *Organization Science,* 14 (5), 2003, 574–590.

PMI, *A Guide to the Project Management Body of Knowledge (PMBoK Guide), Fifth Edition,* Hoboken, NJ: Project Management Institute, 2013.

K. Polanyi, *The Great Transformation: the political and economic origins of our time,* Boston: Beacon Press, 1944.

M. Polanyi, 'Science and reality', *Synthese,* 5 (3), 1946, 137–150.

M. Polanyi, 'The stability of beliefs', *The British Journal for the Philosophy of Science,* 3 (11), 1952, 217–232.

M. Polanyi, 'Sense-giving and sense-reading', *Philosophy,* 42 (162), 1967, 301–325.

M.J. Polonsky, 'A stakeholder theory approach to designing environmental marketing strategy', *Journal of Business and Industrial Marketing,* 10 (3), 1995, 29–46.

C. Porath, D. MacInnis and V. Folkes, 'It's unfair: why customers who merely observe an uncivil employee abandon the company', *Journal of Service Research,* 14 (3), 2011, 302–317.

J. Porter, 'Forward', *Industrial Megaprojects: concepts, strategies and practices for success,* E. Merrow, Hoboken, NJ: Wiley, 2011.

A. Portes, 'Social capital: its origins and applications in modern sociology', *Annual Review of Sociology,* 24, 1998, 1–24.

W.W. Powell, 'The transformation of organizational forms: how useful is organization theory in accounting for social change?' *Beyond the Marketplace: rethinking economy and society,* R.O. Friedland and A.F. Robertson (eds.), New York: Aldine de Gruyter, 1990a, pp. 301–329.

W.W. Powell, 'Neither market nor hierarchy: network forms of organization', *Research in Organizational Behavior,* 12, 1990b, 295–336.

C.K. Prahalad and G. Hamel, 'The core competencies of the organization', *Harvard Business Review,* 63 (3), 1990, 79–91.

C.K. Prahalad and V. Ramaswamy, 'Co-creating unique value with customers', *Strategy & Leadership,* 32 (3), 2004, 4–9.

B. Prasad, *Concurrent Engineering Fundamentals, Volume I: integrated product and process organization,* Englewood Cliffs, NJ: Prentice Hall, 1996.

L.M. Prati, C. Douglas, G.R. Ferris, A.P. Ammeter and M.R. Buckley, 'Emotional intelligence, leadership effectiveness, and team outcomes', *International Journal of Organizational Analysis,* 11 (1), 2003, 21–40.

L.M. Prati, A. McMillan-Capehart and J.H. Karriker, 'Affecting organizational identity: a manager's influence', *Journal of Leadership & Organizational Studies,* 15 (4), 2009, 404–415.

A. Prencipe and F. Tell, 'Inter-project learning: processes and outcomes of knowledge codification in project-based firms', *Research Policy,* 30 (9), 2001, 1373–1394.

PricewaterhouseCoopers, *Human Capital Management Practices Outside the UK,* 2003, www. berr.gov.uk/files/file38843.pdf, 2003. Accessed 16th September 2013.

S.D. Pryke, *Social Network Analysis in Construction,* Chichester: Wiley-Blackwell, 2012.

S.D. Pryke and H.J. Smyth, 'Scoping a relationship approach to the management of projects', *Management of Complex Projects: a relationship approach,* S.D. Pryke and H.J. Smyth (eds.), Oxford: Blackwell, 2006, pp. 21–46.

P. Puranam and B.S. Vanneste, 'Trust and governance: untangling a tangled web', *Academy of Management Review,* 34 (1), 2009, 11–31.

H. Raiffa, *Decision Analysis: introductory lectures on choices under uncertainty,* Oxford: Addison-Wesley, 1968.

D. Ravasi and M. Schultz, 'Responding to organizational identity threats: exploring the role of organizational culture', *Academy of Management Journal,* 49 (3), 2006, 433–458.

F.F. Reichheld, *The Loyalty Effect,* Boston: Harvard Business School Press, 1996.

W. Reinartz, M. Krafft and W.D. Hoyer, 'The customer relationship management process: its measurement and impact upon performance', *Journal of Marketing Research,* 41, 2004, 293–305.

B.D. Reyck, Y. Grushka-Cockayne, M. Lockett, S.R. Calderini, M. Moura and A. Sloper, 'The impact of project portfolio management on information technology projects', *International Journal of Project Management,* 23 (7), 2005, 524–537.

M. Riemer, 'Integrating emotional intelligence into engineering education', *World Transactions on Engineering and Technology Education,* 2, 2003, 189–194.

P.S. Ring and A.H. Van de Ven, 'Structuring cooperative relationships between organizations', *Strategic Management Journal,* 13 (7), 1992, 483–498.

H.W. Rittel and M.M. Webber, 'Dilemmas in a general theory of planning', *Policy Sciences,* 4, 1973, 155–169.

T. Ritter, I.F. Wilkinson and W.J. Johnston, 'Firms' ability to manage in business networks: a review of concepts', *Industrial Marketing Management,* 33 (3), 2004, 175–183.

S.P. Robbins, *Organization Behavior,* New York: Prentice Hall, 2009.

A. Roberts, J. Kelsey, H.J. Smyth and A. Wilson, 'Health and safety maturity in project business cultures', *International Journal of Managing Projects in Business,* 5 (4), 2012, 776–803.

R.D. Roberts, G. Matthews and M. Zeidner, 'Does emotional intelligence meet traditional standards for an intelligence? Some new data and conclusions', *Emotion,* 1 (3), 2001, 196–231.

K. Robinson, *Out of Our Minds: learning to be creative,* Chichester: Capstone, 2001.

S.L. Robinson, 'Trust and breach of the psychological contract', *Administrative Science Quarterly,* 41, 1996, 574–599.

H.O. Rocha and S. Ghoshal, 'Beyond self-interest revisited', *Journal of Management Studies,* 43 (3), 2006, 585–619.

A.G.L. Romme, 'Making a difference: organization as design', *Organization Science,* 14 (5), 2003, 558–577.

A. Ropo and E. Sauer, 'Corporeal leaders', *The Sage Handbook on New Approaches in Management and Organization Studies,* D. Barry and H. Hansen (eds.), London: Sage, 2008, pp. 469–478.

D. Rosete and J. Ciarrochi, 'Emotional intelligence and its relationship to workplace performance outcomes of leadership effectiveness', *Leadership & Organization Development Journal,* 26 (5), 2005, 388–399.

J.B. Rotter, 'Interpersonal trust, trustworthiness, and gullibility', *American Psychologist,* 35 (1), 1980, 1–7.

D.M. Rousseau, 'New hires perspectives of their own and their employer's obligations: a study of psychological contracts', *Journal of Organizational Behavior,* 11, 1990, 389–400.

D.M. Rousseau, 'Why workers still identify with organizations', *Journal of Organizational Behavior,* 19, 1998, 217–233.

D.M. Rousseau and R. Schalk, *Psychological Contracts in Employment: cross-national perspectives,* Thousand Oaks, CA: Sage, 2000.

D.M. Rousseau, S.B. Sitkin, R.S. Burt and C. Camerer, 'Not so different after all: a cross-discipline view of trust', *Academy of Management Review,* 23, 1998, 393–404.

R.T. Rust and A.J. Zahorik, 'Customer satisfaction, customer retention, and market share', *Journal of Retailing,* 69 (2), 1993, 193–215.

I. Ruuska, K. Artto, K. Aaltonen and P. Lehtonen, 'Dimensions of distance in a project network: exploring Olkiluoto 3 nuclear power plant project', *International Journal of Project Management,* 27 (2), 2009, 142–153.

I. Ruuska and T. Brady, 'Implementing the replication strategy in uncertain and complex investment projects', *International Journal of Project Management,* 29 (4), 2011, 422–431.

M. Saad, M. Jones and P. James, 'A review of the progress towards the adoption of supply chain management (SCM) relationships in construction', *European Journal of Purchasing and Supply Chain Management,* 8 (3), 2002, 173–183.

M. Sako, *Prices, Quality and Trust: inter-firm relations in Britain and Japan,* Cambridge: Cambridge University Press, 1992.

J.W. Salacuse and J.Z. Rubin, 'Your place or mine', *Negotiations Journal,* 6 (1), 1990, 5–10.

J.E. Salk and B.L. Simonin, 'Beyond alliances: towards a metatheory of collaborative learning', *The Blackwell Handbook of Organizational Learning and Knowledge Management,* M. Easterby-Smith and M.A. Lyles (eds.), Oxford: Blackwell, 2003, pp. 253–277.

P. Salovey, 'Epilogue: the agenda for future research', *Linking Emotional Intelligence and Performance at Work,* V.U. Druskat, F. Sala and J. Mount (eds.), Mahwah, NJ: Lawrence Erlbaum Associates, 2006, pp. 267–273.

P. Salovey and J.D. Mayer, 'Emotional intelligence', *Imagination, Cognition and Personality,* 9 (3), 1989, 185–211.

C. Sauer and B.H. Reich, 'Rethinking IT project management: evidence of a new mindset and its implications', *International Journal of Project Management,* 27 (2), 2009, 182–193.

A. Saxenian, 'Beyond boundaries: open labor markets and learning in Silicon Valley', pp. 23–39. *The Boundaryless Career: a new employment principle for a new organizational era,* M.B. Arthur and D.M. Rousseau (eds.), Oxford: Oxford University Press, 1996.

L.R. Sayles and M.K. Chandler, *Managing Large Systems: organizations for the future,* New York: Harper and Row, 1971.

H. Scarbrough, J. Swan, S. Laurent, M. Bresnen, L. Edelman and S. Newell, 'Project-based learning and the role of learning boundaries', *Organization Studies,* 25 (9), 2004, 1579–1600.

T. Schakett, A. Flaschner, T. Gao and A. El-Ansary, 'Effects of social bonding in business-to-business relationships', *Journal of Relationship Marketing,* 10, 2011, 264–280.

E.H. Schein, 'Organisational culture', *American Psychologist,* 45, 1990, 109–119.

E.H. Schein, *Organizational Culture and Leadership,* San Francisco: Jossey-Bass, 1996.

J. Schepers, A. De Jong, K. De Ruyter and M. Wetzels, 'Fields of gold: perceived efficacy in virtual teams of field service employees', *Journal of Service Research,* 14 (3), 2011, 372–389.

F.L. Schmidt and J.E. Hunter, 'The validity and utility of selection methods in personnel psychology: practical and theoretical implications of 85 years of research findings', *Psychological Bulletin,* 124 (2), 1998, 262–274.

E. Schofield and H.J. Smyth, 'Trust between project sponsors and project managers in a large public sector organization', *Paper presented at EURAM 2012,* 6th–8th June, Rotterdam, 2012.

D.A. Schön, *The Reflective Practitioner: how professionals think in action,* New York: Basic Books, 1983.

F.D. Schoorman, R.C. Mayer and J.H. Davis, 'An integrative model of organizational trust: past, present, and future', *Academy of Management Review,* 32 (2), 2007, 344–354.

E.F. Schumacher, *A Guide for the Perplexed,* London: Jonathan Cape, 1997.

H.M. Schwartz and S.M. Davis, 'Matching corporate culture and business strategy', *Organizational Dynamics,* 59, 1981, 30–48.

W.R. Scott, 'Approaching adulthood: the maturing of institutional theory', *Theory and Society,* 37 (2), 2008, 427–442.

W.R. Scott, 'The institutional environment of global project organizations', *The Engineering Project Organization Journal,* 2, 2012, 27–35.

W.R. Scott and V.R. Lane, 'A stakeholder approach to organizational identity', *Academy of Management Review,* 25 (1), 2000, 43–62.

R. Sennett, *The Corrosion of Character: the personal consequences of work in the new capitalism,* London: Norton, 1998.

M. Sfeir, A. Siegling and H.J. Smyth, 'Measured and self-estimated trait emotional intelligence in a UK sample of managers', *Personality and Individual Differences,* http://dx.doi.org/10.1016/j.ijproman.2014.03.005, 2014.

M.E. Shaw, *Group Dynamics: the psychology of small group behavior,* 3rd edition, New York: McGraw-Hill, 1981.

Z. Shehu and A. Akintoye, 'Major challenges to the successful implementation and practice of programme management in the construction environment: a critical analysis', *International Journal of Project Management,* 28 (1), 2010, 26–39.

A.J. Shenhar, 'One size does not fit all projects: exploring classical contingency domains', *Management Science,* 47, 2001, 394–414.

H.A. Simon, 'A behavioral model of rational choice', *The Quarterly Journal of Economics,* 69 (1), 1955, 99–118.

H.A. Simon, *The Sciences of the Artificial,* Cambridge, MA: MIT Press, 1969.

H.A. Simon, 'Rational decision making in business organizations', *The American Economic Review,* 69 (4), 1979, 493–513.

S.B. Sitkin and N.L. Roth, 'Explaining the limited effectiveness of legalistic "remedies" for trust/distrust', *Organization Science,* 4 (3), 1993, 367–392.

M.A. Skaates and H. Tikkanen, 'International project marketing as an area of study: a literature review with suggestions for research and practice', *International Journal of Project Management,* 21 (1), 2003, 503–510.

S.F. Slater and J.C. Narver, 'Market orientation and the learning organization', *Journal of Marketing,* 59 (3), 1995, 63–74.

D.P. Slevin and J.K. Pinto, 'The project implementation profile: new tool for project managers', *Project Management Journal,* 18 (4), 1986, 57–71.

A. Smith, *The Theory of Moral Sentiments,* 1984 edition, Indianapolis, IN: Liberty Fund, 1759.

H.J. Smith, R. Thompson and C. Iacovou, 'The impact of ethical climate on project status misreporting', *Journal of Business Ethics,* 90 (4), 2009, 577–591.

G.L. Smithers and D.H.T. Walker, 'The effect of the workplace on motivation and demotivation of construction professionals', *Construction Management and Economics,* 18, 2000, 833–841.

H.J. Smyth, *Marketing and Selling Construction Services,* Oxford: Blackwell Science, 2000.

H.J. Smyth, 'Competencies for improving construction performance: theories and practice for developing capacity', *The International Journal of Construction Management*, 4 (1), 2004, 41–56.

H.J. Smyth, 'Trust in the design team', *Architectural Engineering and Design Management*, 1 (3), 2005, 193–205.

H.J. Smyth, 'Competition', *Commercial Management of Projects: defining the discipline*, D. Lowe and R. Leiringer (eds.), Oxford: Blackwell, 2006, pp. 22–39.

H.J. Smyth, 'Developing trust', *Collaborative Relationships in Construction: developing frameworks and networks*, H. J. Smyth and S. D. Pryke (eds.), Oxford: Wiley-Blackwell, 2008a, pp. 129–160.

H.J. Smyth, 'The credibility gap in stakeholder management: ethics and evidence of relationship management', *Construction Management and Economics*, 26 (6), 2008b, 633–643.

H.J. Smyth, 'Construction industry performance improvement programmes: the UK case of demonstration projects in the 'continuous improvement' programme', *Construction Management and Economics*, 28 (3), 2010, 255–270.

H.J. Smyth, 'Marketing, programme and project management: relationship building and maintenance over project lifecycles', *Proceedings of the CIB World Building Congress 2013: Construction and Society*, 5th–9th May, Brisbane, 2013a.

H.J. Smyth, 'Deviation, emergent requirements and value delivery: a marketing and 'business development' perspective', *Proceedings of the IRNOP 2013: Innovative Approaches in Project Management Research*, 17th–19th June, Oslo: BI Norwegian Business School, 2013b.

H.J. Smyth, *Market Management and Project Business Development*, London: Routledge, 2015.

H.J. Smyth and A.J. Edkins, 'Relationship management in the management of PFI/PPP projects in the UK', *International Journal of Project Management*, 25 (3), 2007, 232–240.

H.J. Smyth and T. Fitch, 'Application of relationship marketing and management: a large contractor case study', *Construction Management and Economics*, 27, (3), 2009, 399–410.

H.J. Smyth and S. Kioussi, 'Architecture firms and the role of brand management', *Architectural Engineering and Design Management*, 7 (3), 2011a, 205–217.

H.J. Smyth and S. Kioussi, 'Client management and identification', *Managing the Professional Practice*, H.J. Smyth (ed.), Oxford: Wiley-Blackwell, 2011b, 143–160.

H.J. Smyth and I.C. Kusuma, 'The interplay of organisational culture with business development for the TMO: service (in)coherence and the implications for marketing', *Proceedings of the CIB World Building Congress 2013: Construction and Society*, 5th–9th May, Brisbane, Australia, 2013.

H.J. Smyth and L. Lecoeuvre, 'Differences in decision-making criteria towards the return on marketing investment: a project business perspective', *International Journal of Project Management*, http://dx.doi.org/10.1016/j.ijproman.2014.03.005, 2014.

H.J. Smyth and P.W.G. Morris, 'An epistemological evaluation of research into projects and their management: methodological issues', *International Journal of Project Management*, 25, (4), 2007, 423–436.

H.J. Smyth and C. Pilcher, 'Developing contractor–client relations is dependent upon respective organisational relations: an exploration through a case of trust within a major contractor organisation', *Proceedings of Cobra 2008*, RICS Foundation, 4th–5th September, Dublin: Dublin Institute of Technology, 2008.

H.J. Smyth and S.D. Pryke, 'Introduction: managing collaborative relationships and the management of projects', *Collaborative Relationships in Construction: developing frameworks and networks*, H.J. Smyth and S.D. Pryke (eds.), Chichester: Wiley-Blackwell, 2008, pp. 1–24.

H.J. Smyth and N.J. Thompson, 'Developing conditions of trust within a framework of trust', *Journal of Construction Procurement*, 11 (1), 2005, 4–18.

H. J. Smyth, M. Gustafsson and E. Ganskau, 'The value of trust in project business', *International Journal of Project Management*, 28 (2), 2010, 117–129.

A. Söderholm, 'Project management of unexpected events', *International Journal of Project Management*, 26, 2008, 80–86.

J. Söderlund, 'Pluralism in project management: navigating the crossroads of specialization and fragmentation', *International Journal of Management Reviews*, 13, 2011a, 153–176.

J. Söderlund, 'Theoretical foundations of project management: suggestions for a pluralistic understanding', *The Oxford Handbook of Project Management*, P.W.G. Morris, J.K. Pinto and J. Söderlund (eds.), Oxford: Oxford University Press, 2011b, pp. 37–64.

J. Söderlund, 'Project management, interdependencies, and time: insights from *Managing Large Systems* by Sayles and Chandler', *International Journal of Managing Projects in Business*, 5 (4), 2012, 617–633.

J. Söderlund and N. Andersson, 'A framework for the analysis of project dyads: the case of discontinuity, uncertainty and trust', *Projects as Arenas for Learning and Renewal*, R.A. Lundin and C. Midler (eds.), Boston, MA: Kluwer Academic Publishers, 1998.

J. Söderlund and F. Tell, 'The P-form organization and the dynamics of project competence: project epochs in Asea/ABB, 1950–2000', *International Journal of Project Management*, 27, 2009, 101–112.

J. Söderlund, A.L. Vaagaasar and E.S. Erling, 'Relating, reflecting and routinizing: developing project competencies in cooperation with others', *International Journal of Project Management*, 26, 2008, 517–526.

J. Solomon and A. Solomon, *Corporate Governance and Accountability*, Chichester: Wiley, 2004.

A.D. Songer and B. Walker, 'General contractor emotional intelligence in the construction industry', *Proceedings of the 20th Annual ARCOM Conference*, 1st–3rd September, 2004, Edinburgh.

H.E. Sørensen, *Business Development: a market-oriented perspective*, Chichester: Wiley, 2012.

J.J. Sosik and L.E Megerian, 'Understanding leader emotional intelligence and performance: the role of self-other agreement on transformational leadership perceptions', *Group & Organization Management*, 24 (3), 1999, 367–391.

F. Spooncer, *Behavioural Studies for Marketing and Business*, Leckhampton: Stanley Thomas, 1992.

G.M. Spreitzer and R.M. Quinn, *A Company of Leaders: five disciplines for unleashing the power in your workforce*, San Francisco, CA: Jossey-Bass, 2001.

R. J. Sternberg, 'Review of D. Goleman, *Working with Emotional Intelligence*', *Personnel Psychology*, 52 (3) 1999, 780–783.

A. Stinchcombe and C. Heimer, *Organization Theory and Project Management: administering uncertainty in Norwegian offshore oil*, Oslo: Norwegian University Press, 1985.

K. Storbacka and S. Nenonen, 'Customer relationships and the heterogeneity of firm performance', *Journal of Business & Industrial Marketing?* 24 (5/6), 2009, 360–372.

K. Storbacka, T. Strandvik and C. Grönroos, 'Managing customer relationships for profit: the dynamics of relationship quality', *International Journal of Service Industry Management*, 5 (5), 1994, 21–38.

J.E. Stryker, 'Identity salience and role performance: the relevance of symbolic interaction theory for family research', *Journal of Marriage and Family*, 30, 1968, 558–564.

R. Suddaby, C. Hardy and Q.N. Huy, 'Introduction to Special Topic Forum: where are the new theories of organization?' *Academy of Management Review*, 36 (2), 2011, 236–246.

M. Suhonen and L. Paasivaara, 'Shared human capital in project management: a systematic review of the literature', *Project Management Journal*, 42 (2), 2011a, 4–16.

M. Suhonen and L. Paasivaara, 'Nurse managers' challenges in project management', *Journal of Nursing Management,* 19 (8), 2011b, 1028–1036.

L.P. Sullivan, 'The role of quality function deployment', *Quality Progress,* 21 (7), 1988, 20–22.

R.Y. Sunindijo, B.H.W. Hadikusumo and S. Ogunlana, 'Emotional intelligence and leadership styles', *ASCE Journal of Management in Engineering,* 23 (4), 2007, 166–170.

J. Sydow and A. Windeler, 'Organizing and evaluating interfirm networks: a structurationist perspective on network processes and effectiveness', *Organization Science,* 9 (3), 1998, 265–284.

H. Tajfel, 'Social identity and intergroup behaviour', *Social Science Information,* 13, 1974, 65–93.

J. Tansey, 'Risk as politics, culture as power', *Journal of Risk Research,* 7 (1), 2004, 17–32.

C. Tansley and S. Newell, 'Project social capital, leadership and trust: a study of human resource information systems development', *Journal of Managerial Psychology,* 22 (4), 2007, 350–368.

D.J. Teece, 'Business models, business strategy and innovation', *Long Range Planning,* 43 (2), 2010, 172–194.

D.J. Teece, G. Pisano and A. Shuen, 'Dynamic capabilities and strategic management', *Strategic Management Journal,* 18, (7), 1997, 509–533.

J. Teicher, Q. Alam and B.V. Gramberg, 'Managing trust and relationships in PPPs: some Australian experiences', *International Review of Administrative Sciences,* 72 (1), 2006, 85–100.

V. Thevendran and M.J. Mawdesley, 'Perception of human risk factors in construction projects: an exploratory study', *International Journal of Project Management,* 22, 2004, 131–137.

M. Thompson, R.J. Ellis and A.B. Wildavsky, *Cultural Theory,* Colorado, CO: Westview Press, 1990.

P.J. Thompson and S.R. Sanders, 'Partnering continuum', *ASCE Journal of Management in Engineering,* 14 (5), 1998, 73–78.

R.K. Thornlike, 'Intelligence and its uses', *Harper Magazine,* 140, 1920, 227–235.

A. Tsvetkova and M. Gustafsson, 'Business models for industrial ecosystems: a modular approach', *Journal of Cleaner Production,* 29, 2012, 246–254.

R. Tuomela and M. Tuomela, 'Cooperation and trust in group context', *Mind & Society,* 4, 2005, 49–84.

R. Turner, 'Towards a theory of project management: the nature of the project', *International Journal of Project Management,* 24, 2006, 1–3.

R. Turner and R. Müller, 'Communication and co-operation on projects between the project owner as principal and the project manager as agent', *European Management Journal,* 22 (3), 2004, 327–336.

M.M. Tuuli and S. Rowlinson, 'What empowers individuals and teams in project settings? A critical incident analysis', *Engineering, Construction and Architectural Management,* 17 (1), 2010, 9–20.

A. Tversky and D. Kahneman, 'Judgment under uncertainty: heuristics and biases', *Science,* 185 (4157), 1974, 1124–1131.

M. Uhl-Bein, 'Relational leadership theory: exploring the social processes of leadership and organizing', *The Leadership Quarterly,* 17 (6), 2006, 654–676.

B. Uzzi, 'Social structure and competition in interfirm networks: the paradox of embeddedness', *Administrative Science Quarterly,* 42 (1), 1997, 35–67.

A.L. Vaagaasar, 'Development of relationships and relationship competencies in complex projects', *International Journal of Managing Projects in Business,* 4 (2), 2011, 294–307.

A. van Marrewijk, 'Strategy of cooperation: control and commitment in mega-projects', *Management,* 8 (4), 2005, 89–104.

D.L. Van Rooy, C. Viswesvaran and P. Pluta, 'An evaluation of construct validity: what is this thing called emotional intelligence?' *Human Performance,* 18 (4), 2005, 445–462.

S.L. Vargo and R.F. Lusch, 'Evolving to a new dominant logic for marketing', *Journal of Marketing,* 68, 2004, 1–17.

S.L. Vargo and R.F. Lusch, 'Service-dominant logic: continuing the evolution', *Journal of the Academy of Marketing Science,* 36 (1), 2008, 1–10.

G. Vickers, *The Art of Judgment: a study of policy making,* London: Chapman & Hall, 1965.

L. Volker, *Deciding about Design Quality: value judgements and decision making in the selection of architects by public clients under European tendering regulations,* Leiden: Sidestone Press, 2010.

A. Walker, *Project Management in Construction,* Oxford: Blackwell, 2007.

A. Walker, *Organizational Behaviour in Construction,* Chichester: Wiley-Blackwell, 2011.

J.E. Wallace, 'Organizational and professional commitment in professional and nonprofessional organizations', *Administrative Science Quarterly,* 40 (2), 1995, 228–225.

L. Walras, *The Elements of Pure Economics: or the theory of social wealth,* 2010 edition, Abingdon: Routledge, 1926.

S. Ward and C. Chapman, 'Transforming project risk management into project uncertainty management', *International Journal of Project Management,* 21 (2), 2003, 97–105.

S. Wasserman and K. Faust, *Social Network Analysis,* Beverly Hills, CA: Sage, 1994.

C. Watkin, 'Developing emotional intelligence', *International Journal of Selection and Assessment,* 8 (2), 2000, 89–92.

G.R. Weaver, L.K. Treviño and P.L. Cochran, 'Corporate ethics practices in the mid-1990s: an empirical study of the Fortune 1000', *Journal of Business Ethics,* 18, 1999, 283–294.

M. Weber, *The Theory of Social and Economic Organizations,* New York: Free Press, 1947.

K.E. Weick, *Sensemaking in Organizations,* Thousand Oaks, CA: Sage, 1995.

K.E. Weick, 'Organizational design and the Gehry experience', *Journal of Management Inquiry,* 12, 2003, 93–97.

V. Wekselberg, 'Reduced "social" in a new model of organizational trust', *Academy of Management Review,* 21 (2), 1996, 333–335.

H. Wells, *An Investigation into the Contribution of Project Management Methodologies to IT/IS Project Management in Practice,* PhD thesis, London: University College, 2011.

H. Wells and H.J. Smyth, 'A service-dominant logic—what service? An evaluation of project management methodologies and project management attitudes in IT/IS project business', *Paper presented at EURAM 2011,* 1st–4th June, Tallinn, Estonia, 2011.

W. Welsch, 'Aestheticization processes: phenomena, distinctions and prospects', *Theory, Culture & Society,* 13 (1), 1996, 1–24.

E. Wenger, *Communities of Practice: learning, meaning, and identity,* Cambridge: Cambridge University Press, 1998.

B. Wernerfelt, 'A resource-based view of the firm', *Strategic Management Journal,* 5, 1984, 171–180.

R. Westbrook and R. Oliver, 'The dimensionality of consumption emotion patterns and consumer satisfaction', *Journal of Consumer Research,* 18 (June), 1991, 84–91.

M. Westner and S. Strahringer, 'Determinants of success in IS offshoring projects: results from an empirical study of German companies', *Information & Management,* 47, 2010, 291–299.

R. Whitley, 'Project-based firms: a new organizational form or a variation on a theme', *Industrial and Corporate Change,* 15 (1), 2006, 77–99.

R. Whittington, 'Strategy as practice', *Long Range Planning,* 29 (5), 1996, 731–735.

J. Whyte and R. Levitt, 'Information management and the management of projects', *The Oxford Handbook of Project Management,* P.W.G. Morris, J.K. Pinto and J. Söderlund (eds.), Oxford: Oxford University Press, 2011, pp. 365–388.

R.W. Wideman, *Project and Program Risk Management: a guide to managing project risks and opportunities,* Newton Square, PA: Project Management Institute, 1992.

K. Wikström, K. Artto, J. Kujala and J. Söderlund, 'Business models in project business', *International Journal of Project Management,* 28 (8), 2010, 832–841.

K. Wikström, M. Hellström, K. Artto, J. Kujala and S. Kujala, 'Services in project-based businesses: four types of business logic', *International Journal of Project Management,* 27, 2009, 113–122.

O. Williamson, 'The vertical integration of production: market failure considerations', *American Economic Review,* 61, 1971, 112–123.

O.E. Williamson, *Markets and Hierarchies: analysis and antitrust implications,* New York: Free Press, 1975.

O.E. Williamson, *The Economic Institutions of Capitalism,* New York: Free Press, 1985.

O.E. Williamson, 'Calculativeness, trust, and economic organization', *Journal of Law and Economics,* 36, 1993, 453–486.

D. Wilson, 'An integrated model of buyer–seller relationships', *Journal of the Academy of Marketing Science,* 23 (4), 1995, 335–345.

G.M. Winch, *Managing the Construction Project: an information processing approach,* Oxford: Blackwell, 2002.

G.M. Winch, *Managing the Construction Project: an information processing approach,* 2nd edition, Oxford: Blackwell, 2010.

G.M. Winch, 'Is project organising temporary?' *Paper presented at EURAM 2013,* 26th–29th June, Istanbul, 2013.

G.M. Winch and R. Leiringer, 'Client capabilities: the developing research agenda', *Keynote Presentation by Graham Winch at the 7th Nordic Conference on Construction Economics and Organisation 2013,* 12th–14th June, Trondheim: Norwegian University of Science and Technology, 2013.

G.M. Winch and E. Maytorena, 'Managing risk and uncertainty on projects', *The Oxford Handbook of Project Management,* P.W.G. Morris, J.K. Pinto and J. Söderlund (eds.), Oxford: Oxford University Press, 2011, pp. 345–364.

A. Windeler and S. Sydow, 'Project networks and changing industry practices: collaborative content production in the German television industry', *Organization Studies,* 22, (6) 2001, 1035–1060.

M. Winter and A. Szczepanek, *Images of Projects,* Farnham: Gower, 2009.

S.G. Winter and G. Szulanski, 'Replication as strategy', *Organization Science,* 6, 2001, 730–743.

L. Wittgenstein, *On Certainty,* G.E.M. Anscombe and G.H. von Wright (eds.), translated by D. Paul and G.E.M. Anscombe, Oxford: Blackwell, 1969.

S.B. Wolff, V.U. Druskat, E.S. Koman and T.E. Messer, 'The link between group emotional competence and group effectiveness', *Linking Emotional Intelligence and Performance at Work,* V.U. Druskat, F. Sala and J. Mount (eds.), Mahwah, NJ: Lawrence Erlbaum Associates, 2006, pp. 223–242.

A. Wölfl, *The Service Economy in OECD Countries,* Paris: OECD Directorate for Science, Technology and Industry, 2005.

E.S. Wong, D. Then and M. Skitmore, 'Antecedents of trust in intra-organisational relationships within three Singapore public sector construction project management agencies', *Construction Management and Economics,* 18, 2000, 797–806.

G. Wood, P. McDermott and W. Swan, 'The ethical benefits of trust-based partnering: the example of the construction industry', *Business Ethics: a European review,* 11 (1), 2002, 4–13.

R.B. Woodruff, 'Customer value: the next source of competitive advantage', *Journal of the Academy of Marketing Science,* 25 (2), 1997, 139–153.

C. Young-Ybarra and M. Wiersma, 'Strategic flexibility in information technology alliances: the influence of transaction cost economics and social exchange theory', *Organization Science,* 10, 1999, 439–459.

A. Zaheer, B. McEvily and V. Perrone, 'Does trust matter? Exploring the effects of inter-organizational and interpersonal trust on performance', *Organization Science,* 9 (2), 1998, 141–159.

D.E. Zand, 'Trust and managerial problem solving', *Administrative Science Quarterly,* 17, 1972, 229–239.

M. Zeidner, G. Matthews and R. Roberts, 'Emotional intelligence in the workplace: a critical review', *Applied Psychology: An International Review,* 53 (3), 2004, 371–399.

V.A. Zeithaml and M.J. Bitner, *Services Marketing,* New York: McGraw-Hill, 1996.

M. Zineldin, 'Co-opetition: the organisation of the future', *Marketing Intelligence & Planning,* 22 (7), 2004, 780–790.

M. Zollo and E. Freeman, 'Re-thinking the firm in a post-crisis world', *European Management Review,* 7, 2010, 191–194.

W. Zou, M.M. Kumaraswamy, J. Chung and J. Wong, 'Identifying the critical success factors for relationship management in PPP projects', *International Journal of Project Management,* 32, 2014, 265–274.

INDEX